PLAS
PITT
LATIN
AMERICAN
SERIES

MEXICO

THROUGH

RUSSIAN

EYES,

1806–1940

William Harrison Richardson

University of
Pittsburgh Press

Published by the
University of Pittsburgh Press,
Pittsburgh, Pa., 15260
Copyright © 1988,
University of Pittsburgh Press
All rights reserved
Feffer and Simons, Inc., London
Manufactured in the United States
of America

Library of Congress Cataloging-in-
Publication Data

Richardson, William, 1947–
    Mexico through Russian eyes,
1806–1940 / William Harrison
Richardson.
        p.   cm. — (Pitt Latin
American series)
    Bibliography: p. 261
    Includes index.
    ISBN 0-8229-3824-3
    1. Mexico—Foreign public opin-
ion, Russian—History. 2. Public
opinion—Soviet Union—History.
3. Mexico—Description and travel.
4. Visitors, Foreign—Mexico—Attitudes. 5. Russians—Mexico—
Attitudes. I. Title. II. Series.
F1228.5.S65R53   1988
972.08—dc19   87-17350
                                    CIP

Portions of this work first appeared,
in different form, in *California History*, *Historia Mexicana*, *The Pacific
Historian*, and in *Mexico and the Soviet Bloc: The Foreign Policy of a
Middle Power*, by William Richardson
and Zbigniew A. Kruszewski, © 1987
by Westview Press, Inc., Boulder,
Colorado.

CONTENTS

ACKNOWLEDG-
MENTS

This work is the product of several years of research and writing carried out at a number of libraries and institutions. It began in 1979 at a National Endowment for the Humanities summer seminar on the Mexican Revolution held at the University of Texas. The seminar's director was Stanley Ross, an eminent Mexicanist, fine scholar, and critical and sensitive evaluator of my participation in the seminar. Until his death in 1985, he continued his interest in my work and helped me pursue my research in the United States and abroad. I owe him a great debt.

The staffs at the Nettie Lee Benson Latin American Library, the University of Texas main library, and the Humanities Research Center in Austin were always helpful and accommodating during my work there in 1979.

In 1980 and 1981 I spent several productive weeks at the University of California at Los Angeles Research Library and at the Hoover Institution in Palo Alto, California. David Heron at the Hoover Institution helped make my stay there particularly rewarding.

The Museum of Modern Art in New York City was the source for much of the visual and film material for the chapter on Eisenstein. Pearl Moeller, supervisor of Special Collections, facilitated my examination of the Eisenstein materials, and Charles Silver of the Film Department arranged for me to view all the film from the Mexican project. The Eisenstein chapter could not have been completed without seeing the Museum's material, and I want to thank the Museum and its staff, as well as Jay Leyda, for permitting scholarly access to it.

Repeated funding for my research was provided by Wichita State University through the graduate division and the university faculty research program. I owe a special debt to the dean of the Graduate School, Lloyd Benningfield, for his support and encouragement. I would also like to thank the staff of the Wichita State University interlibrary loan office for their continuing assistance in obtaining arcane materials for me.

I spent the 1982–1983 academic year at Moscow State University working on this project under the sponsorship of the International Research and Exchanges Board and the Fulbright-Hays Program. I want to acknowledge these programs for their financial and logistical support. My Soviet hosts were cooperative and helpful, and I owe thanks to the staffs at the Lenin State Library and the library of the Academy of Sciences' Institute of Latin America (especially Anatolii Borovkov) for their assistance. The archivists at the Central State Archive of Literature and Art (TsGALI) were more than helpful and provided me with all the material I requested from them. Several other people in Moscow deserve special mention. For Eisenstein materials, Naum Kleiman of the Eisenstein Memorial Study was an always accessible and informative source, and I will long remember his kindness and concern for my work. Vera Kuteishchikova of the Institute of World Literature and Lev Ospovat of the Union of Soviet Writers helped put me straight about a number of issues, and were tolerant of my sometime tiresome questions, as was S. Ia. Serov of the Institute of Ethnography, who helped me ferret out obscure sources and who gave me some useful criticism of my earlier research. I would also like to acknowledge the important work done by Aleksandr Sizonenko, a pioneer in the study of Soviet-Mexican relations.

Special mention must be made of Elida Litavrina of the Faculty of Modern and Contemporary History of Moscow State University for her help and enthusiasm and her unceasing willingness to help me carry out my project. Without her assistance, this book would have been considerably more limited in scope and depth.

The staff at the Mexican Embassy in Moscow, most particularly the cultural attaché, Zarina Martínez Lacy, were very helpful. Their openness, resourcefulness, and encouragement aided my work greatly, as did their allowing me to use material in their small but remarkably complete library.

I spent the 1984–1985 academic year at the University of Kansas as a visiting professor of Soviet and Latin American Studies, and was able to use my time there and the university's excellent library to do the first drafts of this work. I owe special thanks to William Fletcher of the Soviet and East European Studies Center, Charles Stansifer of the Center for Latin American Studies, and Norman Saul of the History Department for making the year in Lawrence a stimulating, comfortable, and productive one.

The Department of History of Wichita State University must also be acknowledged for allowing me two years' leave of absence during my work on this book. The leaves meant that other members of the department had to work harder and were faced with additional demands on their time, and they should know that I appreciate their support and that of the university.

Final editing and preparation of this manuscript for publication was done by the excellent staff of the University of Pittsburgh Press. Catherine Marshall, in particular, was an extraordinarily conscientious editor and critic who improved my original manuscript considerably. I am grateful to Cole Blasier for initially suggesting I send the manuscript to the Press.

Portions of this study have appeared in different form in *Historia Mexicana, The Pacific Historian,* and *California History.* I appreciate those publishers' permitting me to use that material here.

Finally, I must thank my wife, Carol, and our two sons, Caleb and Micah, for allowing me to spend hundreds of hours away from home working on this manuscript, whether in my office at Wichita State University, or several hundred miles away. They accompanied me for many of the research trips and adjusted to circumstances with which only scholars of Russian history are faced. Without their support, I might never even have conceived of attempting this project.

Lastly, I would like to dedicate this book to the memory of my parents, who were never quite sure of what I was after with it, but who nevertheless supported me in whatever way they could. I wish they could have lived to have seen its completion.

While I owe a great deal to all those mentioned above, all errors of fact and interpretation are, of course, my own.

A NOTE ON TRANS- LITERATION

There are several methods for transliterating Cyrillic characters into English, but the one most accessible to American readers is that of the Library of Congress. I have used a modified version of that system. The only significant changes are that in family names *ii* is rendered by *y* in the text, but by *ii* in the notes and bibliography; I have also omitted the apostrophe indicating hard and soft signs. In titles of prerevolutionary works or journals, I follow modern Soviet orthography rather than the former spelling. Some names that have become Anglicized are given in the form most familiar to American readers: Leon Trotsky rather than Lev Trotskii, Wrangell rather than Vrangel.

MEXICO
THROUGH
RUSSIAN
EYES

INTRODUCTION

Europeans have been fascinated by Mexico since the time of Cortés's conquest of the Aztec empire, and first-hand accounts of the country date from Bernal Díaz del Castillo's history of the victorious Spanish campaign. The Spaniards, Frenchmen, Germans, and Englishmen who came to Mexico during the three centuries of Spanish rule found a country that was at times much like Europe, at others entirely different. This perception of duality was something on which all later visitors would comment. Independence marked a great change in how foreigners and Mexicans saw the country. Mexican observers believed their nation was to be the preeminent power in North America, that it would provide an ideal model for the rest of Latin America, with regard to self-respect, prosperity, and cultural advancement. This was rarely how Mexico was seen by outsiders, however, and during the course of the nineteenth century, as more Europeans as well as increasing numbers of North Americans visited the country, the distance between what Mexicans hoped for and the reality described by foreign observers grew. As these travellers reported on their journeys in books and periodicals, foreigners came to have what they felt were highly informed sources of information about the Mexican republic.

By the end of the nineteenth century, widely held stereotypes of Mexicans and their country had developed in the minds of non-Mexicans. These were not always negative, but they also were not exclusively positive. While they were not overly favorable toward Mexico's social and governmental system, for example, they did find human aspects of Mexican life to counterbalance these failings. Some of the greatest contrasts of interpretation appeared abroad during the presidency of Porfirio Díaz. Many outsiders condemned Díaz's political and social system outright. Others contended he was providing Mexico with its first genuine opportunity to become a great and prosperous nation. The Revolution and the postrevolutionary decades of the 1920s and 1930s elicited similar responses from foreign observers. To some the Revolution meant that the chains of the past had been broken in Mexico, never to be reforged. Others felt no compunction in declaring men like Zapata and Villa, Obregón and Calles, agents of the Devil himself, or at least of the Russian Bolsheviks. Cárdenas's apparent radicalism only intensified the arguments among foreign observers, and their evaluations of Mexico continued to diverge until World War II. With the end of the Cárdenas sexenio, Mexicans became more cautious and traditional in their approach to solving their country's problems, and the rest of the world became less interested in the evolution of the Mexican revolutionary process. Mexico no longer seemed quite as unique as it had in the past.

The list of books and articles written by visitors to Mexico is surprisingly long, a reflection of the number of travellers themselves as well as the size of the potential audience. Major works were written by Alexander von Humboldt, John Reed, Max Frisch, Fanny Calderón de la Barca, D. H. Lawrence, Malcolm Lowry, Graham Greene, Antonin Artaud, Aldous Huxley, and Ramón del Valle-Inclán, among a long list of others.[1] Readers who quickly lost interest in events in China or Africa seemed to have an abiding desire to read about Mexico's colorful pre-Columbian past, its turbulent period of revolutions and civil wars, and utopian or catastrophic speculation about its future. The audience was large as well because some of the best known and most talented foreign literary figures, especially from Britain and the United States, wrote about Mexico, either in works of fiction or in travelogues describing their stays in the country. Each observer described Mexico in terms his countrymen could understand and appreciate. Humboldt was interested in Mexico's natural riches and in how they were being exploited, in the country's Spanish colonial administration, and in the beliefs and practice of the Spanish Catholic church.[2] The French came to examine native Indian spirituality, and the Spaniards hoped to see how Mexico differed from Spain, once the long period of Spanish rule had ended. No group wrote more about

Mexico than did the Anglo-Americans, however, and for U.S. writers and observers, especially, the country was a constant source of inspiration, stimulation, even repulsion.³ Citizens of the United States first came to Mexico as representatives of a nation that was its southern neighbor's principal competitor for political, military, and economic dominance on their continent, but by the end of the nineteenth century U.S. observers often saw themselves as Mexico's tutors, and the United States as the standard by which Mexicans should be judged. Those North Americans most critical of the Porfiriato welcomed the outbreak of the Mexican Revolution with enthusiasm, but many more U.S. citizens saw with trepidation and disquiet the prospects of radicalism overflowing Mexico's border with the United States. In whatever period, North Americans were rarely indifferent toward the country and were not always objective in their evaluations. They often travelled under difficult circumstances, and a few rendered Mexico a great service in uncovering and promoting the country's native pre-Columbian heritage. It was this Indian past of Mexico, in fact, that attracted most U.S. visitors, and they admired it more than they did any other aspect of the country. Most of them had little love for their neighbor's modern mestizo culture, for the corruption of the government and church, or for the lack of "energy" of the population, about which they repeatedly complained. Most favored Porfirio Díaz's imposition of "law and order" and his support for economic development financed by foreign investment, but most were similarly shocked at the cruelties of his regime. For many of them, too, especially the writers, Mexico was an escape into "another country" which was satisfyingly different from their own and which would allow them the solitude they needed to deal with the problems confronting them.⁴ This was particularly true in the 1920s and 1930s, when U.S. and British writers, fleeing disillusionment in their own countries, described Mexico in terms directly opposite to those used by their more partisan contemporaries concerned more with politics and social reform than with the "soul" and moral or spiritual regeneration. Above all, however, for the majority of European and U.S. writers, Mexico remained forever alien, and they frequently had difficulty suppressing feelings of superiority toward it. No matter how long they lived in the country nor how well they knew it (and some knew it very well), Mexico remained remote and strange in ways that

England or France never would to North Americans or Germans, or Vienna and Rome to Frenchmen or Englishmen. Almost none of these foreigners were ever assimilated into Mexican life entirely, and few extended to it their unqualified affection. However sympathetic they wanted their understanding of the country and its people to be, there always existed a gulf separating them.

One group of foreigners who visited and described Mexico did not feel this sense of alienation nearly to the extent their Western European and North American contemporaries did. These were the Russians who travelled through Mexico in the nineteenth and early twentieth centuries and who described and depicted the country in journalistic essays, in poetry, even in the cinema. Russian travel accounts in general are not widely appreciated outside the Soviet Union today, and those by Russians who visited Mexico are little known even in the USSR. Yet Russian and Soviet citizens, not all of them professional writers by any means, have given unique descriptions of other parts of the world,[5] and unlike Western Europeans and North Americans, have had a much more sympathetic comprehension than might be expected of the historical experience of peoples like the Mexicans. In addition, because of tsarist censorship, what Russians wrote about Mexico before the revolutions of 1917 was relevant as much to Russia itself as to prerevolutionary Mexico. After the Bolshevik Revolution, Russians were somewhat less empathetic toward Mexican developments, and like their U.S. colleagues, Soviet visitors frequently saw themselves as teachers. Even then, however, they believed they were teachers of a people who had suffered the same exploitation as had the Russians themselves.

This Russian sympathy for Mexico was encouraged by the similarity of the two countries' experiences, or at least by the perception that there had been a surprising concurrence of developments in their histories. Russians were among the few foreigners who understood the importance Mexico's history played in defining the country's modern view of itself, and neither Russians nor Mexicans ever permitted their knowledge of the past to recede into their unconsciousness.[6] The similarities seemed obvious to any Russian or Mexican who studied the two nations' histories: in medieval times, the Mongols had launched a bloody conquest of Russia, the Aztecs of much of Mexico; Spanish rule and the expansion of Muscovy had brought vast national territories under a single centralized government; serfdom had become entrenched in Russia at about the same time the *encomienda* and peonage system had grown in Mexico; Peter I's attempts at reorganizing Russia paralleled the plans of the Bourbons to rationalize Mexico's administration; each country had an established dominant Christian church; liberalism and an effective bourgeoisie had never become strong in either nation; Juárez's reforms of the 1850s seemed remarkably similar to Alexander II's; at the end of the nineteenth century both countries' aristocracies attempted to modernize their nations at a time of deteriorating peasant income and standard of living; both experienced revolutions in the second decade of the twentieth century, and both stepped back from continuing radical change early in the 1920s; finally, in the 1930s, even if to considerably different extents, Russia and Mexico moved again toward revolutionary transformation, under Stalin and Cárdenas.[7] In addition, of course, for centuries there were great extremes of wealth and poverty in both countries, a privileged and educated intelligentsia opposed to government policies had grown up, there was a sense of backwardness and inferiority toward Western Europe, and both nations had been defeated in war at important and relatively recent periods in their history. No one would have said that the two countries' experiences were exactly the same, and Russians on the scene in Mexico were constantly aware of how different their two countries were, particularly during the postrevolutionary period. Still, to many Russians, Mexico seemed more like their own homeland than did almost any other European country, and certainly any Anglo-American country.

This sense of a common background extended beyond those who had first-hand experiences in Mexico to those who read of their visits or who heard them speak of their travels there. All the visitors discussed in this book were influential to one extent or another in determining a Russian, then Soviet, view of Mexico. While it is true that some few books about Mexico had been translated from Western European languages into Russian, Russians on the whole learned what they did about the country from the articles written by the individuals discussed below, or from accounts in the Russian press about them. For Russians, there were, quite simply, no other sources of information about Mexico. Some of the visitors were exceedingly well known in Russia, and their observations about Mexico reached a large percentage of the country's literate, educated population. Others were less popular, and their impact on the reading public is more difficult to determine. Yet, to whatever degree a generally held view of Mexico existed in the Russian Empire before the revolutions of 1917, and in Communist Russia afterward, it was the result of the activities of the people discussed here. Some influenced the Russian public primarily, others wrote recommendations they hoped their governments would follow.

The individuals chosen for this study were selected because they had first-hand experience in Mexico and because they had something to say publicly or in reports to their superiors about what they had seen. Not all the Russians who ever travelled in Mexico are considered, or even mentioned. Those selected were highly literate, generally well-educated, often held important government positions or were at least potentially influential, and in some cases, were touched significantly by their experience. The first Russian citizens to describe Mexico in the nineteenth century were employees of the Russian American Company, and most of them saw only the Spanish, then Mexican, territory of Alta California. Nikolai Rezanov and many of his colleagues desired annexation of the region to the other Russian possessions in the Pacific and were not favorably disposed toward much that they saw in colonial California. Their feeling of superiority was more characteristically Western European than Russian and was not typical of the attitudes that were expressed by Russian visitors of the later nineteenth century. Even then, not all of them were unrelentingly harsh in their evaluations, and few condemned Mexican California absolutely. The first substantial description of central Mexico came from Baron Ferdinand Wrangell in the mid-1830s, in the form of a diary published in one of the most popular journals of the time. He too was not positively impressed, but his criticisms centered on Mexico's political system and its republican form of government, which he disapproved of on principle. Yet upon his return to St. Petersburg, even he added his voice to those in the government calling for improved political and economic ties with Mexico. His interests were those of the Russian Empire, but he also hoped that the benefits of better relations would reach the ordinary Mexicans with whom he sympathized and whom he admired, however much he may have looked askance at the administration of President Santa Anna.

In any case, his journey was interesting and his account lively, and was the only major Russian one to appear until the Porfiriato.

Five writers published valuable descriptions of their visits to Mexico during the presidency of Porfirio Díaz. S. K. Patkanov was a scientist whose sociological analysis of life in Yucatán was one of the most complete, if condemnatory, of anything written about the area by any foreigner. S. D. Protopopov, G. A. Devollan, and P. A. Tverskoi were all journalists. Protopopov pretended at least to be highly favorable about what he saw in Mexico, Devollan was balanced in his praise and criticism, and Tverskoi predicted disaster if nothing were done to reform the country's social and political inequalities. The last of these five, Konstantin Balmont, was concerned almost exclusively with ancient Mexico and with what remained of it in the present. A poet, mythologist, and enthusiast for all that was exotic, he had more influence on the Russian reading public than any of the others in creating a popular prerevolutionary picture of the country. What impact these men may have had on tsarist policy toward Mexico at the time is problematic, but it seems likely that their work, added to the official reports of diplomats and trade representatives, encouraged the steady growth of Russian-Mexican ties during the Porfiriato.

Mexico presented a very different face to Russians after the two countries' revolutions, and the Soviet citizens who travelled there during the 1920s were highly political in their orientation and analysis. Stanislav Pestkovsky and Aleksandra Kollontai were both ambassadors accredited from the new Soviet state, and they had varying degrees of success in dealing with the Mexican government and in carrying out their charges. Their approaches to the country were quite dissimilar: Kollontai had little to say about Mexico, but was the focus of enormous attention in the press and among the diplomatic corps while she was there; Pestkovsky, upon his return to the USSR, wrote the first two major Soviet books about Mexican history, in which he examined the country from a rigidly Marxist-Leninist point of view. The third significant Soviet citizen to visit Mexico during the 1920s was the modernist, avidly revolutionary poet, Vladimir Mayakovsky, who described the country in prose and poetry that were inimitable, and almost untranslatable. If the Soviet government listened often with skepticism to Kollontai and Pestkovsky, the Soviet urban population read Mayakovsky with enthusiasm, amusement, and fascination, and all of them in their own ways laid the foundations for Soviet *meksikanistika*.

No Russian visitors to Mexico were as well known as the final two to be discussed, Sergei Eisenstein and Leon Trotsky. Eisenstein's aborted attempt at capturing Mexico on film earned him attention throughout the world, although it was not entirely favorable, least of all in the USSR. His imagined Mexico was more multifaceted and more intimately felt than that of any other Russian. It was not limited by prejudice, and Eisenstein himself lived through a profound emotional and intellectual transformation while attempting to make his *Que Viva Mexico!* Moscow's knowledge of Eisenstein's activities in Mexico was limited in the extreme, and his work there became well known in the Soviet Union only after his death. Last of all, there was Trotsky. Those who know nothing about Russian-Mexican contacts in general are aware of Trotsky's brief stay in Mexico City and of his murder there by an agent of the Soviet secret police. Trotsky had little to say about the country which granted him his last place of refuge, but he was given such publicity in the USSR and in the West that he cannot be ignored, particularly since he was the only Russian of importance who was in the country during the important years of the late 1930s.

For several reasons this study concludes with Trotsky. The most important is that with the outbreak of World War II, relations between Mexico and the USSR changed greatly, and contact between the two countries grew enormously. Mexico was no longer an exotic land to Russians, and its historical experience began to diverge greatly from that of the USSR. Then too, in the years following the war, Russian visitors' accounts of Mexico, in whatever medium, were simply not as interesting, as idiosyncratic, or as high in quality as they had been before. Soviet academic scholarship on Mexico, on the other hand, increased greatly and was impressively sophisticated and knowledgeable, but it lacked the élan and peculiar character of the works produced previously. As it was, Soviet views of Mexico in the 1920s were already in the process of becoming dangerously one-sided, and a clear bias was obvious in later works. In addition, after about 1929, Soviet analyses of Mexico (and of much of the rest of the world, for that matter) were put into a Stalinist straightjacket that was not removed for over two and a half decades. Trotsky escaped by his involuntary exile, and Eisenstein was not subjected to Stalinist constraints until his return to the Soviet Union in 1932.

Russians have provided a highly unusual and almost ignored perspective on nineteenth- and early twentieth-century Mexico. What other foreigners found unbearable and frustrating about Mexico, Russians rarely did. The purported "laziness" of Mexicans and their inefficiency bothered Russians very little. One of the most critical of Russian observers, Wrangell, mentioned that the inns he found in Mexico, for example, were far superior to many of those he had been forced to endure while travelling about Russia, and even his colleagues in the Russian American Company at times had positive comments to make about the *californios*. Russians were rarely uneasy in the way other visitors were, and unlike Anglo-Saxon writers, in Paul Fussell's phrase, Mexico rarely made them "go all to pieces."[8] Rather, like Eisenstein, they felt more at home in Mexico than almost anywhere they had been. Almost none of them spoke really enthusiastically about Mexico's colonial past, as North Americans so often did, and most of them wanted fundamental change in the country, even if they disagreed on the form that change should take. They were as moved by the country's natural beauties as anyone, and they could be as puerile and superficial as any writers from the European or North American penny press. But there was always an intimate interaction between them and their own experience, and Mexico. Despite intermittent uncertainties, they possessed a sense of identity and understanding that no other nationality had. In describing Mexico, they were often, sometimes too often, speaking of themselves and their homeland, whether tsarist or Soviet. This internal dialogue flavored all their works about the country and guaranteed them a perspective and point of view unlike that of any other foreigners.

1
THE EARLIEST
ACCOUNTS

California and the Russian American Company

It was not until the eighteenth century that Russians first wrote about Spanish America, and none of the earliest works were based on first-hand experiences. While translations of Western European books about the New World had appeared in Russia, nothing substantially original by a Russian was published until the middle of the century.[1] The *Sankt-Peterburgskie vedomosti* (*St. Petersburg News*), for example, included an article on Bartolomé de Las Casas in one of its 1735 issues and a series of articles about California, based on Spanish reports, in 1741.[2] On one occasion, the respected and prolific Mikhail Lomonosov mentioned briefly the "Castilian" move across the oceans, and in a 1752 poem he condemned the Spanish "looting of the wealth of the Americas," but by all indications, did not refer to the subject again.[3] More extensive treatment was provided by the playwright Sumarokov in *Razgovor v Tsarstve Mertvykh: Kortets i Motetsuma* (*A Conversation in the Kingdom of the Dead: Cortés and Montezuma*), a dramatization of the European-Aztec confrontation. Oddly enough, considering the eighteenth century's fascination with "noble savagery," he depicted Montezuma as a tyrant and Cortés as an example of wisdom, courage, and kindness.[4] Sumarokov wrote about Mexico again in 1759, though only briefly.[5] In the middle of the century, Mexico remained an exotic and distant land.

In the 1770s and 1780s, Russian interest in the New World grew. Nikolai Novikov's press issued a number of translations of books dealing with Spain and Spanish America, and Novikov himself wrote a certain amount about the New World.[6] One other private publisher, P. I. Bogdanovich, included a series of general articles on Spanish

America in his journal, *Akademicheskie Izvestiia (Academic News)*, in 1781.[7] Only one other work of note about Spanish America was published in Russia in the eighteenth century: Ivan Krylov's opera *Amerikantsy (The Americans)* was derived from a play by Voltaire. The action takes place in Spanish America and expresses a strong sympathy for the native peoples.[8] Krylov's critical view of conditions in the New World anticipated an attitude toward Spanish rule in America that was more typical of Russians in the eighteenth and nineteenth centuries.

With the exception of these few works, little on New Spain appeared in the Russian press or in the works of Russian writers.[9] What marked the turning point of Russian interest was the arrival of Russians in California at the beginning of the nineteenth century. Russian commercial and territorial expansion had led to the establishment of trading centers in Alaska, Hawaii, and at Fort Ross in Alta California. As Russians became actively interested in Spanish North America, so too did the Spanish viceregal government in Mexico City become concerned about Russian encroachment on territories claimed by the crown of Spain. Moreover, the decision to promote Spanish and Mexican settlement of Alta California was at least partially motivated by fear of Russian expansion to the south.[10] The rulers of New Spain were determined to discourage the Russian interlopers. The Anza expedition to Monterey in 1774 and to San Francisco the following year, extending the territory under effective Spanish control beyond the small settlement Portolá had established at Los Angeles, was seen as an essential step in protecting those areas.[11] The confusion of the Napoleonic era, and above all the emergence of Russia as a great power after the defeat of France, intensified Spanish fear for California. Spain, and later independent Mexico, would never feel entirely comfortable with its Russian neighbors to the north, and fears of Russian attacks from Kamchatka or Alaska were constantly present in their minds.

This concern intensified when, in 1799, several large Russian fur companies in the northern Pacific were consolidated into one firm, to be known as the Russian American Company.[12] The company proposed to promote trade, establish fur-hunting bases, and explore and colonize the lands south of Alaska. The Spanish feared that the Russian American Company was more than simply a commercial venture, that it "reflected Tsarist intent to make the Pacific a Russian 'inland sea.' A logical expression of this fact was the Russian plan to claim and hold the largely unoccupied lands on the Pacific Coast nominally claimed by Spain."[13] It was as representatives of the Russian American Company that the first Russians to visit and describe New Spain arrived there. Their accounts of California would be among the most extensive, if not most favorable, written by any Europeans about the region and its peoples.

Certainly the best-known Russian voyage to California during this period of Spanish-Russian rivalry was the Rezanov expedition of 1806. Nikolai Petrovich Rezanov was an ambitious, influential, and already distinguished veteran of the Russian military and civil service, a participant in the first Russian voyage around the world. In the spring of 1806, as a representative of the Russian American Company, he sailed from the company's Alaskan headquarters at Sitka to buy desperately needed grain at San Francisco, despite Spain's forbidding its colonies to trade with foreigners.[14] Accompanied by several officers who would later publish their own accounts, Rezanov attempted to make the most favorable impression possible on the *californios* and gave them numerous gifts that were intended to disguise the Russians' "distress and needfulness"[15] in Alaska. The Russians' reception was mixed: the missionaries were clearly very interested in purchasing Russian goods, but politically the situation was dangerous. In Europe, Russia and Spain appeared to be on the verge of war, and California's governor and his military staff were uncertain about how to respond to Rezanov's requests for trade and better relations. Rather than permitting Rezanov to travel to the capital at Monterey, the *commandante* of San Francisco told Rezanov that Governor Arrillaga would travel north to meet with him. It was a decision Rezanov found enlightening: "Thereupon I recognized the suspicious nature of the Spanish government, which at every point prevents foreign visitors from gaining a knowledge of the interior of the country and from observing the weakness of their military defenses."[16] On the basis of the little he had seen, Rezanov had already put together a plan that would permit the Russian American Company to establish a special relationship with California: he told the governor that he would return to St. Petersburg and ask Alexander I's government to send him to Madrid, where he would arrange for trade to begin between Russia and

Spain and their respective possessions in the New World. His report to Petersburg reflected the sincere enthusiasm he expressed to Arrillaga:

> This, gracious sire, is our first experiment in trade in Nueva California, which, at a low estimate, may amount to a million rubles yearly. In the future the needs of our American possessions will be supplied; Kamchatka and Okhotsk, with grain and other provisions; the Yakuts will not be obliged to carry grain long distances; the government expenses for army and navy supplies will be diminished; the price of bread in Irkutsk will be much lower when a considerable portion of grain, formerly shipped to the distant provinces, can be kept at home for local consumption; the custom-house will bring new revenue to the crown; the industries of interior Russia will receive a new impulse when the number of factories will have to be increased on account of the California trade alone, and in the meantime ways will be found for trade with India by way of Siberia, and your excellency may believe that with a good and well-considered beginning all this will be brought about in a short time.[17]

He added that his hopes had been strengthened by the genuine friendship the Spaniards expressed toward him and his crew and by the fact that they all agreed on their mutual dislike of the high-handed ways of the "Bostonians," who also frequented the waters of California. Linked to Rezanov's hopes for better relations with New Spain, and intertwined with the negotiations he had begun, was his now famous love affair with the daughter of the commandant of the presidio of San Francisco. Whether his affection for Concepción Arguello was sincere or not, his courting her had immediate benefits for his mission, once the initial uproar over his marriage proposal had died down: it was agreed that since he was to be a relative of the Arguellos, the proscription against trading with foreigners would not apply to him. In addition, and perhaps more valuable, was the decision that as a future relative, he would also be allowed to read all official (and secret) documents kept by the Arguellos.[18]

Rezanov refined his plans during the six weeks he spent in California. He would return to Petersburg by way of Siberia, carry out the promises he had made to Concepción and her family, then be back in California within two years, so that the marriage could take place. From there, he would travel through Mexico, examining port facilities and interior trade routes, and meet with the viceroy in Mexico City to negotiate trade agreements that would benefit both New Spain and the Russian Empire. What he did not intend to tell anyone in Mexico was that he had also recommended to the Russian American Company's directors that California above San Francisco be seized and added eventually to Russia's more northerly possessions.[19] In any event, none of these dreams was realized, since Rezanov did not complete his journey across Siberia: he died in 1807 at Krasnoyarsk, and his plans died with him.[20]

One of Rezanov's hopes did find fruition: what was envisioned as a permanent Russian colony north of San Francisco was established in August 1812 at Fort Ross. In 1808 Ivan Kuskov had been sent south to determine the best site for the new settlement, and in November 1811 he left Sitka for California. Construction was begun eighteen miles north of Port Rumiantsev (now known as Bodega Bay) in March 1812, and the fort was officially dedicated the following summer.[21] Soon after news of the fort reached San Francisco, Spanish officials began to demand that the Russians leave territories on which they were considered to be trespassing.[22] Yet despite this official hostility, surreptitious trade between the missionaries and the Russians continued and even grew as more Russian goods became available.

Protests ceased after Mexico declared its independence from Spain in 1821, and soon a number of agreements were reached between the Russian American Company and the new government in Mexico City: sea-otter hunting by Russians was regulated in 1823, for example, and five years later a treaty allowing Russian purchases of salt at San Quintín in Baja California was signed.[23] Yet while relations improved, growing commercial ties between the Russians and Mexicans were not sufficient to turn the Fort Ross colony into a viable economic enterprise. From their mistakes in Alaska the Russians had learned how to avoid alienating the local Indians, and could discourage an armed attack with their superior military strength, but they could never succeed in producing the kinds of agricultural products they needed for Alaska and Siberia. Economically the colony was a failure, and in the end, after twenty-nine years of occupation, the company sold the fort to Johann Sutter and abandoned the site in December 1841.[24]

The company had neither annexed the area, as Rezanov had recommended, nor increased greatly its trade with independent Mexico. The sale marked the beginning of total Russian withdrawal from the New World.

   This period of fairly intensive Russian contact with Spanish and Mexican settlers in California produced the first substantial Russian descriptions of the area. The most detailed was the widely-known account written by Count G. I. Langsdorff, who arrived in California with Rezanov aboard the *Juno* in 1806. Langsdorff had been born and educated in Germany and had lived in Portugal before he joined the Kruzenshtern-Lisiansky expedition around the world. Later he became a famous scholar (he was elected a member of the St. Petersburg Academy of Sciences in 1812) and explorer, leading a Russian expedition into the interior of Brazil in the 1820s, after having served as Russian consul in Rio de Janeiro. In California, Langsdorff described carefully all he saw, but was particularly interested in the missionaries and their proselytizing Christianity. On the whole, and unlike many Russian observers of Catholic Mexico, he was favorably impressed by the monks and priests he found at work in California. Yet, with his cynicism toward religion, he was surprised that so many of the priests believed even the most extravagant and unlikely miracles of the Mexican church:

> Our cicerone, Father Joseph [José Antonio] Uria, who was, generally speaking, an intelligent and well-informed man, and who seemed to have a sound and accurate judgement among most subjects, understanding that I was a naturalist, took me by the hand when we were in the chapel, and made me take notice of a painting, which represented the *Agave Americana*, or large American aloe, from the midst of which, instead of a flower stem, rose a holy virgin, by whom, as he assured me, many extraordinary miracles were performed in the sequel. This he related with an air of such firm belief in the story, that I could not help thinking if the belief was really not assumed, this was the greatest miracle the Virgin could have wrought. From courtesy, however, I joined in his admiration of the circumstance, expressing at the same time my extreme envy of the painter, who had seen so great a natural curiosity with his own eyes.[25]

Few Russians would be as kind as Langsdorff was toward the missionaries, but many would share his slightly condescending attitude toward their religion.

If the Franciscan priests were gullible in questions of dogma, Langsdorff believed, their wisdom in operating the missions themselves was praiseworthy: "the monks conduct themselves in general with so much prudence, kindness, and paternal care towards their converts, that peace, happiness, and obedience universally prevail among them."[26] After having visited the church at San Francisco and the missions at San José and Santa Clara, Langsdorff wrote that they were all well run, economically successful, maintained nicely, and on the whole, that they were admirable enterprises:

> When one thinks that . . . two or three monks take upon themselves a sort of voluntary exile from their country, only to spread the Christian religion, and to civilize a wild and uncultivated race of men, to teach them husbandry and various useful arts, cherishing and instructing them as if they were their own children, providing them dwellings, food and clothing, with everything necessary for their subsistence, and maintaining the utmost order and regularity of conduct . . . when all these things, I say, are considered, one cannot sufficiently admire the zeal and activity which carries them through so arduous a task, or forbear wishing the most complete success to their undertaking.[27]

What makes these exceedingly kind words most notable is that they seem to have been repeated by no other Russian or Russian-employed visitor. A considerably more typical view was expressed by the seaman, Vasilii Petrovich Tarakanov, who described his experiences with the priests of a southern mission, probably the one at San Fernando:

> From all I saw I must say that the Spaniards are bad men and that their priests in place of living humbly and in a Christian manner, are bent altogether on making money. They oppressed everybody for the sake of filling their coffers. They were not virtuous in any respect and in place of taking a wife as our Orthodox priests do, they have to do with a great many women—both Spanish and native—and they have many children running about the Missions which they call soldiers' orphans, but they are the offspring of priests, who all belong to some order of monks and cannot marry.[28]

Tarakanov had been captured on an illegal fur-hunting expedition near San Pedro and held prisoner for some time at the mission he described. The fact that after his release he told his experiences to an Orthodox priest, who then wrote them down, undoubtedly flavored his evaluation of what he saw. Still, his opinions were more consistent with other Russian views of the Mexican Catholic church during these years than were the tolerant and sympathetic ones of Langsdorff.

If Langsdorff was positive in his descriptions of the Franciscans, he was less favorable toward much else. He described the California Indians in great detail, but said they were among the least capable of native North American peoples with whom he had come into contact. He found European visitors constantly surprised to discover that the Indians did not rebel against their mission captivity, but he explained their resignation by their intellectual "simplicity," concluding that "in stature no less than in mind [they] are certainly of a very inferior race of human beings."[29] While individuals, he noted, might try to escape from the missions, as a group they did not, because they recognized they were in fact unable truly to free themselves. Brightening this generally gloomy picture, he added that despite their general inferiority, there were some differences among the tribes he observed. The Indians at San José, for example, were more attractive and more creative than their cousins at San Francisco.[30]

If the local Indians were noticeably more backward than elsewhere along the Pacific Coast, so too were the Spanish Californians in Langsdorff's eyes, at times consciously and deliberately so. He shared Tarakanov's point of view in this respect: "Anything in the line of grain or kitchen vegetables grow there without much care and the Spaniards could live in plenty all their lives were they not so lazy, but many of them are very poor and live no better than the natives."[31] Much of this sloth Langsdorff attributed to the excess of cheap labor. He was struck by the complete absence of windmills, for example, and concluded that such labor-saving innovations were not considered valuable by the mission padres, who needed above all to keep large numbers of Indians busy. Windmills, they feared, might lead to idleness and sin. Understanding their motivation did not justify such deliberate backwardness, however, which he considered inexcusable.

Like many other Russians, Langsdorff found a certain amount of pleasure in pointing out how, under a more ambitious administration, California could be made productive and profitable. The absence of boats on San Francisco Bay, he wrote, was encouraged by the local authorities, and was "strong proof of the great negligence of the government."[32] He had travelled to San José and discovered that the journey was three times longer by land than by boat. Other signs of backwardness were more the results of isolation than of sloth: there was an absolute lack of medicines and medical care at the missions for the Indians, for example, and the difficulties associated with childbirth and venereal and other diseases were compounded by the primitive way of life of the population. Langsdorff was even led to question Rezanov's hopes for expanded trade, since it appeared to him that California desperately needed many of the same products that the Russian American Company did. He added that much more favorable than trade with the Californians would be the establishment of a colony north of San Francisco, and his recommendations were seconded by Lt. N. A. Khvostov, who wrote his comments in the ship's log. Khvostov reported that he had examined the shore north of San Francisco Bay "under the pretext of searching for two runaway soldiers," and that he had found a number of good sites for a Russian settlement. His comments were ones with which Langsdorff undoubtedly agreed:

> Once established at Bodega, the Russians could . . . extend their settlement to the northern shore of San Francisco Bay. The Spaniards, as [religious] fanatics, are not interested in industries; they do not even have a rowboat, and the frigates which deliver their supplies are not interested in the north shore either. Yet I saw cattle, many antelope, a great number of wild goats, bears and plenty of wild fowl; I also saw wild wheat, peas and beans growing, so it seemed, without cultivation from seeds evidently scattered a number of years ago for an experiment and left in the care of nature and the good climate.[33]

Langsdorff, Khvostov, and their shipmates felt that Russians could better exploit the potential of a land wasted by the *californios*. They saw California's development under Spanish rule with dismay, although generally they made only favorable comments about the local administrators of San Francisco and their kind, generous, and gracious families. The dream of seizing the north shore of San Francisco Bay would be repeated many times, but it remained en ephemeral hope.

It was almost ten years before other Russians wrote extensively about California. In October 1815, the *Riurik* arrived at San Francisco under the command of naval Lt. Otto Von Kotzebue, operating under a commission from Count Rumiantsev. The conditions Von Kotzebue and his crew found inspired several descriptions of life in California during the final years of Spanish rule. Von Kotzebue's own report on social and economic conditions was almost entirely negative. To him, the local Indian population was hopelessly ignorant and backward:

> We . . . found several hundred half-naked Indians kneeling, who, though they understand neither Spanish nor Latin, are never permitted after their conversion to absent themselves from mass. As the missionaries do not trouble themselves to learn the language of the Indians, I cannot conceive in what manner they have been instructed in the Christian religion; and there is probably but little light in the heads and hearts of these poor creatures, who can do nothing but imitate the external ceremonies which they observe by the eye.[34]

Unlike Langsdorff, Von Kotzebue expressed suspicion and disfavor toward the religious administration: "The missionaries assured us that it was difficult to instruct [the Indians], on account of their stupidity, but I believe that these gentlemen do not give themselves much trouble about it. They also told us that the Indians came far from the interior of the country, and voluntarily submitted to them (which we likewise doubted)"[35] Von Kotzebue wrote that he quickly discerned general dissatisfaction with the current condition of the colony, with the soldiers being especially vocal in their unhappiness. They told him that they received no pay for long periods of time, for example, and that they lacked decent clothing and a wide range of essential goods from Europe. California, it appeared, had been forgotten by Madrid and Mexico City, and the *californios* were still doing nothing to take advantage of the region's potential. Indeed, it appeared the country had declined since Rezanov's and Langsdorff's visit. With the harsh conditions in the Russian American Company's northern possessions in mind, Von Kotzebue concluded that "it is to be regretted that this fine and fruitful country should lie entirely useless."[36]

Also sailing on the *Riurik* was Adelbert von Chamisso, a French-born botanist who described California in his book, *Voyage Around the World*. Chamisso was as disappointed as Von Kotzebue:

> California lies without industry, trade, and navigation, desert and unpeopled. It has remained neglected, without any importations from Mexico, during the six or seven years of the war between Spain and its colonies. The ship from St. Blas, which formerly brought supplies to these settlements yearly, arrived in Monterey only while we were there. The missions possess some bad barks in the harbour of San Francisco, built by foreign captives. Even the Presidio has not a single boat; and other havens are no better off. Strangers catch otter-skins even in the Spanish harbors; and only a smuggling trade, which the new governor of California, since his appointment (fourteen months ago) has tried to suppress, furnishes this province with the most indispensable articles.[37]

Chamisso was exceedingly critical of the mission system and of what he said was Indian slavery. Like Langsdorff, he was alarmed at the death rate among the mission Indians, caused, he felt, by the lack of any real medical knowledge on the part of the priests and their general indifference toward their charges: "The contempt which the missionaries have for the people, to whom they are sent, seems to us, considering their pious occupation, a very unfortunate circumstance. None of them appear to have troubled themselves about their history, customs, religions, or languages."[38] To be sure, there was widespread economic decline in the California missions during the years of the Insurgency in New Spain. The limited communication between California and the rest of Mexico increased the sense of isolation and abandonment felt by the *californios*. Yet Chamisso's attitude to the missions was qualitatively different from Langsdorff's. Langsdorff had made an attempt to understand the causes of California's backwardness. Chamisso rejected it as deliberate stubbornness: "A windmill of the Russian American Company's settlement creates astonishment, but does not find imitators. Some years ago, when artizans [sic] were brought here at great expense to teach the necessary arts, the Indians profited more by their instructions than the *gente rational* (rational people) as the Spaniards call themselves."[39] Chamisso's shipmate, Louis Choris, described the San Francisco settlement as well. His paintings of local foods, celebrations, and tools provided a more complete picture of what the crew of the *Riurik* found in San Francisco, but he shared Chamisso's impressions of California in 1816: it was a colony abandoned to corruption, backwardness, and laziness.[40]

The last description of Spanish California written by a Russian appeared as the result of Vasilii Mikhailovich Golovnin's visit to Monterey in 1818. Golovnin, a naval officer, one-time prisoner of the Japanese, and future vice-admiral, had been sent to Russian America to examine the company's treatment of the Indians in regions under its control. In September 1818, he arrived in California on board the *Kamchatka*. His account emphasized California's positive features. He wrote that he was especially touched by the "extreme courtesy and kindness" of the reception given by Governor Solá and Commandante Estudillo, for example.[41] Provided with horses and an armed escort by the governor, he explored Monterey's surroundings. Mission San Carlos, south of the presidio, he found to be poor and ordinary, although the food and hospitality there were pleasant, and the music and singing of the local Indians were rather touching. Geographically, Golovnin wrote, California was a "blessed region."[42] Its main drawback was the backwardness of its native peoples.

Golovnin decided that he could best understand the California of 1818 by comparing his observations with those written by the French explorer La Pérouse in 1786. Golovnin could discern no political development at all, and found there to be little change in the Spaniards' treatment of the Indians. The governor's charge was to protect California from foreign invasion, to maintain the prohibition against trade with foreign states, and to aid in the conversion of the Indians. Nothing more was required in La Pérouse's time, and nothing more was done in his own, Golovnin wrote. The condition of the Indians had changed since La Pérouse's visit, however: there were noticeably fewer of them at San Carlos for example, and those who were there no longer lived in huts, but in structures that to Golovnin resembled cattle pens: "can one possibly call it anything but a barnyard for domestic cattle and fowl? Each . . . small [section] is occupied by an entire family; cleanliness and tidiness are out of the question: a thrifty peasant usually has a better-kept cattle-pen."[43] Unlike many of his Russian compatriots, Golovnin did not blame the Indians for their miserable state. He did not see them as a retarded, inferior race, nor were they lazy or unproductive. On the contrary, with the proper training, they could master all sorts of skills, and "if they could be taught by good crafts-men, they probably could be the equal of Europeans."[44] Such praise for the Indians was so rare as to be almost unique among Russians visiting California, the majority of whom saw few prospects for a race rapidly dying out.

Like all his countrymen, Golovnin was impressed by California's productivity, and he stressed that crop yields at the missions were in "proportions unheard of in Europe"[45] Still, he wrote that he was "astounded and annoyed" at the "laziness and negligence" of the local inhabitants, and gave numerous examples of their incompetence: they refused to raise certain crops that could be useful additions to their fields; their use of ox-driven wagons was almost medieval; their ig-norance of current techniques of plant growing and tending was enor-mous, and their failure to take advantage of the opportunities offered for fishing was most unaccountable, since they appeared to love fresh fish:

> they are very fond of this food, but out of habit, it seems, cannot overcome the laziness that has become part of their nature. Can one possibly imagine that in the main settlement and port of this region, frequently visited by foreign ships, there is only one half-rotted boat and another rowboat quite beyond use? The former is the governor's official boat and therefore cannot be used for fishing. This boat was severely damaged by the surf on the beach because it did not have a boat anchor, as the Spaniards did not know how to manufacture such a complicated object.[46]

Such failures were especially repugnant to a man so accustomed to sailing, and he found it particularly surprising since most of Califor-nia's contact with Mexico was by ship and the seas around San Fran-cisco and Monterey were so rich with marine life.

What impressed Golovnin most in Spanish California was its poten-tial. He described at length the products the region could grow or manufacture and export to other areas of the Pacific Basin, adding that there was "enough grain and cured meat to supply all of our East-ern Siberia," if only the Californians would take advantage of the op-portunities offered them. These possibilities were limited most by the local administration, which acted according to the demands of the Spanish model it felt compelled to follow, and was in "a most pitiful and contemptible state." By altering that model, Golovnin felt, a great future would be possible for California: "I feel that with a different type of administration California could soon become an important, enlightened, and even wealthy region."[47]

What Golovnin said about California was little different from what Russian visitors had written twelve years before, or from what Russians would say about Mexico up to the Mexican Revolution of 1910. It was poorly administered by an incompetent governmental and religious sytem that did not permit the area to attain its full potential, and this failure, particularly the absence of industry and the wastefulness of agriculture, was felt perhaps more strongly by Russians from Alaska and Siberia than by any other foreigners.

After Mexico became independent, it faced many of the same problems as under Spanish rule, as well as a multitude of new ones. One continuing fear was the threat posed by English, United States, and Russian expansion in the direction of California. The Russians at Fort Ross were a particular irritation, but Russian hopes to expand south to San Francisco Bay were thwarted by the construction in 1823 of Mission San Francisco Solano to give added protection (along with Mission San Rafael, built in 1817) to the northern shore of the bay. Yet thousands of new foreigners appeared in Alta California with the opening of the territory's ports by the new Mexico City government. Russian comercial activities in California expanded. In 1826 the Russian American Company opened a permanent commercial agency in Monterey, and in the mid-1820s it was reported that most of the European goods sold in California originated with the company.[48]

A few Russians were still interested in something more than trade, and one in particular, naval Lt. Dmitrii Zavalishin, made rather more than a half-hearted attempt to convince the Russian government to move forcibly toward adding California to the Russian Empire. The nineteen-year-old Zavalishin arrived in California on the *Kreizer*, which was circumnavigating the earth in 1823 and 1824.[49] The ship had visited Fort Ross, and Zavalishin, as purchaser of provisions, recognized the obvious productive superiority of the land to the south. He decided on his own initiative that the company should annex more of California in the interests of improving the firm's economic strength. Knowledgeable and having been well educated in Moscow, Zavalishin studied Mexican California carefully. He discussed its physical isolation from Mexico proper with the local inhabitants in an attempt to gauge their feelings about their position. His report to St. Petersburg stressed that it would be best for California and the company if the territory were to submit voluntarily to Russian rule. Since he believed Britain and the United States would not allow this, however, he recommended that, based on what he knew of *californio* sympathies, the most realistic first step would be the creation of an independent California. The Russian American Company could then be ceded territories to the north, east, and south of this newly independent state, and a friendly Russian fleet in San Francisco Bay would deter any attack from the outside. The Russians would provide trade and economic aid, the grateful Californian government would allow its Russian friends to settle in increasing numbers in the new nation, and eventually California would be Russian. Zavalishin's hopes were those other Russians had expressed decades before: that the northern Pacific would become a Russian sea. Zavalishin informed his superiors that he had already converted at least a few *californios* to his side, "some through fanaticism, others through cupidity, others still through hate for the republican government, and the rest by inspiring them with misgivings with regard to England."[50]

Despite his encouraging reports, nothing came of Zavalishin's plans. When he returned to Petersburg at the end of 1824 and presented his memo to the government, there was some discussion of the suggestion. While the Russian American Company was in favor of the plan, the Foreign Ministry was not, arguing that its execution might alienate the United States and Great Britain at a time when such antagonism would be dangerous for Russia. The plan was dropped, and California was left to its own resources, although the few Russians who visited there during the next two decades constantly commented on how useful the region could be to Russia's Pacific possessions. Zavalishin himself became involved with the Decembrist revolt, was arrested in 1825, and exiled to Siberia. His writings on California were published only in 1865.

Zavalishin was apparently too busy hatching plans for the future of California during his visit there to devote time to describing the territory in any detail. Otto von Kotzebue, on the other hand, who was in the San Francisco Bay area on a return visit at about the same time, devoted several pages to California in his *New Voyage*. He was no more impressed in 1824 than he had been in 1815. He began by attacking with great fervor what he said was the degradation of the local Indians by their Spanish masters:

> The fate of these so called Christian Indians is not preferable even to that of negro slaves. Abandoned to the despotism of tyrannical monks, Heaven itself offers no refuge from their sufferings: for their spiritual masters stand as porters at the gate, and refuse entrance to whom they please. These unfortunate beings pass their lives in prayer, and in toiling for the monks, without possessing any property of their own. Thrice a day they are driven to church, to hear a mass in the Latin language; the rest of their time is employed in labouring in the fields and gardens with coarse, clumsy implements, and in the evening they are locked up in overcrowded barracks, which, unboarded, and without windows or beds, rather resemble cows' stalls than habitations for men. A coarse woolen shirt which they made themselves and then receive as a present from the missionaries, constitutes their only clothing. Such is the happines which the Catholic religion has brought to the uncultivated Indian; and this is the Paradise which he must not presume to undervalue by attempting a return to freedom in the society of his unconverted countrymen, under penalty of imprisonment in fetters.[51]

Von Kotzebue's sympathy for the Indians was not as great as it might appear, however. Some pages later he wrote that the many tribes of California Indians "are all alike ugly, stupid, dirty, and disgusting."[52] He saw almost nothing of value among either the Indians or the missionaries.

Von Kotzebue moved from his attack on the mission social system to give a brief account of recent political developments, explaining that during the Insurgency and the fighting for independence in Mexico, California had remained loyal to the king in Spain, and the only reason it joined with Mexico was that the Spaniards had neglected it. He was aghast at how little had been done in the territory since his last visit and repeated his stringent criticisms of the *californios'* failure to exploit the potential of their land. He visited Santa Clara, which he called an "arcadia" where the "most luxuriant harvest might be reaped" if an industrious population were established there. He added that the lack of boatbuilding in a region where the finest wood grows "is a striking proof of the indolence of the Spaniards and the stupidity of the Indians."[53]

Von Kotzebue's hopes for California were similar to Zavalishin's. He noted that he had travelled to Fort Ross by land with several *californios*.[54] One of these was the commander of the San Diego presidio, José María Estudillo, who told him of his dislike for the missions and their proprietors, and who explained to him the *californios'* sense of frustration at the ineffectiveness of the national government in Mexico City. Von Kotzebue found that the Russians and the *californios* got along well together at Fort Ross, with the Russians providing services such as iron-smithing that the *californios* could not do for themselves. He added that "I confess I could not help speculating upon the benefit this country would derive from becoming a province of our powerful empire, and how useful it would prove to Russia."[55]

Finally, since he too no doubt hoped to interest the government in Petersburg into taking a more active stand with respect to California, he compared Russian and Spanish approaches in dealing with the native peoples of the regions they had colonized:

> The more striking the contrast between the two nations in their treatment of the savages, the more ardently must every friend to humanity rejoice on entering the Russian territory.
>
> The Greek Church does not make converts by force. Free from fanaticism, she preaches only toleration and love. She does not even admit of persuasion, but trusts wholly to conviction for proselytes, who, when once they enter her communion, will always find her a loving mother. How different has been the conduct both of Catholic priests and Protestant missionaries.[56]

His conclusion was predictable: "Should the blessings of civilization ever be extended to the rude inhabitants of these regions, the merit will be due to the Russian settlements, certainly not to the Spanish missions."[57] Von Kotzebue was no friend of the Catholic church and its mission system, and like Zavalishin, he had great hopes for the expansion of Russian influence on the west coast of North America. His devotion to Russian Orthodoxy was that of a convert, and his dedication to Russian imperialist expansion equalled it in enthusiasm. Although Russian administrative and religious policies toward native peoples in Siberia and North America were more enlightened and tolerant that those of the Spanish, Von Kotzebue's highly critical account of Mexican California must be evaluated in light of his own obvious religious and nationalistic prejudices.

A more satisfying and balanced view of California, although by no means one that was entirely positive, was published by Kirill Timofeevich Khlebnikov in the journal *Syn otechestva (Son of the Fatherland)* in 1829.[58] Khlebnikov lived in America for sixteen years as an employee of the Russian American Company, visiting California annually to buy grain for the Alaskan settlements. His knowledge of Spanish aided him in making many acquaintances, especially among the local priests. Khlebnikov gained an understanding of the area which was more complete and objective than that of other visitors. His articles were sober, concise, and to the point, with sections devoted to the mission system, the military administration, the climate, agricultural production and animal husbandry, the way of life of the *californios*, trade, the Indians, and communications with Mexico. He was particularly concerned with natural history, and he gave considerable attention to local geography, flora, and fauna.

Most striking in Khlebnikov's account was his description of the lives of the population, which was as critical as anything Von Kotzebue wrote. The Californians were, for example, "a lazy, untidy people, of limited capability,"[59] and their children were as untidy and irresponsible as their parents. The men played cards or held cockfights, but did little else: "if they can get Indians from the missions to work, [they] walk around with arms folded, telling the Indians what to do. There is hardly a skilled mechanic among them." Some had become farmers with the opening up of foreign trade, but "very, very unwillingly do they give up their laziness."[60] The soliders were undisciplined, and violence, theft, and gambling were frequent. The present condition of California was not encouraging, Khlebnikov concluded: trade was almost nonexistent because the inhabitants did not see its value and the missions had come to share this view; the territory was isolated because the ship from Mexico arrived only once every two or three years; the Indians were like children, since most of their needs were provided for by the area's natural abundance, and the intelligence and cleverness required to survive in more strenuous climates were unnecessary. All told, Mexican California was still in its infancy as a nation. Much was needed for it to reach maturity, but the Mexican and Indian Californians could not accomplish this transformation alone. Only with the proper foreigners settling there could California develop a real civilization of its own.

This steady, and by now monotonous litany of Russian disappointment in how California was administered by the Spaniards and Mexicans continued until shortly before the area was annexed to the United States.[61] Baron Wrangell, as will be seen in the following section, was as critical as were his predecessors of what he found in Monterey and San Francisco. In 1840–41 I. G. Voznesenskii visited San Francisco, San Rafael, Santa Clara, and Sutter's Fort, but despite some fascinating sketches of the local population, wrote little that was new. His diaries, and the naturalist's collections he made along the coast of Baja California near Loreto and Isla Carmen, which might have provided a unique view of that area, were unfortunately lost.[62]

On the whole, then, Russians were extremely critical of Spanish and Mexican California, and particularly of its population, whether native or immigrant. Its potential riches, they felt, were not being developed by its backward and lazy inhabitants. The Russians' criticisms of the military, the civil administration, and above all the mission system can best be understood in light of the fact that many of them reached the California coast after long stays in the north, during which they constantly suffered from the cold and were quite often on the verge of starving. All the Russians believed that a more energetic people, or at least a more imaginative and ambitious administration, was needed in California. It is not surprising that some tried to encourage Russian exploration and settlement. They saw California as a potential garden of Eden; they never understood that for Spain, and then Mexico, it was an uncomfortable, remote, isolated frontier. California offered little to Mexico, but might give Russians a great deal. This more than anything else determined the Russian view of Mexico's northernmost territory.

Wrangell's Journey Through Mexico in 1836

Until the mid-1830s Russian contact with Mexico had almost entirely resulted from trade with California. In the absence of diplomatic relations, Russian ignorance of all but the new republic's northernmost territories remained almost complete. Descriptions of California did not tell much about the "real" Mexico to the south. The first Russian to describe central Mexico was Baron Ferdinand Wrangell (1796–1870), who made an extensive journey from San Blas to Veracruz in 1836, at a time when much of importance was happening in the country. He kept a diary of his journey, and upon his return to St. Petersburg published a book and several articles about his travels in Mexico. Wrangell's career had been distinguished. Born in Pskov, he had twice taken part in Russian voyages around the world (in 1817–19 and 1825–27), had been made a corresponding member of the Academy of Sciences in 1827, and from 1830 until 1835 was given leave from the Imperial Navy to serve in Sitka as governor of Russian America.[63] He was then ordered to return to St. Petersburg to take up a new post. Normally, Russians in North America returned to Europe by sea, or overland across Siberia. Wrangell selected a slightly different route, however. Both he and the Russian American Company's directors believed the time had come to increase commercial, and if possible, political contacts with the new Mexican republic. It was felt that much could be accomplished if Wrangell were to return to St. Petersburg by way of Mexico. There he could meet with government officials and initiate discussions leading to increased and more profitable trade between Mexico and the Russian possessions in America. Very possibly, he could take the first steps toward an exchange of ambassadors as well. Although Wrangell's negotiations yielded no substantive results, his visit was significant because of what might have been accomplished, and because his description of Mexico was the only major source of information about the country written by a Russian citizen for several decades. His published accounts provided Russian audiences a rare view of a tempestuous period in Mexican history: the liberal government of Gómez Farías was overthrown in April 1834; in 1835 Texas had declared its independence; and the following year Santa Anna marched north to defeat the rebels. It appeared that Mexico was in serious danger of political disintegration. Wrangell himself saw little prospect that the country could avoid disaster.[64]

Ostensibly, Wrangell's purposes in visiting Mexico City were to expand Russian trade with California and Mexico and to clarify by legal compact the boundaries of the Fort Ross colony. He hoped to convince Santa Anna's government to make San Francisco Bay the colony's southern boundary. In return, he was prepared to promise that Russia would at last extend diplomatic recognition to Mexico. On the basis of correspondence with Governor Figueroa of California, Wrangell had been led to believe that the Gómez Farías government was interested in improving relations with Russia. Further Russian advances into California could thereby be forestalled, and Mexico would gain a powerful ally in territorial conflicts with Britain and the United States. Other Russians had made similar suggestions to St. Petersburg in the past, of course, and each time the Foreign Ministry rejected them. Wrangell knew that he would need to exercise care in dealing with both governments. In the end, he was given his government's permission to travel to Mexico in order to "enter into discussions on the confirmation of the convention on our rights to the shore of New Albion, on the expansion of our authority to such boundaries which may be restricted [and] about the permanent establishing of trade on known rules in both Californias and on the other coasts of Mexico."[65] However, the Foreign Ministry made it clear that Wrangell would be travelling as a private person. He might represent the Russian American Company, but not the government of Tsar Nicholas I. Diplomatic recognition of Mexico was a question too important for him to handle alone.

Wrangell, his wife, and their young son sailed on the *Sitka* for California in November 1835. In Monterey he expected to obtain the passport and letters of introduction necessary for his journey from his friend, Governor Figueroa. It was Figueroa who had first suggested the journey, and he had given Wrangell a description of the best itinerary to follow.[66] Wrangell was distressed to learn that Figueroa had died only shortly before his arrival, however, and the interim governor was less favorable toward the Russians. Wrangell decided he might be more successful in obtaining the required documents and permissions in San Blas, which was considerably closer to the capital.

Wrangell's visit to Monterey was therefore brief, but it did allow him to observe first-hand the changes so rapidly overtaking California. He found, for example, that secularization had ruined the economic viability of Mission San Carlos. Its appalling deterioration was countered, on the other hand, by impressive growth and construction in Monterey. With independence, California's ports had at last been opened to foreign ships and settlement, and Monterey was over-whelmed by American and English merchants and seaman. Wrangell was certainly struck by the declining role of the Russians in California, and must have felt that Russian activity there might soon be eclipsed should nothing be done to reinforce it. Undoubtedly, his mission in Mexico gained greater importance in his eyes after his stop in Monterey.

Wrangell's anxiousness to reach Mexico City was frustrated almost immediately in San Blas. The port's commandant was in Tepic, forty miles away, in the mountains, when the *Sitka* arrived, but Wrangell was told that a message requesting his return would be sent to him. In the meantime, he was asked to complete a number of forms required of foreigners by the central authorities. Wrangell also learned that his Russian passport, despite its being signed "by a Vice-Chancellor of the Russian Empire,"[67] would not suffice for passage through Mexico. Instead, he would need special permission for the journey from Mexico City, which would probably require six weeks. The commandant's assistant recommended that Wrangell and his party stay in San Blas and enjoy the town's hospitality while awaiting a response from the capital. The region's fresh fruits and vegetables were indeed appealing, but Wrangell did not intend to remain there long. Almost immediately he began sending messages to contacts in Tepic, asking them to use their influence to obtain permission for his party to proceed inland.

As a town and port, San Blas was an enormous disappointment. Three warships anchored there, formerly Spanish property, were slowly falling apart, and Wrangell found in them a metaphor for what he saw as the creativity and energy of viceregal rule now being replaced by the decay and decline of independence. Like the ships, Wrangell wrote later, the town and presidio were literally disintegrating, their only good features the remnants of colonial times. The government's officials were incredibly lax in their duties: an English naval vessel had been anchored offshore for several days, he learned, but the port commander had not yet seen fit to come down from Tepic to deal with it. On the whole, San Blas was a distressing, gloomy place, and when word came that the English consul in Tepic had obtained official approval for them to travel there, Wrangell and his family left gladly.

The journey overland by horseback was uneventful, although Wrangell recalled that the distant sight of coconuts, bananas, and sugar cane made their first day's diet of tortillas and beans unappealing. On the second day they climbed into the mountains, the vegetation changed to corn, maguey, and fruit trees, and their richer diet of spicy foods and exotic fruits was more tasteful. Unlike San Blas, Wrangell found Tepic quite attractive: "the tidiness of the streets, which were paved and which even had sidewalks, the whitewashed walls of the houses, with green trees scattered between them, the activity of the people— all this was a treat for our eyes, grown tired as they had of the monotony of the country in which we had spent the last six years."[68] Despite appearances, however, something was not quite what it should be: the city did not appear to be a particularly healthy place, and hundreds of people had died from a recent cholera epidemic; there was no doctor, no hospital, no teachers, no school, and since they had been drafted to fight in Texas, not even any soldiers in the town.

It was in Tepic that Wrangell had his first opportunity to talk with the local inhabitants about conditions in the republic. Wrangell and his family stayed in the house of the British consul, Eustaquío Barrón, and met a number of people through his intervention. Wrangell wrote that on the basis of his discussions with Barrón, the city's other foreigners, even with the "simple people," he was led to believe that in general the new republic and its government were viewed with distrust and dismay. Politicians were seen to be interested only in their personal wealth, and the military officers and the bureaucrats were felt to be, without exception, corrupt. Wrangell admitted that Mexico's economy appeared to have improved in some respects since independence. Nevertheless, the nation's legal system and its military and political structure had all declined and been corrupted by the republic's promised "freedom," and the country still faced numerous unsolved problems. The general consensus, he wrote, was that life had been better under Spanish rule.

That Wrangell was so critical of Mexico, and that those he talked to reinforced his evaluation, is not surprising. Yet in his analysis, he did not take into account the enormous destruction the country experienced during the Insurgency and the struggle for independence, as well as the years of economic and social dislocation resulting from them. These were events of the past, and he gave little credence to them as ameliorating factors in his evaluation of conditions in the mid-1830s.[69] If what he wrote about Tepic was any indication of his views of Mexico at the time, it could not be expected that he would view the rest of the country any more positively.

Overcoming obstructions placed in his path by Tepic's *alcalde*, Barrón succeeded in obtaining permission for Wrangell and his party to move on to Guadalajara and Mexico City. Of the parts of Mexico through which he travelled, it was perhaps this area of the country that Wrangell liked most. While the roads were frequently rocky and in bad repair, the countryside and natural surroundings were extraordinarily beautiful, he wrote. He could not avoid constantly comparing his experiences in Alaska with what he found in central Mexico. A neat and tiny *posada* in an unexceptional village, for example, with its tasty food and pleasant surroundings, was of a sort almost never encountered in Russia. There was nothing in Siberia to compare to the town of Ahuacatlán, with its stone church, its houses with windows, its benches, gardens, streets, and its bread. European-style bread was not often encountered in rural Mexico, and tortillas had never satisfied the Russians' taste for bread. Outside Guadalajara they were met by a carriage sent at the orders of Barrón's agent, Manuel Luna. It was the first one, Wrangell noted, that he or his family had seen in six years. They continued their journey in greater comfort through the maguey fields in the vicinity of Tequila and on to a military post some distance from Guadalajara. There a detachment of soldiers was to escort them into the city and protect them from the local bandits, although Wrangell remarked that judging by their disorderliness and unkempt uniforms, they might easily be thieves themselves.

Because his son had become ill, Wrangell and his wife remained several days in Guadalajara, in a house prepared for them by Luna in a fashionable section of the city. Thus he was able to describe Guadalajara in some detail. He wrote again that he could discern only decline in comparison with what had apparently existed before independence; only traces of good taste and luxury remained, for example. The people of the city he found quite interesting, and once more, he relied on them for his understanding of the area's condition.[70] Luna was a Spaniard and had lived in the city for twenty-five years, becoming a commissioner for merchants throughout the country, even though he could neither read nor write. A foreigner, he was a great commercial success. Wrangell added that most Mexicans, on the other hand, seemed to lack the energy and initiative to be a success in business. What Wrangell had feared in California, he believed he saw confirmed in Guadalajara. Like other foreigners writing on Mexico in the 1830s, he saw little Mexican enthusiasm for the kind of entrepreneurial activity he felt necessary for the country's future.

By the middle of February his son had recovered, and the family left by coach for Mexico City.[71] As before, he described the countryside in glowing terms, its organ cactus, pepper trees, and variety of vegetables continually impressive. The party passed Guanajuato, had a glimpse of the Valenciana mine, stayed a night in Irapuato, and came quite near the "very pretty" towns of Salamanca, Dolores, San Miguel, and Celaya. They stayed overnight in Querétaro, which they found appealing. Even so, it was a town that had suffered greatly during the Insurgency because of its sympathy with the Spaniards, and it was depopulated and still in great disrepair. On the whole, Wrangell was much more positive in his evaluation of the Bajío, the area north of Mexico City, than of the western part of the country. Nearing the capital, he recalled, he and his family were captivated by the sight of the two snow-covered volcanoes in the distance and by the nicely landscaped road leading into the city. Equally notable however, were the numerous fields, gardens, and haciendas which had been destroyed during the Insurgency, desolate areas where little recovery yet had taken place. They arrived in Mexico City in the rain and darkness and settled into a hotel owned by foreigners.

Wrangell hoped to arrange meetings with government officials as soon as he could, but was immediately frustrated. President Santa Anna could not receive him because he was in Texas, attempting to quell the rebellion there. Wrangell next tried to see the interim president, General Barragán, with whom he hoped for some success: Barragán was reported to be an honest, decent man, and Wrangell had several letters of recommendation from Barragán's friends. Difficulties remained, however. Wrangell still had no documents legally permitting him to travel through the country, and the general Mexican distrust of Russians was encouraged by British and French diplomats who had no intention of allowing the Russians to further their influence in Mexico City. Making things worse for Wrangell was that Barragán was ill and soon died. The foreign minister, José María

Ortiz Monasterio, was temporarily bedridden, so all business was suspended, and for the time being, Wrangell was able to do nothing official in the city.

Wrangell finally decided to approach Ortiz Monasterio by letter, hoping later to be allowed to see him in person. His message recounted his correspondence with Figueroa and noted the hopes expressed by *californios* and Russians for increased commercial relations between Mexico and the Russian American Company. The principal focus of the letter, however, was in a number of specific requests: that the company be allowed to obtain grain and food in Alta California and salt from Baja California, that otter hunting by Russians be allowed, and that Russian ships be permitted to trade freely at all Mexican ports, on both coasts. In exchange, Wrangell offered the company's Alaskan facilities to Mexican ships for trade and repairs, and the training at Novo-Arkhangelsk of Indian and *californio* children in skills that would be useful to them upon their return home. All this, Wrangell concluded rather grandly, would be of great value for the economic advancement of the northern Pacific basin and for those countries along its shores. He mentioned nothing about diplomatic recognition, but he hoped the series of proposals would appeal to the economic aspirations of the government.

Eventually, through the intercession of Friedrich von Gerolt, the general consul of Prussia and a man highly respected in Mexico, Wrangell was given an audience with the new interim president, José Justo Corro. Wrangell repeated his requests and added that Russian friendship could be useful for Mexico, especially with the growing encroachment of the Hudson's Bay Company in the north. Not surprisingly, considering the magnitude of the problems facing Mexico, Corro responded that for the present, relations between their two nations should continue as before. Any new information or requests should be put in writing by Wrangell and would be considered in due course. With that bureaucratic dismissal, the meeting ended.

While awaiting a formal written response to his proposals from the foreign minister, and disappointed in the interim president's evasiveness, Wrangell wrote in his diary some of his most caustic comments on Mexico and its government. Throughout his journey he had tended to believe everything negative he had heard about the government and the military. His experiences in the capital reinforced his growing prejudices. He wrote that he found incredible and unconscionable the banditry, theft, and lawlessness that existed everywhere in the republic. The decline of public morality could be seen in the great number of murders of ordinary people, he added, murders most frequently the result of drunkenness. In Wrangell's eyes, President Santa Anna was little more than a simpleton, as his foolish certainty that he would be able to defeat the Texans indicated. In general, Wrangell described the nation as being in a miserable state:

> Although Mexico seemed destined to be the richest land in the world, at present it is in a pitiable condition; the state's expenditures are twice the size of what they were at the time of the Spaniards, [and] the income from customs would easily cover expenditures if everything would [reach] the treasury, but smuggling and theft have grown indescribably. Santa Anna is the biggest smuggler in the land and there is no official in the entire government who cannot be bought. The Mexican entirely lacks any conscience or sense of honor, he suffers from a deficiency of education, of a clear intellectual sense, he has no direction to his energy and he is happy only when his most immediate personal needs are being satisfied.[72]

Wrangell's frustrations with the government are clearly reflected in this excerpt from his diary, and these were some of the most negative comments he made about Mexico. On the other hand, and despite his almost complete disillusionment with the country, he did find the capital a pleasant, even a beautiful city, its houses attractive and tasteful, and the interiors of the churches, especially the cathedral, exceedingly rich. Above all, he wrote, "Chapultepec was for me the most attractive as a traveler: the view of the city and surroundings was enchanting, and the . . . ancient cypresses . . . made an impression that is indelible."[73] Other comments he made about the city seconded these, although there was no doubt in his mind that appearances could not compensate for governmental and economic ineffectiveness.

Finally, on the fourteenth of March, Wrangell received an encouraging letter from Ortiz Monasterio informing him that the government would be pleased to increase trade and other relations with the Rus-

sian American Company in California and that it was prepared to carry
on conversations with official representatives of Tsar Nicholas I. He
was told as well that a message had been sent to the Mexican ambassador in London instructing him to initiate such discussions with a
Russian diplomat there as soon as the tsarist government expressed
interest in such conversations. Wrangell knew that Mexico did not
favor trade with countries that had not extended it diplomatic recognition. By implication, he concluded, the Russian American Company's fortunes in California and Mexico would depend on the establishment of official relations between the Mexican Republic and
the Russian Empire.

There was nothing more for Wrangell to do in the capital, and he
soon left with his family for Veracruz. From there a ship would take
them on to the United States and Europe. With a military escort to
protect them from bandits, they travelled by carriage to Cholula, then
on to what Wrangell described in his diary as the "hateful" city of
Puebla, notable for its "fanatical Catholicism."[74] Few Russians cared
for Mexican Catholic Christianity, and Wrangell voiced no exception
to their general view. On the second day, the escort left them, apparently because they themselves were fearful of thieves, and Wrangell's
party travelled on through rain, fog, and cold to arrive at a "second
Sitka," the "ugly and unpleasant" city of Jalapa. For unclear reasons,
the party stayed in Jalapa for several days, although Wrangell quite
obviously found little that was attractive in the town. Jalapa and its
surroundings typified another impression that he had come to feel
about all Mexico: "it is notable everywhere [here] that no love for the
beauties of nature is to be found, nor any pleasure in living on the
land."[75] It seemed to Wrangell that the old Spanish urban customs,
particularly the turning away from nature of Spanish domestic architecture, had been transferred almost intact to Mexico, with little con-
sideration for the great physical differences between the two nations.
At this point in his journey, Wrangell's antipathy to Mexico's government influenced all his analyses, and he even considered it worthwhile to criticize the "love of gossip" that he found so offensive among
Mexican women.

During his unexpectedly long stay in Jalapa, Wrangell had an opportunity to read press accounts of the recent fighting in the north

between Santa Anna and the Texans. His reaction to the news from San Antonio de Béjar restated some of his earlier criticisms of the corruption of Santa Anna's administration:

> In Jalapa we learned . . . of Santa Anna's capture of Béjar in Texas and afterwards of the Alamo fortress, which was taken by storm, at a cost of about 300 soldiers, 50 officers and 2 generals, while 150 Texans defended this insignificant fortress and were slaughtered. The pompous announcement in the government newspaper, the promises of reward to the families of the dead, the praise of General Santa Anna as a military genius, immortal, benemerito, etc., the cannon shots, Te Deum, and all sorts of festivities were intended to give this insignificant event the appearance of great importance; [but] since the Texans are now [even] more embittered [than before], it seems likely that if Santa Anna does not soon turn around and invade [and occupy] the country again, the whole [Mexican] army will [eventually] be destroyed.[76]

The adulation of Santa Anna in the newspapers was especially odious to Wrangell, since he believed the inefficiency and dishonesty of government officials throughout the country were but reflections of the president's conduct. What he saw at the port of Veracruz only seemed to confirm his opinions. He noted that a U.S. packet ship docked in the harbor had just been bought by the Mexican government for the Texas expedition. The government paid 14,000 "piasters" for it, 10,000 to the former owners and 4,000 to the local official who "arranged" the purchase. Wrangell added that it was obvious to any seaman that the ship needed extensive refitting and that it was unlikely that the work could be completed before the Texas campaign was over. Nonetheless, enormous amounts of federal money were being expended on it, foolishly, solely to line pockets of local grafters, Wrangell felt. Finally, shortly before leaving Mexico, and apparently in amazement, Wrangell remarked that on the basis of what he had observed, Mexico's entire navy consisted of two ships of war, a single corvette in the Pacific and a schooner in the Gulf of Mexico. For a man who had devoted much of his life to naval affairs, it was an appalling, unforgivable, and highly dangerous situation for Mexico.

Wrangell and his family had made the descent from Jalapa to Veracruz without incident, although they did encounter a coach from the coast that had been robbed only minutes before meeting them. They were all relieved to reach the sea, and in mid-April, they sailed on a U.S. vessel for New York. Within two months of leaving Mexico, they were again in St. Petersburg.

Diplomatically and economically, Wrangell's mission was a failure. Soon after his return to Petersburg, he reported to the Foreign Ministry that if Russia would recognize Mexican independence, Russian possessions in California would be safe, and eventually significant growth in trade between the two countries could be expected. He stressed that one of Mexico's greatest fears in 1836 was that the Russians might be preparing to seize California; recognition would make them considerably more secure. The ministry listened to Wrangell's report with interest, but did not respond to his suggestions positively. While the government was willing to authorize Wrangell to talk to Mexican officials informally about matters of mutual concern, it was not committed to the Russian American Company's further expansion into California. Above all, Nicholas I did not approve of dealing with revolutionary governments. Consequently, and despite Wrangell's recommendations, Russian diplomatic recognition of a Mexican government did not take place for decades. Wrangell knew that with this political failure, economic relations had no real chance for success either. Trade negotiations did begin in London, but the Russian American Company soon decided that Fort Ross and the Russian colony in California were not sufficiently profitable. It eventually withdrew from North America, but Mexico soon found that the United States posed a greater threat than Russia ever had.[77]

Wrangell's journey might have resulted in expanded ties between Russia and Mexico. In the end, however, its significance lay in Wrangell's subsequent writings and in his views of the republic. Central Mexico was a mysterious land to most Europeans, and to Russians it was still almost unknown. With Wrangell again in St. Petersburg, his journey created great interest in the capital and throughout the empire. Almost immediately Nikolai Grech, editor of *Severniaia pchela* (The Northern Bee), asked Wrangell to write about his trip for the journal. Wrangell complied, and in the fall of 1836 a series of articles appeared that were published later the same year as a separate book under the title, *Ocherk puti iz Sitkhi v S. Peterburg F. Vrangelia* (Sketch of a Journey from Sitka to St. Petersburg by F. Wrangell).[78]

By all indications, Wrangell had done considerable reading about Mexico before he arrived in San Blas: his diary indicated familiarity with Poinsett's *Notes on Mexico,* Ward's *Mexico in 1827,* Humboldt's *Political Essay on the Kingdom of New Spain,* as well as with other less well known books. In addition, on earlier trips to California he had talked about Mexico with Governor Figueroa and with William Hartnell, the Russian American Company's agent in San Francisco. Yet while his preparations were exemplary and methodical, it was the first-hand experience of Mexico that inspired his comments and evaluations, written first in his diary and then published.

Like other visitors, Wrangell was moved by the country's rich natural beauties. Being a practical man, he was appalled that so little had been done to exploit Mexico's immeasurable resources, however, including its human population. He described Mexican society with care, and he came to see that the greatest strength of Mexico was its simple, rural people. They lived polite, peaceful lives of quiet hope, he wrote, their only weakness being to follow so closely the advice and leadership of the Catholic clergymen: "The priests, along with the innumerable monks, are a true evil for the country; superstition, immorality, [and] intolerance are fostered and promoted by this ill-bred class."[79] Wrangell wrote little about religion and its practice in Mexico, but his general hostility to it is striking. His only other comments about religion pertained to California. Surprisingly, he found the missions there to be admirably administered, and he was dismayed at what he felt were the negative results of secularization. Yet California was very different from central Mexico, and Wrangell was probably most impressed by the Franciscans' economic efficiency in a frontier region and not by their religious devotion.

Wrangell's evaluation of government officials paralleled his view of the clergy. They were some of the worst he had encountered in his extensive travels, he wrote, and from them Mexico's population suffered greatly. Much of the country's misery derived from these officials and from the unfortunate form of government which had been adopted there: "A pretty republic, whose chief is Santa Anna, the biggest thief, the most unconscionable braggart [of all], a man completely ignorant; no opposition exists in the Chamber [of Deputies], and none in the press. Nothing is done for public enlightenment, nothing for order and security; the conduct of business is tepid, carried on in an unbelievable fashion, the direct consequence of the representative [form of] government . . . everything is based on personal interest."[80] What Wrangell was describing, of course, was a newly independent nation suffering from backwardness and from the rule of men who had had no administrative experience during colonial times. It was a pattern that would be repeated throughout the world over the next century and a half, but not one Wrangell understood. It should perhaps be reiterated as well that Wrangell never seemed to appreciate fully the extent of destruction and dislocation Mexico had suffered during the century's second decade. Nor did he fully understand the nature of Mexico's economy, either before or after independence. But for a Baltic German serving in the Russian Imperial government, none of this mattered greatly. If Russia, with its backwardness, corruption, and bureaucracy, could be expected to be reformed, Wrangell reasoned, so could Mexico.[81]

Above all, Wrangell's writings emphasized the decay and decline he saw in Mexico. Everything was worse than it must have been under Spanish rule, he assumed. Wrangell was no believer in democracy, or in republican forms of government, and Mexico appeared to confirm the weaknesses of both. He wrote that not only had nothing new been built since independence, everything had fallen into disuse and abandonment. In Wrangell's eyes, all that kept the country from sinking into barbarism was the activity of foreigners. Even more discouraging, these energetic foreigners were despised and hated by native-born Mexicans. Here again, Wrangell's judgment may have been flavored by the fact that he had associated primarily with foreigners in Mexico, and that much he learned about the country was through them.

Perhaps most interesting to Wrangell was that he believed he had come to Mexico at a turning point in the nation's history. The country was on the verge of a great crisis: "In general, in my opinion," he wrote in his diary, "the preservation of Texas is of enormous importance for the Republic, and its loss would have great consequences for Mexico."[82] More broadly, he felt, the rebellion in Texas was only a symptom of the problems facing Mexico, and there was more than Texas at stake. The U.S. ambassador told him that his government had agents in San Francisco and Monterey prepared to seize California at any time. Other members of the diplomatic corps in the capital maintained that if Texas were lost, New Mexico, Sonora, and California would all become independent and eventually be annexed to the United States. It was clear from Wrangell's diary, and his reports to the Foreign Ministry certainly stressed as well, that he believed Mexico's loss of its northern territories would be catastrophic. He sensed, however, that because of the country's condition, the corruption and self-interest of the government and army, and lack of any real national feeling on the part of the people as a whole, such a disaster was inevitable. No one in the republic seemed capable of comprehending the threat or of combatting it effectively.

For Wrangell, as for many Europeans and Americans, and not the least his Russian American Company colleagues, Mexico was a country of great potential. Its people and its land demanded more than its government and political system offered. His discouragement at what he saw there was matched only by his frustration at the limited imagination of his own government. While Wrangell hoped that Russia might be able to gain something from Mexico's possible dissolution, he was perhaps most disappointed that his government refused to recognize the great possibilities inherent in the fact that Russia and Mexico were neighbors in North America. His view of central Mexico corresponded closely to his predecessors' descriptions of Mexican California. Their prejudices were similar, as was their pessimism about Mexico's future. They were also the most typically "European" in their approach to Mexico and the least sympathetic of all Russian and Soviet writers in their evaluation of the country, its government, and its way of life. This may have been because many of them had non-Russian ethnic backgrounds, were only partially assimilated into Russian life, or were only employees of the Russian American Company, and not Russian citizens. It was their analysis that dominated the opinion of Russians for many decades, however. Despite their criticisms, Wrangell and at least a few of his predecessors left one positive observation in the minds of the readers of their articles and reports: in general, Mexico's wealth was in its people, people who provided a justification for at least a limited optimism for the future.

2
THE
AGE OF
PORFIRIO
DÍAZ

Early Visitors

Few Russians travelled to Mexico between 1836 and the beginning of the Porfiriato in 1876. Accounts appearing in the Russian press were almost entirely translations of works by Western European or U.S. writers. The last Russian of any importance to write about Mexican California was Aleksandr Markov, who published several articles and a book about his experiences in the region in 1845.[1] He described California in terms similar to those his compatriots had used, but was especially impressed by the *californios'* standard of living. The richness and variety of their food and the extravagant furniture they had obtained through trade distinguished them from the Russian colonists to the north. Like earlier travellers, Markov was also moved by the uncommonly good feelings expressed toward the Russians by the inhabitants of Yerba Buena and was particularly proud of his Russian citizenship. "The Russians enjoy special respect in that country compared with other foreigners on account of [their] kind and civil treatment of the natives. The name of a Russian serves in the distant precincts of the Eastern Ocean as an emblem of good-heartedness, civility, honesty, and enterprise."[2] One might ask whether the *californios* were expressing genuine feelings or merely a general friendliness toward foreigners. No doubt a certain amount of exaggeration was involved on Markov's part as well. He seems to have been an unusually good-natured man, and he constantly met people in California who told him how much they admired the Russians. Even so, it is interesting that Markov and other Russians considered their treatment of the local population to be the feature which distinguished them from their European and American counterparts.

Markov also wrote about a brief visit he made to Mazatlán on behalf of the Russian American Company, to exchange money to buy salt at Isla Carmen. He claimed that no Russian ship had docked at Mazatlán before, so his articles gave Russian readers their first description of the city and its people, who themselves had had little opportunity to meet Russians. Mazatlán's tropical surroundings made Markov and the ship's crew feel they were from a different world, and Markov recounted that the port commander's wife refused to believe their tales of the snow and cold, privation and discomfort of Yakutsk. Walking around town, he and his shipmates were amazed at the oranges, lemons, figs, bananas, and sugar cane that grew almost wild. The prices for the fruit piled in the street or displayed in the central market and private shops were incredibly, but satisfyingly low. Goods from everywhere seemed to be available, and Markov was gratified to find that canvas with a Russian trademark sold easily and at a high price. He was told by a shopkeeper that Mexicans liked to buy foreign items (as did Russians, Markov interjected) and especially Russian canvas, since it had a reputation for quality. The canvas was in short supply, and Markov lamented the failure of Russians to market their goods in Mexico, where he was convinced a significant profit might be realized.[3]

Markov admired Mazatlán's thriving economy, but was happiest, perhaps, with its social life, which had no parallel in the Russian colonies to the north. The city's three-storied main hotel was filled with attractive furniture and crowds of well-dressed people eating ice cream, drinking coffee, and playing cards, chess, and billiards with a grace and elegance he had not seen for some time.[4] The populace promenaded the streets in the evening, and the visiting Russian sailors serenaded the crowds, albeit a bit drunkenly, with traditional Russian songs. The local inhabitants were hospitable, polite, and curious.

The stop in Mazatlán was a pleasant experience. Loreto was more disappointing, and the salt beds at Isla Carmen were too wet to allow collection, but to Markov the journey was not a failure because of the taste of civilization he had had in Mazatlán. He did nothing to help his audience understand better Mexico's economic or political problems, but he wrote the sort of colorful travelogue that Russian readers enjoyed in the 1840s and 1850s, a description of the tropical coast of Mexico that almost none of them would see for themselves.

Markov's account of Mexico and California was the last written by a representative of the Russian American Company. After the company's withdrawal from California, there was little reason for Russians to visit Mexico, particularly since the two countries had no diplomatic contacts and almost no commercial ties. The Crimean War focused Russian concerns on affairs in Europe and the Near East, and during the War of the Reform and the French Intervention, Mexico was involved in its own domestic affairs. The psychological distance between Russia and Mexico came to approximate the geographic distance, and politically the Russian imperial government clearly acknowledged the special role played in Mexican affairs by the United States. Surprisingly, however, there were a few individual Russians who travelled through Mexico during the century's middle decades. They came not on diplomatic or commercial business, but for scientific reasons. They were followed, subsequently, by other Russians who visited Mexico during the Porfiriato, both before and after the establishment of diplomatic relations between Russia and Mexico in 1890. Their writings are particularly interesting since they found much in common in the two countries' historical experience and current hopes and desires. While they presented a picture of the country that was in many ways similar to that of other foreign visitors during these years, they possessed a sense of identification with the aims and intents of the Mexican government and a sympathy with the population that few Western European or U.S. analysts had. Some depicted Mexico progressing at a rate faster than their own country, others saw a regime exploiting its population more unmercifully than did their own. Few are indifferent. Most importantly, their essays were published in some of the most influential and widely read Russian periodicals.

With the exception of Markov, the Russians who travelled in Mexico in the forty years after Wrangell wrote little of more than superficial interest about what they encountered. A. G. Rotchev spent two days in Acapulco in 1853, for example, but left no substantive description of the city.[5] In 1850, P. N. Golovin also stopped in Acapulco while on a journey to Alaska, and in a series of letters to his mother, wrote briefly about the city. He said that Acapulco's setting was superlative, with an excellent harbor and mountains covered with lush vegetation. The town itself, however, was only a collection of small houses beneath a fortress that, while it might have been impregnable to Santa Anna, could easily be taken by no more than "a hundred and fifty Russian sailors."[6] The only unreservedly favorable comment he made about Acapulco concerned the Hotel Louisiane, run by a French-woman, which served the ship-weary passengers chicken, fresh eggs, steak, and wine, and provided remarkably congenial surroundings. Otherwise, he concluded, the town had little to commend it, and the prospect of travelling on to San Francisco was all the more appealing.

Two groups of scientists were considerably more productive in contributing to Russian knowledge of Mexico than were the three travellers mentioned above. In the early 1840s, V. F. Karvinsky led an Academy of Sciences expedition to study the botanical curiosities of central and northern Mexico. The journey was made difficult by local political impediments and recurring transportation problems, but Karvinsky and his assistants succeeded in bringing back to St. Petersburg many living specimens of native plants. The collection included cacti and fruit, dried plants, and an extensive dendrological selection that were important additions to the academy's knowledge of the botany of the New World.[7] Of equal significance was the 1874 journey through Central America by the renowned scholar, geographer, and climatologist, A. I. Voeikov, as part of an expedition around the world. While in Mexico he visited the Mayan cities of Yucatán as well as central and southern Mexico. His studies of the region provided data that contributed greatly to his later reputation as the creator of the study of climate in Russia. The Russian Geographical Society's newsletter carried the first report of his travels in 1875, and in 1884 his book *Klimaty zemnogo shara* (*Climates of the Earth*) synthesized his travel observations.[8] The article concentrated on his ten-day stay in a small village in southeastern Chiapas, an area he found particularly interesting. The region had long been in decline economically, but when Voeikov arrived it was becoming more prosperous as a result of the introduction of coffee cultivation. One recent settler, who seemed representative of a new positive and productive activity in the region, impressed Voeikov by his cleverness and energy. Previously, Voeikov was told, few whites had moved there because of the area's banditry and backwardness. Now that conditions were improving, more knowledgeable and industrious farmers were arriving, and there were expectations of further progress. Travelling with his new acquaintance to the coast and into the mountains, Voeikov found the vegetation richer and denser than any he had seen elsewhere, and he commented that the people they encountered were consistently friendly and helpful. The local villagers were generally poor, but always willing to share whatever they had, even if only tortillas and beans. Without exception, they were gracious, goodwilled, and cheerful. To Voeikov, the study of climate was useful only to the extent that it could be applied to men's lives. In the best tradition of nineteenth-century Russian humanistic science, he hoped to use what he learned to help mankind improve itself. In the case of the people he had met in Chiapas, he felt that if they could be instructed by trained outsiders, their future would be better than their past, their lives made richer and more comfortable. His sympathy for ordinary Mexicans was reminiscent of Wrangell's, but he was considerably more optimistic about the future of Mexico and its people. This optimism helped distinguish Russian expectations for Mexico during the Porfiriato from the pessimism so often expressed by Russians in the early nineteenth century.

Patkanov in Yucatán

Travel for Russians to Mexico was not made easier by the tsarist government's failure to establish diplomatic relations with a regime it considered illegitimate. Recognition was extended to the government of Emperor Maximilian in 1865, but no ambassadors were exchanged, and relations were abrogated with Maximilian's execution.[9] This political awkwardness, added to the difficulty of travelling through Mexico, meant that Russians interested in Latin America often went elsewhere. Political ties to a stable government in Brazil encouraged Russian travel there and to the neighboring republics of Argentina and Uruguay. Some fairly lengthy studies of that region were written by Russian visitors who, by the beginning of the twentieth century, were particularly interested in the condition of Russian emigrants to Brazil and Argentina.[10] It was only at the end of the 1880s that Tsar Alexander III's Foreign Ministry decided to exchange ambassadors with Mexico. It was felt that with Mexico's new stability under Porfirio Díaz, and with Russia's growing international aspirations, recognition would be profitable. Finally, in 1891, embassies were opened in St. Petersburg and Mexico City, several consulates were established, and official relations were begun.[11] With permission to enter Mexico easier for Russians to obtain, and with the rapid expansion of transportation facilities in the country, one of the busiest periods of Russian travel to Mexico began.

The first Russian to describe Mexico during the 1890s was the geographer and ethnographer, S. K. Patkanov, who came to Mexico to examine the Mayan ruins in Yucatán. He wrote about his journey in essays published in the general-interest *Nabliudatel (Observer)* in 1894 and the more specialized *Zemlevedenie (Agriculture)* in 1896.[12] Normally, Patkanov's audience consisted of specialists or scholars, but on this occasion he wrote as an involved layman interested in all aspects of the life and society of Yucatán. Well respected by his colleagues if not well known outside his profession, his essays about Mexico fascinated his readers.

Patkanov justified his interest in Yucatán by explaining that coming to the peninsula and not visiting its ancient Mayan cities would be like visiting Egypt without seeing the pyramids. But, he added, travelling in Yucatán was considerably more dangerous than in Egypt. Heat, reptiles, insects, and other dangers and inconveniences meant that few archeologists succeeded in reaching the ruins, and almost no tourists had the courage even to undertake the journey. And indeed, Patkanov was the first Russian to describe first-hand both the remains of Yucatán's past and the way of life of its present inhabitants.

Travel to the peninsula almost proved to be an epic itself. Patkanov's steamer, the *Orizaba*, was first delayed by a storm in Veracruz, then with better weather, sailed to Tampico to take on cargo for Yucatán. Patkanov described Tampico as one of the most miserable places he had ever been: it was too hot to visit the town during the day, and there was nothing to do at night. The mosquitos were terrible, although he admitted that they were no worse than those which swarmed around St. Petersburg in the summer. In the end, he wrote, his entertainment in large part consisted of watching the Indians and mestizos loading and unloading the ship. Once underway, the ship's engine broke down and the ship rocked at sea idly and nauseatingly for several hours while it was repaired. At last the ship reached Progreso, Mérida's seaport, and Patkanov and his first-class travelling companions were taken ashore on a small steamship, while the second-class passengers travelled by sailboat to the port. After a superficial, rather ceremonial customs inspection at the end of the pier, Patkanov boarded the narrow-gauge railroad that took the passengers to the mainland, then on to Mérida, several miles inland. Patkanov wrote that he was immediately impressed by how different the Yucatecos seemed in comparison to their countrymen from the central plateau. Both men and women dressed entirely in white, although the women's scarves, necklaces, and *guepiles*—their loose blouses—added some color to their attire. Their clothing, so different from the multicolored clothing of central Mexico, seemed to emphasize the fact that they were lighter-skinned and more handsome than the Mexicans from the north. The Yucatecos differed too in identifying themselves first with Yucatán, then with Mexico. While Patkanov was visiting a market in Mérida, a group of soldiers from the north entered the building, and a cry went among the vendors that "mejicanos" had appeared. They immediately covered their goods and refused to sell to the soldiers or their families. The federal army's reputation for theft was one reason for the merchants' reaction, of course, but Patkanov felt that a strong sense of local patriotism was at work as well.

Patkanov told his readers that he had learned a great deal about Yucatán just from the two-hour train journey to Mérida. The flat rows of maguey grown for henequen indicated to him an inadequacy of the rain needed for normal agriculture. The *hacendados'* houses, because of the palms and leafy trees hiding them, were like oases among the fields of maguey. One hacienda, quite near the railroad tracks, was not excessively rich, built of stone and only one story high, but was covered with flowers and surrounded by bananas and coconuts, so that the total impression was one of luxury. The neighboring village consisted of small houses with grass roofs, open doorways, and no windows. He wrote that from the village's poorly dressed Indians and the bronze "cherubim" in little short shirts he concluded that these were the homes of the hacienda workers. Patkanov noted that there were some indications that at least one *hacendado* had tried to improve his workers' housing, but that he did not really understand the lives of the people he employed, and the attempt failed. Two rows of sturdy stone houses with red tile roofs had been built, but they were insufferably hot and stuffy. The Indians quite sensibly refused to live in them, and they had been abandoned by the time

Patkanov saw them. Introducing inappropriate technology was common in much of the world at the end of the nineteenth century, of course, and no doubt Patkanov was reminded of attempts so often made by Russian landowners to improve the lives of their local peasants. Knowing nothing about the real lives of the peasants, they were met with mistrust by those they wanted to help. In the end, it appeared to Patkanov that the results were the same in Russia and Mexico. These attempts did show a certain amount of good will on the part of at least some of the landowners of Yucatán, however. Although misconceived, the stone houses were nonetheless one of the few examples Patkanov found of upper-class concern for Yucatán's peasantry. They did little to ameliorate his highly critical evaluation of Yucatecan society.

The crush of salespeople, beggars, carriage drivers, and *cargadores*—porters capable of carrying enormous loads—meeting the train in Mérida made it difficult for the passengers to leave the train, but after a short delay, Patkanov hired a carriage to take him to a hotel recommended by a travelling companion. As a geographer, Patkanov was especially interested in how human beings adjusted their way of life to variations in climate, particularly to hot and humid climates like Yucatán's. He found Mérida's solutions to such difficulties often ingenious: the carriages were designed to assure maximum openness, as were the train, the Indians' houses, and the stores, which had no glass in their windows. Even the inhabitants' clothing, of lightweight cotton, reflected this devotion to openness. His hotel, despite a number of deficiencies, was designed to promote ventilation, and his bed and furniture suited the climate admirably, as well. As a Petersburger, coming from a metropolis of southern and western European palaces built in inhospitable surroundings with a perverse disregard for the natural environment, Patkanov was particularly impressed by how Mexicans had adapted to tropical weather.

As a city, Mérida was not quite what Patkanov expected. Its principal square was disappointing compared to the fine one in Veracruz, although he admitted that some of the side streets leading into it were attractive and fairly lively. Always interested in how people lived, Patkanov gave the city's houses special attention. He found one major distinction between the homes of the rich and the poor to be the flowers and vegetation that surrounded them. The acacias, mimosas, oleanders, bananas, and orange trees that almost buried the huts of the poor stood in stark contrast to the severely cropped and trimmed vegetation found outside the mansions of the rich. The poor had developed a form of housing that fit the climate perfectly. The wealthy had imported fashionable European styles which had no functional relationship to the place where they were built. Patkanov came to believe that this lack of flexibility, this glorification of European ways of doing things, as well as the refusal to adapt to the demands of the climate, were indications of other deficiencies in the Yucatecan upper classes. He did not have to look far for other similarities between the lives of the Russian gentry and the upper classes of Yucatán.

One feature of Mérida that surprised Patkanov was the lack of a sense of "busyness" about it, even in comparison with Mexico City. Another was the dominance of foreigners in local commerce. The main bank in town was an Anglo-American concern, and most of the shops selling household goods were owned by Germans, the largest European enclave in the city. As in the past, the Yucatecan attitude toward foreign businessmen was entirely negative. Mexicans saw foreigners' success as being largely the result of chance or accident, and foreign businessmen and industrialists were accused of "sucking out the country's vital juices."[13] Still, there were few purely Mexican enterprises. While a number of Mexican-owned pharmacies operated in the city (a response to Yucatán's unhealthy climate, Patkanov felt), Mérida had no real industries with the exception of hammock-making, and nothing meaningful was done to raise the area's productive capacity. The city's overall atmosphere of quiet and inactivity seemed genuinely reflective of its economic reality.

Patkanov also found travellers' facilities remarkably limited for a city of fifty thousand inhabitants, though he soon learned that most business visitors stayed with friends or associates. Since there was no real tourism in the area, hotels and restaurants catering to them were not necessary. The local foods were tasty, but the water, naturally, was not safe to drink, since its germs would produce dysentery and a variety of fevers.[14] The weather was too warm to permit pulque manufacturing, so the only safe beverages were beer and red wine. These were generally too expensive for most of the population, of course, and the diseases transmitted through water and unsanitary utensils were a constant feature of the lives of Yucatán's poor and uneducated. Nor did Mérida offer much entertainment. When Pat-kanov asked the manager of his hotel what there was to do in the evening, the manager laughed and said that it was no secret that life in Mérida was boring for "educated people." His comment Patkanov took as typical of so many of the mestizos he had met in Yucatán. They were constantly trying to be "European," "educated," or "civilized" in comparison to the Indians, but they ended up being nothing more than parodies of the foreigners they hoped to emulate, neither Europeans nor Mexicans. Patkanov would have preferred them to be themselves. He had seen the same attitudes among Russians, and he approved of it no more in Yucatán than in Russia. Finally, abandoning any thought of amusement, Patkanov took a walk around the deserted dark streets of the city, then sat for a while on the balcony of his hotel. Mérida, with its daytime crowds of Indians, was in the evening transformed into an "Arab-like" town of absolute silence. Patkanov retired early, although the insects, thin walls, and patio noises made sleeping difficult in the hotel.

The next morning, he was up early to visit the markets. One of them, El Siglo XIX, he described as a "spectacle" because of its great variety of foods and stallkeepers. He was most impressed by its cleanliness, however: "Everything is clean here, beginning with the white clothing of the vendors and market women and ending with the tables on which the foods are laid out. In light of the circumstances prevailing in similar markets, ignoring the large accumulation here of meat, fish, sea creatures and other products, maintained at high temperatures, one could hope for nothing better."[15] Another feature of the market that appealed to Patkanov was the quiet that prevailed there. There was no screeching or shouting, he wrote; business was conducted "peacefully and in an orderly way, as in the most repectable stores." He had never seen anything like it in Russia.

In another market near the hotel that specialized in cloth, he was surprised to meet two women who belonged to a Syrian settlement not far from Mérida. The Syrians had become Catholics and adopted the way of life of the Yucatecos, but through their native energy had become great successes: "Thanks to their enterprising nature, love of work, and facility in trade, the Arabs for all their small numbers, have come to dominate almost all this market and carry on, in addition, a very active street-hawking trade."[16] Such infusions of outside blood seemed to Patkanov to be exactly what Yucatán needed to invigorate its economy and its mestizo population, who suffered from a malaise of lethargy not typical either of the Indians or of the foreigners.

Patkanov visited the city's mestizo sections immediately after seeing the markets, and was not pleased at what he saw. The white walls and wooden furniture glimpsed in the mestizos' houses were attractive enough, but the bored girls sitting in the windows seemed to have nothing to do. Pianos were a necessity, he learned, as they were in Russia among middle and upper class families, and every "educated" mestizo girl was expected to be able to play something when guests were present. Otherwise, it appeared to Patkanov that their lives were empty: "Up at the very grate of a large window sitting on a stool or rocking chair there will be a pale mestizo girl in a wide white blouse fanning herself, looking at passersby. Nearby will be an open book or, more rarely, some sort of handiwork to which she will resort if she becomes bored with gazing off into space . . . one only has to glance at the tired and apathetic faces of such girls to understand how horribly bored they are."[17] Intensifying their boredom was the fact that these mestizo girls were not permitted to work, nor were they even supposed to be out in the town during the day. Tied to their homes, they stubbornly expressed no interest in domestic tasks, nor in any kind of self-improvement. They read Spanish translations of popular French novels, played a few well-rehearsed light pieces on the piano, gossiped, or went for carriage rides in the evening. "In general," Patkanov wrote, "it is difficult to imagine anything more purposeless and boring than the lives led by women here."[18] The chief respite from their tedium was the Sunday afternoon and evening music and promenading that took place in the plaza, giving the women an opportunity to appear in society and to meet and flirt with members of the opposite sex. Again, Patkanov had seen the same wasted lives in the Russian provinces, among the daughters of the gentry and nobility. What he criticized so openly in Yucatán he would have liked to criticize in Russia.

Patkanov did not blame the women of Mérida entirely for the sad state of their lives, because he recognized that Mexico, like Russia, was a country dominated by men. Indeed, he attributed much of the responsibility for women's fates to the husbands and fathers who were rarely at home during the day, but who spent all their time either at work or drinking and socializing with their male friends. Wives were left at home in what amounted to enforced isolation. Their prospects were not encouraging, Patkanov felt.

As a social scientist, Patkanov was naturally interested in Yucatán's class structure. The Europeans, he observed, had come to Yucatán searching for wealth, and the richest of them were the descendants of the conquistadores of the sixteenth century. The Indians, the lowest class, had to work to survive and could hope for nothing beyond bare subsistence. The mestizos made up several sub-classes between the Europeans and the Indians, with distinctions based on wealth and skin color.[19] They dominated trade and merchandizing, although a considerable percentage of the merchant population consisted of resident foreigners or recent immigrants. The foreigners, mostly Germans from Hamburg or Bremen, were all prosperous, and had tried hard to become accepted in Mérida's mestizo community. They all spoke Spanish, had arranged marriages for their children into local business and landowner families, and had on the whole been able to overcome the traditional Mexican mistrust of foreigners through their efforts. Few other foreigners were as accepted as the Germans, Patkanov noted. Russian readers were no doubt interested to learn that their own admiration for German energy and industriousness was shared by the Mexicans of Yucatán.

On several evenings Patkanov was invited to the homes of members of the German community, and through them he succeeded in meeting many of the "most notable" people of Yucatán. His last evening in Mérida, for example, he spent in the company of his German friends and some "young mestizos from good families" drinking beer and dining at what turned out to be a surprisingly good and tasteful French restaurant.[20] One acquaintance was Teoberto Maler, whom Patkanov described as the best educated of all Mérida's foreigners, the only one he encountered who had no interest in commerce. Maler had come to Mexico with Maximilian and now devoted his retirement to photographing Yucatán's pre-Columbian ruins. It was Maler who helped Patkanov plan his journey to the archeological sites further inland and who suggested that he first visit Uxmal.

The early stages of the journey to Uxmal, a hot train ride through a barren landscape, revealed again the agricultural poverty of the region. The villages through which the train passed were poor, and no livestock or horses could be seen. Since they could grow nothing, the inhabitants of the villages had nothing to sell, and as a consequence, could buy nothing in return. Mérida's prosperity could not counterbalance the abject poverty of the countryside, Patkanov felt, and he believed the strains between the two boded ill for Yucatán's future.

At a stop for lunch at Tecoh, Patkanov sampled some corn tortillas, which he found to be better than the corn cakes of the Caucasus. Late in the day, surrounded by "swarms of fireflies," he arrived at Ticul and was taken to the house of a local *hacendado*, where he was given the overseers' office as a bedroom. His continuing fascination with the adaptability of the local population was intensified when he saw how easily the office was converted into a bedroom, merely by hanging a hammock.

The next morning, Patkanov ate breakfast at a local *fonda* (inn) and set out for the ruins, accompanied by the mayordomo of the hacienda on whose lands the ancient city lay. The journey was uneventful, but of some interest to Patkanov because of the sparse, butterfly-filled forest and maguey fields through which the road passed.[21] Shortly before sunset, they arrived at the hacienda of Uxmal and made preparations to visit the ruins the following day.

Patkanov found Uxmal to be extremely impressive, but he was disgusted to learn that the site had long been scavenged by souvenir hunters and antique sellers. He was moved by the view from on top of one of the pyramids, and the silence, broken only by grasshoppers chirping, seemed to carry him into the past, summoning up visions of the city at its height: "Scenes from ancient Mexican life continued to impose themselves one after another into my imagination." His reverie was broken only by an Indian yelling out a warning about a poisonous snake slowly slithering from the nearby ruins.[22]

Patkanov was surprised that the modern Indians of the area were not interested in speculating about the history of the ruins, that they cared only about guiding foreigners around the area or discussing the price of pilfered carvings in Mérida. Their lack of any close feeling for the achievements of their ancestors puzzled him at first. After some thought, however, he concluded that the reason for their indifference was to be found in their own more recent history, and especially in the Spanish conquest, which was roughly contemporaneous to the Russian conquest of Siberia. A comparison of the two, he wrote, might be instructive for Russian readers. In Siberia, even at the end of the nineteenth century, the native peoples had a sense of their past and its traditions. Their Russian conquerers had been more humane than the Spaniards had been in the New World and had not forced an immediate change in the way of life of the native peoples who came under their control. On the contrary, they were only slowly and partially assimilated into the European way of life, and as a result, they felt no alienation toward their past or hatred of the new Russian settlers. In the New World, in contrast, the Spaniards had forced a complete, radical change in the lives of the native peoples. The results had been widespread poverty and a loss of historical identity on the part of the modern Indians of Mexico. All that was preserved from the past, Patkanov wrote, was Indian hatred for the conquerers who usurped their land and exploited their labor.

Patkanov was not entirely accurate in his account of the conquest of Siberia, but by comparison, the Russians there had imposed a much less radically different way of life on the native population than had the Spanish conquerers in the New World. The American natives had become much more demoralized than the people of Siberia. It seems likely that Patkanov was once more teaching a lesson to his Russian readers by example: during the 1880s and 1890s Russification of the minority nationalities in Alexander III's empire was official governmental policy. Many of the native peoples of Siberia were on the verge of losing their identity, a prospect that Patkanov certainly viewed with alarm and concern. He undoubtedly believed that by stressing the positive achievements of earlier Russian administration in Siberia, and comparing that rule with what he saw as the almost totally negative Spanish colonial domination of Yucatán, that he could encourage his readers to recognize the dangers of Russification. Criticizing the government directly was not possible; doing it indirectly, in *Zemlevedenie*, was.

The modern Indians of Yucatán were also alienated from the rest of the society of which they were a part. Patkanov was surprised to learn that few of them spoke Spanish, that it was used outside urban areas only as a second language if at all, and that lack of understanding between the Indians and the other social classes was to a great extent rooted in this communication problem. Furthermore, their religion was not the Catholicism of the Europeans, but a combination of Christianity and traditional local beliefs. It was a mixture typical of rural Mexico, and it intensified the separation of the Indians from the mestizos and Europeans. They also were industrious, hard-working, and reliable, unlike the mestizo middle class of Mérida. Above all, Patkanov decided, the Indians' poverty, exploitation, and landlessness separated them most from the rest of Yucatecan society.[23] That the Indians could not be happy with their miserable condition was obvious. Ominously, their smoldering discontent could even be sensed by those in authority in Yucatán and by any foreign visitors capable of looking beneath the surface. Yet the whites and mestizos of the cities were rarely sympathetic to the Indians' plight, or willing to improve it. The mayordomo at the Hacienda Uxmal told Patkanov that at heart the Indians were ungrateful for what they had been given. Even though the mestizos and Europeans provided them with work, land, and food, he said, they still hated them. Nothing could be done to remedy that psychological antipathy. The typical *hacendado* attitude, Patkanov added, was that the Indians' position was in fact quite good, that they had no justification for complaining about their lives. Patkanov was appalled at the lack of understanding and the increasing polarization between the landowners and their workers, between the educated and wealthy, and the poor and exploited. Again, his outrage must be seen in Russian terms as well. Much that he found offensive in Yucatán could also be seen in rural Russia. Exposure of injustices in Mexico would be read by informed Russians as criticisms of Russian conditions as well.

In addition to Uxmal, Patkanov visited other Mayan archeological sites, including Ticul, Zayi, Kabah, and Tabi, but he described them less extensively. From the ruins, Patkanov returned to Mérida, purchased a few souvenirs,[24] then left for Havana, New York, and at last, Russia. His concluding remarks about Yucatán summarized all that he had seen there, and in them he speculated on the area's future. Yucatán was fascinating historically and archeologically, he wrote, but it was distressingly poor, and he saw little that could be done to improve its basic economic structure. He was impressed by the ways the Europeans and the natives had adapted to what was not a friendly or pleasant climate and compared the colonists favorably to other Europeans who had settled in tropical countries. Fundamental to understanding Yucatán, he wrote, was that its isolation from the rest of Mexico was psychological as well as geographical. The Yucatecos had considered themselves different from other Mexicans for centuries and had maintained an identity that gave no indication of weakening. Most unsettling about Yucatán, however, was that its social structure appeared essentially unstable. No true sympathetic understanding existed between classes. The Indians hated the wealthy, and the mestizos and whites were contemptuous of their "social inferiors." This social tension could be seen in the haciendas, built as small fortresses, constructed not to protect against foreign invaders, but against rebellions by the haciendas' own Indians. Such fear did not augur well for the future of the established social structure. To Patkanov, the blame for this stagnant and increasingly frightful situation had to be attributed to the mestizo middle class. They were unimaginative and insufficiently energetic to take advantage of economic and political opportunities. Their failure had led to the success of the foreigners who had come to dominate business and economic life. In a healthier society, he concluded, foreigners would not have played so important a role.

Like other visitors to Yucatán during the Porfiriato, Patkanov believed that basic and fundamental change was needed. Should it not come from above, he felt, it was inevitable that radical change would come from below. Unlike other writers, who felt their differentness and even their superiority to the Yucatecos, Patkanov identified the similarities between his own society and that of Yucatán. His criticisms were relevant to the current condition of Russia: the peasants were alienated and exploited; members of the Russian gentry often lived lives of emptiness and frivolity; the only entrepreneurial energy injected into the Russian economy seemed to come from abroad. Above all, in the 1890s in Russia there was a feeling that conditions could not long continue as they had, that the need for fundamental change would become stronger and stronger until something would have to be done. In writing about social and economic abuses in Mexico, Patkanov was writing about them in Russia. Should there be no reform, Patkanov feared that the solutions to the distortions of both societies would be radical and perhaps highly destructive. Neither country would be the same afterward.

Protopopov: Northern and Central Mexico in the Mid-1890s

Patkanov's technique of criticizing Russia by describing Mexico was used by another Russian visitor who was in Mexico at about the same time. Sergei Dmitrievich Protopopov was a widely travelled liberal journalist whose essays appeared in several popular Russian periodicals. He had recounted for Russian readers his journeys to Europe and North America, the Near East, the Mediterranean, and Central Asia in a series of always interesting and entertaining essays. Originally from Nizhnyi-Novgorod, by the mid-1890s Protopopov lived in St. Petersburg and wrote for *Russkoe bogatstvo (Russian Wealth)*, a journal headed by his close friend, K. G. Korolenko.[25] Reporting from the United States in the summer of 1893, he became curious about Mexico. He also knew, with a good reporter's sensitivity, that little had appeared in Russian about the country, and he decided to return from San Francisco to New York by train, through Mexico. He kept diaries during his travels, and used two of them as the basis for an account of his trip to Mexico, published in *Russkoe bogatstvo* in 1896.[26] Why it took this article three years to appear is unclear. Korolenko wrote Protopopov that the essay was not being prepared editorially for publication until August 1896, due in part to censorship problems. Russian journalists always had to be concerned with how the government's censors might respond to material critical of the current state of affairs in Russia, and presumably, *Russkoe bogatstvo*'s editorial board was involved in preliminary censorship of their own. Protopopov had apparently had trouble with the censorship in the past, as had most liberal Russian journalists, and he was aware of the restraints placed on Russian writers. He had become adept at disguising what he wanted to say about Russia by describing other countries. His account of Mexico was written in this way, and the sophisticated Russian, accustomed to reading between the lines, would see much of Russia in Protopopov's articles.

Protopopov admitted at the outset that he had very little idea of what he would find in Mexico.[27] He knew no Spanish and was uneasy about the physical dangers and tropical diseases he might encounter there, he wrote. He later admitted (with a rather droll sense of humor, perhaps) that travelling in Mexico was no less comfortable than travelling in Russia. He rode by train from San Francisco to Los Angeles, then east to Arizona and to the U.S.-Mexican border at El Paso. He had been greatly impressed by everything in the United States, and the American railroads were no exception. The civilized comfort of the Pullman sleeping cars, the efficiency and courtesy of the porters, and the openness and lack of pretense he found in the smoking car, were positive aspects of life in the United States. Describing briefly the history of Arizona, and in an expansive mood, he wrote that the foreign visitor could not but be impressed by the energy of the Anglo-Saxons in transforming what they had found in North America, adding that "it is difficult to deny that [they] are the best colonizers in the world."[28] His enthusiasm for the United States would recur in his work over the next several years, and certainly affected his evalua-tion of Mexico.

After a perfunctory customs check, Protopopov crossed the border. The landscape of cacti, interspersed with fields of corn and beans was not unlike what he had seen in the United States. The train continued to be run by a U.S. crew, English was spoken, and dollars were used as currency. What was different were the small houses, usually with no doors or windows, and the crowds of naked children playing out-side them. The adults were unlike their U.S. counterparts as well. They dressed differently, and physically, he added, they "resemble our gypsies, although they often are darker."[29] Protopopov noticed how much poorer the Mexicans were than the Americans, even though the country looked as productive on one side of the border as the other. As a journalist, of course, he often relied on interviews to gather information or to confirm impressions, and he asked the porter if the Mexicans he saw out the windows were in fact as poor as they looked. The porter said that, on the contrary, they were poorer than they looked, adding that pigs in the United States lived better than they did. One problem, he continued, was that all but a few Mexicans were uneducated, and that they still lived as their ancestors did hun-dreds of years ago. Recently, and encouragingly, some changes for the better had taken place: "Many Americans have come here, all these railroads were built by them, and generally the Americans teach the Mexicans how to live, how to till the soil, raise livestock, build towns, irrigate the fields and extract minerals. But for the present life will be hard for the Mexican."[30] A U.S. businessman from San Fran-cisco, speaking with an enormous cigar in his mouth, contradicted the porter's assessment, however. He told Protopopov that the Mexi-cans were willingly poor, that they lived badly because they were lazy, they had no real desire to work. When they obtained even a piece of bread, they walked away from their jobs and refused to return until they were hungry again. Protopopov admitted that his prejudice toward such businessmen made it unlikely that he would agree with such an evaluation. Consequently, he was gratified to hear from the porter, in private sometime later, that when Mexicans could get any work, they would spend all day at the most demanding labor for almost no pay. Calling them lazy, the porter whispered, was both wrong and insulting. Protopopov's sympathies, like Patkanov's in Yucatán, were from the beginning quite obviously with the poor.

After stops at Torreón, Zacatecas, and San Luis Potosí, where he was able to catch glimpses of Mexican life, Protopopov remarked that the one thing that impressed him most were the police. Armed from head to toe, they must have been more hindered than helped by their sabers, revolvers, and spurs; they were like no other policemen he had seen anywhere else in the world. On the whole, Protopopov found the journey not upleasant. The towns became more attractive as the train moved south, and there were waving children and strawberries and flowers growing alongside the railroad tracks to add color to a landscape which in the north had been sere and often forbidding. With the exception of the cigar-smoking businessman, Protopopov found the people on the train to be politically astute and lacking the awkwardness and self-consciousness so common in Russia.[31]

Protopopov's observations about what he had seen since leaving El Paso were as relevant to conditions in Russia (and the United States) as they were to Mexico. He admired the United States' political system and what he had learned of its citizens' recent entrepreneurial energy in Mexico. He added that it appeared U.S. citizens had accomplished more in Mexico in thirty years than the Spaniards had in three hundred, but he explained that Mexicans and U.S. citizens needed to work together:

> One should not think . . . that the Mexicans of today . . . are not able. On the contrary, as a people they are very talented, energetic, and diligent. But these are all personal qualities: none of them have the initiative, the organizing capabilities which distinguish the Anglo-Saxons from all the earth's races as the entei prising man par excellence. If you were to increase the Mexican population ten percent by adding Englishmen to it, then it could be said with certainty that Mexico would astonish the world with its rapid growth.[32]

Protopopov told his readers that he would advise the governments of the United States and Mexico to collaborate in settling Anglo-American colonists in Mexico as soon as possible. The colonists would start new industries and businesses, and the country's productive ability would rise dramatically. Protopopov's social Darwinism is less acceptable today than it was at his time, but it should be remembered that his recommendations were directed to Russia as well as to Mexico. While he wanted to energize Mexico, he believed that such social and economic planning might pull Russia out of its backwardness and sloth as well: he was as critical of Russians as he was of Mexicans. There was no doubt that his admiration for the Anglo-Americans was enormous, but he shared it with many Russians. Now that they were no longer competitors of the U.S. or Britain in North America, Russian approval of their economic enterprise grew, and Protopopov's glowing praise was impressively different from Russian attitudes during the first half of the century.

In his general discussion Protopopov repeatedly depicted the country in a more favorable light. He wrote, for example, that public education in Mexico was at a level higher than in Russia, that 60 percent of all the children in the republic were enrolled in school. This was certainly not true, and Protopopov could not himself have believed it. He was less interested in presenting an accurate picture of Mexico than of encouraging Russian readers to wonder why in a poor country like Mexico education would be making such headway while in Russia, a country aspiring to world power and influence, education had not kept up with the country's needs and had even been periodically discouraged by government officials. Extensive education stimulated publishing, and in Mexico, Protopopov wrote, the press was strong and operated in complete freedom, with no censorship. The wide variety of journals and newspapers conveyed a generally cultured, principled, and businesslike tone. Again, the veracity of Protopopov's description is open to question, but to Russians contending with a rigorous censorship and a press that was often stodgy and conservative, Mexico's might appear admirable. Politically, too, the Mexico described by Protopopov could only compare favorably with Russia. Díaz's administrative competence was well known in North America, Protopopov wrote: he had organized the army, built railroads, straightened out the nation's finances, insisted on strict legal-ity, promoted agriculture, even reduced his own salary by half. The country's republican form of government functioned well, he wrote (somewhat deceptively), with the senate and congress true representatives of the will of the people. Freedom of religion was guaranteed by the constitution and protected by the government.

Protopopov's initial conclusion about Mexico was inescapably optimistic: "Even someone travelling quickly through Mexico can readily see that a new life, one that is young and energetic, is emerging from the ruins of the old." He was not concerned that his picture was inaccurate, and of course his praise was echoed at times in the European and U.S. press. He was writing with the intent of reforming Russia, which could boast of almost none of the achievements Protopopov claimed for the Porfirian regime. Alexander III was one of nineteenth-century Europe's great reactionary monarchs, and Nicholas II gave all indications of continuing his father's policies. The political and civil guarantees promised by the Mexican constitution were no more than dreams in Russia. Protopopov hoped Russians would be acutely embarrassed at their own economic and political backwardness in comparison with what he called the "young Mexican republic." He expected Russians to ask themselves why they had to be the victims of political repression when Mexicans did not.

As part of his general introduction, Protopopov gave his readers a brief outline of Mexican history. Fairly accurate on the whole, his summary stressed two features of the past particularly. First, he found more than a few praiseworthy features in the pre-Columbian cultures of Mexico and was less enthusiastic about the results of the Conquest than were many foreign visitors. Second, and like most Russians, he was extremely critical of the Catholic church in Mexico. During the three centuries of Spanish rule, he wrote, the church played a negative role in national life: it "damaged Mexico by supporting eveything reactionary, by speaking out against any kind of free thought [and] . . . enlightenment"[33]; it had always sided with the conservatives and the Spaniards. It was only under Díaz that its power was at last declining. As an example of this diminishing influence, he noted that he had stopped in at the church of San Diego in the capital, where he found a "monk" trying to intimidate people with his "bony fingers and fanatical eyes." Only women and children were frightened by him, however, and Protopopov expected that soon even they would overcome their fear.

When he arrived in Mexico City, Protopopov took a coach from the train station to the Hotel Iturbide and was surprised to find that here the surroundings were more "European" than "American." As in Europe, the "historical layers" of the past could be seen in Mexico City. In the United States, he had found, everything was contemporary, built within the last generation. In Mexico City the visitor could encounter a two-hundred-year-old church standing immediately adjacent to a building constructed in the latest "Chicago" style. He checked into his hotel, then left to join the crowds celebrating the anniversary of the Grito de Dolores. He soon found himself taken up in the crowd's enthusiasm and considered himself fortunate to have arrived in the capital on such a holiday.

The next morning, Protopopov set out to explore the city. The cleanliness of the streets belied the riotous celebration of the day before, and as he walked, he decided the city could be compared to any in Europe. Strolling to Chapultepec Park was particularly pleasant, he wrote. The statues, the carriages of the wealthy, Díaz's palace itself, all provided the city with ornaments that embellished it nicely. The Aztec relics in the National Museum were interesting enough, as was the tree of the Noche Triste, but the National Picture Gallery was disappointing because it held only religious paintings. A service in the richly ornate cathedral seemed to him to confirm Voltaire's comment that the Catholic mass was "opera for the poor." He described the markets near the Zócalo in some detail in his diary, but he dismissed them in his article as being akin to those of the poorer Tatar sections of Baku.

From the central districts, Protopopov travelled out to the city's environs. He took a horse-drawn streetcar to Guadalupe, and while he found the view of the mountains and of Lake Texcoco worthwhile, the church itself he did not find attractive. He did admit that seeing the image of the Virgin on Juan Diego's cape was something he would not have missed, despite his anticlericalism. He also visited Tlalpam, Coyoacán, and finally Xochimilco, where he took a walk in what he described as the extraordinarily beautiful countryside. There too he was encouraged about Mexico's future: he asked the young train station manager why it was that Mexicans were so poor in what appeared to be such a wonderfully productive land. The manager told him the Mexico actually had only just recently attained genuine independence, and that now it would be busy building a new country with enthusiasm and optimism. This was how Protopopov wished to remember Mexico. Shortly afterward, he wrote, he dreamed that there were no countries, no capitals, no nations, no classes, but only people living and striving together for a life that would constantly improve. It was a dream inspired by Mexico, he said, but one he hoped would come true for all nations.

Protopopov soon left for New Orleans, with vivid memories of the "original, young, and sympathetic Mexican Republic."[34] Anyone familiar with Mexico in the 1890s would have had to admit that his picture of the country was greatly idealized. While he was genuinely and sincerely pleased by much that he saw, his motivation in describing the country so positively was to criticize Russia. What he wrote about the church, the Díaz government, the expanding economy, the personal freedoms enjoyed by Mexicans, and the rosy future was not meant solely to inform Russians about Mexico. He wanted Russians to ask why their country failed to measure up to his description of Mexico's level of personal and political freedom. In the end, one wonders how much Protopopov really understood during his visit to Mexico. The modern reader cannot escape the suspicion that he saw only what he was determined to see, and what he wanted to tell his Russian readers. To a considerable extent, and his clear sympathy with the Mexican people notwithstanding, Protopopov's account tells more about his analysis of Russia than about the country that ostensibly was the subject of his essay.

Devollan in "Montezuma's Kingdom"

It was in 1905 that the next first-hand Russian account of Mexico appeared in the Russian press. In that year, Grigorii Aleksandrovich Wollant's article "V tsarstve Montezumy" ("In the Kingdom of Montezuma") was published with a large number of photographs and illustrations in *Istoricheskii vestnik (Historical Herald).*[35] Wollant was best known to the Russian public by his pen name, Devollan; not much more is known about him. He apparently intended the article to be one of a series about Mexico, but since only the first installment appeared, the description of Mexico is incomplete. Devollan was neither as critical of Mexico as Patkanov nor as favorable as Protopopov. His article was more balanced, but to a great extent was no more than a typical tourist's view of Mexico. It appeared at about the same time as Balmont's essays, however, and as will be seen in the following section, helped in producing a new appreciation of Mexico in the Russian reading public.

To avoid spending seventeen days at sea between St. Nazaire and Veracruz, Devollan had decided to take a ship to New York, then travel five days by rail to Mexico City. He explained that he had two reasons for preferring a trip by train. Like many Russian children, he had read voraciously the adventure stories of Mayne Reid, many of them set in northern Mexico, and he hoped to see the locales for himself. He also felt that travel by rail would allow him to appreciate better the contrasts between the United States and Mexico, the two "political powers" in North America. The differences were apparent soon after crossing the border, he wrote, in clothing most of all: the "national costume" worn by the *rurales* (rural police) was particularly picturesque, unlike anything he had seen in the United States; the women's custom of carrying their children inside their own clothing was also highly unusual and attractive. As much as anything else, he wrote, these traditional ways of dressing distinguished Mexico from Europe and the United States.

Travelling farther south, Devollan found his image of Mexico gaining color and dimension as he gazed out at the burros, the cactus-covered countryside, and the oasis-like towns. He was fascinated by the fields of maguey and wrote detailed and knowledgeable descriptions of the manufacture of pulque, mezcal, and henequen.[36] Despite his curiosity about Mexico's northern desert region, however, his overall evaluation of the area was quixotic. Zacatecas he said he liked, because of its rich mineral deposits and its Church of the Remedios, to which pilgrims came on their knees in reverent awe. Torreón, on the other hand, he described as a town forgotten by God and humankind both. He saw hope for the town only because a fellow passenger told him that an influx of U.S. capital was imminent and that from it Torreón would become an important industrial center. Devollan's evaluation of Torreón was probably flavored by the fact that he had not expected the northern desert to be so extensive. He wrote that he was relieved to see green plants and gardens surrounding the railroad tracks as the train moved south. He marvelled especially at the variety and availability of tropical fruits and flowers for sale at the last stations before Mexico City. In spite of his preliminary reading, he admittted that the real Mexico still held surprises for him.

Before describing the capital, Devollan attempted to give his readers what had become the standard preliminary summary of Mexican history and geography. Less a scholar than a journalist, however, he recounted the widespread contentions of those who believed that the ancient civilizations of Mexico were remnants of Atlantis, that there could have been contacts between America and Asia, that the Toltecs were perhaps Chinese. He himself suggested that because of apparent similarities between certain Otomí and Chinese words, a comparative study of Asian languages and the ancient Indian languages of Mexico might be undertaken. Even if these earlier contacts could not be proved, he speculated, later interaction between America and the Old World might still have occurred. Like many others at the time, he wondered whether the cross-like symbol associated with Tlaloc, the rain god, might not have shown the influence of Christianity, and whether the legend of Quetzalcóatl could have arisen from St. Brendan's arrival in Mesoamerica on one of his many journeys. Devollan's fascination with these questions reflected that of his readers, particularly at a time when "decadence" and Symbolism were growing in popularity in Russia. The more recent history of Mexico was of less interest; he had little to say about the period from Cortés to Porfirio Díaz, to whom he abruptly moved his narrative. And the Porfiriato was a blessing in comparison to what had preceded it, he wrote: "In [Díaz's] government the country has finally been able to rest from bloody disorder and internecine conflict, and under the beneficial influence of peace and quiet an era of material construction and prosperity has begun."[37] Unlike Protopopov, whose enthusiasm was pure guile, Devollan was sincere in his praise for modern Mexico. Looking at the present in comparison to the decades of uncertainty preceding Díaz's presidency, he saw only progress.

If Devollan was entirely favorable toward Díaz, his impressions of Mexico City were both positive and negative. The streets were wide and clean, with old decorated churches and the new "United-States-style" office buildings providing striking contrasts to the patios, gardens, and fountains of houses built in the traditional way. The capital's social customs and class structure always seemed to interest Russian visitors, and Devollan was no exception. The ordinary people of the city, those who now sat on the benches placed by Maximilian along the Paseo de la Reforma for the use of the upper classes, were dirty and unkempt on the whole. Still, the contrast betwen them and the upper classes, who passed through streets decorated with classical statues to promenade along the Paseo, provided a picturesque view for the visitor, Devollan wrote, and all the people, rich or poor, were unfailingly gracious. Devollan found very little to distinguish Mexico's upper classes from those in Europe or the United States, and women were completely up to date in their knowledge of fashion.

Like Patkanov, Devollan described the way of life of Mexican women with some relish since it was so unlike that of Russian women and remarkably conservative for the first decade of the twentieth century. He found that women rarely left their houses during the day (those who did were almost always foreigners, he pointed out), but generally sat at their windows, watching passersby. He was amused at the evening promenades in Chapultepec Park: every family that considered itself part of the capital's *beau monde* felt it necessary to be there, so that in certain sections of the park traffic had become completely unmanageable. Unlike Patkanov, however, Devollan saw none of this in a negative light. The customs were quaint and old-fashioned, of course, but he saw nothing in them that warranted extensive criticism.

The working classes, since they were much less "European" than their social "superiors," were of even greater interest to Devollan. Their clothing was more picturesque, and the tasks they performed were more varied. He noticed that the difficulty of their lives made them old before their time: Indian women, for example, so attractive when they were young, came to resemble what Europeans could only describe as witches when they grew into late middle age. He was shocked to see how poorer Mexicans were used as beasts of burden. Everywhere, he wrote, one could see *cargadores*, workers carrying enormous boxes, piles of wood, even large pieces of furniture. He included in the article a photograph of a man carrying a huge agglomeration of pots on his back to illustrate his point. He found, too, that people rather than vehicles did all the household moving. This was especially surprising since electric streetcars seemed to go everywhere in the city. They were so common, in fact, that they were employed as hearses, giving Mexicans in death, he remarked wryly, an equality they never attained in life. Everything negative in Devollan's account was counterbalanced by something positive. The weather was always pleasant (he repeated the saying that there was no climate in Mexico, just the sunny and the shady sides of the street), and the food stalls on the streets meant that anyone could afford tasty and inexpensive food. Market day meant free entertainment for the Indians, a holiday during which the process of selling was more important than making a profit, where drinking pulque and seeing friends and strangers were worth more than building up a fortune. Finally, he added, it appeared to him that Mexico's tradition of religious and national fiestas kept the lives of the poor from being as miserable as they might appear to Europeans. Holidays and celebrations were numerous, and the crowds always took part in them enthusiastically, although he heard that some religious holidays were celebrated much less solemnly than they had been in the past.[38] The Day of the Dead, however, had lost none of its traditional popularity. The lighting of candles and the picnicking on loved ones' graves was something he had not expected to be as widespread as it was. It was a strange and unique ceremony, he wrote, one typically Mexican, and one that helped lower-class Mexicans reconcile themselves to their lot.

Having dealt with Mexico City's social strata, Devollan next described the capital's tourist sights. He saw the archeological museum, the National Palace, the cathedral, the suburbs of Coyoacán, Xochimilco, and Guadalupe, and the park at Chapultepec. He was pleased to find that travel was so convenient in the Valley of Mexico and decided to visit other cities as well. He told his readers that in contrast to earlier times, all Mexico was now accessible to travellers because of the Díaz government's stress on law and order. A visitor could safely journey anywhere in the country. Devollan went first to Puebla, then planned to visit Oaxaca as well. He was rapturous about Puebla, more so than about any other Mexican city.[39] He wrote that its clean streets, beautiful churches, palaces, and colorful plazas made it a town that seemed to have been built by angels. It was a remnant of old Spain, and the city had a sense of permanence found nowhere else in North America, particularly not in the United States, where everything was temporary at best. In Puebla the genius of Spain remained, Devollan wrote, embodied in the cathedral and other churches, and in the Church of the Remedios built atop the pyramid of Cholula. He was less enthusiastic about Oaxaca, which he reached after a stop at Tehuacán. The trip was comfortable enough, and being exposed to a number of new kinds of fruits he had never seen before was refreshing. Oaxaca reminded him of Tiflis, in the Caucasus, he wrote, and the display of archeological finds in the city's museum, especially one figure of a "Mongol in a Chinese costume," led him to further speculation on the possibilities of pre-Columbian contacts with China. Oaxaca's market was rather different from ones he had seen elsewhere and needed a more thorough cleaning. On several occasions Devollan had commented on the Indians' lack of cleanliness in general. This was an area into which Díaz's reforms had not yet reached, he felt, though he certainly believed they would. Finally, Devollan went from Oaxaca to visit the famous *ahuehuete* tree at Tule and the archeological site at Mitla. Most impressive of this part of his article were the several excellent photographs of the ruins, some of the first to have appeared in the Russian press.

Devollan's article ended rather abruptly with his account of Mitla. He certainly intended to write a series of essays on Mexico, but the subsequent sections were never published, possibly because of the upheavals associated with the 1905 revolution in Russia. Although disjointed and incomplete, his description did reflect what can be assumed to be a view of Mexico fairly typical of the Russian intelligentsia in 1905. Devollan was favorable toward the Díaz regime, but not excessively enthusiastic, and he maintained a distance from what he found in Mexico that had not been true of Patkanov or Protopopov, both of whom became emotionally involved to a surprising extent in what they were describing. No Russian had given as full a picture of life in Mexico City as Devollan had. It was detailed, relatively balanced, and objective; and it contained striking photographs, apparently taken (or commissioned) by Devollan, which are among the best reproduced in Russia at any time during the twentieth century. However, the article was no more than superficially analytical, and it had the disadvantage of appearing at a time when Russians had more immediate concerns than speculation about a country halfway around the world. Furthermore, those interested in Mexico would prefer to read Balmont's essays and poetry. Still, Devollan wrote for an important journal that reached the homes and offices of a significant sector of the Russian population, and in doing so, he kept an awareness of Mexico alive in Russia.

The Mythological Mexico of Konstantin Balmont

"The country of red flowers, discovered in a mind intoxicated by the Sun and enamored of the Moon, and the Evening Star, the Morning Star. A country of multicolored flowers and of birds with bright feathers, azure, green, the shade of all precious stones. A country of bloody spectacles and of refined reverence, of legends truthful and of reality improbable, of colorful hieroglyphs and pyramid-shaped cathedrals, of slow words and the quick knife, of eternal Spring—eternal Autumn. A country whose history is a tale, whose fate is a sad poem, sadder than a poem by Edgar Allen Poe. A country deceptive, betrayed, sold-out, conquered by prophecy, by a genius, by a woman, by a horse, mutilated irretrievably by a pale-faced centaur, carrying destruction, devastation, and a hypocritical religion, along with deadly contagious diseases, everywhere he penetrates—to India, to Oceania, to the Peruvian idyll, and to this downtrodden Country of Red Flowers."—Konstantin Balmont, "Strana krasnykh tsvetov"[40]

On May 5, 1913, the uncommonly popular Symbolist poet Konstantin Balmont returned to Russia from an extended exile abroad. Two days later he delivered a public lecture at the invitation of the Moscow Literary Artistic Circle and the Society of Free Esthetics, the first he had given in Russia in years.[41] His topic was ancient and modern Mexico, and much of what he said was inspired by his trip to Mexico in 1905. His enthusiastic audience at the evening meeting must have reminded Balmont of earlier days: "The usual throng of awed women peered at the poet as he sat regally dressed in a black frock coat with a high, stiff collar and a flowing black silk cravat that spread luxuriously over his starched shirt. Splendidly coiffured, emerald-studded and wearing a golden pince-nez on a silk ribbon, Balmont savoringly intoned exotic names from Aztec history, and the audience nodded in deep appreciation."[42]

Balmont had returned to Russia bringing Mexico with him, as a part of his creative sensibility. He considered travel essential to his creative life, and he was fascinated especially with the unusual, the exotic, and the primitive. By the time he delivered his lecture on

Mexico, he had visited Africa, South Asia, the Pacific, the United States, and had traveled repeatedly about Europe. Yet his trip to Mexico, and the memories of that experience, seemed to be of particular importance for him, and the influence of the country and its people could be seen on Balmont and his work for the next two decades.[43] Mexico was unique for him, but because of its past, not its present. Indeed, he came to despise modern Mexico as a Europeanized bastardization of a once great and noble civilization. Mexico differed from all other countries because of its pre-Columbian accomplishments. He went there to learn about ancient Mexico and, he hoped, to be inspired by the Maya, Toltec, and Aztec monuments of the past.

Balmont was a highly productive writer, and on the basis of his visit to Mexico he published a travel journal, a considerable number of essays and poems, and several translations. All were read widely because of his great popularity. Young people worshiped him. He was renowned as a spokesman for modernist poetry and for his verbal pyrotechnics, his assonance, alliteration, vibrancy, and rhythm. As if emulating the ideal of the decadent, *fin de siècle* poet, he had lived a life of extremes, one devoted to sin, excess, and sensuality, although his exuberant self-confidence rarely permitted him to share in the pessimism common in Russian Symbolism. His fame was so great that some of his contemporaries found themselves describing the early years of the century as the "Balmontian epoch of Russian poetry."[44] His numerous collections of verse were awaited eagerly by a Russian reading public increasingly enamored of Symbolism and modernism. Balmont was known as well for his opposition to the repressiveness of the Imperial Russian government. His public reading of an anti-government poem, "Malenkii Sultan," in March 1901, for example, compelled him to take an extended journey to Western Europe. Indeed, the pattern of much of the rest of his life was determined by his literary productivity and political notoriety.

No one doubted Balmont's popularity, but even before he was preparing his departure for the New World, several Russian critics believed he was on the verge of losing at least some of his poetic talent, that he had reached a creative impasse. Valerii Briusov, at the time Balmont's only competitor for the allegiance of the majority of the modernist reading public, expressed this attitude in a letter to a friend:

It is strange: everyone suddenly felt emancipated when Balmont left. There were so many merry faces in the aisles that it became embarrassing. And earlier, at the farewell dinner, there were even malicious rather than merry words spoken. Balmont was very sensitive to this and repeated several times: 'But I'm actually leaving!' When he left it was as though a period of sorts had ended in our literature. He had reigned regally for ten years over our poetry. But now the staff fell from his hands. We had gone far ahead; he had remained in one place. Perhaps he is a giant among us . . . but he is in the past. . . . We are going ahead![45]

Balmont himself gave no indication of fearing any diminution of his talents or influence, but in his unceasing search for novelties, he must have believed that Mexico would inspire work equal to any he had done previously.

As we have seen, even though more was being written about Mexico at the turn of the century, the country was still not well known in Russia. Its exoticism did appeal to the *fin de siècle* Russian culture of which Balmont was such a significant representative, however. For Balmont, speculating on the mysteries of the past became an obsession, one stimulated by his knowledge of numerous modern and ancient languages, his infatuation with Theosophy, sunworship, paganism, and in the case of the Maya of Yucatán, with the vague belief that their civilization was all that remained of submerged Atlantis. Mexico was thought to be uncivilized and primitive, and to Balmont, it was immensely appealing as a destination.

He left Moscow late in December 1904 in the company of the well-known translator, Elena Konstantinovna Tsvetkovskaia, who subsequently became his third wife. By the end of January, they were already at sea, en route to Veracruz. It was an ominous time for a Russian to travel. The country was at war with Japan and beginning to dissolve into revolution, with the likely prospect of much blood being spilled in the streets. Balmont's awareness of political developments in Russia, and the peculiar form of homesickness it engendered in him, would play an important role in flavoring his view of ancient and modern Mexico. He wrote in his journal that while his voyage to the New World reminded him once again of pleasures long forgotten, events in Russia were constantly on his mind; that though he did not write about them, "He who knows me will know how I feel."[46] He loved Russia, he added, and wrote that he believed in its future, even in the face of its present turmoil.

His first experience with Mexico overwhelmed him, and he said in his journal, that "writing would be as hard for me as if I were trying to do it while sitting in the theater."[47] The flowers, the sea, Veracruz itself, the birds, the landscape, and the people in general were all extraordinarily unlike the gloomy, wintry Russia he had left behind. After spending ten days in Veracruz, he moved on by train to Mexico City, arriving there at the beginning of March and settling into a systematic preliminary study of the literature on ancient Mexico. He had read Prescott's *History of the Conquest of Mexico* while crossing the Atlantic, and in the National Library (which he said he visited twice every day) he devoured all he could find on Mexico's past: Bernardino de Sahagún, Karl Lumholtz, Augustus Le Plongeon, William H. Holmes, the *Popol Vuh*, Charles Etienne Brasseur de Bourbourg, Mariano Veytia, J. L. Stephens. He hoped to understand as intimately as possible the peoples and cultures existing in Mexico before the arrival of Cortés. He continued his research in the National Museum and received considerable practical (though at times inaccurate) advice from the curators there.

Despite what he considered a somewhat lackadaisical attitude on the part of the administration, Balmont learned a great deal at the National Library, and was duly impressed by the archeological wonders of the National Museum.[48] Yet the capital did not appeal to him on the whole. The Sunday *corrida de toros* in Chapultepec Park began pleasantly enough, he wrote, but quickly degenerated into a "vile, terrifying slaughterhouse," and it was several hours before he recovered from what proved to be the most unpleasant of all the experiences he had in Mexico.[49] News of recent massacres in Russia did nothing to lift his spirits, and he wrote in his journal that he regretted his absence from the "unforgettable page in history," however bloody, through which Russia was living. Mexico City itself he described as ugly, only a "caricature of European cities."[50] It had been ruined by the Spaniards, who had destroyed all that was uniquely Mexican and unimaginatively Europeanized what was left. Expecting to discover at least some remnants of the glories of ancient Tenochtitlán, he found instead "a city of impoverished Aztecs with white faces, silent and voracious, who drink their pulque in stinking thatched huts. Rags, misery and bare feet that would never be seen in Moscow. . . . The conquistadors, who had no pity [even] on the stones, should be damned."[51] In remote Mexico, the Europeans, whom Balmont described as "unscrupulous barbarians," had defiled all that was fine in the indigenous culture. This was an important theme for Balmont, but one about which he was inconsistent, even contradictory. While he decried the destructiveness of the Spaniards, he nevertheless felt an odd affinity with Cortés: he mentioned that he first saw Veracruz through Cortés's eyes, and that later he felt that "between Cortés and me there is such a similarity of character that it was strange in a mystical way for me to read the pages [in Prescott] describing him."[52] And later, despite paragraphs of evocative, highly sensual descriptions of Mexico's natural surroundings, he could write that one still could not compare the wonders of "our beautiful Europe" with those of such "barbarous" countries as Mexico. Finally, Balmont's contradictory response to Mexico was revealed in his flat rejection of the mestizo mixture of Indian and European that had become the dominant racial type in Mexico:

> In [Mexicans] you too often feel a subordinate, subjected race, and they so frequently are cur-like. This cross-breeding of Indian blood with Spanish has by no means improved the Indian type. Mexicans borrowed all the bad qualities of the Spaniards (laziness, coarseness, cruelty), but I have not seen that they have actually succeeded in adopting the noble traits of the Spanish caballero, with his courage, sincere action, and vigorous passion.[53]

Balmont's ideal Mexican was the Indian, the one most untainted by Europeans, and, to him, the true descendant of the builders of the pyramids. In Balmont's eyes, the Indians maintained their nobility wherever he encountered them. In the capital, for example, it was not the Europeanized middle class who visited the National Museum, but the Indians, their faces raised in awe and respect before the old gods. Similarly, Balmont remarked,

> it is moving to talk with a simple Aztec about the beauty of the colors of the poppy, of the nobility of Cuauhtémoc, who silently submitted to torture and did not tell Cortés where the national

treasure was buried. It is moving to see how affectionate [and] tender women are with their husbands here, the lover with his beloved, whether they walk soberly, or more often, drunkenly staggering around the cantinas, in the poor quarters . . . where the descendants of the people who created the colorful hieroglyphs drink the wretched, miserable pulque.[54]

Balmont described the Indian market at Pachuca as being a marvelous spectacle, and an old Indian woman's graciousness in Cuernavaca he saw as yet another indication of all that was fine in the Indian character. Oaxaca in particular seemed to be the Mexico he had come to experience, truly Mexican, he wrote, because it had so little that was European. On an excursion to the nearby ruins at Mitla, he encountered what he termed a great "panorama" of Indians coming to market, and he wrote in his journal that for him the combination of their clothes, eyes, hair, and faces made the experience the most beautiful, exotic, and unforgettable he had had in the New World. It was these people's ancestors who had created what was most valuable in Mexico. In Balmont's mind, nothing the Europeans had done in the past in Mexico or were doing under Porfirio Díaz could compare to what remained of the great Indian civilizations. The symbol of contemporary Mexico, he wrote Briusov, was the dessicated "momias" of Guanajuato. A popular tourist attraction, the mummies represented better than anything else he had seen what he considered the sterility and emptiness of modern Mexican life, particularly that lived by the middle classes and those who directed the country's government.[55]

Balmont's purpose in Mexico was to visit the country's archeological sites, and he devoted his time in the capital almost entirely to research on this subject. While living in Mexico City, he was able to make short excursions to nearby sites, as well. Teotihuacán and Xochicalco he considered to be works of genius, and he used them as inspirations for much of his subsequent poetry on Mexico. Yet, in the Valley of Mexico so little remained of the Aztec and Toltec past he had rigorously studied that he decided to travel south and east, to visit the extensive Mayan ruins of Tehuantepec and Yucatán. They were still primitive areas, and Balmont hoped they would preserve some of the romance and mystery of the ancient past that seemed so difficult to find in Mexico.[56]

By the time he left the capital for the Isthmus of Tehuantepec, Balmont had developed an almost unconscious aversion to colonial and modern Mexico. Puebla was the "most uninteresting" town he had seen, essentially because of the multitude of Catholic churches there. It was redeemed in his eyes only by what was left of a pyramid dedicated to Quetzalcóatl. The trip by steamer from Veracruz to Frontera began pleasantly enough, but once at sea, it proved to be a more frightening adventure than Balmont had imagined possible.[57] About Frontera his opinions were mixed: the tropical heat was exhausting, but the cicadas, the "green walls" of mimosas, bananas, and coconut palms, the iguanas, crabs, fireflies, and above all, the hummingbirds, were striking in their beauty.[58] Leaving Frontera for the ruins was both more and less complicated than expected. The guide he had hired to lead him to Palenque was one of the stupidest persons he had ever encountered, and he found the information given him in Mexico City about the dangers of visiting the area at least thirty years out of date. Still, there was no doubt that the ruins were worth the misery involved in reaching them.

Balmont was so moved by his experiences in the ancient Mayan cities during the following days that he entered nothing in his journal until his return to Mexico City. He explained that unusual impressions and exotic images had come so rapidly that he had had no opportunity to assimilate them and put them on paper. His feelings were complicated, too, he wrote Briusov, by a subconscious sense that he had already been in the ruins, many centuries before.[59] He was ecstatic about Palenque. He felt privileged at being one of the few Europeans to have seen the ruins with his own eyes, but he wondered sadly how long the unprotected temple reliefs would survive in the open air.

Balmont and Tsvetkovskaia travelled from Frontera to Progreso by steamer. They arrived hours behind schedule, and Balmont wrote that the problems with scheduling helped him gain insight into what he called "American" ways of doing things in Mexico. He met the governor of Yucatán, a generous and pleasant man, and Edward Thompson, the U.S. consul and part-time archeologist, who invited the visitors to stay in his house near Uxmal. Here Balmont gave his enthusiasm and imagination full rein. The ruins were magnificent, diminished neither by time nor human beings. Uxmal's mysteries he found akin to those of Egypt, Babylon, or India. Its architecture was unequalled, he wrote later, the view from the Pyramid of the Magician one of the most striking he had yet seen, the once beautiful and busy city below now engulfed in lush, tropical vegetation. In one structure he discovered a half-buried statue, its face that of a beautiful woman of "Egyptian-Jewish" type, with an expression reminiscent to Balmont of H. Rider Haggard's She, "who must be obeyed."[60] These impressions, recorded in his notebook, all later found their way into his poetry and essays on Mexico.

Balmont was more general and less enthusiastic about Chichén Itzá than Uxmal. By the time he arrived there, he must have become tired of travelling under such primitive circumstances. The town officials at Dzitas near the ruins reminded him of those in Gogol's *Inspector General,* although he wrote that he was unable to regard them with Gogol's humor. What he liked most about Chichén Itzá was another of Thompson's houses, which had a marvelous view of the ruins. Its quiet peacefulness provided the perfect surroundings for reading Thompson's fine collection of books, while lying in a hammock and intermittently looking out at the remains of the ancient city.[61] Balmont apparently spent more time relaxing at Chichén Itzá than writing about it, but his stay there did contribute to the emotional and inspirational background of his subsequent works.

By mid-June, Balmont had returned to Mexico City, and the concluding entries in his journal reflected the affinity he felt with the spiritual vision of the ancient peoples of Mexico. He was especially taken with the largest remnants of the pre-Columbian civilizations, the pyramids. They appealed to him because of their orientation toward the sun and the sky, their openness to the "face of nature," their "love of height," and the views they provided of the distant horizon:

> I climbed the Pyramid of the Sun [at Teotihuacán], which is larger than the famous Pyramid of Cheops. But it was not the size of this pyramid that struck me, nor the recognition that this enormous thing was thousands and thousands of years old, but that the vanished people who had built it truly understood that cathedrals, in which one's thought strives for the Sky, must climb to the Skies and be open to the stars, must be remote from the buildings in which people eat, drink, do business . . . as high and soli-

tary as eagles, as century-old trees, as mountain heights. . . . I understand that at one time it was easy to pray in cathedrals, and that it was easy . . . to feel one's unity with the world.[62]

Balmont's discussion of the pyramid temples compelled him to write about the widespread pre-Conquest practice of human sacrifice as well. Examining it from the point of view of those who were prepared to die in expectation of a union with the sun, then rebirth as birds, he concluded that being sacrificed to the sun in such circumstances was not as abhorrent to the Indians as Europeans believed. As he learned more about ancient Mexico, Balmont came to feel that the world of the pre-Columbian Indians was a beautiful one, attractive in both its natural and human aspects. If it was not paradise, it was infinitely closer to it than was the modern Mexico he had come to know in 1905.

Balmont and Tsvetkovskaia departed by train for the United States in June and in the fall he was again in Moscow, working on a translation of Shelley for the Znanie publishing house. Because of the unsettled political situation, he did not remain long in Russia. He left for Paris at the end of 1905 and returned only when the government issued a general amnesty in 1913 on the occasion of the three-hundredth anniversary of Romanov rule.[63] His Mexican travel journal was published in installments in Vesy (The Balance), and he was beginning to write the essays and poems that would appear in various periodicals and books over the next few years. His published journal gave his readers an immediate impression of his travels, but his later works provided a more balanced picture of his attitudes to Mexico and were better indications of how he understood what he had seen there.[64]

Much of the prose and poetry inspired by his journey to the New World appeared initially in such journals as Vesy, Iskusstvo (Art), and Zolotoe runo (The Golden Fleece), but the first collection was published in 1908. A lengthy section of Ptitsy v vozdukhe (Birds in the Air) was entitled "Maya," and was the first extensive body of verse to appear in Russian dealing with Mexican and Mayan themes. The poems were extravagantly musical and introduced exotic Mexican names into the Russian language.[65] Zovy drevnosti (Summons From Ancient Times), published in 1910, dealt with "cosmological" themes from many of the world's cultures. The section on Mexico was a cycle of poems devoted to the origins of the gods and goddesses of the pre-Columbian peoples, retelling the tales Balmont had heard or read in Mexico.[66] The poems were accompanied by notes which showed a highly sophisticated understanding of current scholarly knowledge about the Mexican past.

The most significant book Balmont published on Mexico, however, was his *Zmeinye tsvety (Snake-like Flowers)*, issued by Skorpion in 1910. The travel notes that had appeared earlier in *Vesy* were reprinted, along with forty-three photographs illustrating the sites and locales Balmont had visited.[67] Of particular importance was his translation of the Mayan *Popol Vuh*, its first version in Russian.[68] Balmont was known as a somewhat none-too-faithful translator, but while subsequent versions of the Mayan epic in Russian would be more accurate, it was Balmont's that first made the work accessible to Russian audiences and attempted to convey its literary quality and emotional impact as well as its meaning.

Of greater interest, perhaps, in *Zmeinye tsvety* were the essays on Mexican symbolism and mythology. In "Tsvetistyi uzor—Meksikanskaia simvolika" ("The Florid Pattern—Mexican Symbolics"), Balmont discussed the significance of numbers, of the cross (associated with Tlaloc, the god of rain), the calendar, and the triangle as symbols in ancient Mexico.[69] "Preobrazhenie zhertvi—solnechnaia mysl" ("The Transformation of the Sacrifice—Thoughts About the Sun"), was concerned with a theme in which Balmont was especially interested. After retelling Peruvian, Siamese, Russian, and Slovak tales about the sun, he added two from Mexico, broadening once more his Russian readers' knowledge of ancient Mexican folklore and religion.[70] "Maiia" ("The Maya") considered with sympathy the belief Balmont shared with others at the turn of the century, that the culture of the Maya of Yucatán was a remnant of that of Atlantis.[71] Probably the best essay in the collection was "Strana krasnykh tsvetov" ("The Land of Red Flowers"), in which Balmont retold the history of the Aztecs' semi-mythical journey from Aztlán to the site of Tenochtitlán, recounted the stories he had learned of Quetzalcóatl and Huitzilopochtli, and discussed the unity of life and death in the ancient Mexican world view.[72] Finally, the book included two retellings of ancient Mayan mythological-historical tales.[73]

Zmeinye tsvety was the most complete, most sophisticated, and most artfully constructed account of ancient Mexico to appear in Russian until the post-Stalin era. Yet Balmont's view of Mexico and the Mexicans was also profoundly individual. Ilya Ehrenburg, for example, who saw and heard Balmont in Paris before World War I, wrote that "he had traveled, it seemed, in every country in the world, but he had seen only one—not shown on any map—which I shall call Balmontia."[74] While Ehrenburg's statement is true in general, Mexico did, nonetheless, prove to be unique in Balmont's experience. He responded to it in a highly personal way, and several important themes are present in his Mexican works. One was nature. Balmont was always effusive in his love of his natural surroundings, and nowhere in any of his travels did he find nature as pleasant as in Mexico, where the attitude of the local population was so in harmony with his own. Mexico was the "land of eternal spring"; the "voice of the earth," with its "melodic refrain, unconsciously conveys us to this picturesque country, where thoughts, plants, and birds are colorful, and where bronze people feel in every flower a creative, singing, fantastic soul."[75] No Russian wrote about this affinity before Balmont. Indeed, visitors like Wrangell had felt just the opposite was true. They all described contemporary, mestizo or European Mexico, however, while Balmont wrote about the country's native peoples, and the pre-Conquest civilization they had created.

Balmont knew that the "bronze people" who appreciated Mexico's natural paradise had lost a good deal of their sensitivity to nature in the centuries following the Spanish conquest. He made no serious attempt to understand the Mexico of the Porfiriato and rejected it outright almost upon arrival. Quite simply, to Balmont, everything that was truly good or admirable in Mexico dated from its distant past. The present was incapable of changing that reality. For Balmont, modern religion was inevitably inferior to the ancient gods and the ancient folklore. That much of this Mexican past existed only in Balmont's imagination did not deter him from his opinion. The pre-Columbian myths and legends, the mysterious architecture and sculpture, provided inspiration for a great deal of his later poetry, even his way of looking at the world. While it is true that he brought much Russian intellectual baggage with him to Mexico, he nevertheless left Mexico with much that was new.

Finally, one theme tied Mexico and Russia together for Balmont—
the omnipresence of blood. He was in Mexico during some of the
most severe fighting and bloodshed of the 1905 Russian revolution,
and Russian developments were constantly on his mind during his
travels. Mexico too had been a land of blood, as he wrote in *Zovy
drevnosti:* "If Egypt is illuminated by the golden, soft-yellow Sun,
Mexico is illuminated completely by the glow of a crimson Sun. In
its hymns you hear only the song of blood."[76] He noted that in the
view of the ancient Mexicans, it was blood alone that men and the
gods shared in common and, as noted above, he came to see the
temple sacrifices with considerable sympathy. For the ancient peoples
of Mexico, bloody sacrifice of human beings had an immediate purpose: it propitiated the gods and allowed life on earth to continue,
and was therefore positive in the terms of the times. In Russia, Balmont felt, only vaguely in 1905, but more clearly by the time *Zmeinye
tsvety* appeared in 1910, all the blood that had been spilled had had
no effect. It had not changed a corrupt and insupportable social and
political establishment. What Balmont could not know was that considerably more blood would flow in both Russia and Mexico over the
next decade and that from it new societies would be born. In neither
case, however, would it be a society or culture that would appeal to
Balmont.

Balmont came to Mexico at a time highly significant for him, for
the country he visited, and for the cultural and political life of his
homeland. He found almost nothing of value in Mexico's post-Conquest
experience, nor did he anticipate great improvement in the future.
He loved a good deal of what he found, and was repelled by much
more. There was little to which he reacted indifferently. Because of
his immense prestige as a poet his impressions were highly influential in Russia, more so than those of any of the Russian journalists
writing during the Porfiriato. Most later Russian visitors to Mexico
knew Balmont's writings, some intimately, and his views directly influenced theirs. At a time of severe political and psychological stress,
he expanded Russia's intellectual borders, beyond Europe and Asia,
beyond the United States. While an interest in Mexico became representative of the escapist exoticism of the post-1905 Silver Age, Mexico later emerged as an image and theme of a certain significance in

Russian intellectual life. That later importance can be traced to Konstantin Balmont's journey to the "country of red flowers" in 1905, and his promoting of the value of the ancient Mexican civilizations.[77]

Tverskoi's "Contemporary Mexico"

The final Russian traveller to write about Porfirian Mexico shared few of Balmont's concerns and interests. P. A. Tverskoi visited Mexico at the very end of the Díaz presidency, in 1910, although he published his account only in 1913, when much of what he had written was no longer current. "Tverskoi" was the pen name of P. A. Dementev, and as his pseudonym suggests, he was a native of Tver. A liberal active in the district zemstvo government, he left home just ahead of the police in 1881, although the specific reasons for his departure are unclear. He moved to Florida, became a farmer, and was soon a success through his activities in a lumber mill, railroads, manufacturing, and the planting of oranges. He later became a building contractor, a land developer, and the founder of the new town of St. Petersburg on the state's gulf coast. In the 1890s he moved to southern California and was actively involved in Republican party politics until his death in 1919. He wrote for Russian audiences fairly regularly throughout his career, and in 1895 he completed an exceedingly laudatory book about the United States.[78] His enthusiasm did not carry over to the Mexico of Porfirio Díaz, however. On the contrary, his criticisms of the Porfiriato were quite severe, in political, moral, and economic terms.

"Sovremennoe Meksiko" ("Contemporary Mexico") appeared in *Russkaia mysl* (*Russian Thought*). It was based on three trips to Mexico, adding up to a total of three months spent in the country. Tverskoi stressed in his introduction that Latin America was isolated from much of the rest of the world, that it was backward and relatively unknown to citizens of other countries, particularly Russians. He explained to *Russkaia mysl*'s readers that his brief article would attempt to provide a concise introduction to the current state of one of Latin America's most important countries. The first section dealt with the political and social life of contemporary Mexico, focusing on Díaz and his regime. He traced Díaz's background, remarking that his bravery in the struggles against the church, the French, and Maximilian had made him extraordinarily popular in Mexico. By 1910, however, it seemed to Tverskoi that Díaz was an unlimited dictator, and that while his policies were often good for Mexico, at times they were not. For example, Díaz had raised Mexico's prestige internationally and had obtained foreign credit by systematizing the country's finances, improving its transportation network, and stimulating industrial development. But "the nation paid a high, often insane price for this investment. To attract this capital, Díaz gave the investors numerous varied governmental subsidies and privileges, even outright monopolies, and in every way pandered to them."[79] This was, Tverskoi wrote, the greatest failure of the Díaz presidency, but it was only the most obvious one.

Tverskoi admitted that Díaz himself was relatively poor in comparison to others in his government. His associates, in their search for wealth, had "prostituted" the nation, to the extent that now anything in Mexico could be bought with enough foreign money. All Mexico's natural resources were for sale, Tverskoi reported, and if the buyer lacked adequate financial backing to qualify for the purchase, it could be assumed that the government would subsidize the purchase for a reasonable, under-the-table fee. British and U.S. investors had been given railroad and mining concessions, banking privileges, and water resources for irrigation, for example, not to improve the overall condition of the country, but to make money for corrupt government officials. Tverskoi's tone became increasingly bitter as he discussed these aspects of the Mexican economy. In his final comments he wrote that Mexico City was crowded with people looking for a fast buck and that the corruption and bribery which flourished in the government was a clear sign that the nation's political establishment had sold itself out to foreigners, that honesty and patriotism were sorely lacking.

Other aspects of Mexico's social and political life Tverskoi also saw as reprehensible. Elections were a farce under Díaz, of course. A well-informed electorate might have changed this, but despite government pretense, public education was at a scandalously low level: "Even though Mexico's financial situation has been brilliant during the last fifteen or twenty years, and the government has spent many millions every year for subsidies and all possible ventures in heavy industry, it has severely neglected all cultural and educational necessities, and the population [has been] deliberately doomed to unenlightened ignorance."[80] The wealthy sent their children abroad to be educated, he learned, and the population as a whole, given no real attention by the government, remained illiterate and poverty-stricken. The country's natural wealth was enormous, with rich deposits of silver, other minerals, and oil which were exploited to benefit the government and foreigners, with the workers laboring long hours and being paid miserably low wages. Díaz's promises of democracy notwithstanding, Mexicans had still not truly known the benefits of freedom, Tverskoi wrote, and the upper classes continued to rule the country in their own interests. The population as a whole was backward and apathetic and lacked the energy to develop the nation's resources. In the long run, he predicted, the industrial program promoted by Díaz would not be advantageous for the country. It would, on the contrary, lead only to strains that might have serious and unsettling results.

To Tverskoi's readers, it soon became obvious that despite his early comments about the achievements of the Porfiriato, his view of Mexico in 1910 was a highly negative one. Above all, he saw little possibility that the lives of the majority of the population could improve without fundamental changes in the economic, political, and social systems. Tverskoi was not a radical, not even a moderate socialist, but a U.S.-style, free-enterprise capitalist. He criticized the Porfiriato on the basis of what he considered to be a pragmatic approach to solving the country's problems. And they were problems, he felt, in overwhelming need of a solution. Once more, in the view of a Russian traveller, Mexico was very like Russia. No doubt Tverskoi would have liked to change Russia as well as Mexico. If both countries suffered from many of the same problems, Tverskoi must have believed, then the outcome for both would be highly unpleasant without fundamental reform. By the time his article appeared in 1913, radical change was underway in Mexico, and the Russian government was being bombarded with demands for reform. Tverskoi offered no detailed solutions for Mexico or for Russia, but acting as a gadfly, he did wish to point out the abuses and weaknesses of the society he found in Mexico. If his Russian readers saw parallels with their own country, so much the better.

The second section of Tverskoi's article described some of Mexico's unusual and unique features. He first gave an overview of its geography and of the kinds of agricultural products grown in various areas. Connected to agriculture and topography were problems of transportation, of course, and Tverskoi included a fairly lengthy description of the difficulties involved in building railroads. He was almost glowing in his admiration for the U.S. engineers who had recently completed construction of a line from the U.S. border to the Pacific coast. He used this example of technological ingenuity to stress the remarkable differences between the two principal nations of North America. He noted that the only parallel he could find anywhere in the world to the U.S.-Mexican border was the frontier between Germany and Russia. This was a comparison that could not have been flattering to Russia since Mexico was shown to be poorer, less economically developed, and on the whole, less effectively "organized" than the United States. One side of the border was purely Mexican, the other entirely "American," with almost no mixture between the two. Tverskoi's picture of life in Mexican towns made the distinction even clearer: the architecture and town planning, the clothing of the population (only the upper classes dressed in European styles), and among other things, the public letter writers all revealed how Mexico differed from the United States. The differences were most apparent among the impoverished lower classes of Mexico, especially the working class. Tverskoi found, for example, that among the poor, women seemed to age and grow stout surprisingly early, that "a twenty-five-year-old often looks like an old woman."[81] Further, he wrote, working people were in bad physical condition in general, no matter what their age. They always had a hungry look, because indeed they did not have enough to eat or drink. In the city, their diet was composed primarily of corn, beans, and peppers, and in the country, these foods were all they ate, although never was there enough food of any sort to forestall hunger and malnutrition. They almost never consumed meat or other vegetables, and few dairy cows, pigs, or chickens were to be seen. Finally, and to make their situation even worse, the poor and the working class had no understanding of hygiene, and they often fell ill. Despite the boasts of the Díaz regime, there was no effective organized medical care in the country, and the number of deaths from ordinary illnesses was remarkably high. Only a correspondingly high birth rate kept the population from declining. Finally, in response to their miserable lives, the population had turned to alcohol, and drunkenness was widespread in the countryside and in the cities. It could not be said, Tverskoi believed, that Mexican society was healthy or that its future was promising.

Tverskoi noted later in his essay that widespread poverty in Mexico affected certain aspects of social life, particularly with respect to women. Like most foreigners, he remarked on the traditional custom of soldiers' taking their families along with them on campaign, and on the independent position many lower-class women held in society. Yet Mexican women were bound by strict social restraints, they had no legal rights, they were usually illiterate, and they played no real part in social life, which was dominated by men. Poor women rarely were wed in church, nor were their marriages even legal in most cases, but they were very religious, and they constituted most of those attending mass. Above all, he intimated, women seemed to be the ones who held families together when husbands and fathers fell prey to the temptations of alcoholism and hopelessness. They were, in short, the great strength of the nation. But for them, as for the society as a whole, Tverskoi saw little that made him optimistic about the future.

It was agriculture and land tenure that Tverskoi felt was at the heart of the problems facing Mexico. Always a man who relied more on practical research than theoretical analysis, Tverskoi noted that he had learned about Mexican agriculture firsthand by visiting several rural areas. In the state of Sinaloa he had spent some time talking with the governor and examining both private and communal agricultural holdings. He discovered immediately that the need for radical land reform was apparent to any objective observer and that the leaders of the country were at last beginning to recognize that fundamental change was necessary. He found it interesting that a large percentage of the rural population still practiced the traditional, communal cultivation of land. No doubt because of parallels he saw with Russia, Tverskoi discussed the communal landholding system at length, noting the large concentrations of land in the hands of a limited number of families. These families, he was appalled to find, treated the people working on their estates somewhat the way Russian landowners had treated their serfs before the emancipation of 1861. The head of the family usually lived in Mexico City or abroad, in Madrid or Paris, and considered his property to be like a medieval fief, despite the nation's laws or its constitution. From his discussions in the northern part of the country, Tverskoi learned that governorships and other important posts were almost hereditary within these families, who were determined to maintain the system even in the face of the clear need for reform.

Tverskoi's criticisms of Mexican rural life were not unique, of course; they had been voiced by a number of other commentators, both Mexican and foreign. His views were interesting, however, because of the similarities he noticed between Mexico and Russia. Both countries exhibited the same entrenched, stultifying, if at times paternalistic, despotism. In the 1860s Russia had reached the point that Mexico was approaching only in the early twentieth century: both now recognized that change was inevitable, and that directed change was preferable to revolutionary transformation. Tverskoi's advice was based on what he had seen in Russia following the emancipation of the serfs. He noted that there had been attempts in Russia to break up the agricultural commune in the hope that a new class of independent yeoman farmers would develop. He did not recommend this for Mexico. First, he advised, the agricultural land should be given to the peasants who tilled it; this step was essential if the country were to avoid disaster in the near future. As in Russia, the land should be given to the communes, and not broken up into individual farms. This would avoid the social and economic disruptions accompanying full-scale agrarian transformation. Subsequent reforms could be tackled only after the agricultural question was solved; and in a similarly systemic way, the changes would have to be consistent with the practices of the past.

Tverskoi devoted the final section of his article to a discussion of recent political developments. He prefaced his comments by expressing a certain degree of hope, writing that despite the inadequacies of the Mexican government, there appeared to be a strong democratic spirit linking the upper class who ran the government and the population as a whole, a democratic spirit that was, in fact, stronger than anything he had sensed in the United States. He was led to feel, he wrote, that this belief in democracy would aid the country greatly in the inevitable times of stress to come. By implication, of course, Tverskoi was again writing about Russia. Russia had no such unity of democratic spirit between the government and the people, despite the fact that every tsar claimed to be a "little father" to "his people." By the time Tverskoi was writing about Mexico, the social unity that had once been present in Russia was almost nonexistent, and his remark about Mexican democracy must have sent something of a chill down the spines of his Russian readers looking for parallels with their own country.

While some aspects of Mexican political life were encouraging, Tverskoi was not optimistic about the provisional government formed after the fall of Díaz by Francisco Madero. Madero came from the old landowning ruling class that had no intention of sharing power with the people. The musicians had changed, Tverskoi commented, but the music stayed the same. Madero had no useful experience in heading a government or running a country, and the same could be said of many of his supporters in other parts of the nation: at best, they were uneducated and inexperienced, at worst, thieves. Tverskoi added that by 1911 it was clear that Madero did not intend to fulfill a single one of his promises with respect to agrarian reform. Worse, he had fallen into the hands of foreign business interests to an extent even greater than Díaz had. Any new government, Tverskoi stressed, in order to maintain its legitimacy in the eyes of the poor and the peasants, would have to end what he called foreign capitalist exploitation. This was true particularly with respect to U.S. firms, since a wave of anti–North Americanism had accompanied the early stages of the revolution. Because Madero had no intention of doing this, a new revolution was inevitable, the product of growing popular indignation with government policies. Madero's presidency, Tverskoi believed, was only the beginning of a long period of trouble and uncertainty.

In an attempt to bring Tverskoi's essay up to date, a short article followed his in *Russkaia mysl*. I. O. Levin's "Novyi perevorot v Meksiko" ("A New Revolution in Mexico") dealt briefly with Madero's assassination, the "decena trágica" (the tragic ten days of the Felix Díaz revolt), and with the assumption of power by Victoriano Huerta. Levin emphasized the significance of U.S. influence on these events and discussed the tradition of U.S. intervention in Mexican affairs. He considered the importance of U.S. economic influence on members of the Díaz government, the theory that Díaz had been overthrown by Madero at the instigation of the United States (acting on behalf of Rockefeller, who was furious at Díaz for granting to a British firm an oil concession which he had wanted), and the possibility of a U.S.

invasion or annexation of Mexican territory. Levin concluded that these rumors and theories were unfounded on the whole and that what the United States really wanted was a commanding role in the Mexican economy. His evaluation was clearly critical of the United States and its role in Mexico's affairs.[82]

Unlike his Russian predecessors in Mexico, Tverskoi had not written a travelogue. Instead, he concentrated on analysis, emphasizing the condition of the country and the ways he felt Mexico could begin to solve its problems. He quite clearly knew a great deal about the country and had a keen understanding of many of the difficulties it faced. His views provide an interesting conclusion to what Russians had been writing about Mexico for over twenty years. Like them, and most other foreigners, he saw great potential, but he agreed with Patkanov that significant change was necessary for that potential to be realized. To a surprising degree, however, Tverskoi's proposals for the future of Mexico tie him, as shall be seen, rather more closely to the Soviet Marxist analyses made during the 1920s than to Patkanov's. His emphases on fundamental, radical land reform and the expulsion of foreign economic interests are the most outstanding examples of this affinity. As a result, Tverskoi was a transitional figure in the evolution of Russian views of Mexico. He looked forward to a changed Mexico, one that would take its place among the advanced and progressive nations of the world and offer an example for other Latin American countries to emulate.

While there were some minor essays dealing with Mexican literature published in Russia during the Porfiriato,[83] it was the essays of Patkanov, Protopopov, Devollan, and Tverskoi, along with the lengthier works by Balmont, that were most important in expressing a Russian view of Mexico during those years. It cannot be said that any single one of these men understood Mexico especially well, and it was obvious from reading their essays that their interpretations were flavored to a remarkable degree by their attitudes toward their homeland. Even their praise for the progressive features of the Porfiriato must be appreciated in the context of what they felt about Tsarist Russia. They approached Porfirian Mexico as outsiders, but rarely with condescension. What they disliked in Mexico they despised in their own country, and if at times their criticism seemed harsh, they were much less condemnatory than many North American or Western European visitors, and certainly less negative than the Russians who travelled to California and Mexico during the early nineteenth century. Protopopov and Devollan, who were the most positive and the most superficial, were the least interesting. Patkanov and Tverskoi, on the other hand, were acidic and uncompromising in their accounts, and their essays remain as memorable to the modern reader as they must have been to their original Russian audience. Balmont, of course, was by far the most critical of modern Mexico, but he too based his evaluations not on some sense of European superiority (even though he did reveal this weakness at times), but on just the opposite feeling. Ostensibly at least, he hated all that was modern, and he especially despised the submission of native cultures around the world to European cultural colonialism. His Mexico was unlike any other Russian's. He understood the country in a special way, and his vision of it was the most unusual of any Russian who visited Mexico in the years before the downfall of Porfirio Díaz. His highly individualistic works transcended the strictly national confines of the essays written by the other four men.

One thing distinguished these writers from their predecessors during the first half of the nineteenth century: they wrote not for a social and political elite, but for what they hoped would be a socially conscious, sophisticated Russian reading public. All of them, too, hoped their writings would influence government ministers or policy with regard to domestic affairs in their own country. The first stage of Russian interest in Mexico, that associated with the interests of the Russian American Company, had been replaced by a second. Russia had changed considerably, as had its approach to Mexico.

3

**THE
NINETEEN-
TWENTIES:
A SHARED
REVOLUTIONARY
EXPERIENCE**

Diplomats, Scientists, Dancers, and Athletes

It is not surprising that few Russians came to Mexico during the second decade of the twentieth century. Disorders and uncertainties discouraged potential travellers, although they must also have heartened would-be revolutionaries in Russia. After 1917, with revolutionary governments in place, however tenuously, in both countries, relations between them began to develop more rapidly than might have been expected. In 1924, Mexico and the USSR extended each other diplomatic recognition, and the Soviet government opened its first embassy in the Western Hemisphere in Mexico City. Once again, as during the Porfiriato, the great psychological distance between the two nations was reduced. Both countries had for years emphasized their commitment to revolutionary change, and both governments now based their legitimacy on popular revolutionary movements. Between 1917 and 1924 only a few Russians found their way to Mexico, but once diplomatic relations were established, a constant stream of Soviet visitors arrived. Many of them wrote about their experiences, and an entirely new picture of Mexico was presented to Soviet readers. The decade of the 1920s was one of great hope in both nations, and Soviet travellers to Mexico expected to find a revolutionary process there similar to their own. In most cases, they were disappointed, particularly as the decade progressed. But through the writings of Pestkovsky, Kollontai, and Mayakovsky among others, Russians came to know more about Mexico than they ever had before, and their understanding of the country was considerably more sophisticated than might have been expected.

The first well-known Russian visitor was the ballerina Anna Pavlova. Shortly after assuming power as president in 1917, in Mexico City, Venustiano Carranza had banned the traditional *corrida de toros* because he felt it was cruel and barbarous,[1] and he was anxious to provide the populace with other forms of entertainment. "Higher" forms of culture fit his desire precisely, and on behalf of the government he invited a number of internationally known performers to appear in Mexico City. Early in 1918 Enrico Caruso sang in the former Plaza de Toros before an enthusiastic audience of over thirty thousand people. Pavlova had also been invited, but a group of U.S. citizens in Havana had warned her about the dangers of travel in Mexico. One of her associates recalled that a telegram was sent to Carranza "asking him to let us know whether Pavlova could consider herself perfectly safe in Mexico and whether he could take her and her company under his protection. A day later we received a reply from Carranza saying that he guaranteed complete safety and had already given the necessary instructions to the authorities of Veracruz."[2] Carranza had issued orders that she and her troupe were to be accompanied by an armed escort of federal soldiers from Veracruz to the capital, a precaution that was not unreasonable considering the still unsettled nature of the country and the fact that not all the former revolutionaries had been entirely pacified.[3]

Despite her initial trepidation, nothing untoward occurred, and by all indications Pavlova was quite taken with the country and its people, particularly the colorfulness of the native dress, and the people's "liveliness" and originality of expression. Her appreciation was reciprocated by the population of the capital. Initially, she had planned to stay in Mexico City only two weeks, but because of her enthusiastic reception, she remained considerably longer.[4] She danced each Sunday in the Plaza de Toros before huge crowds and on other days appeared in smaller theaters.[5] She performed her standard repertoire, commissioning additional dances from Mexican composers and choreographers. Her "Fantasía Mexicana," based on a libretto by Jaime Martino del Río, included her interpretation of three typically Mexican pieces: "China Poblana," "Jarabe Tapatío," and "Diana Mexicana." The costumes, settings, and choreography were by the young Adolfo Best Maugard (who worked with Eisenstein over a decade later), and the music was composed and arranged by Manuel Castro Padilla.[6] The dances were a predictable success in Mexico City and were added to Pavlova's permanent repertory.

If Pavlova was disappointed by one thing in Mexico, it was Carranza, who was rather less exotic than she had hoped: "[We] were very surprised . . . when we saw Carranza himself. We had imagined that the president of the Mexican Republic would be a dusky Mexican, with a cruel, tyrannical face, dressed in an exotic uniform covered with gold lace, but instead we saw what looked like a German professor, bald with a long silvery beard and wearing spectacles."[7] Most Europeans probably would have expected the kind of president Pavlova did. Her slightly surprised disappointment indicated that she, like so many other foreigners, had no truly informed understanding of the kind of country Mexico was during these years. Despite her own clear opposition to the Bolsheviks, her visit did make Mexicans more aware of Russian cultural traditions.

More significant than Pavlova's visit in encouraging contacts between Russia and Mexico were two developments that took place in the late teens and early twenties. One was the formation of a Mexican Communist party, eventually affiliated with Moscow's Communist International, and the second was the establishment of diplomatic relations between Mexico and the USSR. The Partido Comunista Mexicano (PCM) was created through the efforts of a number of foreigners and Mexicans in 1919. It had a precarious existence during its first few years because of poor leadership, a recurrent lack of funds, and its limited influence and contact with radical worker and peasant groups beyond Mexico City, Veracruz, and a few other urban areas.[8] Despite the enthusiasm of a small number of intellectuals and artists, the PCM relied on the Comintern and the government of the USSR for much of its financial and moral support. The Soviet embassy, which opened in Mexico City in the fall of 1924, was responsible for a considerable amount of the party's success in the middle years of the decade and for its survival after it was outlawed in 1929. A Mexican Communist party organization meant that Russians would more readily be invited to Mexico and that they would receive a friendly welcome. It meant too, that in the face of the suspicion of many in the government, Soviet visitors would be able to make contacts with representatives of various social groups. The PCM was important in assuring that the visitors would be given more than a tourist's view of Mexico.

It was more difficult to establish diplomatic relations between Russia and Mexico than it was to create a Mexican Communist party. As the Civil War in Russia appeared to be reaching a favorable outcome for the Bolsheviks, the new government in Moscow began to make a concerted effort to break out of the "diplomatic blockade" it felt had been imposed by the Western powers and to strengthen its international position, despite its support for the Comintern and international Communist revolution. Mikhail Borodin had attempted to establish relations through negotiations with Carranza in 1919, but had no success.[9] In 1922, a Soviet trade delegation was sent to Mexico in an attempt to obtain recognition in exchange for a favorable commercial treaty. Again, the meetings were not productive, although one member of the delegation, D. E. Dubrovsky, was quite well received in Yucatán, where he participated in the ceremonies swearing in the new socialist governor, Felipe Carrillo Puerto.[10] In the end, discussions in Europe and the United States between Soviet and Mexican representatives yielded more positive results: on August 4, 1924, Mexico City announced through its ambassador in Berlin that it had agreed to accept to nomination of S. S. Pestkovsky as ambassador. Mexico thus became the first New World nation to extend diplomatic recognition to the Soviet Union.

From the beginning, the new embassy promoted exchanges between Mexico and the USSR. It established contact with leftist labor leaders and intellectuals and assisted in forming the new Sociedad de Amigos de la URSS. It held special receptions, showed recent Soviet films, and subsidized Mexican publishers wishing to issue translations of Russian and Soviet works of literature. The embassy's financial assistance to the PCM allowed the party to quadruple the size of its newspaper, El Machete, and it financed a series of trips by PCM members to the Soviet Union, later paying the costs of publication of accounts of their travels. News of the embassy's activities reached the Soviet Union as well, and as Mexicans began appearing at Comintern congresses and at celebrations marking the anniversaries of various Soviet revolutionary events, there was a growth of interest in Mexico among the Soviet public. New translations of books about Mexico were published in the USSR,[11] and because of the visits of such artists as Diego Rivera and David Alfaro Siqueiros, Russians learned about the Mexican muralist movement. And soon, of course, an increasing number of Soviet scholars, poets, and scientists began planning visits to Mexico.

Cultural contacts between Mexico and the USSR continued to grow during the second half of the decade, but their political relationship was strained. While diplomats at the embassy were defusing potential conflicts with the Mexican government, Comintern agents working with the PCM were provoking them. The Comintern was not particularly knowledgeable about Mexican affairs and frequently sent instructions to its Mexican affiliate to carry out policies that proved to be counterproductive.[12] The PCM, which might have given informed advice to the leaders of the Comintern in Moscow, rarely was able to do so because of factional infighting and an increasing isolation in Mexican society. By the late 1920s, the Mexican government was formally protesting to the Soviet government the activities of the Comintern (by 1929, the Comintern had officially labeled the Mexican government "fascist," "reactionary," and an agent of the colonialist powers and was ordering Communist parties around the world to resist it with force) and the consistently hostile attitude of the Soviet press to the Mexican government. Behind the Comintern's newly militant line were the resolutions passed at its Sixth Congress in Moscow in 1928, calling for disciplined opposition to all reformist socialists, bourgeois nationalists, or "pseudo-progressive" governments like Mexico's. The isolated but "uncompromising" militant Bolsheviks of 1917 were chosen as the model for the PCM to follow. Good state-to-state relations between Mexico and the USSR fell victim to Stalinist extremism.

As relations worsened, the role of the Soviet ambassador became increasingly important. As the first representative of his country to Mexico, Pestkovsky was not overly sensitive to Mexicans' pride in their own revolution; he considered them citizens of a "semicolonial" nation, frequently lectured them on how a genuine revolution might be made in Mexico, and as we shall see, after his return to the USSR, wrote two books that were highly uncomplimentary to the governments of Plutarco Elías Calles and Alvaro Obregón. Aleksandra Kollontai, who followed him in 1926, was constantly on the defensive against attacks on her activities instigated by the semiofficial Mexican labor union confederation and the U.S. State Department. While her personal contacts with Calles and his government were pleasant enough, her political difficulties multiplied the longer she stayed in Mexico. Her successor, Aleksandr Makar, was compelled to devote most of his time to reassuring the Mexican government and press that he was there as a legitimate diplomat, that he was not involved in antigovernment agitation or activities. Internationally and domestically, however, the situation continued to deteriorate. An ill-conceived armed revolt ordered by the Comintern in 1929 led to the outlawing of the PCM as part of a full-scale anti-Communist campaign by the government that included the arrest and imprisonment of all the important PCM leaders. Despite his geniality, openness, indeed apparent popularity, there was nothing Makar could do to stop the Mexican government from breaking relations in 1930. What one eyewitness called "a hysterical red-hunt" followed the diplomatic break, and the Mexican government was condemned by the Comintern and ridiculed by the Soviet press.[13]

Although the Soviet diplomatic staff in Mexico City could not salvage the official relationship between the two governments, it left a legacy of good-will. And it facilitated visits by a number of Soviet citizens who wrote and spoke about Mexico when they returned to the USSR. In June 1925, a group of six oil engineers travelled from Baku to Mexico to study the Mexican oil industry, and in the late summer and early fall of the same year, B. F. Dobrynin travelled throughout the territory of the republic, describing its climate, population, and geography more thoroughly than any previous Soviet writer. He published his account in *Zemlevedenie (Geography)* in 1926.[14] The most important Soviet scientific expeditions of the 1920s to Mexico, however, were those organized by the Leningrad Institute of Applied Botany, under the directorship of the justifiably renowned botanist and geneticist Nikolai Ivanovich Vavilov.

The first expedition, in the fall of 1925, was headed by Iu. N. Voronov. Its assignment was to investigate the varietal composition of plants cultivated in Mexico and to determine the centers of their origin, especially those which were grown at the time in the USSR. It was hoped that such research would uncover ways to improve crops in the Soviet Union.[15] Accompanying Voronov was S. M. Bukasov, who published the best account of their journey around the country in *Vozdelyvaemye rasteniia Meksiki, Gvatemaly, i Kolumbii (Cultivated Plants of Mexico, Guatemala, and Colombia)*. His description of the expedition and its discoveries and investigations was remarkably complete and attentive to detail. It included a fairly extensive study of Mexican crops and plants, the nation's climate and ancient cultures, its agricultural regions, and its historic and present-day populations. Bukasov gave detailed descriptions of such typical plants as papaya, avocado, henequen, agave, and chocolate, but was interested as well in how the products of these plants were used. At one point, he included a drawing of a *molinillo* and a description of how the implement was used to whip the chocolate that was so common in the Mexican diet.[16] The expedition travelled throughout Central Mexico, the Bajío, and the Tehuantepec region, and the photographs published in *Vozdelyvaemye rasteniia* show an intense interest in almost every aspect of human interaction with Mexico's natural surroundings. Although Bukasov's account certainly was not read by many in the USSR, it was an important indication of the kind of interchange of scientific data that resulted from the establishment of relations between Mexico and the USSR.

The last important scientific expeditions of the period—to Central Mexico in 1930 and the Yucatán peninsula in 1932–33—were headed by Vavilov himself. Their purpose was to discover whether pre-Columbian methods of agriculture still existed in the New World. Vavilov had visited the United States in 1921 as part of this project, investigating agricultural techniques on Indian reservations in the West and Southwest. On the basis of his Mexican research he concluded that Mesoamerica and the Peru-Bolivia geographic unit, the two principal agricultural type-regions of the New World, showed no indications of botanical contact with the Old World, and that because of botanical evidence, there was no reason to think that there had been any cultural contact between the civilizations of the Old and New Worlds.[17] Vavilov's research in Mexico coincided with the work of two Mexican agricultural experts from the Chapingo agricultural school in the Soviet Union, and the mutual profit accrued from the experience was great. Since relations between Mexico and the USSR had worsened by 1930, however, and because the United States was generally unfriendly toward him, Vavilov's later journeys were difficult. During his stay in Mexico he was constantly under attack in the local newspapers, for example, accused of coming to steal Mexico's national treasures. He was forced to wait for some time at the U.S.-Mexican frontier while the border patrol decided if he posed a threat to the stability of the United States, even though the U.S. embassy in Mexico City had given him a visa.

Two other Russian visitors to Mexico during this period should be mentioned. In 1925, A. G. Kniazev and I. M. Freidberg, recent graduates of the Institute of Physical Culture in Moscow, rode their bicycles through Mexico as part of an around-the-world trip. As unexpected as their appearance in Mexico was, they were given a friendly welcome and made honorary members of the Mexico City bicycle club. The most interesting product of their visit was their 1929 book, *Vokrug sveta na velosipede (Around the World on a Bicycle)*, a considerable part of which dealt with their adventures in Mexico.[18]

The two had set out from Moscow, crossed Siberia to Japan, then sailed on to San Francisco, finally reaching Manzanillo in October 1924. After almost being denied permission to land because they lacked the financial resources required by Mexican law, they discovered on shore that there were no good roads leading up to the central plateau, that the weather was insufferably hot, the mosquitoes ferocious, and that no one spoke anything but Spanish. They soon adjusted to the local diet of tortillas, peppers, and fruits, however, found the local *kvas* served in the cantinas quite refreshing, and with the help of the always friendly people, managed to reach the Soviet embassy in Mexico City within three weeks, where they were given a warm welcome by Pestkovsky and his family.

While in the capital, they visited a Mexican trade school and found it quite similar to ones in the USSR. Members of the working class relaxing in the parks on Sundays, they said, were always curious about them and helpful. One thing they found unusual was that the few workers' clubs they visited seemed to be used solely by children; they also noticed that since workers could not afford theaters, they spent their free time promenading in the parks. What they did not seem to understand was the importance of traditional customs to all Mexicans, of whatever class. They were surprised at how religious all the people were and that the Catholic priests could demand, successfully, as much as they did from their parishioners. Above all, they were as appalled by the *corrida de toros* as almost all other Russians were.

Having completely exhausted their financial resources by the time they reached Mexico City, the two cyclists lived at the embassy in constant hopes of finding some way to finance the remainder of their journey. The opportunity finally presented itself with the arrival of the Voronov expedition at the end of the year. Needing assistants, the expedition hired the two bicyclists to accompany them into the jungles and mountains of the south. Kniazev and Freidberg did not find the jungle insects, scorpions, and snakes too attractive, but as always, the people in the villages, with their openness, kindness, generosity, and friendliness, made up for any inconveniences. Indeed, the two criticized one of the expedition's directors for his refusal to socialize with the local people, feeling that he was not doing his best to make friends for the Soviet Union.

Having made enough money to continue their journey, Kniazev and Freidberg set out for the United States, still a fascinating destination for Soviet citizens. After several hot and dry days, they reached Laredo, only to be told that they would need special permission from Washington before they could be granted visas to enter the country. They waited ten days, and were refused; they appealed, waited twelve more days, and were refused again; another appeal, another ten days, another refusal. An attempt to cross the border at Piedras Negras produced the same answer from the local U.S. authorities. In the end, the two decided to ride down to Tampico and to continue their trip by boat to Europe, leaving the United States for some indefinite future.

Kniazev and Freidberg did not tell Russian readers much that was new or unique about Mexico. The appeal of the book lay in its lack of sophistication, its warmth, and its generally openhearted tone. It was representative of a still fairly optimistic period in Soviet history, and its picture of Mexico was on the whole a positive and friendly one. Pestovsky, Mayakovsky, and Kollontai would be much less generous in their evaluations of the country.

S. S. Pestkovsky: Diplomacy and a Scholarly Marxist Evaluation of the Mexican Revolution

By the time Stanislav Stanislavovich Pestkovsky and his family left Moscow for Mexico City in September 1924, he had already had an active career as a revolutionary. Born in 1882, the son of a minor Polish nobleman who had lost his fortune, Pestkovsky joined the Lithuanian social democratic party and soon became a vocal and active supporter of the revolutionary branch of social democracy.[19] He spent eight years in tsarist prisons in Siberia, but was engaged during much of his time in confinement with writing on Polish history. He was particularly interested in Polish aspects of the 1905 revolution, and his Marxist interpretation of events showed the obvious influence of his teacher, M. N. Pokrovsky. Pestkovsky escaped from Siberia in 1913 and until 1917 lived in London, where he worked with the Bolsheviks in exile. Despite some disagreements with Lenin during these years (he supported Rosa Luxemburg against Lenin during the meetings of the Second International, for example), he was a firm advocate of the Bolshevik seizure of power in Petrograd in October 1917 and was appointed commander of the unit sent to occupy the Central Telegraph Office. His first assignment in the new government was as commissar of the telegraph, but he was soon appointed assistant commissar of nationalities, under Stalin. He worked in Kirgizia for a short while, became head of the political office for the western front in 1920, and in 1921 was made president of the Commission on the Soviet-Polish border.[20] Both his training and experience had been in revolution and revolutionary administration. However much the Mexican government may have been truly "revolutionary" in 1924, it still would have found it easier to work with a professional diplomat than with a professional revolutionary. What Pestkovsky saw in Mexico, what he did there, and what he wrote about Mexico's revolution were all functions of his previous experiences and prejudices. Pestkovsky approached Mexico on his terms, not Mexico's.

Arriving by ship in Veracruz, Pestkovsky was given an enthusiastic reception by the local leftists and Communists, to whom his radical credentials were more appealing than they were, possibly, to most of the government officials in the capital. One observer described him as "a big booming man with gnarled tobacco teeth showing through a dark beard . . . brusque, tactless but jovial . . . very obstinate, aggressive and quick tempered."[21] Another saw him perhaps more accurately as "a solemn owl of a man, kindhearted in friendships and personal relations; he wore a Russian-type beard and looked as dignified as his position required."[22] The Mexican press had been particularly interested in him and had given much attention to his impending arrival. In the face of considerable speculation, Pestkovsky proved to be precisely the sort of man many Mexicans expected him to be. If his physical presence was disappointing, he compensated for it with his revolutionary enthusiasm and self-confidence.[23]

A thunderous welcome awaited Pestkovsky at the fashionable Hotel Regis in the capital, and he was forced to appear on his balcony to wave to the crowd in the street, which held banners proclaiming support for the Russian Revolution. A week later, on the seventh anniversary of the October Revolution, he presented his credentials to President Obregón in the National Palace. His speech emphasized his gratification at being chosen "to represent Russia's workers and peasants" in Mexico. He stressed the feeling of solidarity he believed the working people of Russia felt for their Mexican comrades, and he concluded by promising to do his best to maintain good and friendly relations between their two countries.[24]

Pestkovsky was uncharacteristically diplomatic at the National Palace, but was more himself at a meeting celebrating the October Revolution held that evening in the National Preparatory School. Pestkovsky was guest of honor, the artist Siqueiros presided, and all the important members of the PCM were present. Pestkovsky spoke about the new society he said was being constructed in the Soviet Union, a society made possible by the success of the revolution, and he asked "Do you want to know why Soviet power triumphed? Because of the indivisible and therefore invincible unity of Russian workers and peasants. Nothing could divide them in the struggle to protect the Soviet power they had created."[25] It was here, only a few days after his arrival in Mexico City, that Pestkovsky gave what would be his basic explanation for the failure of the Mexican Revolution: the lack of worker-peasant political unity. All that he said and wrote afterward only expanded this basic idea.

Pestkovsky, his family, and the embassy staff soon settled into the house that had been rented for the mission. From the beginning the embassy had a series of visitors, and many radical and liberal Mexicans were anxious to make contact with Pestkovsky and his colleagues. As the U.S. Communist Bertram Wolfe recalled, the new embassy was one of the most popular in Mexico City: "Strange to relate, since they were customarily bored stiff by all the dull diplomatic parties that they had to give each other, to which everybody came in formal wear and engaged in evasive small talk, the members of the diplomatic corps looked forward to and enjoyed Pestkovsky's unusual, mixed parties, where they could talk to undiplomatic guests about undiplomatic things, and the entertainment might be full of surprises."[26] The embassy's staff, with their own personal peculiarities, added a certain variety to the scene as well, as did Pestkovsky's wife and energetic little daughter. Considering, too, the Soviet travellers who not only checked in at the embassy, but often ended up staying there for financial reasons, the legation must have been a constantly interesting place.[27]

While he himself was a social success, Pestkovsky's relations with the Mexican government were uneven at best. In some ways he was an admirable ambassador. He was comfortable with all the basic European languages and quickly learned Spanish, which he used to study as much about Mexico as he could, putting together a fine collection of books on Mexico for the embassy library. He travelled throughout the country and raised the prestige of the Soviet government by speaking and appearing in many places where no Russian had ever been seen.[28] On a certain level, too, he was able to work effectively with various branches of the government. His dealings with the Secretariat of Foreign Relations were proper, and he found them to be cooperative at all times. He was also able to promote trade, and almost doubled the amount the USSR bought from Mexico during his two years in Mexico City. Yet, as was mentioned earlier, official relations were hurt by the Soviet government's close ties to the Comintern and the nebulous distinction between government policy and Comintern policy. Foreign Commissar Chicherin's speech of March 3, 1925, calling Mexico a "convenient political base," did not improve Pestkovsky's standing with the Calles government, and Calles himself was never notably favorable toward Pestkovsky.[29] Similarly, relations with the CROM (the Confederación Regional de Obrera Mexicana, the Regional Confederation of Mexican Labor) and its head, Luis Morones, were unfriendly. On one occasion Pestkovsky criticised the CROM "as a reactionary organization opposed to the true interests of the workers and peasants of Mexico."[30] Similarly, First Secretary Khaikiss, speaking at a CROM banquet, said the organization consisted of reformists and traitors and that Soviet workers considered anyone wanting close relations with the American Federation of Labor in the United

States (as the CROM leadership did) to be unsupportive of the best interests of the workers.[31] There could be little hope that Morones and Pestkovsky would get along successfully, although it was Kollontai who would bear the brunt of most of the CROM's opposition to the presence of a Soviet embassy in Mexico.

Pestkovsky was not an overwhelming success diplomatically in Mexico, and through his vocal support for Comintern policy and Soviet government interests, he may have hastened the day when the Mexican government would break relations with the Soviet Union. When he returned to Moscow in 1926, however, he had accumulated an impressive fund of knowledge about Mexican social and political history, more perhaps than any Russian then living. He used this information over the next several years, no doubt at the encouragement of the government and the Comintern, to do a considerable amount of writing about Mexico and Latin America. Most important were his two books on Mexico, the first major Soviet studies of the country. Pestkovsky apparently finished both books in mid-1927, and they were published the following year. The first, written under the pseudonym Andrei Volsky, was entitled *Istoriia meksikanskikh revoliutsii (A History of Mexico's Revolutions)*. Pestkovsky dedicated the study to Pokrovsky, his "dear teacher," and in the preface promised that the book would be the "first attempt at writing a study of the Mexican revolutionary movement from the point of view of a materialistic understanding of history." The second book, *Agrarnyi vopros i krestianskoe dvizhenie v Meksike (The Agrarian Question and the Peasant Movement in Mexico)*, ostensibly written by "D. Ortega," was the first Marxist analysis of the decades-long struggle of the Mexican peasantry for land and freedom and was dedicated to the "revolutionary leaders of the Mexican peasants who died in battle against the landowners and the foreign imperialists."[32]

Both books are the result of considerable reading, scholarly research, and a surprisingly extensive knowledge of Mexico and its past. Bertram Wolfe pointed out that since the embassy in reality had very little business to transact, Pestkovsky and his staff had a great deal of time to spend on their own pursuits. Pestkovsky himself used his time well. His books' weaknesses derive not from inadequate research or a selective citation of facts to suit preconceived Marxist formulae but from having to use unreliable sources of information. He confessed this in the forward to *Istoriia meksikanskikh revoliutsii,* but added that he nonetheless had been able to use the essential primary and secondary materials. He said as well that he had been scrupulous in his own observations and in discussions of recent events with Mexicans who had witnessed them personally.[33] He pursued his research and writing with great acumen and imagination, and with admirable dedication, although he often shared with European and North American archeologists some fanciful ideas about pre-Columbian life in Mexico.[34] He also made a fairly extensive collection of photographs of Mexico, and several of them illustrate each text. Some were of traditional "picturesque" scenes; others were of events which Pestkovsky attended or participated in and were of political interest to Soviet readers. To a new generation of Russian readers who knew little about Mexico and its revolution, Pestkovsky's text and photographs provided a valuable source of information. They were also excellent examples of the new, Marxist interpretation of history that Pokrovsky and his students were so enthusiastically promoting in the USSR during the 1920s.

Pestkovsky began both books with overviews of Mexico's natural surroundings, discussing geography, climate, and natural resources. He described briefly the population's poverty and illiteracy and ended with a summary of Mexico's current social, political, and economic situation. His section dealing with pre-Columbian Mexico was what might be expected from an early Soviet, Marxist historian: the tribal development of the Aztecs from a society practicing primitive communism to a more complicated one characterized by merchant guilds, feudalism, and peasant agricultural collectives tied in nicely with the teachings of Pokrovsky's school. The arrival of the Spaniards helped stimulate the economic evolution of Mexico, grown static under the Aztecs, along the path Marx had described. The Spaniards, however brutal their conquest and their exploitation of the peasants, were agents of history and proved to be effective colonizers and administrators, in Pestkovsky's view, although he qualified his praise by remarking that all their administrative talent still could not keep them from losing their colonies in the end. One important factor contributing to the stability of Spanish colonial rule in Mexico was the Catholic church. The church was an institution of such great power and influence, Pestkovsky wrote, that "the Spanish crown was a weapon in

the hands of the Catholic church and the gentry. Thanks to its organization, the church in the colonies, even more than it did in Spain,
ruled over the government and the gentry."[35] The church was extremely
wealthy, in part because it mercilessly exploited the labor of the Indians in a fashion not unlike that of the ancient Egyptians (although
Pestkovsky added that their demands were no worse than those of
the Aztec priests). Yet it also gained the support of the masses of Indians because of its clever incorporation of the old native rituals into
the new Mexican Catholic religious practice, and because the Spanish priests lived with the Indians, spoke their languages, and even
helped them escape from the excesses of the Inquisition. Eventually
the Indians became fanatically devoted to the imported religion. Pestkovsky added that not all Indians came under Spanish rule; those who
lived in the mountains and far in the north maintained their independence up to the end of the nineteenth century. This was an important point, he felt, since it was Indian resistance to the Porfiriato that
helped bring on the social revolution accompanying the political revolution which began in 1910.

Pestkovsky intended to focus his books primarily on the events of
the twentieth century and did not write a great deal about the colonial period. He did wish to make a social and economic analysis of
the reasons for Mexico's independence movement, however, since he
believed that most traditional interpretations of the Insurgency had
mistakenly emphasized political and philosophical considerations. He
hoped to examine it using Marxist dialectical analysis. By the end of
the eighteenth century, Spain and its empire were hopelessly backward economically, he wrote. Spain's trade monopoly with its colonies and its increasing inability to compete with other European nations in the face of the bourgeois capitalist expansion of Britain,
France, and Holland were forcing it into a state of stagnation. Mexico suffered as much as any other colony, Spain taking all it could
and giving nothing in return for the minerals its richest possession
produced. Society, too, was frozen. Those holding power were unable to provide any real solutions for the colony's social immobility.
Little had changed in Mexico for centuries, Pestkovsky believed: the
clergy were the source of political and economic wealth and power;
the lawyers, government officials, and military officers made up the
gentry, but were little more than a middle-layer proletariat; the In-

dians were exploited by everyone, and the *ejido*, the Indian communal landholding system, was nothing more than a means used by the crown and large landowners to control them more effectively. Pestkovsky admitted that he had simplified pre-independence Mexican society and that it could not quite so conveniently be put into the limited social categories he outlined. Even so, he believed that it was in this lack of social mobility that the stimulus for the independence movement could be found.

Pestkovsky wrote that for the Indians, the Insurgency was a social and racial struggle against their white exploiters. The political independence espoused by the liberal bourgeois *criollos* was little more than words to them. They were a local petite bourgeoisie and had no interest whatsoever in improving the condition of the peasants. Pestkovsky insisted too that however noble their aspirations and policies, the Insurgency leaders Allende and Hidalgo should be evaluated historically on the basis of their failure to satisfy the demands of the Indians. Finally, Pestkovsky came to two fundamental conclusions about Mexico's independence movement. First, as traditional non-Marxist historians claimed, it was a national revolution. It was not organized by a "national" bourgeoisie, however, even though the Mexican *criollo* intelligentsia did see itself as "American" and not Spanish. Second, and closely tied to the first, the revolution was agrarian and social. Yet the peasants were completely unconscious of their role: since there was no industrial proletariat to organize the peasants and lead them on to political victory, their goals of land reform and social emancipation could not be achieved.

The weaknesses in Pestkovsky's argument are immediately apparent. At the time of the Insurgency, no country had an industrial proletariat strong enough to carry out a revolution, even in conjunction with the peasantry, a union which was itself highly unlikely. What Pestkovsky hoped to do was to indicate the direction in which he was leading his readers. The Bolshevik Revolution of 1917 was to be the model for Mexican and Latin American revolutionaries. While Pestkovsky did present an adequate and generally accurate account of the Insurgency, he was more concerned to introduce the basic dialectical and social arguments he would use in discussing issues of more current relevance in Mexico. He made no attempt to disguise his agreement with the Comintern's assertion that the Bolshevik experience

in Russia was to be the model for Communists around the world. Pestkovsky remained first of all a revolutionary, and only secondarily a
historian.

Mexico's bourgeois revolution took place only under Juárez, Pestkovsky contended. During the three and a half decades following independence, a church-dominated conservatism ruled the country. Its
failure was to be seen in the enormous losses of territory to the United
States and in the increasing amounts of foreign capital invested in
Mexico as the century progressed. The liberal reform created new
possibilities, but ones that were not entirely expected: "Objectively
the liberal revolution of 1857 in Mexico was a bourgeois revolution.
It destroyed Mexican feudalism, the legacy of Spanish colonization,
and created the foundation for the economic and political role of the
bourgeoisie. But since a large-scale bourgeoisie did not develop in
Mexico, this revolution in the final reckoning opened the path to the
conquest of Mexico by foreign finance capital. The invasion of imperialism worsened even more the position of the Mexican peasantry."[36]
The peasants, the Indians, the *rancheros,* with no money and no farm-
ing implements, could not buy the land newly made available, and
they found themselves exploited once again.

Mexico had won political independence, but the introduction of
foreign capital soon made it a semicolonial state. Intimately involved
in this development was Benito Juárez who, for all his heroism and
honesty, was an unwitting agent of the economic forces of history:
"Although he did not understand that the essential basis for the national independence of the Mexico of that time was the development
and strengthening of the Mexican national bourgeoisie, he unconsciously, objectively, worked in the direction of creating such a basis."[37]
From Pestkovsky's point of view, a strong national bourgeoisie would
have been able to withstand the pressures pushing Mexico toward
semicolonialism. The political complexities of the time worked against
Juárez's support for Mexican national political and economic power,
however. By accepting aid from the United States in the struggle
against Maximilian and the French intervention, for example, Juárez
had unfortunately led U.S. business and political leaders to assume
that they should have a monopoly on foreign economic penetration
of Mexico. Finally, the system created by Porfirio Díaz destroyed whatever hopes Juárez had for Mexico's economic independence.

To Pestkovsky, the Porfiriato was an attempt to recreate the old semifeudal land system that had existed before independence, except that the great haciendas were now to be maintained through an alliance of large landholders and foreign capitalists. Díaz's attacks on the old Indian communities, especially his anti-Yaqui campaigns, were typical of the ruthlessness of native and foreign capital during these years. By any standard, Pestkovsky wrote, the Porfiriato was an unmitigated disaster. It nonetheless attracted foreign capitalist investors: the government was stable, it was anxious to cooperate in the exploitation of Mexico's natural resources, and whenever a question arose of whether a project should be built more for the benefit of Mexico than for foreigners, it always favored the foreign investors.[38] Díaz, Pestkovsky wrote, was in the "pocket of the American capitalists" as early as the 1870s and never renounced the connection. His finance minister, Limantour, was only "an agent of the powerful Speer and Company (New York–London) trust."[39] Pestkovsky estimated that Díaz's indifference to foreign exploitation of his own compatriots, and his government's persecution of the Indians, the workers, the lower classes in general, meant that 90 percent of the population lived in poverty and cultural backwardness. He concluded that there was one positive aspect of the Porfiriato: "social conflict, strengthened by the rapid accumulation of capital and the expropriation of the peasantry, had created favorable conditions for the appearance of the workers and peasants in the social-political arena of Mexico."[40] This growth of political consciousness was not as extensive as Pestkovsky would have hoped, and he pointed out that it was not as great as in Russia during the same years. It was the beginning of a historic process, however, and Pestkovsky wrote that the radicalization of the Mexican *campesinos* was the foundation for the eventual, if only partial, success of the Mexican Revolution.

Like all Russians writing or thinking about Mexico in the years after 1917, Pestkovsky constantly compared developments in Russia with those in Mexico. If they saw Porfirian Mexico as similar to Nicholas II's Russia, they understood the Mexican Revolution in terms of their Russian experiences. Pestkovsky believed that through his Marxist analysis, and because of his Russian experiences, he could comprehend more clearly than Mexican or Western bourgeois analysts why it was that by the late 1920s the two revolutions had taken such different paths. Committed to the Soviet model for political and social revolution, he gave continuing attention to the question of how events in Mexico differed from those in Russia and why these differences determined the outcome.

By 1910, Pestkovsky wrote, the workers, the peasants, even the intelligentsia[41] were prepared to join a rebellion against Díaz. Mexico's semicolonial position was by that time clear to everyone. A large mass of the rural population had been proletarianized by Díaz's policies, and Pestkovsky described in some detail the techniques of intimidation used by the *rurales* in the countryside, the methods of exploitation on the great haciendas, and the steady immiseration of the rural population. He devoted a long section in *Agrarnyi vopros* to the campaigns against the Yaqui in the northwest and their resistance to central authority, taking them as an example of the continuing opposition to Díaz's rule that began spreading throughout the country. Pestkovsky was especially interested in the motivations of the liberals, who at first assumed Díaz would surrender without a fight. When the need for military action became apparent, however, they recognized that a liberal revolution could not succeed without the support of the peasants, the only armed and sincerely revolutionary group in the country. Needing peasant support, Madero and the liberals made vague promises of land reform, but they soon began to fear social revolution and decided to stop the increasing radicalization of the peasants. It was at this point, Pestkovsky felt, that the true revolutionaries, the peasants, had an opportunity for success. They possessed enough revolutionary enthusiasm to make their movement triumph. What they lacked, however, was essential: they were undisciplined and disunified, and they had not had a proper ideological education. While the Zapatistas did exhibit a certain degree of organization, and even attempted to put together an agrarian program, more typical of the peasant revolutionaries were the Villistas, whom Pestkovsky saw as followers of an anarchist bandit with no political sophistication whatsoever.[42]

Pestkovsky examined each of the movements carefully in his attempt to uncover the reasons for their failure. Each was exclusively local in character, he found. Their limited sense of national geographical consciousness hindered their ability to join with peasant groups from other regions or, even more unlikely, with urban proletarian revolutionaries. In alliance with the liberal bourgeoisie the peasants could have achieved at least partial liberation. Yet had they made their revolution "hand in hand" with the workers, as the Russian peasants did, then they would be finally and irrevocably free of the dead weight of the past. Unfortunately for the peasants, Mexican workers suffered from the same limited imagination as their potential comrades: they were unable to recognize the possibilities available to them because they had been inadequately and incorrectly educated politically.

Because he felt the Zapatistas were the strongest and most viable peasant movement in Mexico, Pestkovsky devoted an entire chapter to them in *Agrarnyi vopros*. They were the most radicalized, he learned, because they came from regions of the most extreme exploitation, areas where the percentage of peasant land ownership was lowest. This made them strong, but limited their national effectiveness. It was true, Pestkovsky admitted, that the "workers'" program adopted by Zapata and his followers in 1916 was an attempt to create some kind of link with the urban proletariat. But in essence it was an "opportunistic" move, Pestkovsky wrote, because "in general [they] were not enemies of capitalism, that is, they were not revolutionary socialists."[43] Similarly, Pestkovsky dismissed the Plan de Ayala, Zapata's program for agrarian reform: while it did have a revolutionary role to play because of the circumstances of the times, the plan itself was not revolutionary because it was not motivated by a properly ideological Marxism. At best, Pestkovsky wrote later, it was similar to the Russian Constitutional Democrats' agrarian program of 1905.[44] It alleviated conditions, but did not solve the basic contradictions of capitalist landholding.

Pestkovsky leveled a number of serious criticisms at the Zapatistas on theoretical and practical grounds, but he made it clear that he did not wish to deemphasize their significance in the revolution as a whole:

> Despite all its inadequacies, despite its isolation from the working class, despite its organizational weakness, the Zapatista movement had an enormous significance not only for the peasantry, but for all of Mexico. The continuation of this movement, from 1911 until 1919, resulted in the strengthening of revolutionary traditions among the peasant masses of Mexico, a strengthening which has been nourished up to this very day. This movement

put the agrarian question at the forefront of the Mexican Revolution, and since that time, the level of the revolutionary nature of any Mexican government or of any Mexican social movement has relied consistently on its relationship to the agrarian question and to the peasant movement.[45]

The Zapatistas' fundamental error was their failure to promote political education, Pestkovsky explained. Quite simply, they did not understand the essential connection between the landowner who ruled their everyday lives (and on whom they focused their hatred) and foreign capital, which Pestkovsky (and the Comintern) said was the true source of their oppression. Associated with this improper understanding of Mexican economic and social realities was the failure of *maderismo*. Madero's constitutionalism could not succeed because Mexico had no socioeconomic foundation for a western-European style government based on law. By hesitating, Pestkovsky believed, by their uncertainty over whether to use force against their reactionary enemies or to grant the wishes of their peasant supporters, the Maderistas lost everything. The conservatives opposed the new Madero government from the beginning, and eventually Madero's failure to act on behalf of the peasants and workers lost him their support as well. Always behind the scenes, however, remained the directing force of international capitalism. To Pestkovsky it was only fitting that in the end Madero was betrayed by Henry Lane Wilson, the "principal tool" of American capitalism in Mexico.

With Carranza, the revolutionary process moved a step forward in a number of ways, Pestkovsky believed. While Carranza was an *hacendado*, he owned and operated his estate as a capitalist enterprise rather than a feudal possession. He was also considerably more pragmatic and less "principled" than Madero had been. Carranza recognized early that he needed worker and peasant support for his constitutional revolution to succeed, but he had no genuine sympathy for such ideas as the "class struggle" and the "advance of the proletariat." He gained worker support by calling for national unity against the usurper Huerta and by taking a firm stand against imperialism, but promised nothing substantial in return. Pestkovsky was naturally interested in the workers' role in this phase of the revolution, and he gave it considerable attention in his books. He especially wanted to examine how the constitutionalists succeeded in bringing the workers over to their side and what the results of this political alignment were. It soon became clear to him, he wrote, that Mexico's professional unions tended to possess a kind of "petit-bourgeois mentality." They rapidly became disillusioned with Zapata and were prepared psychologically for the 1914–15 agreement with Carranza. It was true that the Casa de Obrero Mundial's creation of the Red Battalions in support of the Carrancistas meant that the workers were being revolutionized, but to Pestkovsky, this radicalization of worker consciousness was less significant than it might appear, since the workers were not being educated politically.[46] Self-defeatingly, the workers had joined a movement that was opposed not to the bourgeoisie but to the peasants, who remained the only real revolutionary group in the country. It was obviously not in the interests of Carranza and his supporters to develop the workers' class consciousness, since doing so would allow the workers to recognize the incongruity of their alliance. The workers supported the slogan "Protect the Constitution and the Revolution," but they were defending them not for themselves but for Carranza and the bourgeoisie, who would rule Mexico once the fighting ended.[47] Worse, the petit-bourgeois tendencies of the trade union leadership continued to grow, Pestkovsky wrote. In 1915, for example, the Casa de Obrero Mundial increasingly adopted anarchosyndicalist positions. With the rise of Morones and other "opportunistic" labor leaders, the workers' movement became affiliated with the U.S. American Federation of Labor and with the philosophy of Samuel Gompers, seen by Communists at the time as an agent of U.S. imperialism and the American bourgeoisie. Carranza had been able to disarm the labor movement as a threat to his "constitutional" revolution through clever political maneuvering, the mistakes of his opponents, the greed of the labor movement leaders, and the lack of political sophistication of the proletariat. It was an impressive achievement, Pestkovsky felt, but one that had helped bring about the eventual failure of the Mexican Revolution.

Carranza avoided Madero's mistakes by promising social justice, a democratic form of government, and an end to economic imperialism. This was particularly important to Pestkovsky, and he wrote that "the Carrancistas . . . were the first to understand to its fullest extent the danger of foreign imperialism and the first to do battle with it."[48]

Such promises were guaranteed to appeal to those who wished to develop a native Mexican middle class and to other sectors of the population as well. Carranza also promised order, and after years of fighting, even those who had the least to gain in real terms from a constitutionalist government wanted a respite from anarchy. While the anarchist spirit of the Mexican proletarians may have been growing, their experience with Villa and Zapata had caused them to value a certain amount of central authority. Carranza understood so well the realities of political power in Mexico that he was able both to encourage and restrain those wanting to insert radical articles into the 1917 Querétaro Constitution. The Zapatistas did not get all they wanted from the convention, for example, but Carranza's acceptance of articles 27 and 123, dealing with labor and agrarian questions, proved that the revolution's momentum had forced him beyond the limited constitutional liberalism he had espoused earlier. Indeed, Pestkovsky emphasized, for its time, the 1917 constitution was very revolutionary. It was written as a response to the fact that the consitution of 1857 had only opened Mexico to foreign capital and colonial neofeudalism, and it aimed at guaranteeing the independence of Mexico in the decades ahead. Pestkovsky added that a decade later, even though most of the tenets of the constitution had not yet been brought into practice, it remained the "revolutionary banner" of the Mexican people, and it had tremendous agitational importance in the rest of Latin America, whose population lived in conditions similar to those in prerevolutionary Mexico.

Pestkovsky was also interested in the fate of the Mexican proletariat during these years of Carranza's political dominance. He found that Mexican labor made a number of important decisions during this time, especially at the El Paso conference of Mexican labor organizations and the AFL. For the first time, the Mexican labor movement played a role in international politics; Mexican labor organizations began what would be continuing cooperation with the Mexican government; a whole epoch of AFL influence on Mexican labor's leadership began. Sadly, Pestkovsky added, the El Paso conference meant as well that by consenting to the first steps in the creation of a Pan-American labor federation, the Mexican representatives were agreeing to the application of the Monroe Doctrine to the American labor movement in general in Latin America. Mexican workers had joined hands with their enemies, Pestkovsky wrote: "If, up to the present, three-fourths of the land in Mexico still sits in the hands of big landowners, then this is the fault not only of foreign imperialism, but also of the Mexican petit-bourgeois government and the yellow 'laborists.'" The labor movement should have joined with the Comintern-sponsored Krestintern or Profintern.[49] By doing so it could have pushed the revolution onward. Instead, its leadership had sold out future gains for immediate benefits.

Nothing seemed to indicate to Pestkovksy the decay of revolutionary ideals more than the presidency of Plutarco Elías Calles. Calles's government he dismissed as a petit-bourgeois militaristic dictatorship.[50] Calles himself was able to maintain his power, Pestkovsky wrote, through a clever manipulation of the fears and desires of the bourgeoisie, the peasants, and the workers. He had, for example, succeeded in dividing the working class into two sectors, and the workers from the peasants. The labor movement's leadership was opportunistic and unprincipled, and by now absolutely petit-bourgeois. The diamonds Morones wore on his hands and chest were a symbol of the movement's degradation. The hopes of ten years before, that a native Mexican bourgeoisie would be formed, had not been fulfilled, and as during the Porfiriato, "all industry, transport, banks, and large-scale trade is in the hands of foreign capitalists."[51] Finally, the land question still had not been solved, because the great estates had not yet been distributed to the peasants. Despite appearances, and the constant barrage of propaganda from the United States, it seemed to Pestkovsky that Calles's government was dedicated to slowing land distribution. Land was given in inadequate amounts to insignificant numbers of peasants. Worse, the peasants lived in horrifying poverty, at a standard of living many times worse than that of Soviet peasants. The peasants were kept from rebelling again only by the efforts of the foreign imperialists, who owned much of the land and used force when necessary to put down any new outbreaks of the peasant movement. Similarly, Pestkovsky contended, the living and working conditions of the workers were so bad that they were constantly on the verge of revolting against the government and its foreign friends, but they were cowed by fear of imperialistic foreign intervention.

In the face of an oppressive government in alliance with foreigners, what Mexico needed most was worker-peasant unity, Pestkovsky

emphasized again. Imperialism was the greatest threat to the workers and the peasants, and they should move first against it, he advised.
Second, they must attack and defeat the landowners and the church,
who constantly encouraged U.S. involvement in Mexico.[52] Finally, the
workers and the peasants must be united in their opposition to the
petit-bourgeois dictatorship of Calles, which had no interest in protecting the lower classes. This need for unity was painfully obvious,
Pestkovsky added, but bringing it about was exceedingly difficult. One
major obstacle was the strength of the "laborists" (the "yellow" unions,
the CROM and its supporters) among the workers and even within
Mexico's progressive political parties: "The Laborists have a very 'revolutionary' program, in which there is even talk of the necessity of
social revolution. But all these noisy phrases coexist peacefully alongside the opportunist practice of 'collaboration with honorable capitalists.'"[53] The "laborists" had gained political influence and were ma-
terially well-off. Having tasted the fruits of political cooperation, they
saw no need to endanger their privileges by antagonizing the government that supported them. Similarly, they gave no attention to the
social and political education of their union members and in fact preferred that they remain in ideological ignorance.

Pestkovsky admitted that at present there were no viable alternatives to the "laborists" among the labor movement. Luckily, he wrote,
the anarchist and Catholic trade unions had no real influence in the
country and had few prospects for growth. A Soviet reader would
naturally wonder about the role of Mexico's Communist party in the
labor movement, and Pestkovsky was frank about its ineffectiveness.
Its greatest weakness, he wrote, was that it was poorly organized. The
PCM's anarchosyndicalist traditions worked against the kind of disciplined organization it needed. Still, the PCM was significant from
an ideological point of view, and Pestkovsky made a number of suggestions as to how it might increase its influence in the future. Central to all of them was unity. The PCM should work to create a single,
united labor front. It must attract the peasant masses around the slogan of giving the landowners' land to the peasants without payment.
It must finally unite the workers and the peasants against foreign imperialism, working particularly with the peasants through the more
radicalized and politically conscious peasant leagues. The peasant-
worker alliance that had led to Bolshevik rule in Russia was the model

to follow in Mexico. It was a message Pestkovsky had emphasized repeatedly in both books, and if he belabored it, he felt, it was because it was a message that had to be learned.

In concluding his two books, Pestkovsky emphasized two points above all. The first was that despite all its failures, which he had so carefully detailed, the revolutionary movement in Mexico had accomplished a great deal. The 1917 constitution had created the most progressive of all the governments of Latin America in a social-political sense, even though the country remained economically backward in comparison to Argentina, Chile, Uruguay, and Cuba. Second, Mexico had a highly important role to play in contemporary Latin America: it was to carry on, perhaps even lead, an intense struggle against foreign imperialism. In Latin America that meant a struggle against the United States. At this stage of Mexico's historical development, imperialism was its greatest enemy. And Pestkovsky sincerely believed, he added, that Mexico might be the first Latin American country finally to throw off the "imperialist yoke."

Pestkovsky wrote little of significance about Mexico after publishing these two books in 1927, with the exception of an article published in *Mirovoe khoziaistvo (World Agriculture)* in 1929. "Grazhdanskaia voina v Meksike" ("Civil War in Mexico") was concerned with potentially significant political changes that had taken place during the previous two years. Mexico's new political spectrum seemed to conform to the Comintern predictions of capitalist political alignments during the United Front period. By the spring of 1929, Pestkovsky wrote, basic regroupings of Mexican political organizations had occurred, and a number of new political alliances had been formed. The progressive landowners of the north had joined with the former "revolutionary" generals, for example. In opposition to them, the Partido Nacional Revolucionario and the central and southern landowners had combined with the middle and petite bourgeoisie to create their own political bloc. Opposing the Portes Gil government were the Catholic conservatives and the "laborists" of the CROM. Portes Gil was supported by the government's petit-bourgeois bloc of bureaucrats, ministers, and intellectuals, a group without a wide social base. Finally, there was a worker-peasant alliance, made up of the National Peasant League, the United Workers' Confederation, and the PCM. Pestkovsky agreed that it was proper for the workers to support Portes

Gil in the face of the March rebellion, which was counterrevolutionary and in favor of the landowners, the capitalists, and the imperialists. Unfortunately, he added, the workers' support for the government did not prevent it from moving to the right once the rebellion was put down, and from using terror against the leftists who had come to its aid. The attacks on the PCM, the divisions on the left, the government pact with the church, and Portes Gil's agreements with the reformist labor unions were all typical acts of a government determined to quiet any leftist radical activity while maintaining its position before the still powerful conservatives. In Pestkovsky's view, conditions in Mexico would have to get worse before they could improve. Again, he concluded sadly, the dialectic of history was at work, but at this point on a downward swing for the workers.

This discussion of Pestkovsky's writings on Mexico is perhaps somewhat misleading because it emphasizes the aspects of his work most immediately relevant to contemporary events. To a certain extent this is excusable since much of his writing was intended to serve agitational ends. All his work was based on sound and fairly extensive research into Mexico's past, however, and that aspect of his writing needs to be stressed. From our standpoint today, it is remarkable how sophisticated and knowledgeable Pestkovsky was about Mexican history, particularly the revolutionary period. He understood social and political conditions in Mexico better than many other contemporary historians, both in the USSR and, to a certain extent, in the West. He was, as he hoped to be at the beginning of his studies, a good student of Pokrovsky. He emulated Pokrovsky's technique and methodology, with its emphasis on the role of the masses and of economic factors in history, while deemphasizing the impact of certain "heroic" individuals. While Pestkovsky discussed Juárez, Porfirio Díaz, Zapata, and Carranza, for example, he believed that they were products of their historical contexts and that they acted in response to the social and economic pressures placed on them. His long chapter on Zapata focused on social analysis and mass psychology. It said little about Zapata as an individual and deemphasized his position in the movement named for him. It was only with Carranza that Pestkovsky discussed personal traits at any length. Yet even here, he hoped to show how Carranza altered his political positions in his own self-interest, but in response to otherwise uncontrollable social developments. It was the people and their interaction with the world of economics that interested Pestkovsky, as it had his teacher, and it was around them that his understanding of the Mexican Revolution turned. Modern Western historians can fault him for the rigid Marxist framework he used to understand Mexico's past, but nowhere in his studies can he be said to have been intellectually dishonest.

A modern reader of Pestkovsky's works also cannot fail to be struck by the extent to which he found the failures of the Mexican Revolution to be rooted in its component movements' inability to unify themselves effectively. To Pestkovsky, as we have seen, the Bolshevik Revolution provided the model for other nations of peasants and workers subjected to semicolonialism and imperialism. The prescriptions he offered for Mexican leftists were firmly rooted in his experience in Russia. The true Mexican revolutionaries had failed because they lacked what the Bolsheviks had painfully achieved over time. Above all, he wrote, no one had promoted ideological, political education in Mexico among the workers or the peasants. The leftists had not done it because they were not themselves a disciplined, ideologically unified group. As a result, the workers and the peasants remained pawns of the bourgeoisie, the liberals, and the foreign imperialists. This unfortunate reality condemned Mexico's revolutionary movement for several years, perhaps decades, to failure and ineffectiveness. Governments such as that headed by Calles would continue to be able to divide all those who suffered under the regime. By keeping them disunited, their ineffectiveness could be assured. Pestkovsky wanted his books to show to Russians that the Bolshevik technique of making revolution was correct, and exportable, and to Mexicans that a true revolution could still be theirs with hard work and determined effort.

If Pokrovsky's Marxist interpretation of history determined how Pestkovsky saw the past, his view of the present was overwhelmingly influenced by Lenin's writings and the Comintern's policies. Nowhere was this clearer than in his interpretation of imperialism. To Pestkovsky, imperialism remained the great villain in Mexico. It perpetuated the conditions of the past, it even revived premodern economic relationships when it was convenient to do so. As always, the imperialists' only interests were profit, not for Mexico, but for themselves and their countries. Undoubtedly this was the least dangerous of Pestkovsky's ideas in the eyes of Mexicans in the government and the labor movement. Anti-imperialism was an important component of government policy in the 1920s and a popular stance among the population as a whole. For Mexicans it was often an emotional reaction to the past, for Russians it was ideological. To Pestkovsky, it was an important stage for the present, but even it would have to be overcome. For the Mexican Revolution to succeed, finally, Pestkovsky believed, Mexico's anti-imperialist nationalism would have to be replaced in the end with a Mexican internationalism, of the sort supported by the Comintern and the Soviet government.

Finally, one last feature of Pestkovsky's analysis of the Mexican Revolution is remarkable. His interpretation is essentially the same as that held today by Soviet historians. Pestkovsky's books apparently missed the denigration of the Pokrovsky school that took place during the 1930s and 1940s in the USSR, and their support for subsequently rejected Comintern policies was conveniently forgotten. Pestkovsky's own fate was more sombre and more mysterious. It is known that he appeared at the Sixth Comintern Congress in September 1928 in the persona of "Banderas," an expert on agrarian movements in Hispanic lands, and that he worked for the Comintern's International Organization for the Aid of Revolutionaries in the late 1920s and early 1930s, and may have been associated with the Comintern's Orgburo. His final years are even more open to speculation: some sources contend that he was arrested and executed during the purges, while others believe he went to Spain to help the Spanish Republican forces and that he died only in 1943 in Moscow.[54] In any event, he remained a nonperson until the late 1960s, and only recently have he and his reputation been rehabilitated. The books, on the other hand, were apparently laid quietly aside until the 1950s, when a new generation of Soviet scholars of Latin America came of age and rediscovered them. Their own studies, more sophisticated because of more complete sources of information, began to be published. Except for a greater emphasis on the individual (Zapata and Villa are given much more prominence in N. M. Lavrov's history of the revolution, for example), the basic interpretations of the revolution are the same. The essential continuity is surprising, and despite the many flaws non-Marxist historians can find in his work, Pestkovsky's achievement remains notable.

Mayakovsky's Idiosyncratic Mexico

Heroism
  is not for now
Moctezuma has become a brand of beer
Cuauhtémoc—
    a brand of beer

—Mayakovsky, "Meksika"[55]

Vladimir Mayakovsky was certainly the most famous Soviet citizen to visit Mexico during the 1920s. Some years before the Russian Revolution, he had already made a reputation for himself among the avant-garde poets of Moscow and Petersburg. He was known as a modernist radical, a hater of all that was old and outdated, and a supporter of fundamental cultural change, in Russia and internationally. He accepted the revolution wholeheartedly, in the hope it would sweep away the stultifying life of old Russia and bring into existence a new society, a new culture, a new world. He designed propaganda posters for the Bolsheviks during the Civil War and with the advent of the New Economic Policy (NEP) accepted a position creating advertising slogans and designs for state-run commercial enterprises. He was a major propagator of revolutionary futurism and was given assistance on behalf of the government by Commissar of Enlightenment Anatolii Lunacharsky. By the middle of the first decade of Bolshevik rule, Mayakovsky had become the spokesman for those modernists who supported the new Soviet state. Not always popular with the people or with other poets and writers (and even politicians, for that matter), he was, nonetheless, the most visible representative of Russian poetic modernism. He consistently attracted large, if not always enthusiastic, audiences in the USSR and was at the center of the continuing controversy between those supporting traditional approaches to the new Communist art and those wanting to create an art and culture entirely unconnected with the past.[56]

Mayakovsky was also well known abroad, through his poetry and personally. Like Balmont, he was a constant traveller and often visited Western Europe. Indeed, travel stimulated his creativity, but almost accidentally, since with the exception of his trips to Paris and North America, he planned none of them extensively in advance. He did feel an inveterate need to move about, and he had an insatiable desire to see how life was lived outside Petrograd and Moscow. He left the Soviet Union almost every year during the 1920s. He read his poetry and gave public lectures throughout Europe, representing the USSR's cultural efflorescence during the NEP. His travel experiences were frequently reflected in his work, and among these, his visit to Mexico and the United States was particularly important.[57] This was his longest stay abroad, lasting from May until November of 1925. He had come to the New World to see the United States, a symbol to Soviet Communists of the industrialized, modern, innovative world of the future. The social system was not one Mayakovsky and his Soviet collegues approved of, and they expected it to collapse of its own contradictions, thereby helping lead the rest of the world to the Communist millennium.[58] It was the vibrancy and creativity of U.S. industry they admired and hoped to emulate within the context of a socialist system. This was the America Mayakovsky went to see.

One reason Mayakovsky visited Mexico was that he believed it would be easier for him to obtain a visa for the United States in Mexico City than in Europe. He also felt that Mexico itself might be sufficiently interesting to justify the trip. He knew that it had recently undergone a revolution of its own that promised a radical answer to the problems of Latin America and that the country was said to have a rich and original revolutionary culture. The appeal of this new Mexico to a poet of such radical credentials can readily be imagined. He found a Mexico considerably different from the one he expected, however, one in many ways more surprising.

Mayakovsky left Moscow at the end of May for Paris, where he made preparations for his journey westward. He knew little about Mexico and learned a great deal from meetings with Alfonso Reyes, Mexico's ambassador to France and a respected intellectual and cultural figure in Europe and in North America. Mayakovsky wrote later that he had long discussions with Reyes about Mexico's past, the indigenismo movement, and the new revolutionary frescoes of Diego Rivera. These conversations clearly stimulated Mayakovsky's interest in seeing the artistic products of the Mexican Revolution. He assumed it would be an art similar, or at least complementary, to that being produced in the USSR, but as he admitted later, it was more Mexican than anything else, and more local than international in its revolutionary message. Reyes arranged for Mayakovsky to be issued a visa, and Mayakovsky proceeded with his plans for the journey. He always enjoyed visiting Paris, although on this occasion an unfortunate event spoiled his stay. His hotel room was burglarized and all his money stolen. The only thing of value the thieves had not taken was his steamship ticket to Mexico. Lamentably short of funds, he was still determined to carry on with the trip, and after scrounging money from friends and acquaintances, he sailed from St. Nazaire for Veracruz on June 21.

It is true that Mayakovsky travelled a great deal, but his biographers generally agree that he was not particularly flexible or enthusiastic once his journeys were underway. His two weeks on ship between France and Mexico ran true to form. He was bored and lonely since he spoke neither French nor Spanish and none of his fellow passengers knew Russian. His isolation was only confirmed when he was refused permission to disembark at Santander because Spain and the USSR had no diplomatic relations. His poem, "Ispaniia" ("Spain"), as a result, was based entirely on his view of the country from the ship. In the Atlantic he became increasingly moody. He wrote his friend and confidante, Liliia Brik, that he was not happy at sea, that at heart he was not a "sea" person, but a dry-land traveller. To pass the time he worked on several poems and began the prose account of his journey that he published in 1926, shortly after his return to the USSR. After a day of pouring rain docked in Havana, the ship at last reached Veracruz on July 8, and Mayakovsky saw Mexico for the first time.[59]

Mayakovsky had not come to Mexico to visit Veracruz, however. He was a dedicated city-dweller, and the principal goal of his journey was Mexico City, for centuries the metropolis of the Americas, and now, Mayakovsky assumed, the center of the revolutionary cultural and political life of Mexico. As a representative of an egalitarian Soviet workers' state, he felt compelled to purchase a second-class train ticket and travelled uncomfortably overnight from Veracruz to the capital. Unable to sleep, he concentrated on the tropical night through which the train passed and wrote the first version of what was probably the best of his Mexico poems, "Tropiki" ("The Tropics").[60] Early the next morning he arrived in Mexico City and was met by the staff of the Soviet embassy and by Diego Rivera. Rivera was still a member in good standing of the PCM at this time, and the foremost representative of the Mexican muralist movement. He guided Mayakovsky around Mexico City, and the two of them were together every day of Mayakovsky's visit.[61] Rivera made a great impression on the Soviet poet, and when Mayakovsky returned to Moscow, he carried along with him reproductions of Rivera's works which he used to illustrate his poetry readings and his lectures on Mexico. Mayakovsky promoted Rivera's works so extensively, in fact, that when Rivera visited the Soviet Union in 1927–28, he found himself already a known and appreciated artist.

Mayakovsky spent his first night in the capital in a hotel, but the next day moved to the Soviet embassy at Pestkovsky's invitation because, as he wrote Liliia Brik, it was nicer there, less crowded, and most importantly, cheap.[62] He still lacked funds, and money continued to be a worry throughout his stay in North America. By all indications, Pestkovsky and his staff were glad to have him as their guest, and life at the embassy became more animated after his arrival.[63] Several receptions and social gatherings were held in his honor, with one almost ending in a duel between Rivera and another guest whom his wife said had insulted her.[64] Mayakovsky became friendly with Pestkovsky and his family and especially with Khaikiss, the only staff member at the embassy to remain at the legation throughout the entire period of Soviet-Mexican diplomatic relations during the 1920s.[65]

Naturally, Mayakovsky was the focus of considerable interest. He and Pestkovsky were invited to visit the secretary of public education, Manuel Puig Casauranc, for example, and after what by all accounts was a friendly meeting, Puig wrote a lengthy greeting in the notebook Mayakovsky carried with him.[66] Mayakovsky was also always anxious to cooperate with the press, both because he was flattered by the interest and because he saw himself as an ambassador of Soviet literature, using his trips abroad as opportunities to publicize the achievements of Soviet culture.[67] He gave *Excélsior* an interview almost immediately, once Rivera agreed to act as interpreter. Fortunately, Rivera understood Russian well enough to translate for the reporter. His way of speaking Russian, on the other hand, was confusing, Mayakovsky wrote later, because he tended to mix up his words "mercilessly." Fortunately, the reporter was satisfied with what Rivera told him. Mayakovsky recounted his trip up to that point, said he was planning to write a book about his journey, and that there was considerable interest in, and discussion of, "the Mexican temperament" in the USSR.[68]

All the Mexicans Mayakovsky met hoped to hear him recite his poetry in Russian, since they understood that reading a Spanish translation was not an adequate substitute. A reporter from *El Universal Ilustrado* commented on how much less forceful Mayakovsky's poetry was in Spanish than in Russian. He had heard Mayakovsky read at the legation and said that Mayakovsky had created something new in poetry by combining the "roja y hermosa."[69] The Mexican press continued to be interested in Mayakovsky throughout his stay and continued mentioning him for some weeks after his departure. In August, *Antorcha* published an essay discussing Mayakovsky favorably in comparison with his Russian Symbolist predecessors, offering translations of "Nash marsh" ("Our March") and "Levyi marsh" ("Left March") and a photograph of Mayakovsky. "Nash marsh" was also published later in the month in *Revista de revistas*, illustrated by a Rivera drawing. Finally, in September, Mayakovsky was the subject of an *Antorcha* article summarizing the evaluation Trotsky had written of Mayakovsky in his *Literatura i revoliutsiia (Literature and Revolution)*, recently translated into Spanish.[70] For a poet visiting Mexico, even one representing a revolutionary new state, the publicity was unusual, and the extraordinary appreciation for his poetry was almost unheard of, as even he himself admitted later when he evaluated the state of poetry in general in Mexico. He was pleased at the attention, of course, but considering the significance he attached to his own career and his place within modern Russian poetry, he was not surprised at his warm reception.

Mayakovsky also became acquainted with a number of Mexican artists, writers, and leftist political figures at the embassy. Rivera said somewhat later that although no one in Mexico had previously read Mayakovsky's verse, they had all heard of him, had come to imagine him as a "red, heroic giant," and were anxious to meet him.[71] Several people Mayakovsky remembered with special affection and respect. Rafael Carrillo, secretary and treasurer of the PCM's central committee and editor of the party newspaper, was a good theoretician and reliable comrade, Mayakovsky wrote, Luis Monzón, Communist senator from Veracruz, visited the embassy while Mayakovsky was there on a number of occasions, often with his eight children. He had been one of the authors of the 1917 constitution and was active in the PCM and in Comintern work as well. Mayakovsky undoubtedly learned a great deal about Mexican family life from Mon-zón. Ursulo Galván, head of the Mexican League of Peasants and representative to the international conference of the Krestintern in Moscow in 1923, impressed Mayakovsky greatly, and he continued to follow Galván's career with great interest. It was Francisco Mo-reno, however, whom Mayakovsky liked best, and who became a sym-bol of the positive and negative features of Mexican political reality. Moreno was a popular Communist deputy from Veracruz and head of the Veracruz railroad workers' union, a politician respected by those who worked with him but hated by his conservative, political enemies. Mayakovsky was less enthusiastic about other Mexican lit-erary and artistic figures he met, and with the exception of Xavier Guerrero, whom he described as a good political cartoonist and a mas-ter of the pencil and the lasso, Mayakovsky had little to say about them later.

Like a dutiful tourist, Mayakovsky visited the capital's major sights: museums, theaters, shops, Chapultepec Park, and a *corrida de toros*. He liked the spectacular natural beauties of Mexico City, but not its weather. He wrote Liliia Brik that he had come to the Valley of Mex-ico "out of season," that it rained half the day and was cold at night. On the whole, he said, it was a "mangy" climate. Worse, the city was at such an extreme altitude that breathing was hard on his heart.[72] Despite these complaints and his physical discomfort, Mayakovsky was quite busy. Official visits, receptions, and interviews took up much of his time, but he continued to write verse and was apparently not quite as "bored" in the New World as he said he so often was in Eu-rope.[73] He sent considerably fewer letters and cables to Liliia Brik than he had during earlier travels and mailed only one letter to her from Mexico, in the middle of July. In it, beyond his comments about the weather, he wrote that the country was different because of its cacti, palms, and other tropical plants, but on the whole, he said, he found it dirty, not very nice, and in fact, boring. Except for these few lines the letter was quite businesslike and instructed her to send the en-closed poems to a number of Moscow and Leningrad periodicals.[74] Brik was beginning to be suspicious of his professed "boredom" and later, when he was in the United States, she became seriously con-cerned about his lack of correspondence.

One reason Mayakovsky wrote little from Mexico was that he spent so much time at the U.S. legation attempting to obtain a visa. He was finally issued one, and after three weeks in Mexico City he left for Laredo by train. He had suspected that he might have difficulties at the border, however, and had taken precautions. He carried nothing possibly incriminating, for example, and he tore out any pages in his notebooks that might mark him in the eyes of the border guards as an agitator or Communist propagandist.[75] Finally, after an eight-hour wait at the frontier (his visa had been declared invalid), and with the help of letters from his New York friend David Burliuk, who had arranged for Mayakovsky to be offered a "contract" as an "advertising artist" with a New York studio, he was admitted to the United States. He immediately boarded a train for New York and a country unlike any he had yet seen.[76]

Despite the fascination of the United States, Mayakovsky did not forget Mexico, and as he wrote and spoke about it over the next several years, he helped to provide Soviet citizens with a contemporary and varied picture of life and culture in Mexico in the mid-1920s. Above all, his views were more influential in shaping a Soviet picture of contemporary Mexico than anyone else's, if only because of his prominence. Mayakovsky had told the *Excélsior* reporter that upon his return to the Soviet Union he intended to write not a politically oriented description of Mexico, but rather an account of the country's traditions and customs, its "popular spirit."[77] Excerpts from a larger work still in progress, to be entitled *Moe otkrytie Ameriki (My Discovery of America)*, appeared in January 1926 in *Krasnaia nov (Red Virgin Soil)*. The Mexican section of the book had been completed the month before in what apparently was quite a rush, due to Mayakovsky's need for money. There were many factual errors in it, it was sloppily organized, poorly proofread, and had several inconsistent and misleading transliterations of Spanish and Mexican names. He was later criticized in *Krasnaia nov* itself for these inadequacies: D. Talnikov wrote in 1928 that in general *Moe otkrytie Ameriki*, and the Mexican section in particular, was written in the "vulgar" tone of a newspaper report and that the hyperboles, declamations, "stage dynamics," and "poster-agitational" style were not suitable for a man who was one of the best Soviet poets. These stylistic weaknesses mattered little to Mayakovsky's wider audience, of course, and his published account of Mexico became one of the most important to appear in the USSR in the twentieth century.[78] Most interestingly, too, it provided the best picture of how Mayakovsky genuinely felt about the revolutionary society he found in Mexico.

The reader of *Moe otkrytie Ameriki* cannot help feeling that from the time of his arrival in Mexico, Mayakovsky was prepared for almost nothing he saw. The six-foot tall Russian poet was amazed immediately by the hordes of "little brown people" who confronted him on the docks at Veracruz. He had expected the tall, noble Indians of James Fenimore Cooper or Mayne Reid, and was shocked to see not only how short they were, but how far they had fallen from their "earlier days of glory." Like other visitors to Veracruz, Mayakovsky found certain aspects of the port curious: the number of shoeshiners (at least five for each person with shoes, he calculated, since the Indians wore sandals) and lottery ticket vendors; the peculiar custom of carrying money about in bags; and the refusal to use paper currency because of the notorious instability of previous governments. He was interested to learn that banditry still existed in Mexico. He wrote, however, that he could sympathize with such brigands, considering his own financial difficulties: "And you, if a bag of gold coins were to jingle before your nose, might it not be to your taste too?"[79] He found the condition of the federal army amusing: the role played in it by corruption and graft, government officials' uncertainty about the precise number of soldiers in the army, and the odd means of providing for troops and their families in the field, all seemed to him a world away from his European experiences. He was pleased to see the red flags of the radical Heron Proal tenants' organization protruding from apartment buildings occupied by poor people refusing to pay rent. Such sights made Mexico seem not so far from what was accustomed to, after all.[80]

While Veracruz held Mayakovsky's interest for the few hours he was there, he was anxious to reach Mexico City, to see how it had been transformed by the recent revolution. There he might feel once more the romantic spirit of his own country's revolution, now increasingly bureaucratized and even partially bourgeoisified by the NEP. He left Veracruz at nine in the evening, and although in the darkness he was unable to make out any of what he was told was remarkable scenery, he was enchanted by the tropical night:

In a perfectly blue, ultramarine night the black trunks of the palms are just like long-haired bohemian artists.

The sky and the earth merge. There are stars both above and below. Two complete sets. Above—motionless celestial bodies, below—creeping and flying stars: fireflies.[81]

Arriving at dawn in the Valley of Mexico, Mayakovsky was presented with a different image. The variety and extent of cacti—the nopal, maguey, the organ pipe cactus—prompted him to remark that "I had never seen such a place, and I did not think such a place could exist."[82]

Never a great naturalist, Mayakovsky was in fact only mildly interested in such geographic and botanic curiosities and was glad to see Rivera at the station in Mexico City, prepared to show him the capital. Mayakovsky's initial description of Rivera was that he was a good shot with a pistol, that he was huge, and that he had a fine belly and a broad, constantly smiling face. The two of them soon became great friends. Immediately after Mayakovsky's arrival, Rivera took him to examine the monuments of the pre-Columbian past, then on to see the recent artistic creations of the revolutionary present. Mayakovsky was extremely enthusiastic about Rivera's own murals in the Secretariat of Public Education and described them in detail, calling them the "world's very first Communist frescoes." He felt he had to point out to his Soviet audience, however, that the reality of revolution in Mexico was not exactly what it might appear from Rivera's works. The frescoes were already under attack from members of the government of President Calles; the United States, which Mayakovsky called the "director of Mexico's affairs," had made it plain that it did not approve of such "agitational painting"; and that "hooligans" had begun defacing the murals. To Mayakovsky, it was ironic (and a little close to home, perhaps) that the revolutionary culture initiated and supported by an earlier government was already under siege in 1925 from those associated with the "official revolutionaries" in Mexico City.

Mayakovsky intended to return to this pregnant theme of moribund revolution, but felt he should first discuss other forms of culture, having begun his essay with art. Decent poetry, he wrote, simply could not exist in Mexico because of a weak public demand. He was appalled to learn that while poems written to popular tunes (the Mexican *corridos*) could be sold for a few centavos when printed on broadsheets and hawked in public places, there was no real audience for "higher" forms of poetry. Even Communist poets like Carlos Gutiérrez Cruz wrote only lyrical poetry. No one seemed to think that poets should be paid for writing verses. Only Ursulo Galván was able to market his poetry, and he did so on broadsheets as part of the PCM's election campaign. Knowledge of literature in general Mayakovsky found to be woefully out of date, and the only popular contemporary European or U.S. works he could find in translation were trashy novels. Theater wallowed in an abysmal state, with crowds flocking only to cheap burlesque reviews and to a cinema dominated by U.S. "cowboy epics."[83]

If he found the traditional forms of Western culture lacking in Mexico, the city's one truly popular spectacle, the bullfight, he considered to be disgusting. He described it in detail, and with more than a little prejudice: "I felt the greatest pleasure when the bull managed to lodge one of his horns between the ribs of one of the humans, avenging his fellow bulls." In the end, he wrote, "the only thing I was sorry about was that it was impossible to mount a machine gun on the bull's horns and train him how to shoot it."[84] He would be happiest, he hinted, when he succeeded in forgetting the entire unfortunate experience.

Mayakovsky considered Mexico City physically interesting, though he was disappointed that there were neither monuments of revolutionary architecture nor remnants of the old Aztec city of Tenochtitlán. The city's cathedral was of some note, but mainly because it was used by "Mexican señoras and señoritas . . . [only] as a passageway, leaving their waiting chauffeurs an impression of religious innocence, while they slipped out through the other side into the embrace of a lover or to walk arm in arm with an admirer."[85] On the other hand, Mayakovsky did admit that Catholicism still thrived despite the hostility of the government. He apparently was not particularly fond of writing about Mexican religion, however, and had little else to say about it.

Mayakovsky said that he soon grew tired of looking at the "historical" houses of the "priests and the rich," and in hopes of obtaining a more balanced impression of the city, he asked his new Communist friends to show him where the poor lived. What he found shocked him. The filth, overcrowding, flooding, and poor clothing were not at all what he had expected. The slow mental and physical poisoning of Indians seeking an escape from their dismal lives in the ubiquitous *pulquerías* was a sign of the revolution's failure. In response to what he had seen, he wrote the poem "Meksika" ("Mexico"), in which he bemoaned the fate of the descendents of the magnificent Aztecs, ruined by conquest, capitalism, and imperialism. They needed a new and more complete Mexican Revolution, one that would help them regain control of their lives, their land, and their natural treasures, stolen from them by foreigners. Probably nothing else in Mexico made him as furious as the condition of the poor Indians in the capital's suburbs. It was an aspect of Mexican life he would never forget.

Mayakovsky mentioned a number of other less unpleasant aspects of life in the capital which he felt might be of some interest to his Soviet audience. The conglomeration of automobiles and buses ("not nearly as comfortable or as spacious as our freight drays") and the insane, warlike competition between drivers, which caused a high number of automobile accidents, he found frightening. Sensitive to advertising because of his own experience with revolutionary and commercial posters, he was surprised to see so little of it in Mexico City. What he noticed most was that Mexicans would buy nothing Mexican, "even a fig-leaf," unless it had the word *barata* ("on sale" or "cheap") attached to it. The Mexican infatuation for expensive, foreign goods he found inexplicable, their use of electricity ostentatious, and their dress extravagant: he was flabbergasted that "even . . . workers . . . smelled of perfume."[86]

Whatever his initial intent had been, Mayakovsky concluded his description of Mexico with a lengthy account of local politics. Certainly one of the most disquieting aspects of Mexican life was that because of the until recently unstable political and military situation, violence seemed endemic. He noted that almost all the men, from the ages of fifteen to seventy-five, carried guns wherever they went. Even Rivera's little daughter napped with a Colt revolver at the head of her couch, and Mayakovsky was told that the police usually shot first and asked questions later. He had grown accustomed to violence in Russia during the revolution and Civil War, yet he felt it was a stage in the revolutionary process that had been overcome there, and it saddened him to learn that it continued to be so widespread in Mexico.

One feature of Mexican political life that constantly confused him, he admitted, was the local definition of the word *revolutionary*. In Mexico the word indicated something entirely different from what it did in Russia, he discovered. The Mexican revolutionary was not an individual with a definite Marxist ideology and program, but merely a person who overthrows authority with a weapon in his hand: "And, since in Mexico, everybody either held power, or holds power, or wants to hold power, they are all revolutionaries."[87] The word, then, signified little. Mayakovsky said that nothing proved this more than those Mexicans who were the official representatives of the interests of the working class. Morones, the "dictatorial" head of the "reformist" labor movement, for example, with his diamond cuff and vest pins, had abandoned the "revolutionary struggle with business" for a "ministerial portfolio." In becoming secretary of labor in the increasingly nonrevolutionary government of President Calles, he too had sold out to the bourgeoisie.

Mayakovsky wrote that the true Mexican revolutionaries, the Communists, did have some excellent and enthusiastic officials, but that their numbers were still too small for them to be effective in politics. While members of the party held office in the federal senate (he gave Luis Monzón as an example), the Communists' position was more clearly indicated by the murder of Francisco Moreno, deputy from Veracruz. Moreno was assassinated in Jalapa soon after Mayakovsky left Mexico, and it was generally believed among Mexican and U.S. Communists that he had been killed by an agent of the governor of the state of Veracruz, perhaps even by order of Calles himself. Mayakovsky had been fond of Moreno and remembered a message Moreno had written in his notebook after hearing a reading of "Levyi marsh": "Tell the Russian workers and peasants that at present we can only listen to your march, but the day will come when following your Mausers there will also begin to thunder our '33s."[88] Moreno's '33 would never fire, and it would take years, Mayakovsky admitted sadly, before the Communist movement in Mexico would gain the strength necessary to pose a serious threat to the "pseudo-revolutionaries" ensconced in the national government.

On the whole, Mayakovsky found Mexican politics filled with eccentricities. Its endemic bribery, the rapid changes of government, and the use of assassination as an everyday political technique were vastly different from what he had known in Russia. He did, however, feel that all the country's quarreling groups were united in a "thirst for freedom, [and] a hatred for [their] subjugators," that is, for the "gringos," the North Americans. While Mexicans had good reason to dislike the United States, Mayakovsky explained, it was unfortunate that the Mexican people as a whole did not understand that "Americans" were not the same as "exploiters." Politically, he believed, as in so many other ways, Mexicans simply were not yet fully mature. Their backward nationalism needed to be replaced by Communist internationalism, the Mexican national flag by the "crimson banner" of Communism.[89] Only then would Mexico be able to fulfill its true destiny and carry out an authentic revolution. It was a view he shared with most other Russians commenting about Mexico in the 1920s.

Perhaps to soften the severity of his criticism, Mayakovsky ended his account by praising the personal friendliness and graciousness of the Mexicans whom he had met. Their warmth and hospitality were without parallel, he wrote, and he concluded, quite sincerely, that he missed them and their openness and generosity greatly. Certainly he did not find similar traits among the efficiency minded, businesslike citizens of the United States.

Mayakovsky had difficulty concluding his essay on Mexico because he had mixed feelings about the country and his experiences there. He left greatly disappointed in the political, social, and cultural backwardness he had seen. Mayakovsky believed that he was the product of the most progressive and forward-looking social and political movement on the globe. It seemed to him that Mexico would take years, possibly decades, to catch up with developments in the Soviet Union. The tension Mayakovsky felt between his vision of a future being created in the USSR and a past so tenaciously holding on to Mexico was not resolved.

Mayakovsky appreciated much that he saw in Mexico: the country's natural beauty; Diego Rivera's revolutionary frescoes; the admirable Mexican Communist Party officials. Yet, this was simply not sufficient to compensate for the poverty, filth, and misery he had seen, and certainly not for the moral and political corruption of the Calles government. To Mayakovsky, there was no doubt that the promise of the revolution was not being fulfilled in 1925. It had sold out to the United States and to international imperialism.

If it was not unique, Mayakovsky's view of Mexico was highly idio-syncratic, as could be expected of one of the most original of Soviet poets. It was special because of its style, which did suffer from the inadequacies described by Talnikov and others among the literary critics of the 1920s, but which also had a strength and expressiveness that were rare among Russian and foreign writers describing Mex-ico. His view of Mexico was also shaped by the nature of his very limited experiences. He spent most of his time with officials of the Soviet embassy or with members of the PCM. Nor did he travel exten-sively, but spent his three weeks almost entirely in the capital, which was not the best place to obtain a full picture of the country. Despite all these drawbacks, however, it was Mayakovsky's view of Mexico and its revolution that reached more members of the Soviet public than that of any other Soviet citizen until after the Second World War. If there was a meaningful general Soviet view of Mexico in the late twenties, it was as a result of Mayakovsky's activities after his return from North America.

Aleksandra Kollontai: Soviet Ambassador to Mexico, 1926–27

The appointment of Aleksandra Kollontai as Soviet ambassador to Mexico was certainly greeted with surprise, perhaps even amusement, in Mexico City. She was the only woman holding a position of im-portance in the diplomatic community in Mexico, and she was the twentieth century's first female ambassador to any country.[90] Her duties were not onerous, and like Pestkovsky, she had considerable time for activities not directly associated with her official position. Unfortunately, her stay in Mexico was brief, and for much of it she was ill, a factor further limiting her effectiveness and her mobility. Her service in Mexico resulted in no major political or economic agreements, nor did she write extensively about the country as Pest-kovsky had. She did, however, leave a legacy of good will that re-mained for many years. In addition, the publicity generated by her stay in Mexico aided in presenting a fuller and more sophisticated picture of the country to the Soviet public and to an international audience fascinated by her activities. She was as much a celebrity as a diplomat, by far the best known of all the representatives of the Soviet government abroad during the 1920s. Her assignment to Mexico led to considerable speculation about Soviet intentions in the New World, and particularly in Latin America, but in the end, her activities were no more nefarious than those of the other foreign diplomats accredited to the Mexican Republic.

To a great extent, Kollontai's diplomatic assignment was greeted with such interest in the West because of her reputation as a revolutionary. She was born in St. Petersburg in 1872, the daughter of a tsarist general. Educated at home by a female teacher who had strong populist sympathies, by 1908 she had emigrated from Russia to devote her life to the revolutionary movement, abandoning her husband, but keeping his name. She lived in a variety of Western European countries and was an associate of Plekhanov, Bebel, and Liebknecht. An early member of the Russian Social Democratic Labor Party, by 1915 she had given her support to Lenin and was promoted to the Bolshevik central committee at the Sixth Party Congress in 1917. She was active in the new Communist government as the spokesperson for women's affairs and in 1922–23 served as secretary of the international women's section of the Communist International. Outside the Soviet Union she was known as a revolutionary feminist, a promoter of free love and sexual license, and a danger to the established order of society. By the early 1920s, she was already becoming disillusioned with the political direction of the new regime, however, and she supported the Workers' Opposition as a means of expressing her dissatisfaction with what she and many others felt was a weakening of democratic principles in the Party.[91] In the summer of 1922, Kollontai asked Stalin for a foreign post for reasons both personal and professional: her marriage to Pavel Dybenko was breaking up and her involvement with the Workers' Opposition, refusing to submit to Party discipline, had alienated her from many in the Party leadership.

Kollontai was first suggested as Soviet ambassador to Canada, but the Canadian government would not accept her because of her revolutionary reputation and probably also because of her sex.[92] In October 1922 she was made a member of a trade delegation to Norway, and she apparently left Petrograd with some relief, looking forward to a new assignment that would permit her to serve the revolution and her country without having to become involved in destructive internal politics. She did not know then that she would spend the rest of her active working life as a diplomat, or that she would not return to the USSR for more than short visits until her retirement in 1945. She remained abroad, hoping the unfriendly attitude toward her at home would soften somewhat, but it never did. Yet her absence, coupled with her refusal to discuss Soviet internal problems while serving in diplomatic posts, may have kept her safe from Stalin's paranoia. She was, in any event, one of the few significant Old Bolsheviks to escape the purges of the 1930s.

Kollontai's work in Norway was highly successful, resulting in a series of trade agreements and an exchange of ambassadors between Norway and the USSR. In the fall of 1926 she was offered the post in Mexico vacated by Pestkovsky. Apparently she had been expecting the appointment, and she had spent some time in Norway studying Mexican culture, economy, and history.[93] She was fifty-four years old, and a new phase in her life was beginning, in a country that seemed as remote from the USSR as any could be.

From the beginning her appointment was not looked on with favor by Mexico's neighbor to the north, and the United States did not disguise the fact that it would do whatever it could to make her stay in Mexico uncomfortable. Her application for a U.S. transit visa, for example, was rejected out of hand by the U.S. embassy in Berlin because "she has been actively associated with the International Communist subversive movement."[94] The U.S. public was probably less antagonistic to Kollontai, however, largely because of the favorable press coverage she had received. A New York Times reporter, interviewing her in Berlin in October, asked how she saw her future work in Mexico. She told him she hoped to bring the Soviet Union closer to Mexico and to other American nations, even to improve relations with the United States, if that were possible. She believed diplomacy had changed from what it had been in the past, that now the diplomat must scrupulously refrain "from propaganda or mixing in the internal affairs of the country to which [he] is accredited."[95]

The U.S. government was unimpressed by such statements, and a request from the State Department that she be refused permission to leave her ship at Havana was granted eagerly by the Cuban authorities. Kollantai was careful in her public comments on the incident, but in a private message to Deputy Commissar for Foreign Affairs Maxim Litvinov in Moscow she wrote that while that Cubans cited an obscure law in refusing her permission to land, what they actually wanted was to prevent her from meeting with Cuban leftists. Placing her under "blockade" in the port proved to her, she told Litvinov, that "the Cubans are vassals of the United States in the fullest sense of the word."[96]

The warmth of her reception in Veracruz encouraged her tremendously, and she soon forgot her unfortunate experience in Cuba. A crowd of students and workers met her, the reporters were friendly, and Governor Heriberto Jara invited her to be his guest in Jalapa, an offer she refused because of the press of time. She was met in Mexico City with equal enthusiasm, and she wrote in her diary that the friendliness and curiosity of the people, their spontaneity, the beauty of the country, all made her arrival seem more like a theatrical production than a diplomatic reception.[97] Unfortunately, the altitude affected her badly, and she asked the embassy staff to take her to a hotel where she could rest while accommodations at the embassy were properly arranged. She was soon suffering from heart palpitations, and she wrote to a friend that even breathing was difficult for her. She never adjusted to the altitude, and she had to ask Moscow for a vacation and a change of assignment by the middle of 1927.

Since she was a good news story, both the local and foreign press were anxious to write about her. The *New York Times* reported on her reception by Mexico City's radicals and interviewed Kollontai herself shortly after her arrival. Once again, she denied U.S. Secretary of State Frank Kellogg's charge that she was only a propagandist and promised that she had come to Mexico City to strengthen friendly relations between the Soviet Union and Mexico. Reporters were impressed by her "seriousness," a trait they had not expected. The Mexican press had been especially sensationalistic in its reports about her impending arrival, and stories about her "collection of Paris gowns and jewels" had been rampant in the capital's newspapers.[98] She was also known as a "sexual revolutionary," and North Americans associated her with a "scarlet" way of life. The appearance in English of her novel, *Red Love*, did not help matters, particularly when she tried to have its publication stopped because she considered the translation inept and felt it would prejudice her diplomatic activity. In the end, all this was overshadowed by her professional, even austere behavior. *New York Times* readers were certainly surprised to read in

"Woman Envoy's Books Far Outnumber Gowns" that Kollontai was a "quiet-voiced, mild-mannered woman" whose trunks were filled almost entirely with books.[99] This was not the Kollontai the press had expected, she wrote Litvinov, adding that she had been able to correct a number of misconceptions the Mexican public held about her. *El Universal*, she told Litvinov, published her interview verbatim, so that her emphasis on the respectable nature of her mission, her interest in trade, and her rejection of the charge of being an agitator, were clear.[100] Similarly, *Excélsior* wrote that based on what they had seen of the new ambassador, Mexicans would appreciate and value her knowledge, her good will, and her high level of culture and sophistication.[101] It appeared that Kollontai had won the press over to her side, and her hopes for her mission must have been buoyed after the uncertainties that had developed en route from Moscow.

Within a few days, Kollontai felt she was already beginning to understand Mexico better. She had read a great deal about the country and its recent history before her departure from Europe, and she hoped that the fine collection of books on Mexico that Pestkovsky had assembled for the embassy library would help fill the gaps in knowledge. Her earliest observations about Mexico—tentative, but straightforward and sincere—were written in her diary. She was surprised at the continuing hostility beteen church and state, but decided that it was a conflict that would not be easily solved. She agreed with Pestkovsky's reports about the need for the Mexican government and people to struggle against U.S. imperialism and foreign capital. As she learned more about Mexico, however, she admitted that these were only some of the difficulties facing the country and that there were many more of which she herself was unaware. From her initial observations, Mexico's prospects were not encouraging.

Her early diary entries indicated that one particularly rewarding aspect of her assignment was the attention given to her gender. She believed that her appointment was an accomplishment shared by women around the globe. It provided a great opportunity to show that a woman could be not only as good a diplomat as a man, but even a better one. She was determined to do the best she could, she added, in the interests of her sex, her country, and the revolution.

Finally, she noted during these first few days that she had begun to appreciate how little Russians and other Europeans knew about

Mexico, and for that matter, about Latin America in general. Eventually she came to feel that every educated person should study Mexico's pre-Columbian past and its twentieth-century revolutionary history. She wrote that she herself was fascinated with the period of the Insurgency and that her favorite figure in all Mexican history was Father Hidalgo. Her affinity with the Mexicans grew as she came to know them better, and in January 1927 she wrote that she believed her work in Mexico would be successful because she had developed a sense of identity with the people and their difficult struggle in the face of the multitude of problems confronting them. She rejected the assertion that Mexico was a backward country with a lazy people, writing that on the contrary, Mexicans were anxious to build a new life for themselves and their country, and that Mexico had a great future. Her initial pessimism had been replaced by a cautious optimism.

On December 24, she presented her credentials to President Calles in a ceremony at the National Palace. She noted in her speech that since recognition, relations between Mexico and the USSR had been only fraternal, sincere, and friendly. She stressed her hopes for continued good relations, based on what she had found to a be a fundamental similarity between the two countries and their peoples: "In all the world there are no two other countries which have as much in common as modern Mexico and the new Russia. This resemblance lies in the role which the working people play in the policies pursued by their countries, it can be noted in their major social and economic concerns, and in the direction of the foreign policy which protects the independence of the nation and is opposed to imperialist tendencies: all these tie our two countries together closely."[102] She expressed the Soviet Union's interest in expanding trade and promised to do her best in this regard. Finally, she added that the two countries' relationship was strengthened by the fact that they both had "revolutionary governments" in a world still hostile to such states.

Calles used the occasion to make a pronouncement on his country's position in the international community. He said that it was true that Mexico was a revolutionary nation. Yet it was the Soviet Union which had created a totally new, unique form of government. Mexico respected the right of any sovereign nation to chose the government or economic system its people wished; it desired to live in peace and concord with all the world's nations and would interfere in no way in any other country's affairs.[103] Calles's message was directed as much to the other foreign ambassadors, and especially to the one from the United States, as it was to Kollontai. Apparently he had decided to get along well with Kollontai, and he was always uncommonly gracious if direct in his dealings with her.[104] While she had little good to say about him once she left Mexico, Kollontai did admit that he consistently treated her well and did whatever he could to facilitate what he considered her legitimate activities in his country.

Calles's government was equally cooperative, polite, and helpful, despite the continuing verbal attacks by the United States on the Soviet embassy as a center of subversion and espionage. On January 21 Kollontai again met with Calles. As before, she wrote Litvinov, he was extraordinarily cordial: "My interview with Calles was very friendly. He thanked me for my efforts to build up our relations on a basis of sincerity and said that he valued the establishment of stable and friendly links with the USSR. He referred to the special nature and character of Mexico's 'revolutionary government' which claims to represent working-class elements and not the great capitalists, and again emphasized that we had many points of contact in the struggle against the imperialist tendencies of the capitalist states."[105] Kollontai used the opportunity provided by the meeting to reject some of Secretary of State Kellogg's most recent "lies and fabrications" and to express her continuing interest in the expansion of trade. She also asked Calles's advice on how she might reach some sort of rapprochement with the CROM. The *New York Times* had reported on the day of her arrival in Mexico City that the CROM leadership had forbidden its members to greet her "on the grounds that Mexican and Russian labor had nothing in common," and nothing had as yet changed their attitude toward her and her government.[106] Calles advised her first to improve personal relations between herself as Soviet ambassador and the CROM leadership. Second, he said, she should make a concerted effort to provide more accurate information about the Soviet government's relationship to the radical Mexican unions. He told her that he believed such steps would undoubtedly help reduce the level of hostility.[107]

Kollontai did meet with Morones, but while he gave her a polite reception, no minds were changed. The CROM remained absolutely opposed to what it saw as unwarranted and unacceptable interference in the internal affairs of Mexican labor by the USSR and its representatives. Morones would not cease advising Calles to guarantee the absolute monopoly of the CROM and the secretary of labor over Mexican workers' organizations. No Soviet ambassador would be able to ameliorate the CROM's hostility toward the USSR and the Comintern in the 1920s.

If Kollontai's political overtures were rebuffed, neither were her hopes for expansion of trade realized. Immediately after her arrival, she began negotiations to buy lead for the USSR, by mid-February she had met with the secretary of agriculture, and at one point she suggested a direct steamship link between Mexico and the USSR to make trade easier and more profitable for both nations. Her enthusiasm was no match for the inertia with which she was faced, however, and trade remained at the same level as under Pestkovsky. Kollontai's promotion of cultural relations was quite successful, on the other hand. She arranged showings of recent Soviet films, organized exhibitions, made a number of friends within the Mexican intellectual and cultural community, and continued to give interviews to representatives of the local and international press.

Since she believed her position was as much that of an intermediary between the two countries as a representative of her own, she felt it her duty to learn as much as she could about Mexico. She surprised her Mexican friends by asking for a list of the best Mexican literature to read, something foreign ambassadors rarely did. She was fond of the works of Diego Rivera, and developed a fine appreciation for Mexico's traditional and modern art. Her fascination with the simultaneously ancient and modern qualities of Mexico's pre-Columbian architecture was at times reminiscent of Balmont's, while at others it prefigured Eisenstein's. She wrote to her friend Tatiana Shchepkina-Kupernik about her impressions in April 1927:

> I saw an ancient temple and the pyramids of the Aztecs. Such majesty! And such bold dimensions. The temple is an arena, without a roof. Straight lines of unending little squares, little quadrangles. But so imposing! A temple whose roof is the sky itself! Above all I was struck by how modern all this is. A stylization by Meyerhold. Straight, cut corners. Endless stairways leading nowhere, little quadratic squares, spread around the main square,

conical cut walls behind which there is nothing (and never was anything!). Such stylization! And the decorations on the stone walls—reliefs? Cubism, the purest cubism. And their power is in the fact that they are not artificial, but [absolutely natural], naive. You would probably consider this the most important experience of all these months [I have spent] here.[108]

The past, the present, Russia and Mexico were intertwined in her mind. When she became most disillusioned with the government of Calles and the failure to realize the promise of the revolution, the wonders of Mexico's past, its physical beauty, and the warmth of its people would reconcile her to her task.

One constantly frustrating aspect of Kollontai's work in Mexico was the continuing and increasing hostility of the United States, directed against both her and the Mexican government. As she explained in a letter to Litvinov early in December 1926, she had been aware of the awkward political situation before coming to Mexico City. She knew that Calles had been accused in the United States of pursuing "Bolshevik policies," particularly with regard to U.S. oil concessions. The day she arrived in Mexico, the government announced that Calles had categorically rejected the U.S. charges that he was a "Bolshevik," but the controversy continued to simmer. She expected her position to be difficult, she wrote Litvinov, since Mexican "reactionaries," as well as the U.S. government, believed she had been sent to Mexico to provide new impetus to Bolshevik propaganda in the New World. Calles's friendliness to her, as well as his outspoken criticism of U.S. policy in Nicaragua, had only inflamed the situation and worsened any chances she might have had to improve relations with the United States and the Mexican conservatives. Kollontai responded to the attacks as effectively as she could, but the pressure was maintained— internationally, by the United States, and domestically, by the established labor movement. Both had good reasons to oppose any furthering of Soviet and Communist influence in Mexico, and each in it own way was effective in accomplishing its goals.

In March, her political dfficulties came to a head because of money sent from the Soviet railway union to aid a strike by Mexican railroad workers associated with the PCM. The strike was generally considered to be directed against the CROM and the government, and neither

Calles nor his supporters were happy with this foreign support for people they believed to be renegades and counterrevolutionaries. Kollontai was summoned to the Secretariat of Foreign Relations and given a note in Calles's name stating that the contribution had to be seen as an act against the government of Mexico since the strike had been declared illegal.[109] On the grounds that there were close ties between the Soviet government and Soviet labor unions, Calles asked that the government of the USSR exert its influence on the Soviet railroad workers union to withdraw its support for the strike. Kollontai found herself in an awkward position, since Mexican law stated that only strikes sanctioned by the government could be considered legitimate. She knew too that strikes organized by unions other than those affiliated with the CROM were almost never granted official recognition. She told the foreign secretary, Aaron Saenz, that she and her government were unaware that the strike was illegal. Because it was against a foreign company, and foreign capital, she explained, and because both her government and Mexico's were opponents of foreign imperialism, she had assumed the strike would be given official sanction. She promised that in the future she would keep Moscow and the Soviet trade unions better informed about developments in Mexico, so that such mistakes would not recur.

The railroad strike was only the beginning of several weeks of controversy. The CROM, especially, intensified its press campaign against Kollontai and the activities of the Soviet embassy. While Calles himself continued to profess nothing but good feelings toward Kollontai and the USSR, everyone knew that the attacks had the president's tacit approval. A CROM protest against the showing of Soviet films as being propaganda for revolution, for example, led to the closing of one of the theaters in the capital and the arrest of its owner. As conditions worsened, Kollontai recognized that her effectiveness as a representative of the Soviet government was declining. She also came to feel that she understood better the nature of Mexico's "revolutionary" government, and although she would not comment publicly on it while in Mexico City, she was later exceedingly critical of Calles and his regime.

With the question of the railroad workers' strike apparently resolved, Kollontai at last followed her doctor's advice that she rest for a few days in Cuernavaca. Her stay there was only a brief interlude in the continuing controversy surrounding her, however.[110] By April, the CROM's attacks on her had grown even more virulent. The *New York Times* reported that the Central Labor Organization of the Federal District, desiring to show that Mexican labor had no sympathy with Russian radicalism, had requested that Calles pronounce Kollontai a *persona non grata* and expel her from the country immediately.[111] Complicating the situation was the fact that the spring of 1927 was an extraordinarily unsettled time for Mexican political leaders: peasants were more vocally expressing their unhappiness with the extent of land reform, relations between the Catholic church and the government were becoming more bitter, and the problems arising from foreign oil concessions were intensifying, leading many in the United States and Mexico to speculate on the serious possibility of American military intervention. Similarly, the international position of the Soviet Union was not encouraging, with the British appearing to be on the verge of breaking diplomatic relations and very possibly launching an extensive and wide-ranging anti-Soviet propaganda campaign. Although during her stay in Mexico Kollontai had probably done nothing illegal, or even questionable,[112] the darkening domestic and international scene certainly had an influence on her position as ambassador. While she believed that she was doing as much as anyone could, she was constantly disappointed by her failure to accomplish more.

The altitude of Mexico City continued to irritate Kollontai's chronic angina. She found breathing the thin air painful and the arid winter climate constantly frustrating: "Everyone has skin like a crocodile from the dryness, and creams do not help. I am a denizen of the Leningrad marshes. I miss the moisture. I long for the water." She admitted as well that she had high blood pressure and other ailments and that she was forced to lie in bed for long periods.[113] Her doctor's prescription for extended quiet and no unnecessary exertion could not be followed, she felt, if she were to do her job adequately. In April Litvinov had suggested that it might be wise for her to consider a transfer to Uruguay, which had the only other Soviet diplomatic legation in Latin America. Kollontai replied that despite her physical problems her working relationship with the government had been improving, and she could still be effective in Mexico. She noted in her diary that while a vacation in Europe would be pleasant enough, she did not feel at the time that a permanent relocation would be wise. On the contrary, she anticipated her tour of duty in Mexico to last between two and three years more. Eventually, she did request that Litvinov approve a vacation for her outside Mexico, and when the permission arrived from Moscow in May, Kollontai had come to the realization that when she left Mexico, it would be for good, although she was not officially transferred until October.

Kollontai sailed for Europe at the beginning of June, after a series of dinners and receptions in her honor. She left Mexico with feelings of great affection for the country and its people. Among her several souvenirs, the ones which meant most to her were a sarape with her initials woven into the pattern, given to her by the textile workers union, and a coconut from another labor organization inscribed "To Comrade Kollontai. The imperialists hate you, the revolutionaries love you. Long live the friendship in our hearts between Mexico and Russia!"[114] In spite of the problems that had confronted her, she felt she had been an effective ambassador. Calles had never been less than cordial, and he had not permitted the series of unfortunate incidents to cloud what she believed were basically good relations between their two countries. She wrote in her diary that, after her six months there, she had begun to see and better comprehend Mexico. She understood, she wrote, that past conditions had forced people to carry revolvers more often than books, but the population now valued the benefits of science and culture. Mexico's children—serious, active, and clever— would help create a new Mexico. And Mexico was now part of her, she wrote: "I am now leaving Mexico. But a small part of me will remain there."[115]

Kollontai completed no extensive analysis of what she had seen in Mexico, but she did offer a few comments during the several months following her departure, and was remarkably outspoken in her criticisms of the Calles regime. In interviews in Berlin she was particularly scornful of Calles and Morones, whom she called "false socialists" who used Mexican labor merely as an instrument of their own ambitions. In the case of Morones, "it is not possible that he can develop communism in any way, when he is exploiting the working classes for his own advantage and that of other groups." The CROM leaders are "a bourgeois crowd directed only by personal interests." The government's persecution of the Catholic church, she continued, was indicative of its general cynicism. It was motivated exclusively by a desire to seize church property: "the attacks against religious institutions are in reality political moves only partly concealed within the pretense of the Querétaro Constitution, which the government leaders of Mexico pretend to uphold as something sacred, and yet are the first ones to mutilate."[116] Kollontai obviously relished the opportunity to say publicly what she had come to believe about the Mexican government and the failure of the revolution. Much of what she said corresponded to current Comintern policy toward Mexico.

In the fall of 1927 Kollontai published two articles in Soviet newspapers which were more balanced in their treatment of Mexico. "Revoliutsionnaia Meksika" ("Revolutionary Mexico") was published in Vecherniaia Moskva (Evening Moscow) in September, and "Meksika—strana problem" ("Mexico—A Country of Problems") in Leningradskaia pravda (Leningrad Pravda) in October.[117] Both articles were intended to be educational, to redress the unfortunate ignorance of Mexico and Latin America among Soviet citizens, and to help them appreciate particularly the significance of Mexico's role in the struggle against U.S. imperialism in Latin America. She noted that most Soviet citizens knew only a few basic facts about Mexico: that it had a government supported by workers' organizations, that it had been carrying on a continual struggle with its neighbor to the north, and that its workers had to fight against the power of foreign capitalism, native landowners, and Catholic priests. However, there was more that should be known, she wrote. Most significant was that the problem of peasant landholding had still not been solved. The Indians had been exploited for centuries; they were poor; the best land had been taken from them; and the struggle in the countryside was now between the landless Indians and the mostly foreign, neofeudal landowners. Even though the government spoke enthusiastically of land reform, the church and the big landowners successfully opposed redistribution. However much they may have been weakened, they were not being forced to give the peasants land. Industry was only sporadically developed, Kollontai noted, although rather like Russia shortly before the revolution, it was concentrated in certain industrial areas. The working class was not large, but it was unified and organized, unfortunately not into Marxist unions, however. Finally, unlike the Soviet Union, which during NEP allowed private enterprise on only a limited basis, the "commanding heights" of the economy lay in the hands of foreigners, and there were few state-run enterprises.

Kollontai concluded her brief survey by expressing her optimism about the future. Mexico was a nation rich in oil, minerals, and beauty, and in the talents and capacities of its people, she wrote. Yet the development of its natural wealth was limited by the reality that foreigners controlled or owned most of the country's industrial and economic enterprises. Still, she believed that despite external pressure, the government of Mexico was steadily moving to the left and that the countries of Central America were following Mexico's example. Working-class and "revolutionary" consciousness in general were growing, if slowly, and she predicted that Mexico would have a leading role in Latin America's revolt against Anglo-Saxon domination, that the "colored peoples" of the New World were announcing to the white race their right to exist, and that Mexico would not surrender to U.S. domination. The struggle would be a difficult one for Mexicans, and as Pestkovsky had said, it would have to be led by the proletariat and peasants. The Mexican bourgeoisie could never carry through a nationalist revolution because of their dependence on foreign capital, and because of legitimate fears of American intervention. The genuine and lasting Mexican Revolution, Kollontai concluded abruptly, had yet to take place.

Kollontai wrote nothing more about Mexico in subsequent years, nor was she involved in general with Soviet-Mexican relations. In December 1927 she was appointed ambassador to Norway, and in July 1930, ambassador to Sweden, a post she held until her retirement in 1945. She spent her last seven years living quietly in Moscow. In 1946, she was awarded the Order of the Aztec Eagle by Narciso Bassols, the Mexican ambassador. He recalled that he saw mementos of her stay in Mexico displayed in her apartment and that she still spoke warmly of her stay in Mexico City.[118] She must have been happy to know that despite the extravagantly contrasting opinions of Mexican politicians toward the Soviet Union and the abrogation of diplomatic relations in 1930, few Mexicans since that time had any criticisms to make of her own actions in their country. Rather she was seen as a sincere, honest, and trustworthy individual by all those who dealt with her.

Kollontai's stay in Mexico did not produce any major diplomatic, political, or economic breakthroughs. Despite her special interest in trade, commerce between the USSR and Mexico never reached meaningful levels. Her attempts at cultural exchange were more successful although, because of constant harassment by the CROM and opposition from the United States, even the most innocuous films and exhibitions were branded as nothing more than Bolshevik propaganda. Her position was unenviable in that she was constantly involved in arguments between the "revolutionary" government of Calles (and its CROM allies) and the leftist branch of the labor movement, which was opposed to the government and had close ties to the Mexican Communist party, the Comintern, and of course, members of the Soviet embassy. Kollontai had to represent the interests of the USSR as a diplomat, but also felt it her duty to support the radical labor movement whenever possible, although it must be said that on the basis of the evidence available, she attempted to carry out all her duties within the restraints of Mexican law. Her health problems complicated every other aspect of her work in Mexico, of course, and were a constant source of irritation.

Kollontai did manage to accomplish something positive as Soviet ambassador, however. The legacy of good will she left between the USSR and Mexico was one of which no other Soviet ambassador could boast. Her appointment received great publicity around the world, and by no means was it only negative. As she herself wrote, her serving as the ambassador of one revolutionary government to another, and her being a woman, symbolized a new order of things, a new world in the making. She may have accepted the position because of difficulties arising from internal Soviet politics, and Calles may have been at times condescending to her because of her sex, but she had managed to overcome these drawbacks to become an effective representative of her country and its ideals during its early years. Because of Aleksandra Kollontai, Mexico did become better known in the USSR and Mexicans derived a more complete understanding of the Soviet Union. In terms of public relations, Moscow could not have made a better choice than Kollontai. Had her health been better, the course of Mexican-Soviet relations during the late 1920s and early 1930s might have been considerably different, although it must be remembered that her work for the Commissariat of Foreign Affairs was continually undermined by Comintern directives. While she may have believed, theoretically, in the Comintern's policies, she often proved able to deflect the impact of some of their most damaging activities. As it was, Mexicans remembered her fondly, as she did them. If she was disappointed by her lack of success in achieving anything concrete in Mexico, she could take solace in this, and that her short stay in the country had promoted the image of Soviet women around the world, had managed to defuse potentially damaging conflicts between the Soviet and Mexican governments, and, she must have hoped, had served the interests of the Soviet and Mexican peoples.

With Kollontai's departure, relations between Mexico and the USSR deteriorated rapidly, and it became increasigly difficult for Russians to travel unencumbered through Mexico. As the Mexican Revolution aged, the government became more suspicious, and the population less enamored, of visiting Russians, although as the case of Eisenstein will show, under the proper circumstances that mistrust and suspicion could be overcome. Political pressure from the United States had helped worsen the relationship between Mexico and the USSR, and Soviet observers by the end of the decade were convinced that their long-held belief about U.S. domination of Mexican economic and political affairs was justified, even confirmed. The twenties remain a period of intense cultural exchange between the two countries, however, and more about Mexico was printed in the Soviet press during that decade than at any time until after World War II. Much of what appeared was political, but much was not. Most striking, once more, was the sympathy expressed by Soviet visitors and writers for the population and its aspirations, if not for an increasingly conservative revolutionary administration. Most Russians felt that Mexico was backward in comparison to Russia during these years, but they expressed great hopes for the country's future, especially within the context of Latin America, where Mexico was seen as a progressive force. Inevitably, because of their highly political orientation during this first decade following their own revolution, these Russians were disappointed in Mexico, and that disappointment reflected the dampening of their enthusiasm for international revolution as the decade progressed. Official Soviet policy, as expressed openly by the People's Commissariat of Foreign Affairs and more surreptitiously through the Comintern, had been a failure in Mexico and throughout Latin America. The series of ideologically motivated, Europocentric political decisions made in Moscow harmed Soviet interests in Mexico greatly because they could not be applied to Mexican conditions. The gradualism and appreciation for local realities no doubt recommended by Kollontai and even Pestkovsky were rejected for contradicting ideological unity and discipline. The Soviet government's political disappointments in Mexico (which were to a great extent brought on themselves) were paralleled by the disillusionment of those Russians discussed in this chapter. Yet more optimistically, it can be said that all the Russians who came to Mexico during the 1920s expressed continuing affection for Mexico and love for its people, and upon leaving, all of them spoke of the abiding impression the country had made on them.

4
SERGEI
EISENSTEIN
AND THE
ETERNAL CIRCLE

Je ne fais pas du cinéma. Je fais du Mexique et du moi. —Sergei Eisenstein,
May 22, 1931[1]

*Finally, Que Viva Mexico!, this history of the change of cultures, presented
not vertically (in years and centuries), but horizontally (as the geographical coexistence of the most diverse stages of culture), for which Mexico is so amaz-
ing, in that it has a province (Tehuantepec) that has a matriarchal society next
to provinces that almost achieved communism in the revolution of the first
decade of this century (Yucatán, Zapata's program, etc.). And, as a central
episode, it had ideas of national unification: historically, in the joint entry into
Mexico's capital of the united forces of Pancho Villa the northerner and
Emiliano Zapata the southerner; and in terms of subject, the figure of the
Mexican woman moving, with the same care for her man, from group to
group of the Mexican troops, all fighting each other, torn with the contradictions of the civil war. She seems physically to personify the image of a single,
nationally united Mexico, opposing foreign intriguers who try to dismember
the nation and set its separate parts against each other.* —Sergei Eisenstein[2]

None of the Russian travellers discussed in this study to this point
remained as long in Mexico as Sergei Eisenstein did, and none was
as changed by the country and its people. Mexico was a profoundly
important experience for Eisenstein, both creatively and personally.
The filming he did there, his way of seeing the world, his emotional
development all combined to create a fundamental transformation.
Mexico marked the end of one period of his life and the beginning
of another. His unfinished film, *Que Viva Mexico!*, was a summary
of his work in cinema during the previous decade and an indication of the direction it would follow for the rest of his life. Yet *Que
Viva Mexico!* was a film unlike all his earlier ones. It was unique and

158

individual, and it owed its uncommon personalism above all to the inspiration Eisenstein found in Mexico. What he uncovered there, and what he attempted to reproduce in his film, was more multi-layered, more mysterious, yet also simpler and more direct than anything seen by Russians writing about Mexico over the preceding century. Few foreigners came to understand Mexico as well as Eisenstein did, and for almost none of them was Mexico the revelation it was for him.[3]

Eisenstein was born in Riga in 1898, the son of a German-Jewish architect father and a Russian mother. His was a cosmopolitan family in a sophisticated city. He was still a boy when his parents were divorced, and their continuing personal conflict did not make his childhood a happy one. His feelings toward each of his parents were mixed, and shuttling back and forth between them, he loved neither without reservation. His mother was often cold toward him, and his father was distant, more interested in training him as an engineer, it seems, than in providing him a proper emotional and moral education.[4] His upbringing was fairly typical for a member of the scientific intelligentsia, but his life changed entirely with the events of 1917. He wrote later that "the Revolution gave me that which is most dear to me in my life—it made me an artist."[5] Like many others of his generation, and after the crucial political experience of the Civil War, Eisenstein became dedicated to the new Soviet state.[6]

In the spring of 1921 Eisenstein enrolled under Vsevolod Meyerhold in the State Advanced Directorial Workshop in Petrograd, and it was there that he was first involved professionally with Mexico. Meyerhold assigned him the decor and costumes for the third act of the Proletcult stage production of Jack London's story, "The Mexican." Eisenstein took his teacher's antirealism and esthetic artifice to an extreme and created a caricatured, commedia dell'arte, surrealist backdrop. The designs had very little to do with Mexico, and B. Arbatov's script depicted the Mexican revolutionary movement in very Russian terms, but it was certainly from his work on this production that Eisenstein derived some of his early ideas about Mexico. Set in the "Mexican town of Los Angeles [California]," the play begins with a small Mexican revolutionary group in exile, considering ways to raise desperately needed funds. A young mestizo worker appears. Unable to express himself adequately, he nonetheless makes it clear that he "burns with an inner fire," that although he is only a teenager, he has already lived through hell. His cold-hearted eyes express only hatred for the revolutionaries' enemies, and there seems little human in him. Finally it is agreed that he will fight in the ring in hopes of winning prize money to help the cause of the revolution. The third act, designed by Eisenstein, takes place at a circus, the backdrop for the prize fight. From Eisenstein's drawings of clowns, Japanese, Salvation Army members, cowboys, prostitutes, old ladies, and dancers, it is clear that he was more interested in the circus milieu than in the boxer and his story.[7] Having never seen Mexico, and with only an uncertain knowledge of California, Eisenstein's set and costumes were more theatrical and Russian than Mexican. But traces of the production would survive in *Que Viva Mexico!*

Eisenstein left Meyerhold's theater amicably in the fall of 1922, when he was admitted to Lev Kuleshov's innovative film workshop. It was in film that he found his life's work, and during the 1920s particularly, he made films which have become classics of the genre. While most of his work concerned Russia's recent revolutionary past, Eisenstein was occasionally reminded of Mexico. He was a great admirer of Douglas Fairbanks, for example, and the *Mark of Zorro*, which was set in California and had many visual references to Spain and Mexico, was a film Eisenstein certainly saw in Moscow.[8] No doubt Fairbanks told Eisenstein at least a little about Mexico during his visit to Moscow in 1926, but Eisenstein heard more from his friend Mayakovsky and was anxious to meet Diego Rivera when he arrived in Moscow in 1927. Eisenstein himself wrote later that his earliest interest in Mexico had derived from a series of photographs of the Mexican Day of the Dead published in the *Kölnische Illustrierte* many years before: Rivera's visit and Mayakovsky's stories stimulated his interest enormously.[9] Rivera gave Eisenstein a book of reproductions of his frescoes, and for a long while Eisenstein imagined Mexico visually in terms of Rivera's painting.[10] One of the first things Eisenstein did in Mexico City was to make still photographs of Rivera's frescoes, and he even made a short film of the Secretariat of Public Education murals. He said later that the frescoes were an important source of inspiration for the initial conceptualization of *Que Viva Mexico!* It should not be thought that Eisenstein was seriously planning a film about Mexico during the 1920s, however. He knew little about it and there seemed no prospects of his visiting the country or of filming there; above all, he had a number of other projects underway which were more immediately realizable. What made a film in Mexico more possible was the contract Eisenstein signed with Paramount Studios to come to North America in 1930.

Eisenstein had been interested throughout the 1920s in travelling outside the Soviet Union for personal as well as professional reasons. It was only in 1926 that he finally went abroad, to Berlin for the premiere of *Battleship Potemkin*. In 1929 he again asked permission to travel outside the USSR. To a certain extent, his request was the result of problems he had had with the editing of *October*, and the difficulties involved in finishing *The Old and the New*, which premiered in Moscow only after he and his associates had left the USSR.[11] Ostensibly, Eisenstein, his assistant director Grigorii Aleksandrov, and his cameraman Eduard Tisse went abroad to examine the new sound technology beginning to be applied to cinema in the West, although Eisenstein soon came to the conclusion that as yet sound had been used unimaginatively at best.[12] The center of new film technology was Hollywood, as Eisenstein realized when he visited the principal film studios in Western Europe. Hollywood films were often vapid and devoid of meaning, he felt, but they did have vitality and used all the most recent technological innovations. It was soon common knowlege that Eisenstein would be interested in working temporarily in California if a studio made him an attractive offer. After talking with agents of several U.S. studios, he, Aleksandrov, and Tisse left for the United States in May 1930, with Moscow's permission. In June they arrived in Los Angeles to begin working for Paramount Pictures under a contract that was very lucrative by Soviet standards.

Eisenstein's experience in Hollywood was not one he remembered with pleasure: he was constantly at loggerheads with the studio's staff and owners over the kind of film he should make. He and Paramount considered seven different projects. Some proposals were turned down immediately by lower-level studio executives; others Eisenstein spent considerable time planning, only to have the final scripts rejected by the studio heads. From the beginning, many observers had warned that the chances of Eisenstein's producing anything of value in the United States were slim. Herbert Marshall wrote in *Moscow News*, for example, that many European filmmakers had been invited to

Hollywood, "but never before has there been such a meeting of the antipodes as in this case. At what point could the Russian engineer-artist and scientific materialist meet the commercial made-to-pattern pseudo-romantic demands of the American financiers?"[13] Grigorii Aleksandrov recalled an exchange with Charlie Chaplin:

"Why did you come to Hollywood" he asked.

"We wanted to find out how films were made here."

"Nobody makes films here," said Chaplin, "here they make money through the aid of films. If you want to see how good films are made, then go to the place where *Battleship Potemkin* was made."[14]

In the end, Marshall and Chaplin proved to be correct. Six months in Hollywood yielded nothing but several uncompleted scripts. Eisenstein was disillusioned with the United States in general, and his experience with Paramount proved to be one of his life's major disappointments. It should be admitted, however, that Paramount was not entirely at fault. Eisenstein had no desire to be a conventional Hollywood director and refused to cooperate with the studio's public relations and publicity staffs. He was indifferent to his employers' concern with box-office receipts, and Paramount was leery of his insistence on using nonprofessional actors. Finally, as the result of a press campaign directed against him by a "Major Pease," Eisenstein became a political embarrassment to the studio. The studio heads began to feel that the best solution to what had become a major headache for them was to have Eisenstein return to the USSR as soon as possible, particularly as the economic crisis of the Great Depression seemed to worsen.

However anxious Paramount was to rid itself of him, Eisenstein did not plan to return immediately to Moscow. On the contrary, he had two alternatives in mind. Initially, he had hoped to travel back to the USSR by way of Japan, where he would make a film about a country which had interested him for several years.[15] More immediately attractive was a suggestion made to Eisenstein's film crew in New York. Rivera had organized a group of Mexican "cultural figures" to invite them to Mexico to make a film about Mexican history and the "life of the Mexican people."[16] The prospect was an exciting one to Eisenstein, and when he returned to Los Angeles to pack up his things, he began studying the country. With the aid of a local book dealer who had, he told Eisenstein, fought with Villa during the revolution, he read a number of books, including Martín Luis Guzmán's *The Eagle and the Serpent,* Louis Stevens's *Here Comes Pancho Villa,* and D. H. Lawrence's *The Plumed Serpent.* He put together a large collection of English-language books on Mexico and obtained several issues of Frances Toor's magazine, *Mexican Folkways,* which were particularly important in his early attempts at conceptualizing his film. The issues he read included articles dealing with Diego Rivera's murals, the photographs of Edward Weston and Tina Modotti, José Guadalupe Posada's prints, José Clemente Orozco's Preparatoria frescoes, as well as essays on Mexican folk music, the *penitentes,* who reenact Christ's journey to Calvary, and the *calaveras,* associated with the Day of the Dead celebration. Eisenstein was soon excited at the possibilities promised by a Mexican film. Within a few days of the termination of his contract with Paramount, and through the intercession of his friend Berthold Viertel, he was discussing with the leftist writer, Upton Sinclair, the possibility of a joint film venture in Mexico. Sinclair was attracted to the project immediately. He wrote later that he had not wanted Eisenstein to leave the United States without having accomplished anything of value.[17]

By the end of November 1930, Eisenstein had signed an agreement with Sinclair's wife, Mary, to make an independent motion picture in Mexico. The filming was to last between three and four months and to cost approximately $25,000; Mary Sinclair's brother, Hunter Kimbrough, was to act as business manager. As it turned out, Eisenstein was in Mexico fifteen months, the film's financing was a constant source of conflict between the Sinclairs and Eisenstein, and Kimbrough was a continuing irritant to everyone.[18]

Early in December, Eisenstein left for Mexico City by train. A *Los Angeles Times* reporter described the scene: "Capricious Hollywood, with but a shrugged shoulder, last Thursday saw enacted the first act finale of one of its strangest dramas. Mexico-bound, departing without fanfare, with but a handful of friends to see him off, was Sergei M. Eisenstein, the Russian motion-picture director, who came to conquer the film capital just six months ago."[19] Eisenstein had not conquered Hollywood, but he did not believe his failure had prejudiced his chances for success in Mexico. He told the reporter that his plans were

to go first to Mexico City, then to Yucatán and the Isthmus of Tehuantepec, and that he would most likely be gone from the United
States about two months.[20] He was, he said, quite excited by the prospect: "Mexico is primitive, close to the soil, its missions alone are
many pictures. One can only make a good film when one has the 'positive approach.' This is possible in a country like Mexico, where the
struggle of progress is still very real."[21] There too, like Mayakovsky,
Eisenstein hoped to experience again some of that heady revolutionary spirit he had felt in Russia over a decade earlier. As his train
pulled away, however, Eisenstein was not the heroic revolutionary
filmmaker he had been depicted as in the press, nor was he entirely
in control of the Mexican project. He had embarked upon what would
be one of the most personally meaningful, but also most frustrating
and disappointing, undertakings of his life.

A week after leaving Los Angeles, Eisenstein and his crew had
settled into the elegant Hotel Regis on Avenida Juárez in Mexico City.
The journey through northern Mexico had been fascinating. The austere landscape was entirely unexpected and therefore all the more impressive.[22] Eisenstein wrote later that what struck him most about the
landscape was its "linearity," a characteristic that stimulated him to
take up drawing, which he thought he had abandoned for good years
before.[23] This had an immediate influence on the type of film he made
in Mexico. He still had no script or plot, and in the early stages of
filming he was preoccupied with composition and movement within
the frame, the result of one of the earliest of his firsthand impressions
of Mexico.[24]

Eisenstein's plans had been congealing only imperfectly in his mind
during the railroad journey south, and he wrote later to his friend Lev
Monoszon that the most difficult part of his work in Mexico was trying to limit what he would film. There were, quite simply, so many
possibilities.[25] He continued to read about Mexico, adding to his growing collection of books.[26] Anita Brenner's *Idols Behind Altars* was by
far the most important in shaping his eventual plan for the film. He
read the book on the train and made extensive notations in it. He was
undoubtedly impressed particularly by the illustrations Brenner had
chosen, primarily photographs by Weston and Modotti. Eisenstein and
Weston did not meet while Eisenstein was in North America, but
Eisenstein's admiration for Weston's work is obvious in what remains

of *Que Viva Mexico!*, at times in the form of an *hommage*, at others as variations on a visual theme.[27] Weston's photographs prepared Eisenstein for what he saw in Mexico during the early days on the train and stimulated his imaginative response to the country's landscape. Eisenstein's Mexico would not be Weston's, of course, not even, on the whole, visually, but there was a clear intellectual interaction between the two.

Eisenstein and his crew began filming almost immediately after their arrival. They saw so much that was potentially valuable, and since they had no specific screenplay in mind, they felt they could not risk missing anything. By December 13, they were working at Guadalupe, on the anniversary of the appearance of the Virgin. That same afternoon they shot a *corrida* at the Plaza de Toros. Eisenstein wrote later that that first Mexican Sunday impressed him most because of the contrast between the "simplicity of the monumental" (the simple clothing of the Indians) and the "impetuousness of the baroque" (the elegant clothes of the bullfighters). Combined, he felt, they suggested nightmarish themes. This basic conflict and unity in Mexican life, seen most clearly on Sundays, he said, was his first real insight into Mexico:

> It was Mexico itself mixing into one Sunday festive element Christ's blood of the Matins in the cathedral with streams of bull's blood at the afternoon corrida in the city arena.
>
> Even tickets for the bullfight were graced with the image of the Madonna de Guadalupe whose quatercentary was marked not only by thousands of pilgrimages and by scores of South American cardinals in scarlet robes, but also by particularly sumptuous bullfights to the glory "de la Madre de Dios."[28]

Eisenstein felt that he understood Mexico better once he appreciated the curious duality of that first Sunday. He later said that through his Mexican drawings, which he was already producing at a furious rate, he hoped to express that duality on paper, to find a mathematically abstract and pure line, and to use that line to depict the sensual relations between human beings. These "sensual relations" became a primary concern, and eventually his drawings reached the bizarre extremes of the series depicting Salome drinking the blood of John the Baptist from a straw or the one dealing with Macbeth's murder of King Duncan. The Mexican inspiration for these drawings was seen best in the extensive group combining themes of St. Sebastian, the *corrida*, and the crucifixion of Christ.[29] Eisenstein never lost interest in what he considered these extremes of Mexican dualism.

In the midst of this flurry of activity, on December 21, Eisenstein and his crew were arrested. The reason, according to Eisenstein, was a fight they had had on the train with a man occupying their pullman compartment. When he refused to leave, Eisenstein and his associates tossed him out physically. As it happened, the man was the brother of the Federal District's chief of police, and he issued a complaint against them as soon as he reached Mexico City. There was more reason for the arrest than this fight alone, of course, because Eisenstein had been preceded by a considerable amount of publicity. There were rumors that he was a Russian agent, not a minor charge since there was still much hostility toward the USSR and its activities in Mexico. Some observers believed he planned to ask for asylum in Mexico, others that he was a German spy. All these suspicions were reinforced by the scurrilous letters "Major Pease" sent the government, accusing Eisenstein of every possible crime. The *New York Times*, reporting the incident, said that Eisenstein had been placed under detention "for examination on the charge of being a communist agent disguised as a movie man," and that the Secretariat of Foreign Relations was considering whether he should be deported: "The police declare that he came to Mexico on a tourist passport, which does not permit work, but that he has transacted business while in the country."[30] No one was sure what the government might decide, but in the end, through the intercession of the Spanish ambassador, Álvarez del Vayo, Eisenstein and his friends were released after a night in jail.[31] Three days of police surveillance, and cables of protest from Albert Einstein, George Bernard Shaw, and Charlie Chaplin, among others, finally resulted in a government announcement that Eisenstein was to be an honored guest in Mexico and that it would give him all the assistance it could for the completion of his film.

On the surface, everything must have looked encouraging to Eisenstein after this false start. However, the government insisted that the filmmakers negotiate an understanding with them over what could and could not be filmed in Mexico. Knowing Eisenstein's reputation, and remembering what other Russian Communists had said about them in the past, they feared that Eisenstein might depict the country and its revolutionary government in a negative light. Eisenstein knew the awkwardness of his position: in the early days of his stay in Mexico, he wrote Monoszon not in Russian but in English, telling him that it would be easier for the Mexican censors to translate and less "suspicious" in general than writing in Russian.[32] Eisenstein also cultivated members of the government, especially Secretary of Education Puig Casauranc and Secretary of Foreign Relations Estrada, although at the same time he maintained his newly established relationships with such radicals as Lombardo Toledano. Hedging its bets, the government in the end decided to appoint an "advisor" who could assure that nothing anti-government or anti-Mexican would be included in the film. Their choice was Adolfo Best Maugard, a man described by one contemporary as being "not in the least revolutionary."[33] He was a good designer, however, the former head of the Federal Department of Art Education and the author of a book on Mexican art. Best's professional and personal relationship with Eisenstein deteriorated after a number of months, but initially Eisenstein must have been pleased with the government's choice. He knew Best's work on Mexican popular arts and was particularly interested in his study of the linear quality of pre-Columbian art and architecture. As much as he might have disliked the idea of a government spy, Eisenstein would certainly have admitted that Best was by far the most helpful and well-informed agent the government could have selected.[34]

One other officially appointed assistant was the young writer and journalist Agustín Aragón Leiva, who was to be Eisenstein's guide, interpreter (none of the Russians knew Spanish well, if at all), and advisor on folklore and history. Leiva also became a great friend and admirer of Eisenstein and translated a number of his essays into Spanish.[35] Other Mexicans attached themselves to Eisenstein not because the authorities wished them to, but because they wanted to study his film techniques. His technical helpers, for example, included Emilio Fernández, who later became an important director, and Gabriel Figueroa, who began his work in film as Tisse's assistant. The most important thing they learned from Eisenstein was for the first time to "see" Mexico in cinematic terms.[36]

At various times, Eisenstein and his crew were visited by the artists Roberto Montenegro, Carlos Mérida, and Fernando Gamboa and his wife Susanna.[37] Eisenstein also renewed his acquaintance with

Rivera, although there was a certain amount of awkwardness about their meetings since Rivera had just been expelled from the PCM. Eisenstein came to know Rivera's wife, Frida Kahlo, and certainly must have seen and liked her highly individualistic work, although, oddly, neither of them commented extensively about the other.[38] Despite Rivera's ambiguous political position, Eisenstein had long before decided to use his works as a model for the visual imagery in at least one part of the film. Moreover, a fresco in the Secretariat of Public Education may have helped Eisenstein decide on how he wanted to employ sound in the film: Rivera's *Corrido de la Revolución* incorporated a poem by Gutiérrez Cruz into a scene depicting a revolutionary soldier singing to a group of his comrades. Eventually Eisenstein decided to choose a specific piece of Mexican popular music as background for each episode of the film. Rivera's politics might have been intermittently offensive to Moscow-allied Communists, but as inspiration for other Communist artists, his painting could still be acceptable.

By December 28, Eisenstein and his crew were again filming, this time a *corrida* in Puebla. By early January, it was decided that they would have to see more of the country for themselves before they would have any firm idea of what kind of film they should make. According to Aleksandrov, this was necessary because they wanted to make a unique film about Mexico: "Our friends tried to acquaint Eisenstein's *troika* with the real life of the people. We went many places located far from tourist routes, and discovered that Mexico which had not yet appeared on screen."[39] As his sketches from this period indicate, many of these locations were the cabarets, bars, and houses of prostitution that were an abiding interest for Eisenstein. His Mexican hosts were less enthusiastic about visiting such places and must have wondered about what Eisenstein really had in mind for his film. No doubt they were relieved when in January it was decided that the crew would begin their travels by going south to Taxco and Acapulco.

While filming colonial architecture in Taxco, Eisenstein met David Alfaro Siqueiros, in exile there at the time for participating in the May 1 demonstrations in Mexico City in 1930. Long a political radical, Siqueiros was nonetheless still in the early stages of his artistic career, and in Taxco he spent much of his enforced leisure systematizing his philosophy of art. Hart Crane Joined Eisenstein and Siqueiros in discussions of the commercialization of folk art in Mexico, esthetics, and the role of art in politics. Eisenstein and Siqueiros agreed that without political revolution, their two countries' revolutionary art could not exist. Each influenced the other intellectually as well. Siqueiros's biographers have traced Eisenstein's impact on the Mexican muralist's views of film imagery and its relations to art in general, and Eisenstein made clear references to Siqueiros's *Praying Women*, *Burial of a Worker*, and *Children's Games* in shots to be used in *Que Viva Mexico!*[40] A year after their meeting, Eisenstein was instrumental (with Brenner, Montenegro, and Crane) in mounting a large Siqueiros exhibition in Mexico City. He also wrote a statement for the show's publicity poster and spoke at the exhibition opening, calling Siqueiros a "marvelous synthesis" of the conception of the masses and its individually perceived representation.[41] Eisenstein admired Siqueiros greatly, his intuitive understanding of Mexico especially. Through his conversations with Siqueiros, Eisenstein believed he would be able to make a truer, more authentic film about Mexico.

From Taxco, the crew continued on to Acapulco, where they met with Pascual Ortiz Rubio, the nation's new president. Hoping to maintain good relations with the government, they spent a week divided between photographing Ortiz Rubio and making plans for filming an episode in the nearby mountains dealing with the revolution. From Acapulco they made a hurried trip by plane to Oaxaca to film damage from a recent earthquake, and in a matter of days they were back in Mexico City.[42] Eisenstein returned to planning the film, taking time out to meet with the *torero* David Liceaga and his brother, and with the composer and conductor Leopold Stokowski. Eisenstein suggested to Stokowski that he might compose music for the film, incorporating Spanish and Indian themes as a way of assuring authenticity. Stokowski apparently liked the idea in principle, although nothing more was spoken of the agreement. Since reading Brenner's *Idols Behind Altars* and seeing Rivera's *Corrido de la Revolución*, Eisenstein had been interested in using traditional Mexican music in the soundtrack. Eventually it was decided that having a Mexican composer do the music would be wisest (and perhaps most diplomatic), and by the middle of the year, Manuel Castro Padilla's name was put forward. Before music could be added, the film would have to have a more precise framework, of course, and at the beginning of 1931 it was at best only a collection of amorphous images.

Toward the end of January the crew left for Tehuantepec, where they were to remain until early March. Filming went slowly, however, because despite vaccinations against typhoid, cholera, and various other fevers, all the crew members at one time or another came down with tropical illnesses.[43] Eisenstein himself was so grateful to recover from one such fever that he had a *retablo* painted, attributing his cure, in a typically Mexican way, to the intercession of the Virgin of Guadalupe. They visited the villages of Jauchitlan and San Blas to film local festivals and were impressed at how little the area had been influenced by Europeans and how much of the old Tehuana matriarchal system remained. Eisenstein was amused to discover that in order to film there, the crew had to obtain a *propusk* (a permission form, or pass, so common in Soviet life) from the head of the village, an old woman. Eisenstein wrote later that many of the frescoes and paintings he had seen in Mexico City seemed to be coming to life in Tehuantepec.[44] He began sketching and produced dozens of drawings depicting life among the Tehuanas. The impact of Tehuantepec on Eisenstein was unexpectedly strong, and as his drawings indicate, he began to feel that the Garden of Eden, if it had existed anywhere, must have been located there.[45] He was fascinated with the area's vegetation and extreme fertility. He often drew human figures in the midst of tropical vegetation; the figures themselves are either plantlike or sinuously reptilian, with an implication of sensuousness and sexuality always present.[46]

The sensuality Eisenstein was so aware of in Tehuantepec was not something he expected to be as much moved by as he was:

> It is here in *tierra caliente* (burning earth) that I come to know the fantastic structure of prelogical, sensual thinking—not only from the pages of anthropological investigations, but from daily communion with those descendants of the Aztecs and Toltecs, Mayas, or Huichole who have managed to carry unharmed through the ages that meandering thought. It determined the astonishing traits of that miracle of Mexican primitive culture, as its tribes, to this day, stand beside the cradle of a cultural era that has not yet begun for them.[47]

He had first felt this new fascination with sensuality and the tropics during his stay in Acapulco:

The tropics responded to dreamy sensuality. The intertwining bronze bodies seemed to incarnate the latent roving of sensuality; here in the over-saturated, overgrown grasping of the lianas, male and female bodies wreathed and intertwined like lianas; they looked in the mirror and saw how the girls of Tehuantepec looked at themselves with black, almond-shaped eyes in the surface of the dreamy tropical creeks, and admired their flowered arrays, reflecting on the golden surface of their bodies. It seemed that embodied in me, and flooded with moonlight, was the rhythmically breathing abundance of the bodies of *esposas de soldados* clasped in the embraces of their husband-soldiers; bodies spread across the whole area of the little eight-sided courtyard of the small fortress guarding the Pacific Ocean port of Acapulco. (Guarding from whom? Unless it be the flights of pelicans, their heads tucked away on one side, plunging like arrows into the amber-colored water of the Gulf.)

The bodies breathe rhythmically and in unison. The very earth itself seems to be breathing, whitened here and there by a veil drawn modestly over a pair among the other bodies, gleaming black in the moonlight, that are not covered by anything. Bodies knowing no shame, bodies to whom what is natural for them is natural, and needs no concealment.

The sergeant and I slowly walk round the narrow parapet, with its narrow loopholes, looking down what appears, from above, to be a battlefield after the bugles have finished sounding the attack, a field of death cast in silver, but is, in fact a vast cornfield where the seed of countless generations of bronzed children is being sown.[48]

Eisenstein must have felt he had lost touch with the romantic feelings of his earlier years. The gentle sentimentality, the love for simple human beings, the overwhelming sensuality indicated by these passages were exceedingly unlike what one might have expected from the director of *Strike* and *October*. Nature, and human beings living in harmony with nature, became for the first time a major concern. In the film shot in Tehuantepec, individual frame compositions reinforce Eisenstein's new appreciation for sensuality, and for symbols of femininity: the ovals and circles of water jars and women's faces

almost overshadow the verticals of palm trees and the knife shapes
of tropical vegetation. The hammocks that had emphasized masculin-
ity in *Potemkin* here take on a more sensual, rounded, and feminine
quality.

Never had Eisenstein's conceptions been as romantic as they were
in Tehuantepec, and many have suspected that his new infatuation
with sensuality was the result of some personal romantic experience
he had while in Mexico. Such speculation is frequently tied also to
the question of Eisenstein's own sexual orientation and the extent to
which it may have impinged on his creative life. Marie Seton contended that Eisenstein absolutely had no romantic involvements while
he was in Mexico, but she was not anxious to discuss forthrightly the
rumors of homosexuality that constantly surrounded him.[49] Eisenstein's biographers have always been more than a little reticent on
this issue, and for understandable reasons: homosexuality, was and
continues to be a serious offense in the USSR, one that could be pun-
ished severely should the authorities wish to. There was also a certain amount of prudery and embarrassment involved as well as a belief that Eisenstein's reputation might be damaged. The question comes
up particularly in Mexico because of his preoccupation with sexuality there, and because he made a large number of sketches of homosexual acts in Mexico.[50] Yet it is probably true that he did not "fall
in love" with any single individual in Mexico and that there as elsewhere he succeeded in sublimating his sexual desires, of whatever
sort, into his other activities. Eisenstein had been greatly impressed
by Freud's contention that Leonardo da Vinci had sublimated his sexual drives into artistic and scientific creativity, and he mentioned on
occasion that this kind of sublimation was basic to his character and
essential to his artistic career.

Eisenstein's fascination with the variety of sexual experience was
clearer during the fifteen months he spent in Mexico than at any other
time during his life, although perhaps this was true only because he
had fewer restraints on expressing those interests in Mexico than in
the USSR. According to his contemporaries, Eisenstein often appeared
rather embarrassed by sex, and had been since he was a youth. It was
felt by some of his amateur psychoanalyst friends that his sketching
and clowning about sex were Eisenstein's means of working his embarrassment out through a kind of therapy. Katherine Anne Porter

mentioned his "bawdy" clowning in her semifictional story, "Hacienda," and there exists a photograph of Eisenstein with a lewd grimace
on his face, "riding" a large cactus which looks a great deal like an
enormous, engorged penis.[51] Eisenstein also had a deep need to understand both the male and female aspects of sexuality and the mutation
of traditional sex roles. His friends always remembered his love for
cheap, erotic theaters, houses of prostitution, and sailors' bars. His
sketches reflected his concerns: he produced dozens of erotic drawings based on the crucifixion of Christ, for example, many of which
were considered "blasphemous" by those who saw them.[52] A series
depicting the procession of the statue of the Virgin in Tehuantepec
included one with a platform bearer kissing one figure and being fel-
lated by another (apparently male) figure. Fellatio was particularly
prominent in the sketches. Christ's having fellatio performed on him
while on the cross by both women and men, appeared time after time
in Eisenstein's drawings.[53] Clearly Eisenstein connected sex with religion in Mexico, and like Mayakovsky, he was interested in the inconsistent role played by the clergy: he did a series of sketches of priests
and their illegitimate children. Eisenstein said later that the contrast
between official morality and the failings of individuals stuck in his
mind because of the "cynical and slightly soiled" priest he had seen
at San Juan de los Remedios near Mexico City, who "went off on his
motorcycle every Thursday, without fail, to Mexico City's brothels."[54]

In many of these drawings, particularly the religious ones, there
was an obvious homoerotic quality. An entire series, for example, dealt
with the relationship between Christ and Judas, which Eisenstein saw
as an extended lovers' quarrel. Elsewhere men are depicted giving
money to other men, clearly with sex in mind.[55] In other drawings
a man is shown masturbating while peering through binoculars at
naked fishermen casting their nets. What all this meant with respect
to Eisenstein's emotional makeup or his psychosexual yearnings and
desires cannot be determined. What can be said, however, is that the
freedom from inhibitions and the lack of social and political constraints Eisenstein felt in Mexico allowed his imagination to develop
unencumbered. He could never have admitted this openly, but secretly he must have been grateful for the opportunity to express his
innermost feelings to the extent he did in Mexico.

As his work in Tehuantepec progressed, Eisenstein decided that at least one section of the film would include scenes celebrating the physical act of love. On the isthmus, this could be done by filming the courting and marriage of a young couple. The idea prompted him to imagine similar relationships in the sections of the film that were to be made in other parts of the country. This male-female theme eventually was to be used throughout the film, and each section, Eisenstein decided, would have two identifiable lovers, whose romantic relationship would take place before a backdrop of the film's overall dramatic development: "Concepción and Abundio, the ideal Indian couple uncontaminated by an alien civilization; Sebastian and María, the victims of the Spanish colonial system of peonage; the matador and a Queen of the bullring, expressive of Spanish colonial life; and Juan and Pancha, lovers involved in the terrible days of the Mexican Revolution."[56]

A more important aspect of the film was also becoming clear in Tehuantepec. It was a problem that for Eisenstein was the main social issue in Mexico—the position of women in society.[57] He felt it first in Tehuantepec, where women held the dominant position and men were procreators, nothing more. For someone as interested as Eisenstein in the varying status of men and women, what he saw among the Tehuanas was a revelation, and he began to question the strength of the machismo he had seen paraded so often in other sections of Mexico. It became one of the principal motifs in his plans for Que Viva Mexico![58]

Early in March, the Tehuantepec filming was completed, and after another brief stay in Mexico City, Eisenstein and his associates left by air for Yucatán. In Mérida, Eisenstein wanted to film a corrida with the Liceaga brothers, who were on their way to Spain for an extended stay. This would form part of the "Fiesta" episode, the first of the "novellas" making up the film. The ceremonial character of the bullfight and the psychological reactions of the audience were essential to Eisenstein's interpretation of the three centuries of Spanish rule in Mexico, giving him an opportunity to depict the typically Spanish, self-centered, idolized matador and his milieu. The matador's world included not only the corrida, but Catholic Christianity as well, a religion imported into Mexico, yet made typically Mexican by the Indians. At Umán and elsewhere, Eisenstein hoped to film what he believed was the duality of Mexican Christianity: the genuine religious feelings of the ordinary believer as well as the evils of the Catholic church's dogma and hierarchy. There is little doubt, as some feared at the time, that he planned to use the footage of Archbishop Pascual Díaz satirically, and many of his other shots of the priests were chillingly critical in intent. Eisenstein treated the religious devoutness of the Indians more sympathetically, however. Such generosity toward religion could be found nowhere in Eisenstein's films before this time. He especially wanted to show how the old and new faiths were interconnected. Traditional pre-Columbian practices had been absorbed into Christian rites, and the Spaniards built Catholic churches above the sites of former temples.[59] The better he understood Mexican Indian Christianity, the less Eisenstein's approach to it was intellectual and scientific. It was more intuitive, an understanding unprecedented in his career. While Eisenstein had always used Christian metaphors in his films, the Mexican experience left him with a more emotional and even religious approach to art.[60]

In his attempt to be true to his subject, Eisenstein utilized Christian imagery and motifs extensively in his work in Yucatán. His screenplay, sketches, and filming all show his fascination with the practice of Mexican religion. He hoped to tie the old Mexican legend of the Lord of Chalma into the film's matador episode, for example.[61] He completed an extraordinary number of religious sketches in Yucatán, many depicting scenes from the Old Testament, but more often dealing with Jesus, and in the churriguerresque style of late colonial Mexico. The drawings which remain indicate that he was interested most in three episodes from the life of Christ: the relationship of Judas and Jesus, discussed above, the miracle of St. Veronica, and the crucifixion. St. Veronica Eisenstein depicted wryly as the "protector of photographers" and the "first photo-reporter" because of the image of Christ that became imprinted on her scarf. Most numerous, and least favorable toward Christianity, were the sketches of the crucifixion, in which Christ was shown as an emaciated and unpleasant figure, with an evil and abnormal influence on human beings. In many of the drawings Eisenstein speculated on Christ's psychological makeup, and in others he approached the crucifixion with a sort of bizarre humor. One series showed Christ reaching into his chest to hand out the "divine message" to his disciples; another had him using a spigot projecting out of his side to give them the blood of his body. To be fair, Eisenstein was not only "perverse" and "blasphemous," as Sinclair might have said. He was also interested in the compositional possibilities of the crucifixion, with its strong verticals and diagonals. All these sketches were Eisenstein's immediate responses to the extremes of Mexican Christianity. Neither entirely Mexican, nor solely Eisenstein's, their influence was seen in one form or another in the film's "Fiesta" section.

It has already been noted that Eisenstein used drawing to work out a number of creative frustrations, and in Yucatán it helped him develop a general outline for the film. He would organize it around novellas which would depict the "living history" of Mexico. The source of this idea lay in Brenner's contention that Mexicans were simultaneously primitive and modern. Eisenstein himself wrote later that in Mexico "we see existing simultaneously side by side *mores* and ways of living which, socially and culturally, correspond to different stages of human society."[62] What he had found in Yucatán seemed to confirm Brenner's belief in the juxtaposition and coexistence of the pagan and Christian. It became the theme around which his plans for the script coalesced.[63] The Mexican past, he believed, could be depicted without distortion and dishonesty by filming the present, and as his assistant Leiva wrote, time itself would be dissolved "into uncertainty and vagueness."[64] Furthermore, Mexico's geographic extremes could be used to show the nature of conflict in the society, and the conditions of social groups making up Mexican life would be tied to it. This was as specific as Eisenstein became about his plans in Yucatán, but this conceptualization was a considerable step forward from the formlessness of his earlier approach.

An important feature of Mexico's past was the Indian civilizations that had flourished before the Conquest, and Eisenstein had come to Yucatán not just to film what remained of Spanish colonial ways of life, but also to record the area's ancient Maya ruins. During March, the crew worked at Celestún, Chichén Itzá, and Izamal, and it was at these sites that Eisenstein began to appreciate firsthand the significance of the image of death.[65] Each of Mexico's cultural traditions, the Indian and the Spanish, had contributed to a unique attitude toward death, he felt. One of the frescoes which had impressed Eisenstein most in Mexico City was Siqueiros's *Burial of a Worker*, depicting men carrying a simple wooden coffin on their shoulders. At

Izamal, Eisenstein decided to incorporate this image into the first section of the film, to indicate how the past dominated the present in Yucatán[66] and to introduce the recurrent theme of death as it dominated Mexican society both before and after the Conquest. He also recreated at Izamal the *penitente* procession of Amecameca, where hundreds of Indians relived the journey to Calvary. On their knees they climbed the steps to the dome of the church and there reenacted the crucifixion. Christ's transcending death seemed to show the Indians that death was an inextricable part of life. Eisenstein shot an enormous amount of footage of these religious and funeral processions in Yucatán, and had he been able to edit them himself, they probably would have been some of the most moving sequences in the film, a clear representation of his more tolerant understanding of religion. They were certainly essential to the ultimate plans for *Que Viva Mexico!*, however somber they might seem.

In May, the crew left Yucatán to work in the central plateau. Filming had already exceeded the time limit specified in the agreement with Mary Sinclair, and Eisenstein was beginning to realize that the project would take much longer than he had originally anticipated. He was determined to go on as long as money was available.[67] Local labor troubles complicated their journey, but eventually the crew reached the pulque hacienda of Tetlapayac, where they would spend four months making the "Maguey" episode.[68] The hacienda belonged to Julio Saldivar, a friend of Leiva's, and was located near Apam in the state of Hidalgo, about two hours by train from Mexico City. Visually, the fields of maguey, the clothing of the Indians, the volcano-dominated landscape, would be perfect for his purposes, Eisenstein felt. What he was not prepared for was his emotional reaction to the hacienda and its people. According to Marie Seton, Tetlapayac was one of the few places in the world where Eisenstein felt completely and immediately at home:

> "The moment I saw Tetlapayac, I knew it was the place I had been looking for all my life," Eisenstein told me.
>
> I remember the tone of his voice. Singularly controlled and modulated even when speaking of his most painful experiences, Sergei Mikhailovich could not speak of Tetlapayac without his voice breaking into tones of excitement and pain though he had

not seen the hacienda for years. He never spoke of any other place, experience or person in such tones. Like a man haunted by a lost love, he would carry in his pocket the letters he received telling him of what subsequently happened at Tetlapayac.[69]

Seton may or may not have been correct in presenting Tetlapayac as the central experience of Eisenstein's life in Mexico, but the hacienda did provide the setting for the principal episode in the film, depicting events leading up to the Mexican Revolution of 1910.

"Maguey" was to combine the still-living traditional beliefs of the Indians with the dramatic story of a group of peons coming to revolutionary consciousness and taking part in the early stages of the revolution. The dramatic development itself was to be fairly straightforward, as we shall see, but the levels of imagery in this section of the film were remarkably complicated in their semiotic references. Eisenstein planned to intercut the hacienda's Corpus Cristi celebration with the main plot line, for example. The three dying revolutionaries were given the same compositional treatment as the Izamal *penitente* crucifixions. The revolutionaries' bodies and blood were to be equated with Christ's. Modern human sacrifice was related to pre-Columbian human sacrifice through the *aguamiel* harvest, at the end of which the maguey dies in the production of life- and oblivion-giving pulque.[70] The shots of the heroine, María, with the maguey cacti behind her were modern, celluloid depictions of the traditional image of the Virgin of Guadalupe. Above all, the composition in this episode was oriented around triangles, with obvious references to the Christian trinity. Although Eisenstein disingenuously insisted that this motif was purely accidental, the triangle was apparently another of his keys to understanding Mexico. According to Seton,

> he said he had been greatly interested in the way the Mexicans (and he thought it was perhaps true of all people) were unconsciously affected by certain ancient forms of composition, for example, the triangle. In regards to this last statement, it is the basis of Eisenstein's composition in the film; and it is startlingly evident in Mexico that numerical symbolism, and the triangle form, runs as a connecting thread between the most diverse tribes and districts, so that, in fact, it becomes the only coherent pattern in a country of the greatest diversity.[71]

Balmont had remarked on this, of course, and Best Maugard had tried to explain it systematically. In Tetlapayac, as elsewhere in the film that was developing in his mind, Eisenstein was hoping to combine still-vital ancient traditions with the country's modern way of life. Above all, he wanted to be the first one to do it in film.

If triangular shot composition was essential to the "Maguey" episode, so too was the juxtaposition of male and female. The sensuous, feminine Tehuantepec episode was in direct contrast to the aggressively masculine maguey novella. Yet even within this novella, Eisenstein constantly contrasted masculine and feminine images. In the sequence devoted to the *aguamiel* harvest, for instance, the maleness of the maguey spikes and knives, and the aggressive thrusting actions of the workers is contrasted to, and complimented by, the femaleness of nurturing, of rounded gourds and white clouds.[72]

Enriching the triangular arrangement and the male-female dichotomy, there was to be a clear evolution of action and composition in this episode. From an extreme simplicity at the beginning, Eisenstein planned to move to an almost "baroque complexity and maximum force"[73] at the end, when the Corpus Cristi celebrations and the revolution were to take place simultaneously. This growth in complexity is expressed even in the visual textures of images, stronger in this part of the film than in any other, and modulated dramatically.[74]

It is possible that the "Maguey" novella became so complex and multilayered because so little of the time Eisenstein and his crew spent at Tetlapayac was devoted to filming. The summer of 1931 was extraordinarily wet, and at times Tetlapayac was completely isolated by the torrential rains. The crew could not film in the rain and were able to plan their work more carefully in advance. Eisenstein previously had filmed anything that might be even remotely useful, but now, because of pressure from the Sinclairs over expenses, he was more careful. As before, he worked out much of his planning for the episode while sketching. He produced an extensive series of sketches of bull crucifixions, of matadors and bulls being crucified together, of Veronica, of Judith decapitating Holofernes, and above all, and perhaps oddly, of Macbeth murdering King Duncan. Several themes were intermingled in the sketches. They depicted remorse, ambition, female aggression, cannibalism (less medieval Scottish than pre-Conquest Aztec), even pregnancy and new life developing from death

(Lady Macbeth was often pregnant in Eisenstein's drawings). But again, most striking in the sketches was the intertwining of sex and death, and of death and life.[75] The drawings were among the most disturbing Eisenstein ever produced, yet their themes derived directly from the work he was anticipating once the weather improved. Unsettling as they were, they had direct parallels in the sequences filmed at Tetlapayac and elsewhere in Mexico.

In the meantime, Eisenstein and his project were being given a great deal of attention in the Mexican and foreign press. In mid-June, an article by A. F. Bustamente in *El Universal Ilustrado* was as much an attempt to assuage the doubts the Sinclairs had about the project as to publicize it. The article included stills from the film, taken in Mérida and Tehuantepec, noted all the important and talented painters, sculptors, musicians, photographers, and writers who had come to visit Eisenstein at Tetlapayac, and stressed that when the film was completed, it would redound to the glory and prestige of Mexico. Bustamente also spoke of Eisenstein's exceedingly upstanding personal life: he was "jovial, intelligent, sensitive, a polyglot," a person who neither smoked nor drank, and who spent all his waking hours working or studying.[76]

Bustamente obviously wished to counteract the increasingly negative reports Kimbrough was sending back to his sister and brother-in-law in Pasadena. Kimbrough's personal relationship with the Russian filmmakers had not been good at the beginning and was not improving. They argued constantly, and soon a barrage of letters was exchanged between the United States and Mexico. Eisenstein attacked Kimbrough as a drunkard and an embarrassment to the project. Kimbrough complained about the unconscionable extravagance of the Russians. As the situation became more and more heated, Eisenstein felt he had to defend his actions to Monoszon, who represented the investment made in the picture by Amtorg, the Soviet trading agency. Eisenstein assured him that they were all working hard and, despite rumors he might have heard, were not living like sybarites.[77] It is more likely Monoszon might have heard other rumors, however. In the eyes of many observers, the constant coming and going of guests and visitors had turned Tetlapayac into less a film site than a kind of permanent circus.[78] Eisenstein suffered from a recurrent illness, Saldivar and his fiancée argued repeatedly about their future, and in July, one of the actors accidentally shot and killed his sister. It was against this background that Kimbrough decided to report in person to the Sinclairs. When he returned, conditions were still essentially the same, except that Tetlapayac's guests now included Diego Rivera, the art historian Elie Faure, the artist Ione Robinson, and the novelist Katherine Anne Porter.[79]

Oddly enough, considering the confusion and agitation at the hacienda, it was at this time that Eisenstein began to put together the first version of the screenplay for Que Viva Mexico![80] He now anticipated a ten-reel film, with music composed by Saldivar (ostensibly, at least, a well-known musician). The basic themes were to be death and love, body and spirit, and the interactions between them. Eisenstein had also settled on a sequence for the film: first would be a prologue (the sequences filmed in Yucatán); second would be "Fiesta" (the Spanish section, incorporating the corrida and Indian Christianity); third, the "Sandunga" (Tehuantepec); fourth, "Maguey" (Tetlapayac); fifth, "Soldadera" (the revolution); and last, "Death Day" (the conclusion tying all the other episodes together). Eisenstein had decided to structure his film around an idea prompted by a chapter in Susan Smith's Made in Mexico about the sarapes of Oaxaca. He had written Sinclair about the idea when it had first struck him: "Do you know what a 'sarape' is? A sarape is the striped blanket that . . . every Mexican wears. So striped and violently contrasting are the cultures in Mexico running next to each other and at the same time being centuries away . . . we took the contrasting independent adjacence of its violent colors as the motif for constructing our film."[81] These "violent colors" also suggested contrasting musical themes, and Eisenstein imagined the film in symphonic terms as well, with the introduction being the largo, "Sandunga" the andante, "Maguey" the allegro tragico, and so forth.[82] At the center of the film would be the two contrasting novellas, "Sandunga" and "Maguey." The other episodes would comment on and complement those two. Eisenstein could not be specific about details, since he knew that Sinclair did not want a "radical" film that would be difficult to market, and there was always the problem of the Mexican government's censorship.[83] Since Eisenstein was never able personally to edit and do the montage on the film shot in Mexico, the script (with a few additions and comments) is the best indication of his plans for *Que Viva Mexico!* and deserves to be discussed in some detail.

The prologue was to depict the link between the past and the present: to show how in Yucatán an earlier way of life still prevailed and to express the old pre-Columbian hopelessness in the face of death. Eisenstein planned to do this by intercutting shots of modern Indians with ancient carvings. The expressions on the faces of the living were to be those of the pre-Conquest sculptures, living faces turned to stone, accompanied by the music of native drums and traditional Mayan songs.[84] The principal action in this episode was to be the funeral sequence inspired by Siqueiros's fresco, and Eisenstein and his crew filmed repeated versions of the procession through the henequen fields. The funeral and the overwhelming presence of death in the prologue, Eisenstein wrote, would only "be revealed in the contents of the four following stories and of the Finale at the end of these."[85] The dead hand of the past would only be raised by centuries of struggle, and by the revolution.[86]

"Fiesta," either the second or third "novella" in the film, was to depict the "weirdness, romance, and glamour" of Spanish Mexico. It would be set in a period shortly before the 1910 revolution, using sequences filmed in Mexico City, Xochimilco, Mérida, Taxco, Puebla, and Cholula. Eisenstein planned to edit this section in such a way as to show the extraordinary richness of the Mexican rococo style. It would include the Santiago *danzantes,* the *penitentes,* the austere images of Jesuit and Franciscan monks posed with skulls, Christian religious symbols of death and its transcendence, and at least sections of a mass said by the archbishop. The religious fervor of Sunday morning would be followed by the *corrida* in the afternoon. The finery and extravagance associated with the bullfight, and the frivolous rendezvous of a picador and his married girl friend, were to be highly romantic, accompanied by the music of marimbas.[87]

"Sandunga" would use the film taken in "dreamlike and unchanging" Tehuantepec, where "time runs slowly under the dreamy weaving of the palms and costumes, and customs do not change for years and years."[88] The episode was to begin slowly, in the early morning, with the awakening first of the parrots, then of the other animals of the isthmus; the monkeys, pelicans, crabs, turtles, and alligators would all establish the dominance of nature over man. Finally humans would appear, Indian maidens in the river, girls in canoes, bringing Gauguin's Tahitian paintings to life, but accompanied by the region's traditional languorous music, the "Sandunga." The young Tehuana, Concepción, ponders her hoped-for marriage to Abundio and prepares the bananas she will sell at the market for the gold coins that will constitute her dowry. In the evening, at a village dance, Abundio and Concepción are engaged officially.[89] The preparations for the wedding were apparently to be shown in great detail: the examination of the dowry by the matchmaker and the groom's mother, the dressing, cooking, joking by the couple's friends (cows dressed in masquerade costumes, goats in bow ties), and always the dominant role of women. The episode was to end with the Tehuanas' traditional wedding customs, and the last shot would show Concepción and Abundio some years later, laughing with their young son, and arranged in the triangle Eisenstein planned to use throughout the film.[90]

Eisenstein hoped to show in "Sandunga" that despite Spanish rule, much of the sensual, innocent world of the Indians still survived in Mexico. "Maguey," on the other hand, would convey precisely the opposite. Like "Fiesta," this episode was to depict events taking place shortly before the outbreak of the 1910 revolution. Eisenstein explained that it was to be characterized by aggressiveness, arrogance, and austerity, its accompanying music the sad and slow "Alabado," sung in the mornings and evenings on the plateau. The plot was simple: a young Indian couple are betrothed, a friend of the estate's owner rapes the girl, the boy fights back, is captured, and killed. Since the bad weather had given him considerable time to experiment with the plot, Eisenstein apparently did not intend to change this basic story line once he returned to California for the final editing.[91] This episode was also the one most influenced by Eisenstein's preparatory reading.[92] Deceptively straightforward in plot and individual frame composition, "Maguey" was certainly expected to be the film's central episode. And for those who have seen all the film saved from the project, the visual imagery of this novella remains the most striking.

Shooting for these sections had been completed for the most part by the time Eisenstein wrote this synopsis. The next novella, however, had received only preliminary planning. Accompanied by the music of "Adelita," "Soldadera" would depict the victory of the 1910 revolution. His approach, Eisenstein wrote Sinclair, was to be that of John Reed, whose descriptions of the revolution would form the basis for much of the novella.[93] As in "Maguey" and "Sandunga," the dramatic development was to focus on a woman. In "Soldadera," it was Pancha, fighting with her husband in the revolution, but for what she was not sure.[94] Eisenstein intended for her to lose one husband, then find another, the struggle continuing all the while. Almost none of this episode was filmed, due to financial arguments with Sinclair and personal conflicts with Kimbrough. This is doubly unfortunate because Eisenstein considered it so important to the film's final makeup, and because he had imagined it in detail. Eisenstein wanted especially to show in "Soldadera" his debt to the works of José Clemente Orozco. He and Orozco never met, but Eisenstein considered his National Preparatory School frescoes in Mexico City the best such painting he had seen anywhere in the world.[95] Tisse wrote as well that the "technique" the crew planned to use in "Soldadera" was based on Orozco. Seton added that even more than Orozco's style, Eisenstein appreciated his imagery, imagery tied to a belief that the earth was governed by two equal but opposed realities, one eternally destructive, the other eternally constructive. These ideas were not adequately assimilated into the film, but since "Soldadera" was never really begun, Eisenstein continued to speculate on how the episode might be worked out. As late as 1947 he was still suggesting refinements to the screenplay that incorporated the inspiration he derived from Orozco.[96] Since Pancha was to unite symbolically the factions struggling in the revolution, Eisenstein felt the failure to film this episode was a special blow to any plans he had for ever completing the film.

Eisenstein wanted the film to conclude with the celebration of the Day of the Dead. This epilogue would tie all the novellas together. Beginning slowly, it would build and accelerate, from a cemetery to a carnival to the film's final message: "The great wisdom of Mexico about death. The unity of death and life. The passing of the one and the birth of the next one. The eternal circle. And the still greater wisdom of Mexico: the *enjoying* of this eternal circle. Death Day in Mexico."[97] This understanding of the equilibrium of life and death was the aspect of Mexican life Eisenstein loved best, and it was the one influenced most by the works of José Guadalupe Posada, whom Eisen-

stein called "the incomparable."[98] The epilogue was to be an odd conglomeration showing postrevolutionary progress, smiling and healthy
children, generals, and the *calaveras*—toys and sweets in the shape
of human skeletons. What Eisenstein had in mind was not entirely
understood by those working with him, and certainly not by Sinclair
and his investors, to whom it seemed terribly morbid. In the film's
first "libretto," Eisenstein had stressed the positive aspects of Mexico
during Calles's rule, but his principal intent was to mislead the government censors.[99] The final shot of the film would be the smiling face
of an Indian boy, Eisenstein promised, and the epilogue was to be
filled with images of life, vitality, and dynamism: revolving wheels,
dancing, the *calaveras*, overflowing barrels of pulque, a celebration
of modern Mexico. Death was to be there as well, however, at the
grave sites, in the skulls, and in the somber black clothes of the priests
and *calaveras* dancers. Eisenstein wanted to connect the two themes
of life and death, but in a way that would make a political statement
not flattering to the government, and perhaps even objectionable to
Sinclair's easily bruised political sensitivities. While the children
would wear skull masks, when they pulled them away, their own smiles
would dominate the screen. The costumed politicians, bishops, priests,
hacendados, and presidents, recognizable from earlier parts of the
film, would remove their masks only to show skulls. Mexico's rulers
were the truly dead, morally and spiritually. Its children were the
country's future. "The film began with the realm of death. With victory of life over death, over the influences of the past, the film ends."[100]

Eisenstein sent this fairly complete screenplay off to mollify Sinclair, hoping that he and his crew could soon complete the remainder
of the shooting, then return to Hollywood for the cutting, editing, and
sound synchronization. At the end of August, with Best Maugard's
resignation and his replacement by Saldivar, the "Death Day" filming
began in Mexico City.

The arguments with Kimbrough and Sinclair, his illnesses, the news
of Mayakovsky's suicide, even the filming of "Death Day" itself made
Eisenstein feel much older than he was.[101] Related was the fact that
the triangular motif, now more clearly indicating the concept of the
eternal circle of life and death, began to play an ever more important
role in the composition for the Death Day sequences. Eisenstein was
becoming increasingly concerned personally with the idea of immor-

tality, of how an individual could overcome death. Death had been a significant theme in all Eisenstein's films, and it had been "overcome" in a variety of ways. His work in Mexico led Eisenstein to believe that for an artist, creativity was a way to overcome the limitations of death, to transcend it.[102] This concept, while not unique to Eisenstein, had an important impact on the film he attempted to make there.

Eisenstein and the crew spent September filming "Death Day," more footage for "Fiesta," and what was hoped to be the final work at Tetlapayac. At the end of the month they visited President Ortiz Rubio to discuss preparations for filming a documentary for the government, part of the price Eisenstein had to pay for its cooperation. In October, Eisenstein, Tisse, and their friend Montenegro set off for the Pacific Coast to do some preliminary work on "Soldadera." Meanwhile, however, relations between Eisenstein and Kimbrough worsened because of the Sinclairs' growing concern about cost overruns. Early in October Kimbrough telegraphed Eisenstein that the Sinclairs were anxious for him to finish his work as soon as possible and return to Pasadena for the final editing. At the end of the month, Sinclair himself wrote Eisenstein, more or less repeating those instructions. Sinclair mentioned that he had persuaded the Soviet film organization Amkino and Monoszon to invest an additional $25,000 in the film, but that Eisenstein would have to send them a detailed budget for the remainder of the picture if he were to be allowed to continue. Sinclair did not attempt to hide his frustration:

> Suffice it to say that I have given most of my time to your problems for eleven months—ever since I dropped everything else and began sending telegrams to keep you from being shipped off to Japan in three days. I have worked so hard and been forced to worry so much that I have had two serious spells of illness.
>
> I have set before me the goal that a great artist was to be permitted to make one picture the way he wanted it. I am sticking to this resolve to the last, but it can only be done in case the great artist will exercise some restraint upon himself.
>
> No doubt you have your heart set upon colossal and wonderful things for the last two episodes, but sit down now with your friends and figure how you can do it upon a smaller scale.[103]

The problem of finances, and the suspicion in Pasadena that Eisenstein was not doing all he could to limit the costs of the film, caused the final break between Eisenstein and Sinclair and led to the destruction of *Que Viva Mexico!*

Most of October and November the crew spent in Mexico City, working on the film commissioned by the government. Progress was slow because of turmoil in the administration in October, and because the crew had to gain the trust not only of Ortiz Rubio, but of the *jefe máximo* himself, Calles. Since Eisenstein hoped to be permitted to use government troops for the "Soldadera" episode, he made a special effort to convince Calles of his good intentions.[104] He apparently succeeded, because the second half of November was spent filming Ortiz Rubio and doing other work commissioned by the PNR. While Eisenstein certainly planned to use this material ironically, his spending so much time with political leaders and following their orders led many onlookers to wonder about his political allegiance.[105] The suspicion grew that he had sold out to a government condemned by the Comintern and was making for them what to all intents and purposes was a fascist film. Leiva wrote to his North American friend, Seymour Stern:

> Eisy [Eisenstein] has got in acquaintance with the racketeer in chief [General] Calles, he is in the film, altogether with the imbecile President [Obregón (sic)] we have. I see this as dangerous stuff for the standing of Eisy among the advanced people, as it is no more a secret that Calles is the wealthiest Mexican, a fascist of the worst kind. . . . I cannot imagine [him] in the film otherwise than in a sarcastic mood. We must refrain from doing any comment until we'll see the film complete.[106]

Making Eisenstein's political position even more awkward was his continuing association with Rivera. Rivera was employed by the government to paint the National Palace staircase fresco, was still isolated from the PCM, and was soon to be denigrated in the Soviet press as an apostate. Such friendship could only compromise Eisenstein in the eyes of Mexican and foreign Communists.

Soon serious concern about Eisenstein's political loyalties developed in Moscow. On November 21, Stalin himself sent Sinclair a letter in which he stated that Eisenstein "is thought to be a deserter who broke off with his own country."[107] The Soviet Union had changed a great deal since Eisenstein left in 1929, and coercion and conformity were much more prevalent. As long as Eisenstein remained in the New World, there was little Stalin could do to control his activities. He did not want Eisenstein to renounce his allegiance to the USSR, but he was uncertain what Eisenstein's plans were. He was apparently using theories and techniques in his Mexican film that were now being discredited in the Soviet Union, and reports from abroad indicated that he was consorting with reactionaries, Trotskyites, and enemies of the Soviet Union.[108] Rumors that the film was becoming a celebration of "fascism" were spreading, and Moscow feared that Eisenstein was preparing to defect. Since he was by far the Soviet film director best known abroad, his defection would not only set an example for other Soviet citizens but would have serious implications for the Soviet Union's international image. Finally, working behind the scenes in Moscow to bring Eisenstein back into line was the new director of the Soviet film industry, Boris Shumiatsky. If the film were completed in the West and released abroad to favorable reviews, Eisenstein's personal prestige would rise and Shumiatsky's attempts at regimenting Soviet cinema would be made more difficult. Much in the USSR was working against Eisenstein, and little was working in his favor.

Complicating Eisenstein's position was an article Edmund Wilson published in the *New Republic* early in November. Wilson praised Eisenstein but criticized the current condition of the Soviet film industry:

> Eisenstein in Mexico . . . was having a free hand for the first time in his life . . . as you watch [the rushes for *Que Viva Mexico!*] you get a new idea of the plasticity of the films as a medium and you are ready to believe that Eisenstein has indeed produced the first real artistic masterpiece of the movies. For Eisenstein is able to work to an extent to which no director not Russian works—instead of with theatrical sets, properties and actors—with the raw materials of life; and he succeeds in absorbing these—landscapes, people, plants, animals, tools, furniture, clothing, and buildings— into his artist's imagination in a way that no Hollywood director has ever been able to do with all the animals and actors especially

trained for him, all the fancy costumes and properties specially
provided, by the Hollywood studios.[109]

As an artist, Eisenstein was flattered, but as a loyal Soviet citizen,
he recognized the danger of what Wilson had written. He wrote Monoszon that he was uncertain about how to respond, but attempted
to reassure him about the speedy progress of his work in Mexico
and about his ideological reliability.[110] Eisenstein finally decided to
write a letter to the *New Republic* protesting Wilson's comments that
Eisenstein had a "free hand" for the first time in his life in Mexico.
He complained that Wilson gave the impression "that those who work
in the creation and development of the Soviet cinema are victims of
a kind of 'forced labor.'" This was a mistake and a slander on the
Soviet system, "the only system which could give free creativeness
an opportunity to expand so enormously." Eisenstein ended by emphasizing his belief that Soviet artists do what they do out of their
"profoundest convictions and opinions," and that he counted himself
among them.[111]

Eisenstein must have hoped he had softened the possible damage
done by the Wilson article, but his situation did not improve with the
passage of time. Sinclair and others defended Eisenstein and his work
to Stalin,[112] but his difficulties with Kimbrough increased, and Amkino
in New York (now headed by V. F. Smirnov, an associate of Shumiatsky) announced suddenly that it was withdrawing the money it had
promised to invest in the film.

In December, Kimbrough returned to Pasadena to confer with Sinclair, and Eisenstein went to Tetlapayac, where he was alone for much
of the month. No doubt he was reassessing his position with respect
to the project, Sinclair, and most importantly, his career in the Soviet
Union. The recurrent fears in Moscow of his possible defection bothered him and there seemed little he could do to dispel them. He had
kept in constant touch with his friends at home by letter and at one
point had asked Pera Atasheva (his future wife) to come to Mexico
to assist him in his work. To some observers in the Soviet capital and
in North America this was an indication that he did indeed plan to
defect, and Moscow turned the request down, not surprisingly. Most
recent writers on Eisenstein believe he never had any intention of
defecting, however, and that his principal concern at this time was

completing *Que Viva Mexico!*[113] Prospects for the project continued
to grow dim. Eisenstein had argued with Aleksandrov about the film's
final editing, and Aleksandrov had left Tetlapayac after a personal
disagreement with Eisenstein over an article published shortly before
in the Soviet press. Alone at Tetlapayac, living in a monk's cell, there
was little to encourage Eisenstein. He must have begun to suspect that
the project was doomed.

The culmination of these uncertainties came with Kimbrough's return to Mexico in January 1932. He and Eisenstein continued to argue
over money. Eisenstein wrote a series of letters to Sinclair asking for
Kimbrough's removal. He explained that he had never been anything
but frugal and hardworking in Mexico, despite what Kimbrough told
his brother-in-law.[114] Soon Eisenstein's friends in Mexico offered to
write Sinclair on his behalf; in response, Sinclair told Eisenstein to
continue his work, which he did despite uncomfortable physical ailments.[115] Finally, the blow everyone must have expected came: on
January 24, Sinclair sent a telegram ordering the crew to return to
California, explaining that the money had finally run out.

At Amecameca, during the final few days of the month, Eisenstein
and Tisse completed some last-minute filming for the "Death Day" sequence. After some additional hesitation, Eisenstein, Tisse, and Aleksandrov set off by car early in February.[116] At Laredo the U.S. border officials refused to admit them for almost a month, citing visa
problems and trunks of what the officers considered pornographic
sketches.[117] At last the three were given transit visas allowing them
to travel only to New York, and then leave the United States. Since
the agreement with the Sinclairs had been that the film would be edited
in Hollywood, it was now uncertain where the work would be done.
By March first, Eisenstein had arrived in New York, and the situation seemed clear to him at least, as he wrote his friend Salka Viertel:
"We hope to cut the film in Moscow. I am really homesick and very
glad about it. I have decided to change the plan of the whole film and
to use everything I have shot, but in a different continuity. I hope it
can be saved."[118] Eisenstein visited friends in the city, arranged to have
some of his Mexican sketches exhibited in a New York gallery in the
fall, and, fully expecting to finish work on the film in Moscow, left
for Europe on April 19, 1932. Shortly before his ship sailed, Eisenstein received a cable from Sinclair: "Bon voyage. All film will follow

on next ship."[119] The film was never sent, and according to Jay Leyda, Eisenstein kept this telegram on his desk, where he could see it, for the rest of his life.

Eisenstein recalled later that he returned to Moscow feeling old and "done for," and went through an extended period of great depression. It seemed he had nothing substantive to show for his stay in the West, and a challenge he had formulated two and half years before came back to haunt him: "To go abroad—it presents the ultimate test that one can set a Soviet citizen whose life has been inseparable from the October Revolution: the test of a free choice. Going abroad offers the final challenge to the creative worker: to prove whether he can really create outside the Revolution, whether he can even exist outside it."[120] It was a challenge he could not yet answer. But in Moscow he was faced with failure. The next few years were probably the unhappiest of his life, made that way by Shumiatsky and Stalin's government: he had a nervous breakdown, his projects for *Black Majesty* and *MMM* were rejected, and his film *Bezhin lug* was shelved for political reasons.[121] His marriage to Atasheva in 1934 was one of the few happy events during these years, but it was a marriage of convenience, of colleagues rather than lovers.

These frustrations in Moscow did not prevent Eisenstein from hoping that it might be possible to get the Mexican footage for editing, however. He knew that he had the support of many people of influence in the United States, and letters he received encouraged his optimism.[122] He initiated a law suit in April 1933, through a New York firm, to force Sinclair to send the film to Moscow for editing and sound synchronizing, after which it would be returned to the United States for distribution.[123] In May 1934, Seymour Stern's *Experimental Cinema* group launched a campaign to return the footage to Eisenstein.[124] Above all, Eisenstein knew that a tremendous amount of sympathy had been expressed for him in the U.S. press. Morris Helprin, for example, wrote in the *New York Times* that *Que Viva Mexico!* would "set a completely new standard in motion pictures." The *New York Sun's* critic wrote that the sequences from the film he had viewed were the best he had ever seen. The *Herald Tribune* said that the film's "visual magnificence" could be appreciated even from stills. Mexican newspapers were equally as effusive, and Bustamente wrote in *Nuestro México* that it was "un himno a nuestras bellezas, una oda a nuestras costumbres" ("a hymn to the beauty [of our country], an ode to our customs"), an evaluation shared by many other Mexicans.[125]

With his friends abroad working on his behalf, Eisenstein wanted to do nothing to endanger the agreement he felt he still had with Sinclair. He tried to avoid Tina Modotti when he returned to Moscow, for example, since she had been expelled from Mexico in 1930 as an undesirable alien and might offend Sinclair and his conservative investors.[126] Meanwhile the controversy grew. In September 1933 the *New Republic* announced that it would print no further letters on Eisenstein's Mexican project unless "our correspondents have something new and important to say."[127] The arguments and negotiations continued, but Eisenstein never was able even to see all the film he shot in Mexico, much less edit it. His disappointment was enormous. In one of his gloomier moods, at the end of 1932, he already admitted that "it looks as if the picture is lost for ever," and it was only in 1936 that he could write to Salka Viertel about his feelings: "I am slowly recovering from the blow of my Mexican experience. I have never worked on anything with such enthusiasm and what has happened to it is the greatest crime, even if I have to share the guilt."[128] The news from North America did nothing to improve his spirits. Sinclair and the investors, in an attempt to recoup at least some of the money they had put into the film, hired Sol Lesser to make *Thunder Over Mexico*, based on an abbreviated version of Eisenstein's scenario. Later much of the film was sold to Bell and Howell for educational shorts, and there was some suspicion that sequences were used elsewhere as well.[129] Few besides Sinclair and the investors were satisfied with the results.

Marie Seton edited a truncated version of the film in 1939, but her *Time in the Sun* was a pale reflection of what Eisenstein intended. Jay Leyda did some work on the footage that the Sinclairs gave to the Museum of Modern Art, putting together several "study films" that he hoped would give students an idea of how Eisenstein's creative mind operated, but these too did not pretend to approximate Eisenstein's original plan.[130] Aleksandrov and Tisse launched a campaign for the completion of *Que Viva Mexico!* in 1957, and in the 1970s, after Sinclair's death, prints of the remaining footage were shipped to the Soviet Union for Aleksandrov to edit.[131] At last, in 1979, three years after he had begun working on it, Aleksandrov's version of *Que*

Viva Mexico! was premiered at the Moscow Film Festival. It was not a great success, and even in the Soviet Union, many viewers considered it only a product of Aleksandrov's increasing senility. Critics abroad were no kinder in public than Russians were in private: it was described as being "silly and sentimental," and edited like a "soap opera."[132] It was a sad conclusion to the history of an uncompleted attempt at capturing a nation on film.

Eisenstein himself never forgot Mexico, of course, and his widow's apartment in Moscow has a large number of the mementos he collected while he was there. Its living room is dominated by a large sarape showing pre-Columbian figures in a traditional Indian design. There are photographs of Orozco, the *torero* Liceaga, Stokowski, and a Mexican soldier; reproductions of shots from the film and of murals by Montenegro and others hang on the walls. A carved wooden cane, gourd bowls, small statues of Christ and Mary, and some imitation pre-Columbian carvings rest on the bookshelves. Most interesting, perhaps, is a series of *retablos* showing Eisenstein's recovery from several illnesses. He continued to sketch Mexican subjects for some time after his return to Moscow and at any opportunity collected books on Mexico.[133] And he continued to think over the possibilities of what could be done with the unedited film should he ever succeed in obtaining it. No matter how he tried, Eisenstein was never able "to overcome death through irony—the death of my own child on whom I lavished so much love, work, and passionate inspiration."[134]

Had it been completed, *Que Viva Mexico!* might be remembered as Eisenstein's greatest film. Yet even the attempt had had an impact on Eisenstein unlike any other of his films, perhaps because he saw in Mexico a projection of his own character, a duality of emotion always in harmony with itself. Its sensuality and its tenderness were constantly contrasted to its brutality and sadism. Even in this brutality, Eisenstein believed he learned about himself:

> Physical brutality, whether in the "ascetism" of monks' self-flagellation or in the torturing of others, in the blood of the bull or the blood of man, pouring over the sands of countless Sunday *corridas* every week, after Mass, in a sensual sacrament; the history of unparalleled brutality in crushing the countless uprisings of the peons, who had been driven to a frenzy by the exploitation

of the landowners; the retaliatory brutality of the leader of the uprising, Pancho Villa, who ordered prisoners to be hanged naked in order that he and his soldiers might be entertained by the sight of the last physiological reactions of the hanged.[135]

Brutality and kindness, complexity and simplicity, an appreciation of the interconnectedness of life and death were all features of the Mexican character that appealed to Eisenstein. Tying all these contradictory emotions together, however, keeping them from resulting in schizophrenia, Eisenstein believed, was the *vacilada*, a peculiar "wicked humor, irony, and that special sort of Mexican wit" that contributed to a unique way of dealing with the contradictions and complications of life.[136]

Mexico meant more to Eisenstein than it had to any other Russian who had been there, and its impact on his life was permanent. It was tragic that he was unable to complete *Que Viva Mexico!*, but as he admitted, the project's failure was as much his fault as it was that of Sinclair or of the capitalist economic and social system. His position politically with regard to changing conditions in the USSR certainly intensified his emotional reactions to Mexico, and he expressed a love for the country that was completely unexpected. While he defined himself as a Soviet artist whose creative life was tied to the experience of the revolution, Mexico remained alive for Eisenstein, a country he never forgot, and one whose people and landscape continued to haunt him. The filming of *Que Viva Mexico!* marked a turning point in his life, the end of the beginning and the beginning of the end. Yet it also marked a high point in that life, and his new understanding of life and death, his appreciation of the idea of eternal recurrence certainly must have helped him better accept the vagaries of life in the USSR in the 1930s and 1940s. Above all, however, Eisenstein's *Que Viva Mexico!* project was an attempt to make a film in Mexico by an enormously imaginative, active, original, and creative genius, a man who could produce images operating on multiple levels of understanding. The richness of Eisenstein's mind is nowhere better to be seen than in what remains of *Que Viva Mexico!* His visual images have directly or indirectly influenced everyone interested in Mexico since his time, whether in the USSR, Mexico, or in other nations. The debt owed to Eisenstein is considerable.

5
POSTSCRIPT:
TROTSKY'S
MEXICO

Murió Trotsky asesinado
de la noche a la mañana
porque habían premeditado
venganza tarde o temprano

Fue un día martes por la tarde
este tragedia fatal,
Que ha conmovido al país
y a todo la Capital

—*"Gran Corrido de Leon Trotsky,"*
sung after Trotsky's death, at the funeral cortege[1]

Although Eisenstein was on fairly good terms with Calles and the Mexican government, most Mexican and foreign leftists found themselves in a difficult situation during the years following the outlawing of the PCM and the vigorous anti-Communist campaign of much of the Maximato. Many PCM members were imprisoned or forced into exile, and foreign Communist visitors were scrutinized carefully before being allowed to enter Mexico. The PCM itselt went underground and remained illegal until 1934, when the new president, Lázaro Cárdenas, allowed it to be active politically once again. Many Mexican leftists found it convenient to disavow any connection with the PCM, even if they did not entirely give up their allegiance to Communism. In 1932, Vicente Lombardo Toledano formed the Confederación General de Obreros y Campesinos de México (General Confederation of Workers and Peasants of Mexico) as a counterpart to the now defunct CROM. It became a center of Mexican leftist political sentiment. Three years later, Lombardo visited the USSR and on his return delivered a series of enthusiastic lectures about his experiences to overflow audiences. At a time when Stalinist Marxism proved enormously appealing to many of those supporting Cárdenas, the favorable views expressed in his book, *Un Viaje al mundo del porvenir (A Journey to the Land of the Future)*, found an equally appreciative audience.

Cárdenas himself was willing to consider adopting some aspects of the Soviet agricultural and industrial model and made an effort to improve relations with Mexican Communists, but he did not reestablish diplomatic relations with the USSR at a time when the Soviet government and the Comintern would have liked such ties. While Mexico and the Soviet Union pursued some common policies with respect to the League of Nations and the Spanish Civil War, their apparent similarity of interests did not lead to an official relationship until World War II. Throughout the 1930s, the most leftist decade in modern Mexican history in the eyes of many observers, and the one most influenced by Soviet ideology, there was no official Soviet representation in Mexico and few Russians went there for any reason. Oddly enough, one of those who did was Leon Trotsky, and Cárdenas's Mexico thus became the last place of refuge for the most vocal opponent of the Stalinist regime.

At the end of 1936 Trotsky had already lived nine years in exile. A hero of the Bolshevik Revolution, the creator of the Red Army, one of the most original and intelligent of the Bolshevik leaders, he found himself in great difficulty because of his intransigence both as a revolutionary and as a foe of Stalin. He had been expelled from Moscow by the Fifteenth Communist Party Congress and had lived in Alma Ata in Central Asia until 1929, when he was deported from the USSR. He moved first to the island of Prinkipo, off the coast of Turkey, then to France in 1933, and then to Norway. He was finally expelled from that country because of pressure from Norwegian conservatives and the Soviet government. It looked as though he had nowhere to go, and Trotskyite groups around the world were desperately searching for a place of refuge for him.

In the midst of this growing concern, on November 21, 1936, Diego Rivera received a telegram from Anita Brenner in New York. Writing on behalf of the Trotskyite Fourth International, she told him that the question of Trotsky's being granted political exile in Mexico, a possibility discussed only in broad terms previously, had become one of life or death urgency. She asked him to use his influence to press the government for a decision. Rivera had been as confused as anyone about the Stalin-Trotsky arguments, but in his case, it is not difficult to see why he was amenable to helping Trotsky, whom he had long admired. His expulsion from the PCM had not encouraged his affection for the Soviet Union's Stalinist government; although he did not join the Mexican section of Trotsky's party until September 1936, emotionally he was a Trotskyite by 1933.[2] Rivera agreed with Trotsky that the rise of the bureaucracy in the Soviet Union had seriously harmed the development of the revolution; he supported Trotsky's championing of revolutionary internationalism and his opposition to the Stalinist program of "socialism in one country." Emotionally, politically, and intellectually, Rivera was prepared to aid Trotsky in whatever way he could, and upon receiving the telegram, Rivera immediately left the capital for Torreón, where Cárdenas was overseeing a land distribution program. Cárdenas willingly granted Trotsky permission to enter Mexico, both from a sense of "revolutionary solidarity," and in accordance with Mexico's policy of granting asylum to political exiles. He requested only that Rivera organize no demonstrations to welcome him. Official permission took some time to be arranged, however: Cárdenas notified the secretary of foreign relations but the secretary refused to carry out the president's orders. It was only after several weeks, following a struggle between the secretary and General Mújica, Cárdenas's close friend and a supporter of the president's decision, that permission for Trotsky to land was formally granted.

The voyage from Oslo to Tampico was pleasant, Trotsky wrote later, although he found the Norwegians extraordinarily circumspect in the way they treated him: he and his wife, Natalia Sedova, were given two hours to pack in Oslo; the crew watched his activities carefully the whole time he was on the ship; the captain refused him permission to listen to the radio; and no one would tell them what their landing point in Mexico would be.[3] After three weeks at sea, on January 9, 1937, he and his wife arrived at Tampico. The reception was friendly, but they had become so nervous that they refused to disembark until they saw some faces on shore they recognized.[4] At last they picked out Max Schachtman, founder of the U.S. Trotskyite movement, and George Novak, secretary of the American Committee for the Defense of Leon Trotsky, and the two of them relaxed. Rivera was ill and could not be there. Instead, he asked his wife, Frida Kahlo, to meet the ship, even though she "detested Trotsky's politics."[5] Once his initial concern and reserve had lessened, Trotsky himself remarked that in Mexico he and his wife "encountered hospitality and attentiveness at every step," and some time later he expressed his thanks to Mexico in a newsreel speech:

> You will easily understand if I begin my short address to you . . . by expressing my warm thanks to the Mexican people and to the man who leads them with such merit and courage, President Cárdenas. When monstrous and absurd accusations were hurled at me and my family, when my wife and I were under lock and key by the Norwegian government, unable to defend ourselves, the Mexican government opened the doors of this magnificent country and said to us: "Here you can freely defend your rights and your honor!" Naturally, it is not sympathy for *my* ideas which has motivated President Cárdenas, but *fidelity to his own ideas;* all the more meritorious, then, is his act of democratic hospitality, so rare these days![6]

Trotsky's enthusiastic gratitude should perhaps have been qualified. Alice Rühle-Gerstel pointed out that Trotsky did not appear to understand the true seriousness of his situation, that Mexico might prove to be the end of his peregrinations: "He was delighted to have been granted asylum in Mexico but . . . he did not seem fully aware of what in fact it meant, namely his salvation from certain death; rather [it was] as if he had an inner conviction that there would always be a way out for him."[7] For the present, however, Mexico appeared to offer great potential. He would remain in the country, he told a reporter, as long as Mexico would allow him to stay.

Immediately upon arriving in Tampico, Trotsky was handed a personal message from Cárdenas saying that he should consider himself a guest of the government. Cárdenas asked in return only that Trotsky pledge not to interfere in Mexico's internal affairs. He readily agreed, and he restated his promise the next day to a reporter for *El Universal*: he would not intervene in Mexican politics nor do anything to interfere in Mexico's foreign relations. He kept his promise, never commenting (openly) on domestic affairs and restricting his political observations to foreign developments, for the most part unrelated to Mexican policy. Trotsky considered this a small price to pay for what he gained. For Cárdenas, it was essential for internal political peace. He had already come under attack from the PCM for granting Trotsky asylum. An editorial in *El Machete* expressed the opinion not only of Mexican communists, but of many other Mexican leftists: "If Cárdenas, as he says, desires the unity of the Mexican people and particularly of the working class, then why has he authorized the entry into Mexico of a man who has struggled against the only popular front in all the world and whose partisans attempt to divide and disunite the labor movement. . . . We severely censure the government's conduct in this case."[8] Cárdenas had known that granting Trotsky asylum would not be popular with many of the groups he depended on for support, but as Trotsky pointed out, he had made his decision at least partially on principle and would not retreat from it. In fact, Cárdenas was playing a delicate political game, with both foreign and internal gains to be made; domestically at least, he had less to lose than might appear on the surface.

Trotsky and his wife had been more exhausted by the journey from Europe than they realized, and Sedova in particular, wrote one observer, was "quite overwhelmed" by the whole experience.[9] She later described to Victor Serge her own state of mind during their first hours in Mexico:

A train provided by the Mexican government [through Mújica's intervention, according to Trotsky] took us through sun-baked country, scattered with palm-trees and cacti. The mountains blazed with splendor. At a small station [La Lechería], Antonio Hidalgo and Fritz Bach, a socialist of Swiss origin and one of Zapata's comrades-in-arms, were waiting to greet us. . . . All security precautions broke down when a crowd of unknown friends swarmed round us, and I tried not to lose sight of the only face I knew—Frida Kahlo's. We were shown a car which we were expected to share with policemen and strangers. Suddenly we felt afraid once again—were they, in spite of everything, taking us to prison? We arrived in a suburb of Mexico City, at a low house painted blue; it had a patio filled with plants, fresh, airy rooms, a collection of pre-Columbian objets d'art and a vast number of pictures. . . . We had come to a different world, the house of Frida Kahlo and Diego Rivera.[10]

This was the "Blue House" in Coyoacán, now the Frida Kahlo museum, where Trotsky and his wife lived for a number of months. Rivera and Kahlo had moved several miles away, to Rivera's house in San Angel, so that Trotsky and Sedova could have their own home. They were all glad to arrive in the cooler air of the plateau and soon settled into something of a normal way of life. It was one that constantly drew them into politics and controversy, however, and placed them before the North American reading public continually. The *Life* magazine photographer who recorded their early days in the house was only the first of many who hounded them over the next few years.

As might have been expected, Trotsky's arrival caused immediate strains in the Mexican left. The Stalinists who dominated the PCM and the new Confederación de Trabajadores Mexicanos (the Confederation of Mexican Workers, CTM), launched a propaganda campaign against Trotsky's presence. He was accused of being in league with reactionaries and fascists. Lombardo Toledano said he was plotting a general strike against the government. The CTM newspaper, *El Popular*, wrote that he was conspiring with the "fascist" Dr. Atl, and with the anti-Cardenistas Cedillo and Vasconcelos, to bring down the government. Trotsky responded to the charges by forming, with his new Mexican friends, a Mexican branch of the Fourth International and by opening a new anti-Stalinist journal, *Clave*. It was announced that *Clave* would be the theoretical review of the Spanish-speaking sections of the Fourth International. Its introductory editorial, probably written by Trotsky, emphasized the value for all the Spanish-speaking world of pure Marxist thought in Mexico: it was only there, the editorial asserted, that Marxist thought was truly free. Above all, *Clave* attacked the CTM and the PCM, the latter with special venom for having been "decisively transformed from the party of the proletariat vanguard into the party of the conservative petty bourgeoisie."[11] Trotsky's allies criticized the PCM and its leadership for blindly supporting the Comintern. Trotsky labeled Lombardo Toledano a "flunky" and a "political dilettante," and in his article, "What is the Meaning of the Struggle Against 'Trotskyism'? (About Lombardo Toledano and other GPU Agents)," he wrote that Lombardo was "one of the most zealous and shameless of the Moscow bureaucracy's agents," that he was contemptible, and only a transmitter of the lies of Stalin and Vyshinsky.[12] Eventually, Trotsky predicted, the totalitarianism of Lombardo and his friends would prepare the road for Mexico to become a fascist state.[13]

It appeared Trotsky was becoming more active in Mexican internal politics than he should have, considering his promise to Cárdenas. Not wishing to endanger his position further, and recognizing that his Mexican enemies were only repeating Soviet charges, Trotsky decided to try something new. In March 1937, an International Joint Commission of Inquiry was set up to discuss and evaluate the charges made against him by his critics around the world, and particularly at the second mass purge trial in Moscow.

The commission's supporters and organizers included John Dos Passos, Sidney Hook, Norman Thomas, and Reinhold Niebuhr. John Dewey headed an investigating panel made up of Otto Rühle, Suzanne Lafollette, and Carleton Beals; a number of representatives from groups throughout the Mexican and foreign political spectrum were invited to attend, although most non-Trotskyite Communists refused to take part. The commission's hearings, held in Coyoacán at the Blue House from April tenth to the seventeenth, were clearly an attempt to clear Trotsky's name. They received great publicity abroad, but less in the Mexican press, since none of the proceedings was translated into Spanish. Some observers considered the hearings only Trotskyite propaganda, since many of the commission's members were known to be sympathetic to Trotsky from the beginning. Beals asked to have his name removed from the commission's membership list after Trotsky flew into a rage in response to a question Beals asked that Trotsky apparently assumed was directed toward embarrassing him with the Mexican government. Beals concluded that the entire proceeding was a pretentious show, without substance.[14] However laudable the purpose of the commission, it only produced more publicity and hostility at a time when Trotsky needed less public exposure. Its closing was greeted with considerable relief by Mexicans from both the political left and right.

Trotsky's stay in Mexico became more awkward when he and Rivera quarrelled and Trotsky moved out of the Blue House. From the beginning, the temperaments of the two men clashed, and both suf-

fered from a bit too much pride and self-confidence, although as van
Heijenhoort remembered, their personalities at times could complement one another: "If they were together, Diego might dominate the
talk, and then Trotsky would take the floor. They would talk mostly
about Mexican politicians, and Diego had a very penetrating mind
for people, for what a person really was. That was a bit different from
Trotsky, who always interpreted things in terms of tendencies, left-
right, all that—abstract concepts. Trotsky enjoyed this side of Diego,
and Diego's insights were useful to Trotsky."[15] What Trotsky could
not abide was Rivera's "fabulous fantasy," although according to Herrera, Rivera made a concerted effort to control his famous and almost unconscious lying in conversations with Trotsky: "For his part,
Diego admired Trotsky's courage and moral authority, and respected
his discipline and commitment. In Trotsky's presence, he tried to
bridle his compulsion to fantasize, and made an effort to rein in his
anarchical ways."[16] Complicating the two men's relationship even
more was the fact that a kind of love affair was going on between
Trotsky and Frida Kahlo, one that had begun after the commission
hearings had ended and continued until July 1937.[17] Yet even this
was not the final cause of the break between Trotsky and Rivera, who
in any case saw much less of each other in Mexico than is generally
imagined. The central issue was Rivera's political transformation. By
late 1938 or early 1939 Rivera had apparently lost faith in Cárdenas
while Trotsky continued to regard him favorably. More importantly,
Rivera had become disenchanted with Trotsky's Fourth International.
It seemed a futile enterprise, proof of Trotsky's vaingloriousness and
self-indulgence. Rivera's resignation from the Fourth International
marked the end of his intellectual flirtation with Trotskyism, although
it took him more than a decade to return finally to the Communist
party. With Rivera's defection, Trotsky lost an important ally in the
Mexican leftist community.

Trotsky constantly received threats against his life, and the new
house, on Avenida Viena in Coyoacán, was soon transformed into a
fortress, guarded by Mexicans and foreigners against possible at-
tackers. The living-room windows, facing the street, were boarded
up; a revolver was placed on every table, and according to a visitor,
"even going to the lavatory everyone takes one with him."[18] Trotsky
and his wife were almost never left alone, and normally were accom-

panied by their bodyguards wherever they went. Trotsky himself spent his time writing, collecting cacti, and caring for the rabbits and chickens he kept on the patio. Occasionally he was able to travel around the country: he visited Veracruz to fish in the Gulf of Mexico, went to San Miguel de Allende and Taxco, visited Guadalajara and Lake Pátzcuaro with André Breton and Rivera, and made several trips to an isolated hacienda in the state of Hidalgo in order to relax and to enjoy some privacy. He was delighted by the richness of Mexico's natural surroundings and wrote enthusiastic letters to his son Leon about the wonders of nature in Mexico.[19]

Trotsky was never able to retreat far from the public eye, however. Many in the press accused him of plotting the conservative-backed Cedillo rebellion of 1938 against Cárdenas; on the other hand, the New York Daily News attributed to Trotsky the presidential decision to expropriate foreign-owned oil companies and stated bluntly that he was the "evil spirit" behind many of Cárdenas's radical acts. Trotsky said the change was absurd, adding that while he thought it a good idea, he had learned of the expropriation himself only by reading the local newspapers.[20] In fact, there was no real contact at all between Cárdenas and Trotsky. Trotsky continued to hold Cárdenas in high esteem, but the two never met.[21] Cárdenas was not a Trotskyite, not even a Communist in the 1930s. If he took a number of radical steps while Trotsky was in Mexico, it was for his own reasons, not because Trotsky acted as an éminence grise.

As he had promised, and despite the constant hectoring by the newspapers for his views on current Mexican political developments, Trotsky refrained from any statements of significance that might endanger his precarious position. In any case, Trotsky told a reporter at the beginning of his stay, he would have needed a year or two, perhaps three, of studying Mexico before he would feel competent to comment on the country.[22] While at one point he did praise Mexico's support for the Republic in the Spanish Civil War,[23] his only major observation on Mexican internal affairs was an article devoted to Cárdenas's economic program, published in 1939. "On Mexico's Second Six-Year Plan" was not published under his name, and it was not seen at the time as being directly attributable to him. Hence it did not violate his agreement with Cárdenas. It was surprisingly critical of government hopes to develop the country economically, however. Trotsky wrote that he saw no "plan" at all in the new program, that it was general, and only glossed over the most important problems. However much the government used Soviet-style terminology, he continued, Mexico's social and economic system was still basically capitalist and would remain so even if the goals of the plan were attained. Its proposals to reorganize the machinery of state were too vague to be of any use, he felt. Above all, Trotsky faulted the plan for failing to deal directly with the most important issue: the need for democratic agrarian revolution. "Complete collectivization" was inconsistent and unreasonable given Mexico's present conditions; the foundations for such a reform would have to be laid first. Mexico should not emulate the Soviet Union's program of forced collectivization, both because of the obvious problems encountered in the USSR, but also because Mexico was further behind in its economic development than Russia had been. Above all, and of foremost importance, he repeated, the peasants needed land: "In short, it is necessary to finish the work of Emiliano Zapata and not to superimpose on him the methods of Joseph Stalin." Trotsky then listed a series of other weaknesses riddling the Six-Year Plan. The agricultural credit program had not been thought through adequately. The industrial growth promised could not be attained because there was no foreign investment to finance it. The government's call for state capitalism in association with foreign investment was not possible in a country as poor as Mexico. Nor would the workers, abused by the government's own labor bureaucracy, support the plan. On the whole, he concluded, the plan was vague and verbose; it needed more strictly limited goals and especially ones that were understandable to the peasants, because the agrarian question remained Mexico's foremost problem.[24] At no other time was Trotsky as outspoken about Mexican domestic politics, and interestingly, the position he took in this article was more restrained, even more conservative, than Cárdenas's and the government's. It was also one that infuriated and further alienated the radical left.

Because of his interest in cultural revolution, Trotsky was also active within the highly original and creative Mexican artistic movement of the 1930s, one that combined both indigenous and modernist internationalist traditions. The Mexican muralist movement of the 1920s had lost much of its drive by this time, of course, yet for Trotsky there was still much in it that might provide examples for the proletarian art he had hoped to see first established in Russia after the Bolshevik Revolution. André Breton visited Trotsky at Coyoacán in 1938, and he and Trotsky held a series of conversations with prominent Mexican artists on the question of the role of art in revolution.[25] These discussions eventually led to the issuing of a manifesto, "For an Independent Revolutionary Art," signed by Trotsky, Breton, and Rivera, although written almost in its entirety by Trotsky. Trotsky in no way approved of Stalinist socialist realism. His views on revolutionary culture were still much as they had been when he was writing *Literature and Revolution* in the early 1920s. In Mexico, he believed, he had found artists who better than any others had fulfilled his ideas of what revolutionary art should be. Like Eisenstein, Trotsky was tremendously impressed by the works of Orozco and after meeting him in person, declared that he was "a Dostoevsky!"[26] It was Rivera, however, Trotsky wrote in a *Partisan Review* article, who was the only truly revolutionary proletarian artist:

> In the field of painting, the October revolution has found her greatest interpreter not in the USSR but in far-away Mexico, not among the official "friends," but in the person of a so-called "enemy of the people" whom the Fourth International is proud to number in its ranks. Nurtured in the artistic cultures of all peoples, all epochs, Diego Rivera has remained Mexican in the most profound fibres of his genius. But that which inspired him in these magnificent frescoes, which lifted him above the artistic tradition, above contemporary art in a certain sense, above himself, is the mighty blast of the proletarian revolution. Without October, his power of creative penetration into the epic of work, oppression and insurrection, would never have attained such breadth and profundity. Do you wish to see with your own eyes the hidden springs of the social revolution? Look at the frescoes of Rivera. Do you wish to know what revolutionary art is like? Look at the frescoes of Rivera.
>
> Come a little closer and you will see clearly enough, gashes and spots made by vandals: catholics and other reactionaries, including, of course, Stalinists. These cuts and gashes give even greater life to the frescoes. You have before you, not simply a "painting,"

an object of passive esthetic contemplation, but a living part of the class struggle. And it is at the same time a masterpiece![27]

Trotsky concluded by pointing out that since Rivera had been expelled from the Mexican Communist party, his works, despite their true revolutionary character and nature, were not acceptable in the USSR, a situation that only proved in Trotsky's eyes the bankruptcy of the Stalinist political and cultural regime.[28] While Trotsky's relations with Rivera were not always the friendliest, their arguments did not diminish Trotsky's admiration for Rivera's work and for the sentiments which inspired it. While he personally may have preferred the works of Orozco, Trotsky believed that Rivera's frescoes fulfilled the needs of revolutionary art better than anyone else's, in Mexico or abroad, and that they came closest to the ideal art Trotsky believed in.

Speculation about art helped Trotsky forget, for a while at least, the growing danger to his life in Mexico. The first serious attack on him took place on May 24, 1940, when a group of gunmen led by Siqueiros broke into the massively fortified house and fired wildly into Trotsky's bedroom, hoping to kill him. The attempt failed, and the would-be assassins escaped. The political atmosphere of the time was indicated by the assertions in *El Popular* that Trotsky had planned the attack on himself as a provocation against Mexico and its government. Trotsky countered their charges in a letter to the attorney general accusing the PCM of instigating the attack. He said that he soon planned to publish a book proving the leaders of the PCM were the "intellectual authors" of the attack. They and their sympathizers in *El Popular,* *La Voz de México,* and *El Nacional,* as well as Lombardo Toledano, had taken part in the "moral preparation of the terrorist act" and should be questioned. Trotsky added that he suspected Siqueiros might have been involved as well.[29] In supplementary statements to the police, Trotsky continued his attempts at helping the authorities pursue their investigation.[30] Neither increased police surveillance nor intensified efforts by his own bodyguards kept Trotsky safe, however. On August 20, he was murdered by a member of his own household in a particularly bloodthirsty manner that was publicized around the world in lurid detail. Trotsky may have been correct in asserting that a climate encouraging his murder had been created by Mexico's unfriendly leftist press, but in the end the murder was accomplished by an agent of Stalin and the GPU, and a foreigner. Mexico was not far enough away from Moscow after all.

Despite one or two lapses, Trotsky had made a determined effort to position himself outside Mexico's internal politics, neither to involve himself in them nor to comment on them. He had, on the whole, kept his promise to Cárdenas. His broader influence, however, was considerably greater, and Trotskyism found receptive audiences in Mexico and throughout Latin America in the years following his exile from the USSR. He arrived in Mexico a hero to some and a counter-revolutionary to others, and by his very presence caused controversy. It is unfortunate that he did not write more about Mexico, since the little he did say showed great insight, intuitive understanding, and imagination at a time when most foreign observers were influenced more by political prejudices than by a desire for pragmatic analysis. Trotsky is by far the best-known Russian ever to have been in Mexico, although chiefly because of his bloody death. His house in Coyoacán is now a museum, and he is buried in its garden. He thereby gains the distinction of being the only Russian visitor discussed in this book who never left the country.

CONCLUSION

Trotsky was not the last well-known Russian to come to Mexico, and most of those who followed had more to say about the country. Indeed, many Soviet citizens travelled to Mexico after 1940. One reason their numbers increased was that in 1942 Mexico and the USSR reestablished diplomatic relations, largely as a result of the outbreak of the Second World War. In 1943 Konstantin Umansky presented his credentials as ambassador in Mexico City and began to build what would for many years be the largest Soviet embassy in Latin America. It sponsored visits by Soviet political and cultural figures in the mid-1940s, and during the Cold War, a period of relative isolation for the USSR in Latin America, a surprising number of Russians visited Mexico. Their accounts appeared in major Soviet journals and in a few short books. The majority of these visitors were tourists or journalists, although a few were scholars. If their comments were better informed and their perspective more sophisticated than those of the earlier travellers, they were also fairly pedestrian and highly predictable.

This situation changed after Anastas Mikoyan's state visit to Mexico in 1959, and particularly with the signing of a cultural and scientific exchange agreement between Mexico and the USSR in 1968. Throughout the 1960s, and especially during the 1970s, greater numbers of Soviet citizens than in the past travelled to Mexico, and they published more, thus providing Russians with an extensive array of sources of information. By the 1970s, the earlier distinctiveness of the Russian interpretation of Mexico was no longer present, however. Russians had become part of an international community, and they saw Mexico much as other foreigners did. The studies of V. N. Kuteishchikova and N. M. Lavrov, A. F. Shulgovsky and M. S. Alperovich helped Russians and foreigners, as well as Mexicans, comprehend aspects of Mexico sometimes ignored by other scholars. They also examined the country from a standpoint considerably unlike that of early Soviet observers and their Russian predecessors. Mexico continued to interest Russians, but little that was written in the years following Trotsky's death was as remarkable as what had come before. Yet quite obviously, the interpretations of later observers were flavored by earlier Russian writing. It was the visitors of the nineteenth and early twentieth centuries who one way or another had established the tone of subsequent Russian analyses of Mexico, and their works were highly influential in forming the preconceptions of later writers, if not in determining their governments' policies toward Mexico. This concluding chapter will attempt to summarize the views of the Russian visitors discussed in the preceding pages, to distinguish three principal phases of Russian interest in Mexico, and finally to comment on an overall Russian attitude toward the country between 1806 and 1940 that will show a continuity in the Russian viewpoint.

At the beginning, the only Mexico Russians knew was Mexican California, and their earliest attitudes toward what was then known as New Spain were determined by their experiences in the country's far northwestern frontier. The first phase of Russia's interest in Mexico was tied closely to its territorial expansion and political imperialism. From Asia, Russia explorers and merchants moved across the Bering Strait to Alaska, then south and east, eventually reaching Hawaii and the lands bordering Spanish possessions in California. Their motivations were both political and economic. Developments in revolutionary and Napoleonic Europe caused them considerable anxiety, as did the need for adequate supplies of food for their growing Alaskan and Siberian settlements. For Russians coming from the north, California was a paradise where almost all the agricultural products they needed so desperately could be grown. To them, it was not the unpleasant, isolated backwater it seemed to its Spanish and Mexican settlers. It was this fundamental difference in point of view that determined the highly critical way Russians looked at Spanish and Mexican rule in California. It should be remembered as well that the majority of the Russian visitors to Alta California were representatives of the Russian American Company, which had a reputation for progressive economic and political ideas, and which would later be a source of Decembrist sentiment. Many of those who wrote about California were highly educated, with upper-class backgrounds, and were influenced by the ideas of the Enlightenment. The result was that most of them were highly critical of what they considered the laziness, unproductivity, and backwardness of the *californios*. The landscape and natural surroundings were wonderful and constantly attractive, they wrote, almost without exception. The Spanish and Indian populations, on the other hand, were in no way equal to their surroundings. The few positive comments that were made were memorable only because they were so limited in number, and also because they came from men who were not necessarily ethnic Russians, but who were sailing under the Russian flag.

Until the mid-1830s, when Russians thought of Mexico, it was really California they had in mind. This was not the "real" Mexico, of course, but it shaped Russian opinion about Mexico until Baron Wrangell's reports of 1836. His comments proved to be transitional, in that his analysis lay somewhere between the early nineteenth-century accounts and those written during the second phase of Russian interest in Mexico, which corresponded roughly to the Porfiriato. Wrangell himself approached independent Mexico with a number of prejudices. He could not, on principle, be favorable toward the Mexican Republic. He did not believe in democracy and thought that independent Mexico ruled itself much more poorly than the Spanish viceroys had. His recommendations to St. Petersburg for diplomatic, consular, and trade agreements with Mexico were purely pragmatic—to benefit the Russian Empire and a Mexico which he hoped would be dominated neither by Britain nor by the increasingly threatening United States. He hoped to strengthen the Russian position in the North Pacific and to expand Russian activities on the Pacific coast of North America while there was still time to do so. An official Russian relationship with Mexico would make this possible. The further Wrangell travelled into Mexico, of course, and the more he saw of the country, the more discouraged he became. The consistently negative instructions he received from St. Petersburg did nothing to raise his spirits. Russian influence would inevitably decline, he felt, because other nations were more ambitious. About Mexico's future he was gloomy in the extreme. He was never overly generous to the country and especially to its political leadership, but he came to believe that Mexico would not have time for its political system to evolve into one of honesty and effectiveness before it would be destroyed by domestic and external forces.

Some historians feel that Wrangell made no attempt to understand the long-lasting impact on Mexico of the fighting and destruction of the Insurgency. Such criticisms have some credence, certainly, but it should be remembered that Wrangell was analyzing Mexico from the perspective of the mid-1930s. The Mexican Republic was pretending to political and economic preeminence in North America; it was a large and potentially wealthy country facing important decisions about its future. Wrangell felt that Mexico had real choices, just as the Russian Empire did. At best, Wrangell hoped that Mexicans themselves might recognize the dangers they and their government were not addressing effectively, and respond to them. At worst, from the Mexican standpoint, he expected Russia to take advantage of the growing power vacuum in western North America. Neither of these possibilities was realized. Russia eventually withdrew from the Western Hemisphere entirely, and Mexico lost its contest for North American supremacy to the United States. Wrangell must have felt a certain bitter satisfaction that his most negative predictions had come to pass. This first period of Russian interest in Mexico ended in disappointment, even disillusionment. Russian imperial expansion in North America had stopped, it was not Russians who would help the Mexicans solve their problems, and the few positive comments these Russians made about Mexico were lost in a plethora of criticism often verging on calumny.

Russian writing about Mexico reached a nadir in the middle decades of the nineteenth century. Mexico was struggling for its national existence against the United States in the 1830s and 1840s and against the French in the 1860s. The latter intervention was to a certain extent a continuation of the bloody internecine fighting between the liberals and conservatives during the 1850s. Russia and Nicholas I had never been particularly interested in improving relations with Mexico or in encouraging travel there, and with the Crimean War and the reforms of Alexander II, the tsarist empire became too involved in its own affairs and in assimilating its own new territories to be concerned with Mexico. Only now and then did Mexico appear in the Russian press, and occasionally writers such as Dostoevsky, Chernyshevsky, and Tolstoy might comment on Mexico.

When Russians again appeared in Mexico, it was during the last third of the century. Russia had changed considerably, with plans for industrialization and economic expansion, and it found a Mexico busy laying the foundations for its own modernization under the firm rule of Porfirio Díaz. In chronological terms, the second phase of Russian interest in Mexico was tied in closely with the period of his political dominance. National Russian political interests played almost no role in the writings on Mexico which appeared in the Russian press. The Mexican Republic was important as a political idea, as a distorted reflection of Russian reality seen through a liberal mirror, or simply as the locale for the working-out of the internal conflicts of Russian individuals.

Russian writers about Mexico during this second period produced some of the most interesting accounts of the country ever published in the Russian press. Their predecessors had been enormously self-confident, exceedingly proud of being Russians (even if only by association), frequently congratulating themselves on being so efficient, generous, and kindly in their colonial endeavors. They had felt much superior to Mexicans and to other Europeans in this area of activity. At the same time they had been realistic and pragmatic in their analyses of what they found in their travels. Only in the plans and projects for what they would have liked to see established in Mexico had romanticism overtaken realism. Their self-assurance and dedication to reason, however insulting it might have seemed to Mexicans, was very much in the tradition of the eighteenth century, although in the Russian case it must be admitted that at least part of the motivation for their bravado must have been their own sense of inferiority toward Western Europe. Very little of this was true of the Russian visitors who came to Mexico at the end of the century. These Russians were almost invariably members of the liberal intelligentsia who wanted to reform Russia, to transform it from a backward into a modern country, and they never hesitated to criticize themselves, if only by implication, as well as Mexico. Indeed, as has been seen, a considerable portion of what they wrote was intended as commentary on Russia as much as on Mexico. Educated Russians had learned to read between the lines in journal articles many decades before. Their sophistication and understanding of subterfuge was something Russian writers about the Porfiriato could utilize for their own purposes.

The essay of Protopopov provides the best example of this technique. His approach was to describe a Mexico that seemed to have little relation to the reality of life during the Porfiriato. Indeed, Mexicans reading Protopopov's essay might have wondered if he was truly talking about Mexico. His comments were almost exclusively positive. Even the government's obvious shortcomings he presented in such a way that the reader thought government-initiated reform was imminent. Clearly, Protopopov expected Russians to ask themselves many difficult questions about how their own country operated in comparison with the growing, democratic Mexico he depicted in his essay. And he knew that he could write whatever he wanted about Mexico since few Russians, and no government censors certainly, would be able to contradict him. He hoped Russians would continue questioning the fundamental tenets of their political and social system as a result of reading his article, and as the attention of the censorship showed, his hopes were not misplaced.

Patkanov and Tverskoi took slightly different tacks. They did not distort reality, but their intent was much the same as Protopopov's. Patkanov was a scientist in the tradition of Lomonosov, a man who felt he owed more to his country and his people than a life devoted to purely scientific research. He believed it his duty as a citizen to leave Russia better than he had found it. Because of press restrictions, he hoped in a small degree to raise questions about Russian life by describing Mexico. He was extremely critical of much he saw, but he felt it his right to be as outspoken as he was about life in Yucatán, condemning much of it, because in private he would say the same things about his own country. He assumed, or at least hoped, that his readers would understand this pretense. An obviously independent and outspoken man, by all indications he was a good and welcome guest in Mexico, despite what one might expect. To him, however, Mexico and Russia appeared to be making many of the same mistakes, in circumstances that would be painfully similar in the eyes of his educated Russian readers. Had he been only a scientist, Patkanov might have been satisfied with commenting on Yucatán's ruins, its vegetation, its climate. His sense of social responsibility compelled him to write extensively on the negative aspects of Yucatecan life under the Porfiriato, however, in the hopes that Mexico and Russia could be changed before a cataclysm overtook them both.

Tverskoi's article appeared many decades after Patkanov's and described a very different Mexico, one on the verge of revolution. An ambitious, progressive capitalist with strong populist feelings, he condemned Díaz's rule and predicted future disasters in response to it. Having abandoned Russia in the face of repression and a lack of opportunity, he had adopted a "booster" point of view toward Mexico not unlike that of many U.S. citizens. His approach to Mexico's problems was essentially pragmatic: if the country did not change fundamentally, it would face revolution. Tverskoi was uncompromising in his prescription for change, but any Mexican listening to his advice might be consoled by knowing that he would offer the same blunt suggestions to his Russian compatriots. Once again, while Tverskoi's criticisms of Mexico were certainly sincere reflections of his own views, they also expressed his attitudes toward what needed to be done in Russia. Neither he nor Patkanov wished to denigrate Mexico, but they were reformers intent on improving the world as a whole. They did not like what they found in Mexico any more than what they had seen in their own homeland.

When all this has been said, it must be reiterated that none of these views and analyses of Mexico reached as many Russian readers as did the poems and essays of Konstantin Balmont. Balmont's popularity was never greater than it was in the years following the 1905 revolution and his trip to Mexico. His books were best sellers, published in editions larger by far than any other modernist works. If educated Russians, particularly the younger generation, knew anything about Mexico, it would be what they learned from Balmont. And interestingly, Balmont did not have to resort to conceit to express his views about Mexico, because governmental censorship collapsed during the first few years following the success of the revolution. He was not at all concerned with modern Mexico, however, and indeed, he rejected it entirely because it was too much like the Europe and Russia he hoped he had left behind. He wanted to uncover the pure, mystical Mexico of the distant past, and he was a traveller as much in time as in space. He and his readers would remember only those aspects of contemporary Mexico that helped them understand and appreciate the country's pre-Columbian past. As more and more Russians hoped to escape into Decadence and Symbolism with the tsarist government's reassertion of authority, ironically Balmont's mythic Mexico was the one that determined the view of the country Russians would carry with them until the 1920s. Only then would the Mexican Revolution define the country in different terms for the Russian population.

Between 1910 and 1920 two watersheds were passed in Russia and Mexico. Both nations ostensibly made breaks with their pasts and created new social and political systems that had no equals elsewhere. While only the least sophisticated saw these revolutions as essentially congruent, many in both nations felt it only natural that the two new states should have official contacts. With the establishment of diplomatic relations, an exchange of visitors soon followed. These post-revolutionary years marked the beginning of the third phase of Russian interest in Mexico. On a political level, the new Soviet government promoted relations with Mexico and encouraged Russian travel there as a way to strengthen its legitimacy as a state and as a revolutionary force. Pestkovsky and Kollontai represented these political interests, and while Mayakovsky and Eisenstein did to a certain extent, their work exemplified as well the personal, idiosyncratic approach to Mexico of Balmont. For all Russian visitors to Mexico during the 1920s and early 1930s, international politics were always relevant to their evaluations, as they had been during the first four decades of the nineteenth century. Thus, this last period has more in common with the first than might have been expected.

Mayakovsky was responsible for the first real popular interest in Mexico during the period of the New Economic Policy, and was the one who, through his journey, made Soviet citizens aware of a full range of social and cultural developments in Mexico. He, like many Russians, expected Mexico to be not unlike the new Soviet Union, although he knew that its revolution was essentially non-Marxist. He imagined as well that Mexico would be making great strides forward socially and economically and was surprised and disappointed when the country did not live up to his highest expectations. Fascinating as Mexico was to Mayakovsky, it nonetheless seemed to be only marginally Westernized, backward, and restrained from further progress by ambitious politicians and the overwhelming influence of U.S. economic imperialism. However kind, generous, and original were the Mexican people, Mayakovsky came to feel, their future could only be assured by the adoption of Marxism-Leninism and by support for international proletarian revolution, based on the Bolshevik model.

This was precisely what Pestkovsky had reported to Narkomindel and the Comintern upon his return to Moscow and what he would write in his books and essays about the country in the years that followed his reassignment. Pestkovsky was probably better informed and more knowledgeable about Mexico than anyone else discussed in this book. What he found in Mexico only tended to confirm what he had believed to be the solution to Mexico's social, economic, and political problems before he left the USSR, however. In his eyes, only the unity of the workers and the peasants against the bourgeoisie and the imperialists would guarantee Mexico the safety it needed to build up a truly egalitarian, eventually Communist system. Pestkovsky was interested in teaching a lesson to Mexicans, and his two books published in Moscow were further reflections of that desire. Those Russians who read his books no doubt knew that lesson well, of course, but through studying *Agrarnyi vopros i krestianskoe dvizhenie v Meksike* and *Istoriia meksikanskikh revoliutsii* they could also learn more about Mexico than they could anywhere else. Pestkovsky's approach to Mexico and its history was "scientific" from a Marxist point of view, and as he had promised, consistently "Pokrovskian." He was not swayed by great personalities, whom he saw as tools of economic interests. On the contrary, his was a history of social groups and the economic relationships between classes. Whatever their drawbacks, his books were the first Marxist interpretations of Mexico's history. His personal fate should not detract from his intellectual and political legacy in this regard.

Undoubtedly, few ambassadors had the leisure to study the country to which they were accredited that Pestkovsky did. Diplomatic duties require a considerable amount of time and little is left for purely scholarly or recreational pursuits. The Soviet ambassadors to Mexico during the 1920s had such opportunities, however, and consequently, it is surprising that Kollontai wrote and spoke so little about Mexico. Apparently, her views were consistent with those of other Russians who did write about Mexico during the 1920s. She, like Pestkovsky and Mayakovsky, for example, privately considered Mexico's government to be made up of "phony revolutionaries" who ran the country for their own good through their agents and their connections with foreign businessmen. All three agreed that Mexico needed a new, genuine revolution, not the agrarian tumult it had had. Kollontai differed from her two fellow countrymen in that she was given much more publicity, because of her importance during the Bolshevik Revolution and her fame and notoriety deriving from the question of women's liberation. It might be added that she differed from them as well in that she made a point of expressing her embarrassment at having known so little about Mexico before her assignment. She commented on this a number of times, adding that such ignorance was surprisingly widespread in Europe and that she would like to see the situation changed. Her veracity was refreshing since Pestkovsky and Mayakovsky rarely admitted afterward that they had known little about Mexico. They might bewail the ignorance of other Russians, but always conveyed the impression that they knew the country well. And they, of course, never hesitated to give Mexicans advice on how to run their affairs, a trait typical of Soviet citizens abroad during the 1920s, most particularly those representing the Comintern.

Probably the single feature that distinguishes Soviet writing on Mexico of the 1920s from what was written about the country elsewhere was the Soviet evaluation of the Mexican Revolution. To Soviet citizens, Mexico had had no real revolution, only a change of government, accompanied by the widespread use of meaningless revolutionary rhetoric. Russia, on the other hand, had gone through genuine revolutionary change and had been transformed. They would readily have agreed with Tverskoi that while the players had been replaced, the music remained the same. It was for this reason that Soviet observers, even when they were most objective, saw themselves as teachers and the Mexicans as pupils. To appreciate this, one must read what was printed in the West about Mexico during these years, especially in the United States and Great Britain, the two nations whose interests were threatened most by Mexico's revolutionary nationalism. Pestkovsky and Mayakovsky no doubt found it ludicrous to hear Calles described as heading a "Bolshevik" regime; to present the Mexican Revolution, in the form they found it in the mid-1920s, as a threat to capitalist free enterprise was equally laughable. Not all in the West failed to see the growing reaction in Mexico's government, but generally in Western Europe and the United States, Mexico was felt to be as radical as any nation in the world during the 1920s. What was "Red Mexico" to the West was "reactionary Mexico" in Moscow, and this became only more evident to Russians as the decade continued. The two revolutions had been different from the outset, and despite the diplomatic verbiage, they moved further and further away from each other as the years passed.

To a surprising degree, Eisenstein was able to incorporate this concept of moribund revolution into his synthesis of all the ideas Russians had had about Mexico since the time of Rezanov. He was as interested in the ancient past as Balmont, and he wanted to understand colonial rule as much as Wrangell and the representatives of the Russian American Company did; his attitudes toward rural hacienda life were as negative and critical as Patkanov's, and he expressed his sense of the need for a true, genuine revolution as avidly as did Pestkovsky and Mayakovsky. However, he showed a greater sensitivity to Mexico, its culture, and traditions than did any other Russian visitor to the country. Mexicans were always appreciative of Russian interest, but those who worked with Eisenstein were amazed at his empathetic comprehension of their country. They said that he helped them see Mexico with new eyes, with a new love and a clearer, more penetrating understanding. Eisenstein assimilated Mexico into his character, to an extent few foreigners, and certainly no other Russian, ever succeeded in doing.

What was extraordinarily sad about Eisenstein's attempt to recreate Mexico on film was its ultimate failure. No more than a few stills from the film were seen widely in the Soviet Union until long after Eisenstein's death, and the disfavor that Eisenstein fell into meant that for many years little could be written about the project in the USSR. Still, even in the truncated, distorted form in which the film exists today, and through the hundreds of stills that survive from the project, the culmination of the best in the long tradition of Russian interest in Mexico can be seen and appreciated in *Que Viva Mexico!*

Because Eisenstein's accomplishment was so impressive, Trotsky's stay in Mexico would be nothing more than a minor addendum were it not for his great historical importance, the publicity he was given throughout the time he lived in Mexico, and his murder. Needless to say, few Soviet citizens know anything about Trotsky's activities in

Mexico, and almost no one read what he wrote there. His life in the country coincided with an awkward period in Mexican foreign relations, and particularly in its relations with the USSR. Not wishing to endanger his refuge, Trotsky carefully avoided any statements which might embarrass his benefactor Cárdenas. If his stay was newsworthy, therefore, it cannot be seen as more than an epilogue to this study of those Russians who had visited and been influenced by Mexico. The third phase of Russian interest in Mexico had ended with Eisenstein.

In the 1980s, because of recent events in the Caribbean and Central America, there is much uneasiness about Soviet intentions in Latin America in general. Many governments around the world tend to believe that their interest is without precedent. This may be true with respect to the majority of nations in Latin America, but not Mexico. Until the success of the Cuban Revolution, Mexico was the Latin American country which interested Russians more than any other. Only Brazil and parts of the southern cone nations have even approached that level of attention. For decades, Mexico has been used by Russian and Soviet writers and political activists for their own purposes. But Russians and Mexicans, despite the great differences separating them from each other, have also long felt a sense of mutual comprehension, even at times of similarity of worldview, but always a great sympathy for each other. Even when Russians were most critical, they often possessed this sense of emotional and moral identity with Mexicans and appreciated similar expressions by Mexicans. By 1940, the educated Soviet Russian public were probably as well informed about Mexico as were most Europeans, and while their interpretation of the country was ideologically determined, it was their intuitive sympathy for Mexico and its people that distinguished their views from those of other Europeans or U.S. citizens. That attitude had been growing since the time of Rezanov's voyage to Mexican California and had been determined to a great extent by the writings and experiences of the people discussed here.

Since the time of Trotsky, relations between the USSR and Mexico have grown and expanded and can be expected to continue to do so in the future, whatever limits might be set by distance and the presence of the Soviet Union's great international competitor immediately next door to Mexico. More than many other peoples, Russians see themselves in terms of their history, and how they understand and react to Mexico and the rest of Latin America in the future will be conditioned by their past analyses. This book has been an attempt to explain how Russians responded to Mexico during the first century and more of the relationship between the two countries.

NOTES
BIBLIOGRAPHY
INDEX

NOTES

The full names of Russian authors are given in the bibliography; only first initials are provided in the notes. For archival materials, *fond* numbers are given first, then *opis* numbers, then finally *edinoe khranilishche*, each separated from the other by a slash.

Introduction

1   See Héctor Sánchez, ed., *México nueve veces contado, por narradores extranjeros* (Mexico City: Secretaría de Educación Pública, 1974).
2   See Brigida M. von Mentz de Boege, *Das Mexicobild der Deutschen im 19. Jahrhundert (1821–1861) im Spiegel der ersten populären Zeitschriften* (Mexico City: 1975).
3   See Drewey Wayne Gunn, *American and British Writers in Mexico, 1556–1973* (Austin: University of Texas Press, 1974); Drewey Wayne Gunn, *Mexico in American and British Letters* (Metuchen, N.J.: Scarecrow Press, 1974); Paul Fussell, *Abroad: British Literary Travelling Between the Wars* (New York: Oxford University Press, 1980); and Alicia Diadiuk, *Viajeras anglosajonas en México: Memorias* (Mexico City: Secretaría de Educación Pública, 1973).
4   Gunn, *American and British Writers*, p. x.
5   See Charles Rougle, *Three Russians Consider America: America in the Works of Maksim Gorkij, Aleksandr Blok, and Vladimir Majakovskij* (Stockholm: Almqvist and Wiksell International, 1976).
6   Gunn, *American and British Writers*, p. 253, says that U.S. and British writers never really understood this sense of history that was so important to Mexicans.
7   See John H. Kautsky, *Patterns of Modernizing Revolutions: Mexico and the Soviet Union* (Beverly Hills: Sage Publications, 1975), for a general discussion of these similarities.
8   Fussell, *Abroad*, p. 158.

1   The Earliest Accounts

1   The translations conveyed the general impression that Mexico was a region populated by intelligent, skillful natives exploited by the Spaniards; see Avrahm Yar-

225

molinsky, *Russian Americana, Sixteenth to Eighteenth Centuries: A Bibliographical and Historical Study* (New York: New York Public Library, 1943).

2 See *Primechaniia k Sankt-Peterburgskim vedomostiam*, 1735. Six issues in 1741 included a series of articles entitled "Izvestiia o Kalifornii."

3 M. V. Lomonosov, *Polnoe sobranie sochineniia*, vol. 8 (Moscow-Leningrad: Akademiia nauk SSSR, 1959), p. 514.

4 Yarmolinsky, *Russian Americana*, p. 39. The play's moral was expressed in Cortés's last words, and were indicative more of Sumarokov's hopes for Russia than for his knowledge of Mexican history: "My kindness toward my allies and the mercy I showed those I conquered, on the one hand, and your pride and your tyrannous treatment of your subjects, on the other, were my chief aids in conquering the Mexican kingdom and in subjecting it to the Spanish crown."

5 See "O Amerike," *Trudoliubivaia pchela*, November 1759, p. 704.

6 See N. I. Novikov's 1783 *Pribavleniia k Moskovskim vedomostiam*; see also V. V. Volskii et al., eds., *Latinskaia Amerika v proshlom i nastoiashchem* (Moscow: Izdatelstvo sotsialnoi-ekonomicheskoi literatury, 1960), p. 349.

7 One was entitled "Ob ispanskikh v Meksikanskoi oblasti seleniiakh"; *Akademicheskie izvestiia* was published between 1779 and 1781.

8 The full title was *Alzira, ili Amerikantsy*, and is republished in I. A. Krylov, *Polnoe sobranie sochinenii*, vol. 2, ed. D. Bednyi (Moscow: Khudozhestvennaia literatura, 1946), p. 668; see Volskii et al., *Latinskaia Amerika*, pp. 351–52 for a summary of the play.

9 One last article should be mentioned: "O Meksike," *Vestnik Evropy* 57 (1811): 77, described the beginning of the wars of independence in Latin America and gave many details about life in Mexico.

10 "Stretched out as she was across the vast distances of the Americas, there is little reason to think that Spain would have been interested in extending her sparsely settled domains into these unknown territories had it not been for disquieting rumors that began to circulate concerning Russian exploration far to the north." C. Alan Hutchinson, *Frontier Settlement in Mexican California* (New Haven: Yale University Press, 1969), pp. 1–2.

11 Spanish disquiet was certainly increased by a book written by Fray José Torrubia, *I Moscoviti nella California*, published in Rome in 1759, warning about Russian designs on California.

12 The best brief summary of the history of the Russian American Company has been given by E. O. Essig, "The Russian Settlement at Ross," *Quarterly of the California Historical Society* 13, no. 3 (September 1933): 191: "The Russian American Company was first organized by Gregory Shelekhof with some two hundred members. The first American colony was established at Kodiak in 1784. In 1788 the Company received exclusive control over the Alaskan district from the Empress Catherine, and in 1799 it was given a monopoly of Alaskan commerce for twenty years under the name of the Russian American Company. Its charter was always regranted whenever it expired and the Company virtually ruled Alaska until December 31, 1861, shortly before the latter was purchased by the United States in 1867."

13 Diane Spencer-Hancock and William E. Pritchard, trans. Ina Kaliakin, "Notes to

the 1817 Treaty Between the Russian American Company and the Kashaya Pomo Indians," *California History* 59, no. 4 (Winter 1980–1981): 307–08.

14 On Rezanov, see Hector Chevigny, *Lost Empire: The Life and Adventures of Nikolai Petrovich Rezanov* (New York: Macmillan, 1937); N. P. Rezanov, *The Rezanov Voyage to Nueva California in 1806*, trans. Thomas C. Russell (San Francisco: Thomas C. Russell, 1926); and Richard A. Pierce, ed., *Rezanov Reconnoiters California, 1806* (San Francisco: The Book Club of California, 1972).

15 Rezanov, *The Rezanov Voyage*, p. 15.

16 Ibid., pp. 16–17.

17 Ibid., pp. 41–42.

18 Langsdorff wrote that Rezanov's only concern was to obtain corn and flour for the Russian settlers in Alaska; G. H. von Langsdorff, *Langsdorff's Narrative of the Rezanov Voyage to Nueva California in 1806*, trans. Thomas C. Russell (San Francisco: Thomas C. Russell, 1927), p. 153.

19 He added that a great opportunity had been missed in 1798, when Russia and Spain were at war, to seize all of California down to Santa Barbara, and that such opportunities should not be passed up in the future; see S. B. Okun, *The Russian American Company*, trans. Carl Ginsburg (Cambridge: Harvard University Press, 1951), p. 121.

20 Concepción became a nun at the news of his death, and she died in 1857 at the convent of St. Catherine in Benecia.

21 A traditional source of information on Russians in California is Hubert Howe Bancroft; see his *Works*, especially vol. 19: *History of California*, pt. 2 (San Francisco: The History Company, 1886).

22 Otto von Kotzebue's arrival in San Francisco in October 1816 was met with a request from the local officials that he convey again to the inhabitants at Fort Ross the Spanish demand that they leave.

23 See the "Fort Ross" section of K. T. Khlebnikov's *Colonial Russian America*, trans. Basil Dmytryshyn and E.A.P. Crownhart-Vaughan (Portland: Oregon Historical Society, 1976), pp. 106–34.

24 In 1802 the Russians had suffered a disastrous attack by the Tlinkit Indians at Novo-Arkhangelsk and learned that cooperation with the local Indians was essential to their survival in North America; as a result, they stressed peaceful relations with the California Indians, and in 1817 signed a treaty with the Kashaya Pomo Indians to protect their position at Fort Ross; see Spencer-Hancock, "Notes to the 1817 Treaty." See also Clarence John Du Four et al., "The Russian Withdrawal from California," *California Historical Quarterly*, September 1933, pp. 240–76.

25 Langsdorff, *Langsdorff's Narrative*, p. 155.

26 Ibid., pp. 157–58.

27 Ibid., p. 161.

28 V. P. Tarakanov, *Statement of My Captivity Among the Californians* (Los Angeles: Glen Dawson, 1953), p. 18.

29 Langsdorff, *Langsdorff's Narrative*, p. 168.

30 Their intricately choreographed and imaginative dances proved the Indians' superiority, Langsdorff believed. Ibid., pp. 194–95.

31 Tarakanov, *Statement*, pp. 21–22.

32 Langsdorff, *Langsdorff's Narrative*, p. 188.

33 N. A. Khvostov, "Extracts from the Log of the Ship Juno," in Pierce, *Rezanov Reconnoiters California*, p. 53.

34 August C. Mahr, *The Visit of the "Rurik" to San Francisco in 1816* (Stanford: Stanford University Press, 1932), p. 59.

35 Ibid., p. 61.

36 Ibid., p. 65.

37 Ibid., p. 79.

38 Ibid., p. 83.

39 Ibid., p. 87.

40 Louis Choris, "Port San Francisco and Its Inhabitants," ibid., pp. 93–103.

41 V. M. Golovnin, *Around the World on the "Kamchatka," 1817–1819*, trans. Ella Lury Wiswell (Honolulu: Hawaii Historical Society and the University Press of Hawaii, 1979), p. 140; not all his officers were so impressed by the reception; see, for example, Litke, ibid., p. 144. For more on Golovnin, see Iu. V. Davydov, *Golovnin* (Moscow: Molodaia gvardiia, 1968).

42 Golovnin was more than a little confused about the geography of California, writing for example that the area's main port was San Blas, and that California's northern border was "definitely 37 degrees latitude," which would have placed it just above Santa Cruz, near Año Nuevo, and about sixty miles south of the Golden Gate. Golovnin, *Kamchatka*, pp. 145–46.

43 Ibid., p. 148.

44 Ibid., p. 150.

45 Ibid.

46 Ibid., p. 153.

47 Ibid., pp. 155, 157. Golovnin admitted that much of what he had written about California he had learned from a local Spaniard well disposed toward Russians, a man who was not happy with his "lazy and inactive countrymen" (p. 147), and one who might even have welcomed a Russian administration. This did not compel Golovnin to retract anything he had said, however.

48 This was Zavalishin's contention; see James R. Gibson, *Imperial Russia in Frontier America* (New York: Oxford University Press, 1976), p. 185.

49 See Okun, *Russian American Company*, pp. 136–40; Ekkehard Völkl, *Russland und Lateinamerika, 1741–1841* (Wiesbaden: Harrasowitz, 1968), pp. 134–38; Glynn Barratt, *Russia in Pacific Waters, 1715–1825* (Vancouver: University of British Columbia Press, 1981), pp. 224–28; and Anatole G. Mazour, "Dmitrii Zavalishin, Dreamer of a Russian American Empire," *Pacific Historical Review* 5 (1936): 26–37. Zavalishin left an account of the journey in "Krugotsvetnoe plavanie fregata 'Kreiser' v 1822–1825 gg. pod komandoiu Mikhaila Petrovicha Lazareva," *Drevniaia i novaia Rossiia*, 1877, no. 5–7. He described California in "Kaliforniia v 1824 godu," *Russkii vestnik* 60 (1865): 322–68, and the Ross colony in "Delo o kolonii Ross," *Russkii vestnik* 62, no. 3–4: 36–65.

50 Okun, *Russian American Company*, p. 137. Zavalishin also made a collection of Mexican and Spanish folksongs; see *Russkii vestnik*, 1865, no. 11: 349, 353–55. One

of the songs, the "Riego Hymn," concerned the recently victorious revolution in Mexico.

51 Otto Von Kotzebue, *A New Voyage Round the World in the Years 1823, 24, 25, and 26*, 2 vols. (New York: Da Capo Press, 1967), vol. 2, p. 80.

52 Ibid., p. 98.

53 Ibid., pp. 88–94 passim.

54 He remarked in passing that the northern shore of San Francisco Bay was not part of California, but was "assigned by geographers to New Albion" (p. 112) despite the Mexican settlements there, thereby suggesting that the Russians might have a good claim to it.

55 Ibid., p. 110.

56 Ibid., p. 124.

57 Ibid., p. 127.

58 K. T. Khlebnikov, "Zapiski o Kalifornii," *Syn otechestva* 174 (1829), bk. 2: 208–27, 276–88, 336–47, 400–10; bk. 3: 25–35. On Khlebnikov, see B. N. Vishnevskii, *Puteshestvennik Kirill Khlebnikov* (Perm: Permskoe knizhnoe izdatelstvo, 1957); see also Khlebnikov's "Vzgliad na polveka moei zhizni," *Syn otechestva* 175 (1836): 299–324, 345–75, 413–28.

59 Khlebnikov, "Zapiski," p. 336.

60 Ibid., p. 325.

61 For an interesting Russian account of California under U.S. rule, see A. G. Rotchev, "Vospominaniia russkogo puteshestvennika o Vest-Indii, Kalifornii i Ost-Indii," *Panteon*, 1854, no. 1: 79–108; no. 2: 93–114.

62 See E. E. Blomkvist, "A Russian Scientific Expedition to California and Alaska, 1839–1849," trans. Basil Dmytryshyn and E.A.P. Crownhart-Vaughan, *Oregon Historical Quarterly* 73, no. 2 (1972): 101–70; and A. I. Alekseev, *Ilia Gavrilovich Voznesenskii (1816–1871)* (Moscow: Nauka, 1977). Voznesenskii was in Baja California in November 1841 on board the *Naslednik Aleksandr*; once every three years a ship was sent down from Sitka to buy salt from local officials at Isla Carmen.

63 On Wrangell's Life, see V. M. Pasetskii, *Ferdinand Petrovich Vrangel, 1796–1870* (Moscow: Nauka, 1975).

64 Wrangell's diary is the source for much of the information here, and is reprinted as F. P. Wrangell, "Dnevnik puteshestviia iz Sitkhi v Sankt-Peterburg cherez Meksiku," in L. A. Shur, ed., *K beregam Novogo Sveta* (Moscow: Nauka, 1971), pp. 190–259. The diary has been published in Spanish; see *De Sitka a San Petersburgo a través de México*, trans. Luisa Pintós Mimó (Mexico City, 1975).

65 Letter from I. V. Prokofev to Wrangell, quoted in Pasetskii, *Vrangel*, p. 138.

66 Shur, *K beregam*, pp. 270–71. Wrangell knew Figueroa from his visit in 1833 to California; see James R. Gibson, "Russian America in 1833," *Pacific Northwest Quarterly*, January 1972, pp. 1–13.

67 Wrangell, "Dnevnik," p. 203.

68 Ibid., p. 206.

69 Ibid., pp. 208–09. As examples of corruption, Wrangell gave the following: government officials' salaries were enormous, and such officials seemed innumerable; of thirty-five soldiers in Tepic, one was a colonel; before the Texas campaign, five

of the sixty-five soldiers were colonels; and the three alcaldes in Tepic behaved like petty dictators to whom the law meant nothing.

70 His knowledge of recent political developments he attributed to a French merchant from Mazatlan whom he had met on the road to Guadalajara.

71 Here and elsewhere in the diary, Wrangell was careful to list in detail all costs involved in the journey so as to give precise figures to his superiors in St. Petersburg and to justify his expenses; quite often he felt he was much overcharged for the services he received; see ibid., p. 222.

72 Ibid., p. 237.

73 Ibid., p. 241.

74 Ibid., p. 243.

75 Ibid., p. 245.

76 Ibid., p. 248.

77 While the fortunes of the Russian American Company declined rapidly, Wrangell's career flourished: between 1840 and 1848 he was director of the company; in 1847 he was appointed vice-admiral, and in 1856, admiral; finally, in 1855 he became head of the Naval Ministry.

78 The articles, "Puteshestvie iz Sitkhi v Sankt-Peterburg" ("A Journey from Sitka to Saint Petersburg"), appeared in *Severniaia pchela* in nos. 240–46 and 259–64 (October and November 1836); the book, published in St. Petersburg, was written in the form of a travelogue, as letters to an old friend (probably E. P. Litke, who had traveled with Wrangell around the world on the *Kamchatka* in 1817–19).

79 Wrangell, "Dnevnik," p. 249.

80 Ibid., pp. 249–50.

81 It is entirely possible, although there is no substantial evidence for this view, that Wrangell's criticisms of the Mexican government and economy were veiled criticisms of Russia at the time. This type of surreptitious criticism was not at all uncommon, and later Russian writers about Mexico were quite clearly doing this.

82 Ibid., p. 250.

2 The Age of Porfirio Díaz

1 He was also known as Aleksei Markov; his articles appeared in *Russkaia slovesnost* in 1849 and were published in book form as *Russkie na vostochnom okeane*, 2d ed. (Saint Petersburg, 1856).

2 Alexei [Aleksandr] Markov, *The Russians on the Pacific Ocean [California 1845]*, trans. Ivan Petroff (Los Angeles: Glen Dawson, 1955), p. 25.

3 The storekeeper told him in private, however, that British merchants had brought the canvas from Brazil, where it had been manufactured with the Russian trademark stamped on it to increase its price; ibid., pp. 194–95.

4 He mentioned that when an Englishman at the hotel lost a game of chess to a Russian captain, he generously and good-humoredly ordered a bottle of champagne to celebrate.

5 A. G. Rotchev, "Vospominaniia russkogo puteshestvennika o Vest-Indii, Kalifornii i Ost-Indii," *Panteon*, 1854, no. 1: 79–108; no. 2: 93–114.

6   P. N. Golovin, *Iz putevykh pisem P. N. Golovina* (St. Petersburg: Ministerstvo morskogo flota, 1863), p. 59; also in English as *Civil and Strange Encounters: The Worldly Travel Letters of an Imperial Russian Navy Officer, 1860–1861*, trans. Basil Dmytryshyn and E.A.P. Crownhart-Vaughan (Portland: Oregon Historical Society, 1983). It was in the same year that S. Danevskaia's *Otkrytie i zavoevanie Meksiki* (St. Petersburg, 1863), a children's history of the Conquest, was published, with several subsequent editions.

7   See B. V. Lukin, "Ekspeditsiia Peterburgskoi Akademii nauk v Meksiku i na Kubu," *Vestnik Akademii nauk SSSR*, 1966, no. 7: 109–12.

8   A. I. Voeikov, "Puteshestvie A. I. Voeikova v tsentralnoi Amerike," *Izvestiia imperatorskogo russkogo geograficheskogo obshchestva* 11, pt. 2 (1875): 152–55.

9   Héctor Cárdenas, *Las relaciones mexicano-soviéticas: Antecedentes y primeros contactos diplomáticos (1789–1927)* (Mexico City: Secretaría de Relaciones Exteriores, 1974), pp. 21–28. Dostoevsky also wrote about this period; see Galina Kogan, "Fiodor Dostoevski, el pensamiento social ruso y la 'cuestión mexicana' en los años sesenta del siglo XIX," *América Latina*, 1975, no. 2: 128–45.

10 See Fedor Smirnov, *Iuzhnaia pri-atlanticheskaia Amerika: Politiko-ekonomicheskie ocherki* (St. Petersburg, 1872), and A. S. Ionin, *Po Iuzhnoi Amerike*, 4 vols. (St. Petersburg, 1892–1902).

11 The ambassadors were Baron Roman Romanovich Rozen and General Pedro Rincón Gallardo; Mexican consulates were established in St. Petersburg, Moscow, Helsinki, Riga, and Liepaja, and Russian consulates in Mexico City, Veracruz, Laguna del Carmen, Monterey, and Guadalajara.

12 S. K. Patkanov, "Po gatsiendam i ruinam Iukatana," *Zemlevedenie* 3 (1896): bk. 1, pp. 79–110: bk. 2, pp. 93–130; bk. 3, pp. 111–42; "V strane maiasov," *Nabliudatel*, 1895, no. 6: 98–130.

13 Patkanov, *Zemlevedenie*, p. 95.

14 He noted, however, that with care, all such diseases could be avoided, and that during his month's stay there he was not sick at all.

15 Patkanov, *Zemlevedenie*, p. 99.

16 Ibid., p. 101.

17 Patkanov, *Nabliudatel*, pp. 118–19.

18 Ibid., p. 119.

19 Ibid., p. 121. Many people, he noted, found the mestizo women of Yucatán to be the most beautiful in Mexico, but he disagreed; they were not as beautiful as Spanish women and appeared to have picked up the negative features of both races, and none of the positive ones. Ibid., p. 127.

20 Ibid., p. 123.

21 This gave Patkanov an opportunity to discuss the henequen industry of the region, its cultivation and processing. Ibid., pp. 103–04.

22 Patkanov, *Zemlevedenie*, p. 115. He was glad to hear that the U.S. consul had been working to preserve the ruins; ibid., p. 112.

23 Their ideas toward marriage and divorce were very liberal by European standards— another indication of their unique position within the society of the peninsula, he felt; ibid., pp. 124–26.

24 Ibid., pp. 120–24. The souvenirs included a hammock, which symbolized to Patkanov one of the positive features of Yucatecan society.

25 See the letters of Vladimir Galaktionovich Korolenko to S. D. Protopopov, 5 May 1894–13 August 1921, TsGALI 389/1/61.

26 Several of Protopopov's journals are kept in TsGALI; the Mexican ones (389/1/3 and 389/1/4) are unfortunately less detailed than the others.

27 It was a country "little known to us." S. D. Protopopov, "Proezdom po Meksike (iz zapisnoi knizhki puteshestvennika)," *Russkoe bogatstvo*, 1896, no. 9: 82.

28 Ibid., p. 85. He added in his notebook that the same thing had been true in Alaska: Russia had lost tremendous wealth by selling the territory to the United States, but had not been able to take advantage of its economic potential in any case; 30 August/11 September 1893, 389/1/3.

29 Protopopov, *Russkoe bogatstvo*, p. 85. He sketched what he saw in his diary to aid his memory; in general, he kept extensive notes and sketches in his notebooks. 2/14 September 1893, 389/1/3.

30 Protopopov, *Russkoe bogatstvo*, p. 87.

31 "In smoking rooms . . . in hotel lobbies, bars, even on omnibuses you can overhear very sensible, intelligent opinions on the most difficult questions of political and social life." Ibid., p. 90.

32 Ibid., p. 91.

33 Ibid., p. 95.

34 Ibid., p. 108.

35 G. A. Devollan, "V tsarstve Montezumy," *Istoricheskii vestnik* 100 (1905): 285–307, 631–57.

36 His photograph illustrating the collection of aguamiel from the center of the maguey plant was strikingly like the images Weston and Eisenstein used in their work more than twenty years later. Ibid., p. 290.

37 Ibid., p. 302.

38 See ibid., pp. 643–46, for a lengthy description of the *posadas*.

39 Ibid., p. 646. It is interesting to compare his impressions of the city with Wrangell's, who found Puebla to be one of the Mexican cities he liked least.

40 K. D. Balmont, *Zmeinye tsvety* (Moscow: Skorpion, 1910), p. 3.

41 The police had forbidden his speaking at the railroad station lest it cause a political demonstration.

42 Rodney L. Patterson, "Balmont," in K. D. Balmont, *Izbrannye stikhotvoreniia i poemy* (Munich: Wilhelm Fink Verlag, 1975), p. 43. The evening also led to a verbal attack and confrontation instigated by the young Mayakovsky, but the argument could not spoil Balmont's pleasure at being home again. Mayakovsky spoke on "Balmont-Meksikanets" on 10 September 1928; see Nikolai Khardzhiev, "Zametki o Maiakovskom. 4. Puteshestvie v Meksiku," *Den poezii* (Moscow: Izdatelstvo sovetskii pisatel, 1969), p. 239.

43 Valerii Zemskov, "Y México surgió cual inspirada visión . . . Konstantin Balmont y la poesía india," *América Latina*, 1977, no. 3: 181.

44 K. Mochulskii, quoted in Martin P. Rice, *Valery Briusov and the Rise of Russian Symbolism* (Ann Arbor: Ardis, 1975), p. 67.

45   P. Pertsov, quoted in Patterson, "Balmont," pp. 34–35.

46   Balmont, "Putevye pisma," *Zmeinye tsvety*, p. 12. The journal was written in the form of letters to someone in Russia. Unfortunately, Balmont's notebooks from Mexico as well as his numerous letters to his then wife, A. A. Andreeva-Balmont, have apparently been lost. See Introduction, Letters to E. A. Balmont, 1904–33, Arkhiv K. D. Balmonta, TsGALI 57/1/145. His "Putevye pisma" are thus the only significant sources of information about his journey. On homesickness as a determining factor in Balmont's rejection of modern Mexico see Luis Mario Schneider, *Dos poetas rusos en México: Balmont y Mayakovski* (Mexico City: Secretaría de Educación Pública, 1973), p. 12. Even while crossing the Atlantic, Balmont was already writing about what pleasant, generous people Russians were in comparison with Germans, Britons, and Frenchmen.

47   Ibid., p. 15.

48   Balmont gave a humorous account of working conditions in the library: hardly anyone was there reading; roosters crowed just outside the windows; doves had made nests inside the building and flew in and out while he and Tsvetkovskaia worked; people smoked while reading, not worried in the least about damaging the books; young ladies typed at their desks disturbing the quiet; and everyone looked at Balmont working as if he were a little crazy; see ibid., p. 16.

49   "Evening—What suffering. I finally cannot endure [any longer] the coarse events which I at one time liked. The bullfight, especially here, where there is no Spanish elegance in the staging, is a vile terrifying slaughterhouse. The bulls were of rare strength and ferocity, and the toreadors [sic] were clumsy and cowardly to an abominable extent. It was as if my senses had been dulled by the sight of the blood and corpses. By accident we sat in the second row up from the bottom, that is just a few feet from the arena, and it was the first time I had seen it all from so close up. Two bulls jumped over the barrier. This could have had serious consequences for anyone in the first or second row, but everything turned out happily. Only these few moments were any good, however, because a few moments later, a bull twice almost raised the scurrying clowns of the odious spectacle onto his horn, but they were saved at the last minute. I secretly hoped for the death of one or another of these outcasts, and the bull seemed to me, as he had in Madrid in the spring, to be a noble animal, dying with dignity. The people were disgusting. The public, boistrously laughing at the dying horses, were a cruel nightmare. I was in hell. I am sick. I cannot bear the sight of people." Ibid., p. 17.

50   Ibid.

51   Zemskov, "Y México surgió," p. 184.

52   Balmont, "Putevye pisma," p. 16. He was especially taken with Cortés's palace in Cuernavaca: "It was evening, the stars were shining; I walked back and forth on the veranda where he was inspired continually by proud and bitter thoughts, looking at the distant masses of the volcanoes." Ibid., p. 24.

53   Ibid., p. 31.

54   Ibid., p. 20.

55   Postcard dated 15 June 1905. Letters to V. IA. Briusov, Arkhiv K. D. Balmonta, TsGALI, 56/3/6.

56 Balmont's sense of the destruction of the pre-Columbian past in central Mexico was much greater than our own because many of the most impressive sites known today had not been excavated in 1905, e.g., Tula, Monte Albán, Cuicuilco, Tlatelolco, and many others.

57 He remarked later that he would someday write a book, *A Handbook for Ill-Fated Travellers Who Wish, in Their Unknowing Imprudence, to Eat, Drink, Sleep, and Wash — On a Mexican Steamship (!!!);* "Putevye pisma," p. 35. Balmont's account is not unlike that in Graeme Greene's *Another Mexico* (New York: Viking, 1939); see esp. pp. 113–22.

58 Balmont frequently described hummingbirds (see "Putevye pisma," p. 256, e.g.), both because of their beauty and because of their importance in Mexican mythology.

59 Postcard dated 19 May 1905. Letters to V. IA. Briusov, Arkhiv K. D. Balmonta, TsGALI, 56/33/6.

60 Balmont, "Putevye Pisma," p. 44; Haggard had been in Mexico in 1891, and ideas for two novels had resulted: *Montezuma's Daughter* (1893) and *Heart of the World* (1896).

61 He was especially glad to find *Hamlet* and *King Lear*, poetry by Coleridge and Burns, and the archeological studies of Le Plongeon and Brasseur de Bourbourg.

62 Balmont, "Putevye pisma," p. 48.

63 Balmont published a number of highly emotional accolades to the revolution, to uprisings, barricades, and other such symbols of insurrection until 1907; they were later collected in his *Pesni mstitelia (Songs of An Avenger)* (Paris, 1907).

64 Patterson, "Balmont," p. 36, has commented that "discriminating readers were increasingly sensitive to the mediocre verse that Balmont usually allowed into his collections." More acidly, D. S. Mirsky felt that most of Balmont's work was worthless: "This includes all his original verses after 1905, most of his numerous translations . . . and all his prose without exception, which is the most insipid, turgid, and meaningless prose in the language." *A History of Russian Literature*, ed. Francis J. Whitfield (New York: Alfred A. Knopf, 1949), p. 433.

65 Vladimir Markov, "Balmont: A Reappraisal," *Slavic Review* 28, no. 2 (June 1969): p. 241. *Ptitsy v vozdukhe* was published by Shipovnik in Moscow in 1908.

66 *Zovy drevnosti: Gimni, pesni i zamysli drevnikh* (St. Petersburg, 1908); the volume included poem cycles on the themes of Mexico and the Mayans.

67 The photographs were of carvings of gods and goddesses from the National Museum, pictures of Indian life, of the Pedregal outside Mexico City, the maguey and organ cactus, the cirio, the archeological sites of Xochicalco, Monte Albán, Mitla, Palenque, Uxmal, and Chichén Itzá. The final page of each section of the book was decorated with pre-Columbian designs and the cover with an illustration of the intricate brick-work of Mitla.

68 See Balmont, *Zmeinye*, pp. 89–207. See also I. Rozhdestvenskaia, "K. D. Balmont: Pisma k E. A. Liatskomu," *Russkaia literatura*, 1975, no. 2: 194. The translation in *Zmeinye tsvety* was accompanied by a highly informed commentary on the *Popol Vuh* which related it to other of the world's epics; see "Peresvety pomyslov," in Balmont, *Zmeinye*, pp. 231–43. The best recent translation of the *Popol Vuh* into Russian was done under the supervision of R. V. Kinzhalov; see *Popol Vukh: Rodo-*

slovnaia vladyk Totonakipana (Moscow-Leningrad: Akademiia nauk SSSR, 1959).
Balmont translated from dozens of languages, modern and ancient: plays by Ibsen,
Wilde, Hauptmann, Maeterlinck, Calderón; stories by Hoffman and Hamsun; much
of Whitman's *Leaves of Grass;* Wilde's "Ballad of Reading Gaol"; primitive and exotic poems; poets from Bulgaria, Lithuania, Poland; the Western lyric poets; and
the complete poetry of Shelley and Poe.

69 Balmont, *Zmeinye,* pp. 53–70.

70 Ibid., pp. 73–87.

71 Ibid., pp. 247–48.

72 Ibid., pp. 3–7.

73 "Nachertaniia tsaritsy Maiev" ("The Account of the Queen of the Maya"), *Zmeinye,*
pp. 211–19; "Slovo maiskogo vaiatelia" ("The Tale of the Mayan Sculptor"), *Zmeinye,*
pp. 223–27.

74 Ilya Ehrenburg, *People and Life: 1891–1921,* trans. Anna Bostock and Yvonne Kapp
(New York: Knopf, 1962), p. 103.

75 Balmont, "Poeziia stikhii—zemlia, voda, ogon, vozdukh," ("The Poetry of the Elements—Earth, Water, Fire, Air"), *Belye zarnitsy* (St. Petersburg: M. V. Pirozhkov,
1908), p. 15; "Pesn boga obnovlennykh polei," ("Song of the God of Renewed Fields"),
Zovy drevnosti, p. 305.

76 Balmont, *Zovy drevnosti,* p. 300.

77 A collection of Balmont's works was published in Leningrad in 1969, with an appreciative article by V. N. Orlov ("Balmont: Zhizn i poeziia," pp. 5–74, in K. D.
Balmont, *Stikhotvoreniia*) but he is still treated diffidently by Soviet literary historians. Latin Americanists value his contribution to their field, on the other hand;
see V. I. Guliaev's *Amerika i staryi tsvet v dokolumbovu epokhu* (Moscow: Nauka,
1968), p. 96, for a quotation by Balmont about Uxmal.

78 *Ocherki Severo-Amerikanskikh shtatov* (serialized in the liberal *Vestnik Evropy).*
He also used the name Demens. Hans Rogger, "America in the Russian Mind—or
Russian Discoveries of America," *Pacific Historical Review* 47, no. 1 (February 1978):
pp. 27–51, notes that "the America Tverskoi discovered for his countrymen had
never been described for them in such concrete and knowledgeable detail, certainly not in such approving terms" (p. 41).

79 P. A. Tverskoi, "Sovremennoe Meksiko," *Russkaia mysl,* 1913, no. 3: 68.

80 Ibid., pp. 69–70.

81 Ibid., p. 25.

82 I. O. Levin, "Novyi perevorot v Meksiko," *Russkaia mysl,* 1913, no. 3: 12–14. One
other article about Mexico appeared early in 1913 in *Russkoe bogatstvo.* N. S. Rusanov's "Obozrenie inostrannoi zhizni: 3. Meksikanskaia revoliutsiia," 1913, no. 2:
365–72, discussed the recent history of the country and described the Díaz government in generally favorable terms, although admitting that changes were needed.
Madero had been unable to bring about the necessary political reform, however,
and Rusanov concluded that up to the present, no revolution had been able to
provide Mexico with the foundations for normal development (p. 372). A contrasting view of the Mexican Revolution can be found in the reports of the Russian
ambassador to Mexico, who clearly sympathized with Porfirismo because of what

he saw as its similarity to Tsarist Russia. See N. M. Lavrov, "La revolución mexicana de 1910–1917 en los documentos del archivo de la política exterior de Rusia," *Latinoamérica*, 1979, no. 12: 13–25.

83 "Literaturnoe dvizhenie v Meksike," *Obrazovanie*, 1900, no. 2, pt. 2: 22, discussed the development of realism as the successor to romanticism in Mexican literature: Mexican literature was now "broader" than it had been in the past; it had superseded the stage of copying foreign models; it was now ready to create an independent life. Several translations of Mexican legends were also published, obviously in response to the popularity of Balmont's work. "Thomas Zhanve" translated three tales for *Novyi zhurnal* in 1907; they were accompanied by two full-page illustrations by Walter Appleton Clark, done in fairly gruesome detail; a slightly different translation of the stories was published in 1906 in *Vestnik*.

3 The Nineteen-Twenties

1 Manabendra Nath Roy, *Memoirs* (Bombay: Allied Publishers Private Ltd., 1964), p. 123.

2 V. Dandré, *Anna Pavlova in Art and Life* (New York: B. Blom, 1972), p. 319.

3 "In those days, everyone carried revolvers in Mexico. In those days no trains ran at night; and no trains ran in the daytime except with an escort train of soldiers in front, and an escort train of soldiers behind." Charles Phillips [Manuel Gomez], "From Mexico to Moscow," *Survey* 53 (October 1964): 37.

4 Alma Reed, *The Mexican Muralists* (New York: Crown Publishers, 1960), says she stayed in Mexico City for one month; Walford Hyden, *Pavlova* (Boston: Little, Brown, and Company, 1931), p. 62, contends she stayed eight weeks.

5 Hyden, *Pavlova*, p. 62, estimates the size of the crowds in the Plaza de Toros at 36,000 people.

6 See John Lazzarini and Roberta Lazzarini, *Pavlova: Repertoire of a Legend* (New York: Schirmer Books, 1980), pp. 166–67. While dancing her famous role as Saint-Saëns' "Swan," she was accompanied on the cello by Pablo Casals, who happened to be visiting Mexico at the time.

7 Dandré, *Anna Pavlova*, p. 319.

8 On the history of the PCM, see among others, Ernst Halperin, *Communism in Mexico* (Cambridge: Massachusetts Institute of Technology, 1963); Karl M. Schmitt, *Communism in Mexico: A Study in Political Frustration* (Austin: University of Texas Press, 1965); Manuel Márquez Fuentes and Octavio Rodríguez Araujo, *El partido comunista mexicano (en el período de la Internacional Comunista: 1919–1943)* (Mexico City: Ediciones "El caballito," 1973); Valentín Campa Salazar, *Mi testimonio: Experiencias de un comunista mexicano* (Mexico City: Ediciones de cultura popular, 1978).

9 Pseudonym of Mikhail Markovich Gruzenberg, 1884–1951; for a good recent biography, see Dan N. Jacobs, *Borodin: Stalin's Man in China* (Cambridge: Harvard University Press, 1981). For further details on his activities in Mexico, see Carleton Beals, *Glass House: Ten Years of Freelancing* (Philadelphia: J. B. Lippincott, 1938), pp. 43–53.

10   I. A. Vasilkova, "Kniga, posviashchennaia vsem, kto delal revoliutsiiu," *Latinskaia Amerika*, 1984, no. 8 (August): 74–80.

11   See L. A. Shur, comp. *Khudozhestvennaia literatura Latinskoi Ameriki v russkoi pechati, 1765–1959* (Moscow: Izdatelstvo vsesoiuznoi knizhnoi palaty, 1960), pp. 147–65. For example, a translation of parts of Azuela's *Los de abajo* appeared in *Vestnik inostrannoi literatury* in 1928, and a two-volume translation of Bernal Díaz's account of the Conquest was printed in Leningrad in 1924 and 1925.

12   See Bertram D. Wolfe, *A Life in Two Centuries* (New York: Stein and Day, 1981), pp. 332–33, for example.

13   Beals, *Glass House*, p. 355.

14   B. F. Dobrynin, "Meksika (geograficheskii etiud)," *Zemlevedenie* 28 (1926): no. 1–2, pp. 35–56; no. 3–4, pp. 45–66.

15   On the expedition, see M. Sh. Fainshtein, "K 50-letiiu pervoi sovetskoi ekspeditsii v Latinskuiu Ameriku (1925–1928)," *Latinskaia Amerika*, 1975, no. 5 (September–October): 134–42.

16   See S. M. Bukasov, *Vozdelyvaemye rasteniia Meksiki, Gvatemaly, i Kolumbii* [Leningrad: 1930), p. 349.

17   See A. I. Revenkova, *Nikolai Ivanovich Vavilov, 1887–1943* (Moscow: Izdatelstvo selskokhoziaistvennoi literatury, zhurnalov i plakatov, 1962), and N. I. Vavilov, "Velikie zemledelcheskie kultury dokolumbovoi Ameriki i ikh vzaimootnosheniia," *Izvestiia gosudarstvennogo geograficheskogo obshchestva* 71, no. 10 (1939): 1487–515.

18   A. G. Kniazev and I. M. Freidberg, *Vokrug sveta na velosipede* (Moscow-Leningrad: Molodaia gvardiia, 1929).

19   See Pestkovsky's *Wspomnienie rewolucjonisty* (Lodz: Wydawnictwo Lodskie, 1961), and A. I. Aleksandrov, "Revoliutsioner, diplomat, uchenii," *Latinskaia Amerika*, 1982, no. 12: 142–44.

20   On all this, see Pestkovsky, "Vospominaniia o rabote v narkomnatse (1917–1919 gg.)," *Proletarskaia revoliutsiia*, 1930, no. 6 (June): 124–31; he includes some especially interesting information about working with Stalin.

21   Beals, *Glass House*, p. 338.

22   Wolfe, *A Life*, p. 341.

23   See A. I. Sizonenko, *V strane atstekskogo orla* (Moscow: Mezhdunarodnye otnosheniia, 1969), p. 16.

24   Héctor Cárdenas, *Las relaciones mexicano-soviéticas: Antecedentes y primeros contacts diplomáticos (1789–1927)* (Mexico City: Secretaría de Relaciones Exteriores, 1974), p. 75. See also Akademiia nauk SSSR, Institut Latinskoi Ameriki, Ministerstvo inostrannykh del Meksiki, *Sovetsko-meksikanskie otnosheniia (1917–1980): Sbornik dokumentov* (Moscow: Mezhdunarodnye otnosheniia, 1981), pp. 25–26.

25   Reprinted in *El Universal*, November 8, 1924; see Sizonenko, *V strane*, p. 19.

26   Wolfe, *A Life*, p. 347.

27   The indigent included Mayakovsky, the physicist Dobrynin (who spent two months at the embassy in 1926), and the two young bicyclists.

28   Rafael Rámos Pedrueza had good things to say about him in *La estrella roja: Doce años de vida soviética* (Mexico City: 1929), for example.

29 G. V. Chicherin, *Stati i rechi po voprosam mezhdunarodnoi politiki* (Moscow: Izdatelstvo sotsialno-ekonomicheskoi literatury, 1961), p. 352.

30 Beals, *Glass House*, p. 339.

31 Robert J. Alexander, *Communism in Latin America* (New Brunswick, N.J.: Rutgers University Press, 1957), p. 326.

32 S. S. Pestkovsky, *Istoriia meksikanskikh revoliutsii* (Moscow-Leningrad: Gosudarstvennoe izdatelstvo, 1928), and *Agrarnyi vopros i krestianskoe dvizhenie v Meksike* (Moscow-Leningrad: Gosudarstvennoe izdatelstvo, 1928). He also wrote the section on Latin America in the first edition of the *Malaia sovetskaia entsiklopediia* and articles on Brazil and Mexico in the *Entsiklopedicheskii slovar russkogo bibliograficheskogo instituta imeni Granat*. Pseudonyms were used for a variety of reasons: most important would have been to protect Pestkovsky's identity should he be sent to other diplomatic posts where his written statements might compromise his purely diplomatic activities or his assignments from the Comintern. Secondarily, the use of a variety of pseudonyms might suggest that the authorities hoped readers would conclude that a number of Soviets were writing about Latin America, and that many Latin American converts to Communism were actively examining the political and social history of the New World from a Marxist standpoint.

33 He used Sahagún's works, for example; collections of colonial documents such as *Las leyes de las Indias*; Móntufar's *Settlement of the Valley of San Juan Teotihuacán*; Humboldt; Lorenzo de Zavala's *Ensayos historicos de la revolución mexicana*; Francisco Bulnes's *La guerra de independencia*; the laws of the Reform; and current books and statistics, including studies of Madero and Antonio Manero's *El antiguo régimen y la revolución*.

34 One of these was a photograph of what Pestkovsky took to be an "ancient Aztec theater" at Teotihuacán (*Istoriia*, pp. 14–15), something that was, of course, very unlikely.

35 Pestkovsky, *Istoriia*, p. 27.

36 Pestkovsky, *Agrarnyi vopros*, p. 30.

37 Pestkovsky, *Istoriia*, p. 54.

38 This was the case with railroad construction, Pestkovsky pointed out: Mexico received a considerable railroad network from foreign investment, but the routes were determined by foreigners for their own economic or strategic reasons, not Mexico's.

39 Pestkovsky made a number of points to support his contention; see *Istoriia*, p. 76, and *Agrarnyi vopros*, p. 34.

40 Pestkovsky, *Istoriia*, p. 92.

41 Whom Pestkovsky said had earlier been "lackeys . . . or local satraps of the central administration." *Istoriia*, p. 90.

42 Pestkovsky, *Agrarnyi vopros*, p. 53; for a description of Villa, see ibid., pp. 80–81; Pestkovsky added that the reason for Villa's falling out with Carranza and Obregón was their attempt to "discipline" Villa's partisans.

43 Ibid., p. 71.

44 S. S. Pestkovsky, "Agrarnyi vopros i krestianskoe dvizhenie v Meksike," *Na agrarnom fronte*, 1927, no. 2 (February): 53.

45 Pestkovsky, *Agrarnyi vopros*, pp. 74–75.

46 On the Red Battalions, see Jean Meyer, "Los obreros en la Revolución mexicana: Los 'batallones rojos'," *Historia Mexicana* 21, no. 1 (1971): 1–37.

47 S. S. Pestkovsky, "Raskol v rabochem dvizhenii," *Krasnyi internatsional profsoiuzov*, 1927, no. 4: 318.

48 Pestkovsky, *Istoriia*, p. 141.

49 Pestkovsky, *Agrarnyi vopros*, p. 92. On the Peasant International and the Red International of Trade Unions in Mexico, see Donald L. Herman, *The Comintern in Mexico* (Washington, D.C.: Public Affairs Press, 1974), pp. 64–66, and Schmitt, *Communism*, pp. 14–15.

50 A year after his two books appeared, he wrote that Calles was a reactionary agent of American imperialism; S. S. Pestkovsky, "Reaktsiia v Meksike," *Put MOPRa*, 1929, no. 11–12 (1–30 July): 23.

51 Pestkovsky, "Raskol v rabochem dvizhenii," p. 316.

52 Here Pestkovsky admitted that the government was carrying on a fight against the church and the largest landowners in the country.

53 Pestkovsky, *Istoriia*, p. 202.

54 See *Sovetsko-meksikanskie otnosheniia*, p. 104, and Sizonenko, *V strane Atstekskogo orla*, p. 34.

55 V. V. Mayakovsky, "Meksika," *Polnoe sobranie sochinenii*, vol. 7 (Moscow: Gosudarstvennoe izdatelstvo khudozhestvennoi literatury, 1958), p. 45. Hereafter cited as *PSS*.

56 For a Soviet evaluation of Mayakovsky's career during the middle and late 1920s, see A. I. Metchenko, *Tvorchestvo Maiakovskogo 1925–1930 gg.* (Moscow: Sovetskii pisatel, 1961).

57 Charles A. Moser, "Mayakovsky's Unsentimental Journeys," *American Slavic and East European Review* 19 (1960): 85–100; S. Snegovskaia, "Maiakovskii za granitsei," *Zvezda*, 1949, no. 4: 157.

58 See V. O. Pertsov, *Maiakovskii v poslednie gody: Zhizn i tvorchestvo (1925–1930 gg)* (Moscow: Nauka, 1965), pp. 5–64.

59 In the meantime, he wrote two poems, "Blek end uait" and "Kristofor Kolomb"; Mayakovsky, *PSS*, pp. 20–23, 31–38. The poems he worked on were "6 monakhin," "Atlanticheskii okean," and "Melkaia filosofiia na glubokikh mestakh," ibid., pp. 9–19.

60 Ibid., pp. 39–40.

61 L. S. Ospovat, *Diego Rivera* (Moscow: Molodaia gvardiia, 1969), pp. 242–50.

62 "Pisma Maiakovskogo k L. Iu. Brik (1917–30)," *Literaturnaia nasledstvo* 65 (1958): 149. Ella Wolfe, in an interview with the author in Palo Alto, California, in June 1983, remembered that it was Mayakovsky's difficulties with money that led to his pretending to have fathered a daughter while in the United States; in fact, she said, Mayakovsky had come to know her and her husband, Bertram, in Mexico City, and had appropriated one of her party aliases as the name of the mother of this illegitimate child; he used the child as an inducement for others to loan him money, promising that he would use it to support his American daughter, but in fact he used it for his own support.

63 Salomon Kemrad, *Maiakovskii v Amerike: Stranitsy biografii* (Moscow: Sovetskii pisatel, 1970), p. 54.

64 Ella Wolfe, interview with the author; Bertram did not identify the party per se, but did recall the episode in his memoirs.

65 At the conclusion of the Mexican section of *Moe otkrytie Ameriki*, Mayakovsky wrote that he, Khaikiss, and his new friend Moreno had planned a trip into the Veracruz mountains; an announcement in *Literaturnaia gazeta* (March 14, 1934) noted that Khaikiss, then a representative of Narkomindel, had given a talk at the Lenin Library on Mayakovsky's trip to Mexico.

66 V. A. Arutcheva, "Zapisnye knizhki Maiakovskogo," *Literaturnoe nasledstvo* 65 (1958): 390.

67 I. I. Uspenskii, *Maiakovskii o burzhuaznoi "kulture" zapada i Ameriki* (Moscow: Gosudarstvennoe izdatelstvo kulturno-prosvetitelnoi literatury, 1950), p. 7.

68 "Notable poeta ruso que llegó a esta capital," *Excélsior*, 10 July 1925, pp. 1, 4.

69 José D. Frías, "El poeta ruso, Vladimiro Mayakowsky," *El Universal Ilustrado*, 23 July 1925, pp. 25, 54; this article also included a photograph of Mayakovsky.

70 Salomón Kahán, "La poesía rusa de la revolución frente a la poesía 'Este Tica'," *Antorcha* 2, no. 1 (August 1925): 17–22; "Trotzki y el poeta Mayakovsky," *Antorcha* 2, no. 2 (September 1925): 20–21. The journal was founded by José Vasconcelos and edited at the time by Samuel Ramos.

71 Ospovat, *Diego Rivera*, p. 242.

72 V. A. Katanian, *Maiakovskii: Literaturnaia khronika*, 3d ed. (Moscow: Gosudarstvennoe izdatelstvo khudozhestvennoi literatury, 1956), p. 234.

73 Edward J. Brown, *Mayakovsky: A Poet in the Revolution* (Princeton: Princeton University Press, 1973), pp. 286ff. He completed "Meksika" on June 20th, and began working on "Bogomolnoe" soon thereafter.

74 These included *LEF*, *Ogonek*, *Izvestiia*, and *Prozhektor*; "Pisma Maiakovskogo," *Literaturnoe nasledstvo*, p. 149.

75 Arutcheva, "Zapisnye," p. 390.

76 On Mayakovsky in the United States, see Charles A. Moser, "Mayakovsky and America," *Russian Review* 25, no. 3 (July 1966): 242–56, and Charles Rougle, *Three Russians Consider America: America in the Works of Maksim Gorkij, Aleksandr Blok, and Vladimir Majakovskij* (Stockholm: Almqvist and Wiksell International, 1976).

77 "Notable poeta ruso," pp. 1, 4. TsGALI 336/5/120, 121, 122 have collections of local newspaper clippings about Mayakovsky's public lectures and readings dealing with Mexico in Iaroslavl, Krasnodar, Saratov, etc.

78 D. Talnikov, "Literaturyne zametki," *Krasnaia nov*, 1928, no. 8: 268. Some other pieces of Mayakovsky's work about Mexico appeared elsewhere: a book of poetry entitled *Ispaniia* included verses dedicated to Mexico; his sketches of Mexico were published in *Krasnaia nov* in 1926; a separate version of *Moe otkrytie Ameriki* illustrated with photographs appeared in 1926; and a book, *Meksika*, appeared after his death in 1933, as did other printings of his writings in subsequent decades.

79 Mayakovsky, *PSS*, p. 273.

80 There was some belief in Mexico City that Mayakovsky had been sent by Moscow to give assistance to Proal, and there was a certain amount of suspicion about his

true aims in Mexico as a result; on Proal, see Mario Gill, *México y la revolución de octubre* (Mexico City: Ediciones de cultura popular, 1976), pp. 65–78, and Manuel Castells, *The City and the Grassroots* (Berkeley and Los Angeles: University of California Press, 1983), pp. 37–48.

81 Mayakovsky, *PSS*, p. 274.

82 Ibid.

83 In his autobiography, Wolfe mentions his wife's trips to the Esperanza Iris puppet theater (at which Mayakovsky was quite impressed); they also accompanied him to the movies and the theater; Wolfe, *A Life*, p. 370.

84 Mayakovsky, *PSS*, pp. 279–80.

85 Ibid., p. 281.

86 Ibid., p. 284.

87 Ibid., p. 286.

88 Ibid., p. 287; Mayakovsky learned of Moreno's assassination from New York's *Daily Worker*: "Mexican Politician Is Assassinated, Causing Sensation," 16 September 1925, p. 2; "Mexican Communist Deputy Murdered," 21 September 1925, p. 5. The second article included the photograph of Mayakovsky and Moreno together and said that Moreno was "assassinated because of his exposure of the traitorous policy of the Calles government."

89 Mayakovsky called the Mexican flag the "watermelon," a reference to the apocryphal story about how the colors for the flag were chosen by Iturbide and Guerrero at the beginning of the nineteenth century; Mayakovsky, *PSS*, p. 290.

90 Her position was not entirely unique. Bela Kun's Hungarian Soviet government had been represented by a woman at the Paris Peace Conference for example, but her assignment had been a short one, and apparently she was ignored by the Allied governments. In this regard, Kollontai's appointment was much more significant.

91 On the Workers' Opposition, see Beatrice Farnsworth, *Aleksandra Kollontai: Socialism, Feminism, and the Bolshevik Revolution* (Stanford: Stanford University Press, 1980), pp. 212–48.

92 Barbara Evans Clements, *Bolshevik Feminist: The Life of Aleksandra Kollontai* (Bloomington: University of Indiana Press, 1979), p. 223.

93 Emilii Lvovich Mindlin, *Ne dom, no mir: Povest ob Aleksandre Kollontai* (Moscow: Politizdat, 1969), p. 394.

94 Clements, *Bolshevik Feminist*, p. 245.

95 "Woman Envoy Hits Intrigue: New Soviet Minister to Mexico Says Business Is Her Aim," *New York Times*, 19 October 1926, section 1, p. 26.

96 Ministerstvo inostrannykh del SSSR, *Dokumenty vneshnei politiki SSSR*, vol. 9 (Moscow: Izdatelstvo politicheskoi literatury, 1964), p. 588. For her public comments see "Reds of Mexico City Hail Mme. Kollontai," *New York Times*, 9 December 1926, section 1, p. 3: she explained that the Cuban refusal to permit her to land "was not due to the American government's attitude, but to the Cuban law which forbids women travelling alone to disembark from ships."

97 Aleksandra Kollontai, "Meksikanskii dnevnik Aleksandry Kollontai," ed. I. A. Vasilkova, *Latinskaia Amerika*, 1979, no. 5 (September–October): 188.

98   Beals, *Glass House*, p. 343.

99   "Woman Envoy's Books Far Outnumber Gowns," *New York Times*, 10 December 1926, section 1, p. 3.

100   Ministerstvo inostrannykh del SSSR, *Dokumenty*, vol. 9, p. 586.

101   Sizonenko, *V strane*, p. 41.

102   Kollontai's speech was published in *El Universal* on 25 December 1926 and has been reprinted in Akademiia nauk SSSR, *Sovetsko-meksikanskie otnosheniia*, p. 31.

103   *Sovetsko-meksikanskie otnosheniia*, p. 32–33.

104   Kollontai, "Meksikanskii dnevnik," p. 189. Kollontai noted in her diary that the day after the presentation Calles had an enormous bouquet of violets delivered to her. She saw this as "a good sign because they say that Calles is not known for courtesy." Ibid.

105   Stephen Clissold, ed., *Soviet Relations with Latin America, 1918–1968: A Documentary Survey* (London: Oxford University Press, 1970), p. 88.

106   "Reds of Mexico City," p. 5.

107   Ministerstvo inostrannykh del SSSR, *Dokumenty vneshnei politiki SSSR*, vol. 10 (Moscow: Izdatelstvo politicheskoi literatury, 1965), p. 24.

108   Letter from Kollontai to T. L. Shchepkina-Kupernik, 11 April 1927, TsGALI, 571/1/755.

109   Kollontai said the amount mentioned was 25,000 rubles, but Sizonenko (*V strane*, p. 49) contends the sum was 50,000 rubles. On the strike, see Elías Barrios, "La Unión soviética y los ferrocarilleros mexicanos," in Gill, *México y la revolución de octubre*, pp. 120–23.

110   Her stay in Cuernavaca was short but interesting. The governor of the state of Morelos had met her in her hotel restaurant and invited her to visit him in the city hall the next morning. She kept the appointment, but the governor was late, and she was finally told that he had been arrested and that it might be best for her own safety if she returned to Mexico City as soon as she could since there might be some violence by the governor's supporters. Indeed, she soon heard guns firing, and fearing capture and the possibility of being held for ransom, she escaped on a bus back to the capital with a group of heavily armed men and women. She was not entirely familiar with this Mexico, and for a few hours she must have had some understanding of why the Calles government might have feared the kind of spontaneous rebellion and violence that still surfaced in the country, and why it was making a determined effort to control any "unauthorized" violence. There are several variations on the details to this account; see Mindlin, *Ne dom, no mir*, p. 394; Clements, *Bolshevik Feminist*, p. 247; and Itkina, *Revoliutsioner*, pp. 244–45.

111   "Want Mme. Kollontai Expelled from Mexico," *New York Times*, 12 April 1927, section 1, p. 23. Specifically, she was accused of sheltering Bertram Wolfe, who had been ejected from Mexico the previous year. Wolfe had become a particular target of the CROM and Calles because of the highly critical articles he had written about the government in *El Machete* and *El Libertador*.

112   This was the contention of Silva Herzog, Mexican ambassador to the USSR, in

1929; see Isabel Palencia, *Alexandra Kollontai: Ambassadress from Russia* (New York: Longman's, Green, and Company, 1947).
113 Letter to N. N. Iakimov, quoted in Clements, *Bolshevik Feminist*, p. 247; letter to Shchepkina-Kupernik, 11 April 1927. Ella Wolfe remembered that Kollontai was forced to spend a great deal of time during the day resting; interview, June 1983.
114 Kollontai, "Meksikanskii dnevnik," p. 195.
115 Ibid.
116 "Madame Kollontai on Mexico," *America: A Catholic Review of the Week* 37, no. 15 (23 July 1927): 342. The editors commented on Kollontai's feelings upon her return from Mexico: "It is somewhat amusing to contemplate the bitter reflections of this Red lady, as she returns disconsolate from the failure of her mission to the darlings of the Russian communists in the New World. She found that, after all their lofty mouthings of love for the proletariat, they turn out to be only vulgar grafters after all." Ibid., pp. 342–43.
117 The *Vecherniaia Moskva* article is reprinted in A. M. Kollontai, *Izbrannye stati i rechi* (Moscow, Politizdat: 1972), pp. 357–60; the *Leningradskaia pravda* article is summarized in Sizonenko, *V strane*, p. 53.
118 Akademiia nauk SSSR, *Sovetsko-meksikanskie otnosheniia*, pp. 46–47.

4 Sergei Eisenstein and the Eternal Circle

1 Jay Leyda and Zina Voynow, *Eisenstein at Work* (New York: Pantheon and the Museum of Modern Art, 1982), p. 61.
2 S. M. Eisenstein, *Immoral Memories: An Autobiography*, trans. Herbert Marshall (Boston: Houghton Mifflin, 1983), p. 260.
3 "There is an old maxim which says: the more a person gives, the more he receives. Eisenstein gave Mexico the most profound part of his artistic inventiveness [and] his philosophical thought. And, in return, Mexico was very generous with him, enriching him with new ideas and insights." V. N. Kuteishchikova, "Serguei Eisenstein y México," *Revolución y cultura*, November 1978, p. 36.
4 His father took him on his first trip abroad, to Paris, in 1906, and encouraged his enrollment in engineering school in Petrograd. Eisenstein said later that his engineering studies gaved him his appreciation for systematic planning and intricate, detailed blueprints. He was also influenced by his reading on the Renaissance and especially on da Vinci. He wrote that he read Freud's writings on da Vinci with great interest. TsGALI, 1923/1/1031, "Avtobiografiia."
5 Quoted by Iu. Pimenov in S. M. Eisenstein, *Risunki/dessins/drawings* (Moscow: Iskusstvo, 1961), p. 8.
6 Robert C. Williams, *Artists in Revolution: Portraits of the Russian Avant-Garde, 1905–1925* (Bloomington: University of Indiana Press, 1977), p. 166. The years of civil war also marked him in ways which help explain his sense of affinity with much of what he found in Mexico, with cruelty, death, and thoughts of immortality being especially significant. Psychological cruelty had been an important component in the breakup of his parents' marriage, and physical cruelty was

an everyday experience during the years of fighting following the revolution. Eisenstein was also concerned, at times almost unnaturally, with death and immortality, to the point that Williams has seen this fascination as a fundamental factor in Eisenstein's worldview. See ibid., p. 176.

7   Eisenstein, Risunki/dessins/drawings, pp. 123–25. For the script, see Meksikanets (instsenirovka po rasskazu Dzhona Rida), in TsGALI 1923/1/778. The director was Valentin Smyshliaev, and Eisenstein's friends Maksim Shtraukh and Judith Glizer worked on the production as well. The one totally realistic character in "The Mexican" was played by Eisenstein's friend, Grigorii Aleksandrov. He was "a revolutionary, remember my words, he is the greatest revolutionary of all of us. I know this is so, I feel it with my heart, I know it with my head. But even so, I don't understand him." Ibid., p. 11. The circus atmosphere of the play reappeared in the Death Day sequence in Que Viva Mexico!. At the end of "The Mexican," the victorious hero was shown alone, spotlighted, with the sounds of marching Mexican revolutionary battalions behind him; in Que Viva Mexico!, Eisenstein filmed some overlapping shots of revolutionary troops marching in the distance toward victory; see the concluding scenes of G. V. Aleksandrov's version of Que Viva Mexico!

8   Eisenstein commented on it in his essay, "Dickens, Griffith, and Film Today." See S. M. Eisenstein, Film Form, trans. Jay Leyda (New York: Harcourt, Brace, and World Inc., 1949).

9   It would probably be a mistake to contend, as Helprin did in 1931, that it was Rivera's visit to Eisenstein's apartment that was the source of Eisenstein's interest in Mexico, and that after Rivera's visit, Eisenstein began to collect all he could about the country. Morris Helprin, "Eisenstein's New Film," New York Times, 29 November 1931, p. 6.

10   The book, inscribed by Rivera, is kept in the Lenin Library rare book division; the date of the inscription is 17 October 1927. V. N. Kuteishchikova, "Diego Rivera y la revolución de octobre," Plural 1 (1978): 49.

11   See Vance Kepley, Jr., "The Evolution of the Eisenstein's Old and New," Cinema Journal 14, no. 1 (Fall 1974): 34–50.

12   As he told a New York Times reporter: "I consider the so-called 'all talkie,' the film with conversation from beginning to end, nothing but rotten trash." "M. Eisenstein's Next Film," New York Times, 16 February 1930, p. 6. The use of color in film was another technique Eisenstein wished to study abroad because he felt it was a way to fulfill the Soviet cinema's didactic charge, to reach the lower classes. What Eisenstein had in mind, he told a Boston Globe reporter, was a new type of film, one that was best understood and appreciated, and best used by the socialist cinema he represented: "The new type of films will have the possibility of guiding not only the emotions of the audience but its process of thought." "Eisenstein Predicts New Type of Film," Boston Globe, 27 May 1930, p. 17.

13   Herbert Marshall, "Moscow Invited to Hollywood," Moscow News, 5 October 1930, p. 7.

14   G. V. Aleksandrov, Gody poiskov i truda (Moscow: Soiuz kinomatografistov SSSR, Biuro propagandy sovetskogo kinoiskusstva, 1975), p. 45. On Eisenstein's experience in Hollywood, see Ivor Montagu, With Eisenstein in Hollywood (Berlin: Seven

Seas, 1968); William Richardson, "Eisenstein and California: The *Sutter's Gold* Episode," *California History*, Fall 1980, pp. 194–203; and G. V. Aleksandrov, *Epokha v kino* (Moscow: Izdatelstvo politicheskoi literatury, 1976), pp. 135–53.

15   Early in his career, Eisenstein had studied Asian languages in Petrograd and in August 1928 had acted as host for a visiting troupe of Japanese Kabuki actors in Moscow; his apartment has a number of mementos of this visit, and much of the work he did in *Ivan the Terrible* can be traced to this interest.

16   Aleksandrov, *Gody*, p. 45.

17   On Sinclair at this time, see *The Autobiography of Upton Sinclair* (New York: Harcourt, Brace, and World, 1962). Oddly enough, by all indications, Eisenstein's first sight of Mexico was Tijuana. Apparently, the day after he arrived from the East Coast he hired a car and asked the driver to take him to Mexico. The city was not what he expected: it was a "row of saloons and bawdiness, a mile of double-barrelled barrooms that desecrated the Mexican soil on which they stood." Helprin, "Eisenstein's New Film," p. 6, and Alfonso Reyes, *A Lápiz: 1923–1946* (Mexico City: Editorial stylo, 1947), pp. 94–99. Although he learned that Tijuana was not typical of Mexico, he remembered it for some time afterward. One of his drawings the next year, from the "Pieta" series drawn in Tehuantepec, uses a play on word sounds to depict what he called a "Pieta Tihuana," a Tehuana woman in elegant dress, with a small Christ in her arms, but with her breasts, sagging stomach, pubic hair, and vagina visible through the front of her dress. TsGALI, 1923/2/1239. Eisenstein was always interested in the contrasts between what society regarded as sacred and profane, and he must have felt that contrast nowhere better than in Tijuana.

18   For the terms of the contract, see Harry M. Geduld and Ronald Gottesman, eds., *Sergei Eisenstein and Upton Sinclair: The Making and Unmaking of Que Viva Mexico!* (Bloomington: Indiana University Press, 1970), pp. 22–23. Money was a continuing subject of disagreement in Eisenstein's correspondence with Sinclair and others; see ibid., and R. Iurenev, "S. Eizenshtein—pisma iz Meksiki," *Prometei*, 1972, no. 9: 196. Kimbrough was described in a Mexican newspaper as a "100 por ciento de americano"; A. F. Bustamente, "Lo que en México hace Eisenstein," *El Ilustrado*, 18 June 1931, p. 25. For Sinclair's account of all this, see Sinclair, *Autobiography*, pp. 262–67.

19   "Eisenstein Says 'Adios'," *Los Angeles Times*, 7 December 1930, part 3, p. 1.

20   That these were indeed his plans was corroborated by a letter he wrote to Esfir Shub; see Yon Barna, *Eisenstein*, trans. Lise Hunter, (Bloomington: Indiana University Press, 1973), p. 166.

21   "Eisenstein Says 'Adios'."

22   This led him to an experience of "unprecedented peace and perfect internal harmony," according to Barna, *Eisenstein*, p. 167.

23   Eisenstein, *Risunki/dessins/drawings*, p. 18.

24   Barna, *Eisenstein*, p. 176.

25   Monoszon was serving as Amtorg representative in New York; see Iurenev, "Eizenshtein," p. 190. His correspondence with Eisenstein is in TsGALI, 2617/1/42.

26   One of the first books he purchased in the capital was an English edition of Azu-

ela's *The Underdogs* that included Orozco's illustrations; the book was marked extensively and by all indications provided much inspiration for Eisenstein's work dealing with the revolution. In a letter to Monoszon in June 1931 (TsGALI 2617/1/42) responding to a request, he recommended several: he noted that Beals's *Mexican Maze* (which he obtained shortly before writing Monoszon) gave him "nothing new" although he said later that it was "a rather good book" (Eisenstein, *Immoral Memories*, p. 192) and the chapters on the church, the government, and caricature he read with great care; *Idols Behind Altars* was "entertaining," but Ernest Gruening's *Mexico and Its Heritage* was better for serious reading; Flandreau's *Viva Mexico* was notable, and Henry Berlein's *Mexico: The Land of Unrest* was interesting as well.

27   Weston lived in Carmel while Eisenstein was in Hollywood and Mexico. Weston's son Brett photographed Eisenstein for the frontispiece to Seton's biography of Eisenstein, and Eisenstein did know Tina Modotti, Weston's former lover, when she lived in the USSR in the 1930s. Many of Weston's Mexican photographs are similar to the shots Eisenstein planned to use in *Que Viva Mexico!* In Amy Conger's *Edward Weston in Mexico, 1923–1926* (Albuquerque: University of New Mexico, 1983), for example, see the photos of the three pots (p. 44), the ollas (p. 54), and the maguey (p. 62). One also cannot help seeing a similarity between Weston's "La Teresina, 1933" (Edward Weston, *The Daybooks of Edward Weston*, ed. by Nancy Newhall [New York: Millerton Press, 1973] vol. 2, no. 20) and some of the poses Eisenstein used for his shots of Christ. While Weston wrote later that he faulted what he called Eisenstein's "very picturesque, rather sentimental approach to the Indian!" (ibid., p. 248), he did say that he was very impressed by *Battleship Potemkin*, which he called "A great picture!" (ibid., p. 56). Finally, among the few photographs of Mexican subjects kept in Eisenstein's apartment in Moscow, one of the most striking is Weston's photograph of Orozco, taken in 1930 and no doubt obtained by Eisenstein while he was in North America (ibid., no. 19).

28   The errors are in the original. S. M. Eisenstein, *Eizenshtein: Risunki*. Vol. 3, *Meksikanskie motivy* (Moscow: Soiuz kinematografistov SSSR, Biuro propagandy sovetskogo kinoiskusstva, 1971), unpaged.

29   Eisenstein wrote that many people believed that much of the stimulus for his drawing derived from Rivera, but in fact it came from the "direct influence of the primitives"; Eisenstein, *Immoral Memories*, p. 45.

30   "May Deport Eisenstein: Mexico Considers Action on Soviet Film Man After Freeing Him," *New York Times*, 24 December 1930, section 4, p. 5.

31   Eisenstein had known Álvarez del Vayo in Moscow during his four visits to the country between 1922 and 1928, and the two of them continued to be friends in Mexico and afterward. Álvarez del Vayo was a patron for the Siqueiros show in which Eisenstein took part in 1932, for example; he was responsible for the showing of *The Old and the New* in Spain after the 1931 revolution (Iurenev, "Eizenshtein," p. 193); and he showed some of Eisenstein's rushes from *Que Viva Mexico!* at the Spanish embassy, on one occasion at a diplomatic dinner whose guests included three Mexican government ministers (the secretary of foreign relations among them) and the U.S. ambassador. Ibid., p. 196.

32   S. M. Eisenstein, letter to Monoszon, 25 January 1931, TsGALI, 2617/1/42. According to Seymour Stern: "Before Eisenstein could shoot a single foot of film on Mex-

ican soil, he had to satisfy the government censor that nothing in the picture would reveal, or any way suggest, the poverty, slavery, and general degradation of the Mexican masses. Film censorship in Mexico is at least as rigid as that of any other country, and more severe than that of most countries. It is virtually impossible for anyone to take even a camera snapshot in Mexico without incurring the interference of the police or some form of bureaucratic displeasure." "Introduction to Synopsis for 'Que Viva Mexico!'" *Experimental Cinema* 1, no. 5 (1934): 3. Stern was overstating the case since the government was more worried about Eisenstein's being a Communist and Russian than about his filmmaking, but the concern did make Eisenstein's position somewhat uncertain.

33 Bertram D. Wolfe, *The Fabulous Life of Diego Rivera* (New York: Stein and Day, 1963), p. 157. On Best, see also Alma Reed, *The Mexican Muralists* (New York: Crown Publishers, 1960), p. 636.

34 In 1935 Best sent Eisenstein an inscribed photograph of himself; see TsGALI, 1923/2/226. Gruening commented that Best "discovered that inherent in the ancient paintings on Mexican architectural monuments were seven fundamental motifs or lines, taken directly by the primitive artists from their impressions of nature." Ernest Gruening, *Mexico and Its Heritage* (New York: The Century Company, 1928), p. 636.

35 The translations were for *Contemporáneos*. Leiva was the founder, with Carlos Mérida and Roberto Montenegro, of the Mexican Cinema Club, and after Eisenstein's departure from Mexico, he sought the title of Eisenstein's "disciple" in the New World. Leiva was extremely hurt that Eisenstein did not answer his letters after his return to Moscow and wrote Eisenstein about how much he was missed in Mexico; TsGALI 1923/1/1913, 1923/2/1817.

36 Emilio García Riera, *Medio siglo de cine mexicano* (Mexico City, 1960), p. 6.

37 Montenegro included Eisenstein in a fresco painted during the first half of 1931 at the College of Peter and Paul in Mexico City; on Montenegro, see Wolfe, *Fabulous*, pp. 157–58.

38 See the photo at the Museum of Modern Art, dated June 1931; see also Hayden Herrera, *Frida: A Biography of Frida Kahlo* (New York: Harper and Row, 1983). Rivera gve Eisenstein a pen and ink drawing through a mutual friend (Guillermo Spratling); the drawing is in TsGALI, 1923/1/2996.

39 Aleksandrov, *Epokha*, p. 141.

40 See I. R. Grigulevich, *Sikeiros* (Moscow: Iskusstvo, 1980). Siqueiros said that "Modern Mexican painting is the expression of the Mexican revolution. . . . without the Revolution there would have been no Mexican painting." Mario De Micheli, *Siqueiros*, trans. Ron Storm (New York: Harry N. Abrams, 1968), p. 2. Illustration no. 8, "Moliashchesia zhenshchiny," 1930; "Burial" was done in 1922; see also De Micheli, *Siqueiros*, pp. 8–9; O.S. Semenov, *David Alfaro Sikeiros* (Moscow: Detskaia literatura, 1980).

41 Ruth Solís, ed., *Vida y obra de David Álfaro Siqueiros: Juicios críticos* (Mexico City: Fondo de cultura económica, 1975), p. 30. On Eisenstein and Siqueiros, see I. A. Karetnikova, "Eizenshtein i Sikeiros," *Latinskaia Amerika*, 1970, no. 5: 146–61.

42 They wanted to market the film in the United States as a way of raising additional money for their project and to publicize their work in Mexico; on this episode,

see Aleksandrov, *Epokha,* p. 141. This work was promoted by Monoszon in the interests of Amtorg, which wanted to protect its investment; see L. Monoszon [L.M.], "Gruppa Eizenshteina v Meksike," *Proletarskoe kino,* 1931, no. 1: 49. The journey was not uneventful since the earthquakes continued while they were in the city, and on their return, their plane almost ran out of fuel because of Eisenstein's desire to see inside the volcano of Popocatepetl. Eisenstein, *Immoral,* p. 211.

43 According to Aleksandrov, the vaccinations also made them quite ill; see his *Le cinéaste et son temps,* trans. Antoine García (Moscow: Progress Publishers, 1976), p. 139.

44 He mentioned Covarrubias's *Four Seated Tehuana Women,* Rivera's *Woman Grinding Maize,* and other works with similar themes by Jean Charlot. Tehuantepec was described by Gruening, *Mexico,* p. 631, and this must have first stimulated Eisenstein's interest in going there.

45 Barna, *Eisenstein,* p. 168.

46 One drawing in particular combines all these: it shows stylized, vegetation-like male genitals, the penis erect, the pubic hair arranged in tropical, pre-Columbian motifs, and a small figure swimming about inside the scrotal sac; TsGALI, 1923/2/1283.

47 Eisenstein, *Immoral Memories,* p. 211.

48 Ibid., pp. 181–82.

49 Marie Seton, *Sergei M. Eisenstein* (New York: Grove Press, 1960), p. 203.

50 Bixby, for example, has found what she feels was a reference to homosexual "cruising" in part of the sequence devoted to the *corrida* crowd's reaction to events in the arena (Barbara Evans Bixby, "The Weave of the Serape: Sergei Eisenstein's *Que Viva Mexico!* as a Multitext," Ph.D. diss., University of Florida, 1979, p. 123), and Eisenstein's sketches of the groupies surrounding the matadors give clear references to homosexuality.

51 See Katherine Ann Porter, *Flowering Judas and Other Stories* (New York: New American Library, 1963), pp. 152–90.

52 This was Sinclair's reaction, and the reaction of the U.S. customs agent in Laredo; see Geduld and Gottesman, pp. 309–10.

53 Sinclair described one of these, see ibid. One sketch combined Eisenstein's interest in prostitution with the crucifixion: "Teresita's Bath" depicted a voluptuous prostitute taking a bath behind which a crucified Christ rises, gazing at her with what would appear to be anything but Christlike interest; TsGALI, 1923/2/1233.

54 Eisenstein, *Immoral Memories,* p. 182.

55 One shows Christ giving money to a boy fisherman and pointing to a hotel up the beach, a transparent reference to Christ's instruction to Peter to be a "fisher of men." Judas is often shown as a black man, very worshipful of Christ; one drawing shows him finding Christ and Mary Magdalen in bed together, another shows Christ throwing him out of his bed in order to get Mary Magdalen in. TsGALI, 1923/2/1228.

56 Marie Seton, "Eisenstein," in *Eisenstein, 1898–1948* (Lyon: Musée de Beaux Arts, 1978), p. 18.

57 "Simply stated, he sensed the importance of woman's position in that country as in no other in the world. Positively, she makes no appearance. But her influence

is as subtle as the Indian's overconquest of the Spaniard." Helprin, "Eisenstein's New Film," p. 6.

58   As Bixby pointed out in her analysis of the episode's "hammock-seduction shot," Eisenstein had moved almost entirely away from the kind of aggressively masculine and politicized filmmaking that had characterized his work in the past: "A young couple replaces the crowd; love replaces politics. The image surprises, for it is reminiscent of Gauguin rather than Leger, a prelapsarian paradise rather than a progressive marching society, of a world where sensuousness and femininity prevail as values over male-dominated materialism." "The Weave of the Serape," p. 225.

59   Eisenstein wrote in *Immoral Memories*, p. 37:

> But here the Catholics do not earn any particular merit. They did not choose these sites. They were the sites of ancient pyramids, at one time crowned with temples by Aztecs and Toltecs.
>
> The wisdom of the Catholics probably lay only in that, having destroyed the temples, they raised churches in exactly the same places, on the peaks of those pyramids, in order not to sidetrack the pilgrims, who for thousands of years had come from all the corners of the land to the foot of these very pyramids.

60   Seton, "Eisenstein," p. 20; see also Williams, *Artists in Revolution*, p. 176.

61   A wife was to be surprised by her husband in her lover's arms at Xochimilco; in great fear, she was to pray to the Lord of Chalma for aid, and instead of her lover becoming an altar, he was to be turned into an old painted crucifix. See "Posleslovie," in S. M. Eisenstein, *Izbrannye proizvedeniia* (Moscow: Iskusstvo, 1964–), vol. 6, pp. 446–52.

62   Eisenstein, quoted in Seton, *Eisenstein*, p. 508.

63   Brenner had commented on the work of the Mexican artist Pintao, for example: "Here all styles are constantly being repeated; there is primitive, renaissance, baroque, conscious and unconscious, all simultaneously." Anita Brenner, *Idols Behind Altars* (Boston: Beacon Press, 1970), p. 94. Eisenstein wrote "me!" in his copy of the book alongside this quotation.

64   A. A. Leiva, "The Destruction of Eisenstein's Mexican Film," typescript in Museum of Modern Art, Gottesman file.

65   Eisenstein and his crew filmed the various pyramids of the archeological sites, and they all were fascinated by the style of the carving and stonemasonry; Eisenstein wrote later (*Immoral Memories*, p. 119) that he had come to agree with those who believed the Mayan style was influenced by its architects' use of marijuana:

> Marijuana, the miracle-working smoke with which the Mexican soldiers stupefy themselves.
>
> There is a theory that the astounding ornamental disintegration of the forms of nature in Aztec, Toltec, and Mayan architecture was either created in a marijuana trance or depict memories of one. A normal conscious condition would hardly be capable of such extravagance.

66   Aleksandrov, *Epokha v kino*, pp. 143–51.

67 He wrote Monoszon that he might have to ask Moscow to extend his leave of absence; Iurenev, "Eizenshtein," p. 192. In the same letter he mentioned that there was some talk of his going to India to make a film of Kipling's *Kim*; ibid., pp. 190–93.

68 A strike in Veracruz meant they had to unload their own trunks from their steamship and were faced with other problems as well; TsGALI, 1923/2/2143.

69 Seton, *Eisenstein*, p. 195.

70 Best Maugard had been speculating on the greater significance of the pulque harvest and must have spoken of his ideas to Eisenstein. The comments he made in an article in 1932 were closely related to concepts Eisenstein hoped to convey in the "Maguey" episode of the film; see Adolfo Best Maugard, "Mexico Into Cinema," *Theatre Arts* 16 (November 1932): 927.

71 Marie Seton, "Treasure Trove," *Sight and Sound* 8, no. 31 (1939): 90.

72 Bixby, "The Weave of the Serape," p. 29.

73 Leyda, quoted in ibid., p. 127.

74 It is here perhaps that Eisenstein owes his greatest debt to his study of Weston's photographs.

75 Eisenstein had done a number of highly stylized and constructivist "Lady Macbeth" sketches after working on "The Mexican" in 1921, and at Tetlapayac he returned to this theme, although the style of the drawings of 1931 shows a clear influence by pre-Columbian, particularly Mixtec, design traditions, interpreted with an art-deco eye. Many depict Macbeth with an erect penis at the time of the fatal blow against Duncan. One shows Lady Macbeth masturbating her husband while he cuts off the head of the king, and often the phallic connotations of Lady Macbeth handing her husband the sword with which he is to murder Duncan are clear and inescapable. TsGALI, 1923/2/1222.

76 A. F. Bustamente, "Eisenstein el magnífico," *El Ilustrado*, 11 June 1931, p. 47. His "Lo que en México hace Eisenstein" summarized Eisenstein's activities in Mexico and reproduced stills from the film; "Los Indios del señor Eisenstein" (*El Ilustrado*, 25 June 1931, pp. 24–25, 43) dealt with the depiction of the Indians in the prospective film and said that Eisenstein was creating a "cinematic poem" in Mexico, one (significantly) "without sex" (p. 43). Leiva published articles in Havana's *Orbe*, and the Los Angeles Spanish-language newspaper, *La Opinión* (5 July 1931) wrote about Eisenstein's claim to have discovered a new world in Mexico's artistic spirit; finally, the Mexican journal *Contemporáneos* included an article by Eisenstein and a series of photographs from the project.

77 Iurenev, "Eizenshtein," p. 193.

78 Gabriel Fernández Ledesma had come to visit with his future wife Isabel Villaseñor, and she found herself cast as the "Maguey" episode's heroine. Fernández was already becoming famous for his studies of folk arts and Mexican toys (he gave Eisenstein a copy of his book on Mexican toys), and he collected a number of Eisenstein's sketches while he was at the hacienda. He also obtained a number of Eisenstein's sketches, depicting him, the musician Castro Padilla, Eisenstein (being crucified), and a series on the death of Werther (these were reproduced in S. M. Eisenstein, *Dibujos mexicanos inéditos* (Mexico City: Cineteca nacional, Secretaría de Gobernación, 1978).

79 The latter two of whom left interesting accounts of their visit. See Porter, "Flowering Judas," and Ione Robinson, *A Wall to Paint On* (New York: E. P. Dutton and Co., 1946).

80 For one version, see TsGALI, 1923/2/41. See also S. M. Eisenstein, *Izbrannye proizvedeniia*, vol. 6 (Moscow: Iskusstvo, 1971), pp. 105–28; see also the 1947 "Posleslovie," ibid., pp. 446–52. For notes and a summary of the Sinclair business, see ibid., pp. 533–38. See also S. M. Eisenstein, *Que Viva Mexico!* (London: Vision Press, 1972).

81 Seton, *Eisenstein*, p. 197.

82 Leiva, "Destruction."

83 TsGALI, 1923/2/47, "Prilozhenie k libretto," written in 1947, published in *Iskusstvo kino*, 1957, no. 5, and in Eisenstein, *Izbrannye proizvedeniia*, vol. 6, pp. 446–52.

84 Originally, Eisenstein intended to incorporate some film he and the crew had made in Michoacán of the fishermen and their "Japanese-like" houses in Pátzcuaro and Janitzio, but decided against it; sketches in TsGALI, 1923/2/40.

85 Eisenstein, *Que Viva Mexico!*, p. 28.

86 Williams has pointed out that death is often used to foreshadow revolution in Eisenstein's cinematic works: "In Eisenstein's films, the death of an individual often heralds the birth of revolution, as, for example, the funeral of the sailor Vakulinchuk in *Potemkin*, which launches the revolution in Odessa. In *October*, made in 1927, Eisenstein again uses death to foreshadow revolution, with the dead horse on the draw-bridge, the massacre on Nevsky Prospect, and the apparent explosion of the baroque statue of Christ." *Artists*, p. 176.

87 Eisenstein, *Que Viva Mexico!*, p. 64. For Sinclair's benefit, Eisenstein wrote that "happy, romantic, is the finale of the story about this ancient and beautiful Spanish holiday" (ibid., p. 67), but undoubtedly the twist of the variation on the miracle of Chalma would have given the episode more of the "weirdness" Eisenstein had mentioned at the beginning of his summary of this episode.

88 Ibid., p. 28.

89 At this point, the narrator was to intrude into the action of the film, addressing Concepción directly: "Why, Concepción, Isn't this what you came for? Is it not what you expected? It is not what you longed for? In reply to the voice of the author Concepción smiles, nods her head in assent." 1931 synopsis of the film; TsGALI, 1923/2/43, p. 9; Eisenstein, *Que Viva Mexico!*, p. 40. The crew had to remove the roof of the room in which the dance was held so that they could film it, and this was one of the expenses Sinclair must have thought excessive; it is remarkable how much like Rivera's paintings and frescoes of a dance in Tehuantepec this sequence would have been. See especially *Baile en Tehuantepec* in the Secretariat of Public Education. The heroine was originally called Trinidad, another indication of Eisenstein's fascination with the triangle.

90 The wedding customs included the mother's announcement that her daughter has become a woman, sky rockets and fire works (Eisenstein used this now hackneyed imagery in *The Old and the New* to indicate the success of the stud bull Foma in impregnating the collective farm's cows), and the turning inside out of the typical and unique headdress of the Tehuanas.

91 Although he did intend to intercut a cockfight with the main story line, he did not mention this to Sinclair because he was afraid Sinclair would object.

92 Henry Berlein's *Mexico: The Land of Unrest* (Philadelphia: J. B. Lippincott, 1914), p. 104, had given him the idea for the episode involving the *jus primae noctis*, among others; Gruening had provided him with the suggestion of burying the three peons up to their necks in the sand and galloping the horses over them in punishment (Gruening, *Mexico*, p. 129), and the use of the "Alabado" had come from Brenner.

93 Eisenstein mentioned this to Monoszon as well; see Iurenev, "Eizenshtein," p. 197; Eisenstein certainly knew Reed's work well (although Eisenstein had only one book by Reed in his library—on 4 October 1928 he obtained a copy of *Doch revoliutsii*, which included the stories "Soldiers of Fortune" and "Peons"—he had undoubtedly read most of Reed's works), and excerpts from Reed's *Insurgent Mexico* (New York: International Publishers, 1969) were an important source of inspiration. One episode in particular he borrowed directly; see pp. 4–5. Reed was not the only source of information for the "Soldadera" episode, of course, and Eisenstein utilized his reading of Azuela and Bierce as well (he wrote later that he felt Bierce's depiction of Villa was closer to the truth than anyone else's; Eisenstein, *Immoral Memories*, pp. 192–93).

94 To the narrator's direct question, in the manner of Christ's question of Peter, of where she was going, she replied, "Quién sabe?"

95 Eisenstein and Orozco missed each other in New York, Los Angeles, and Mexico City, but Eisenstein did have a copy of Weston's photograph of Orozco inscribed "Para mi amigo, Sergio Eisenstein" (dated "1930 Mexico" and kept today in his apartment in Moscow); in November 1933 Orozco and Alma Reed sent him a volume of Orozco's works, and earlier, Orozco had sent a copy of Susan Smith's *The Glories of Venus: A Novel of Modern Mexico* (New York: Harper and Brothers, 1931) that had his illustrations in it. Leiva wrote about Eisenstein's affection for Orozco's works in a letter: "When looking at his frescos, after having looked at every other that is here (Mexico City), he exclaimed with religious devotion and complete sincerity: 'Orozco is the greatest painter in the world.'" Leiva, letter to Mrs. Reed of Delphic Studios, quoted in Walter Gutman, "News and Gossip," *Creative Art* 8 (March 1931): 94.

96 He felt he could be clearer about his intent with respect to Pancha's fate. To make the plot more interesting, and at the same time more typical and more unexpected, he would have liked to have changed the script, he said:

> Let us add that this new version did not seem to us to constitute proof of a lack of political conscience or indifference of the Mexican woman Pancha. All to the contrary!
> Her first husband belonged to the army of Pancho Villa.
> Her second—to the detachments of Emiliano Zapata.
>
> In the definitive version of the scenario, Pancha's growth represents Mexico, which, passing from hand to hand, gradually rises to the conception that strength does not reside in dispute, but uniquely in the union of all the people against the forces of reaction. (Seton, *Eisenstein*, pp. 506, 507)

97 Ibid., pp. 209–10.

98 Karetnikova, "Eizenshtein i Sikeiros," p. 152. Eisenstein apparently first learned about Posada from Toor's book on him which he bought in Mexico City in mid-December, and from Brenner's chapter devoted to him in *Idols Behind Altars*, which Eisenstein marked carefully. Eisenstein also admitted to being influenced by Holbein and Daumier and suspected that Posada might have known their work as well because of the French influence in Mexico during the time of Maximilian.

99 See TsGALI, 1923/2/43, p. 30; Eisenstein, *Que Viva Mexico!*, pp. 74–75. It depicted modern life, factories, harbors, airplanes, industrialization, technology:

> And the nation's leaders, the President, generals, secretaries of State Departments. Life, activity, work of new, energetic people . . . but if you look closer you will behold the same faces.
>
> Faces that bear close resssemblance [sic] to those who held funeral[s] of antiquity in Yucatán, those who danced in Tehuantepec; those who sang the Alabado behind the tall walls, those who danced in queer costumes [sic] around the temples, those who fought and died in the battles of revolution.
>
> The same faces
> but different people.   (Eisenstein, *Que Viva Mexico!*, pp. 76–77)

These faces were of great importance to Eisenstein and were mentioned throughout his notes for the film; TsGALI, 1923/2/40.

100 Eisenstein, *Que Viva Mexico!*, p. 77. While many foreigners felt only horror and disgust at the Death Day celebrations, Eisenstein understood them the way Mexicans did, in a positive sense; Malcolm Lowry was writing *Under the Volcano* at the same time Eisenstein was making his film, for example, and its central theme was death, but it was treated entirely negatively. In one version of the conclusion (1932) Eisenstein makes an attempt to fit Stalinist constraints: "They know that the Mexican proletariat will grow and become stronger and that only under its leading role and with its help will an unorganized peons' rebellion be directed toward a real revolutionary channel and be crowned with a final class victory." TsGALI, 1923/2/46, p. 9.

101 Letter to Monoszon, 25 January 1931; TsGALI, 2617/1/42.

102 See Williams, *Artists*, pp. 176–77. Kepley pointed out that in *The Old and the New*, the death of the bull Fomka was intercut with "gloomy shots of skulls which symbolize the inevitability of death and the futility of trying to conquer death through mysticism. Death is conquered through the act of reproduction, however, as Fomka's offspring survive to replenish the herd." Kepley, "Eisenstein's *Old and New*," p. 48.

103 TsGALI, 1923/2/1832.

104 Eisenstein apparently planned to show Calles some of the film and was introduced to him through Álvarez del Vayo. Eisenstein was also interested in meeting Calles because of his reputation in Mexico. Eisenstein had a copy of McCullagh's *Red Mexico*, and the sections about the Church-state conflict he read with interest. Curiously, the copy in Eisenstein's library in Moscow had two sections of the book removed: "Mexico and Russia" and "The Dzerzhinsky of Mexico." On Calles, see Geduld and Gottesman, p. 125.

105 Much filming took place at and around the presidential residence at Chapultepec. There are a number of photos preserved at the Museum of Modern Art, including shots of Ortiz Rubio and even Calles; Ortiz Rubio gave Eisenstein an inscribed photograph of himself, dated 23 November 1931; TsGALI, 1923/1/2977. Leiva wrote that Eisenstein had told him his views on the possibility of another revolution in Mexico:

> [He] explained revolution as a stroke of destiny; he pointed out revolution as the only way to complete the fusion of all our dispersed elements in an [sic] unified whole. There are many kinds of revolution; he was clever enough to realize that after the enormous energy expenditure of the 1910 Revolution there are very few probabilities for a coming one of the warlike type.
>   "I consider communism impossible in Mexico for many years; to have it, your country need [sic] at least ten years of a strong, hard capitalism"— he said to me once.
>   (Leiva, manuscript in Gottesman file, Museum of Modern Art)

106 Letter of 7 January 1932, quoted in Seton, *Eisenstein*, pp. 211–12.
107 Geduld and Gottesman, p. 212.
108 The suspicion that Eisenstein might have had Trotskyite beliefs is interesting, and Eisenstein's reputation has been made more respectable in this regard by the manipulation of information in his TsGALI archive to protect him from the earlier charges. In TsGALI's copy of Sinclair's letter of 16 November 1931 to Eisenstein, a long section referring to Eisenstein's attitude toward Trotskyism has been cut out; the complete text of the letter was published in Geduld and Gottesman, pp. 207–08, and the excised portion is as follows: "For everyone who has talked to us about the matter knows stories which you are said to have told about your troubles in Russia. For example, there is the story that you make Trotsky the hero of "Ten Days That Shook the World," and that just as the picture was completed the break with Trotsky came, and you were compelled to mutilate the picture and cut out the hero. There is the detail that at one place in the picture Trotsky appeared with his back turned to the audience and that the audience recognized him and applauded. I don't know if any of this happened, nor do I know if you told it. I only know that that is what people in Hollywood are repeating as having been told by you." Whether Eisenstein himself excised this section of the letter is uncertain. TsGALI, 1923/2/1833.
109 Edmund Wilson, "Eisenstein in Hollywood," *New Republic*, 4 November 1931, p. 321; reprinted in his *The American Earthquake* (Garden City, N.Y.: Doubleday, 1958), pp. 397–413.
110 Iurenev, "Eizenshtein," p. 198. At about the same time, and in a similar mood, he told Helprin that he had to be back in the Soviet Union in February to make a film celebrating the fourteenth anniversary of the October Revolution. Helprin, "Eisenstein's New Film," p. 6.
111 Original copy, p. 2, TsGALI, 2617/1/42; see also S. M. Eisenstein, "A Mexican Film and Marxian Theory: A Communication," *New Republic*, 9 December 1931, pp. 99–100.

112 Geduld and Gottesman, pp. 212–14. Stern noted in 1934 that he and others were aware in 1931 that Eisenstein had to conceal some of his ideas for the film which would offend the Mexican government and that the official scenario had to be written in the "apple sauciest way" so as to avoid doing this; Stern, "Introduction to Synopsis," p. 4. *Variety* wrote in March 1932 that *Que Viva Mexico!* was "reported to be of a very liberal nature"; "Barred from U.S. Serge Will Cut Film Abroad," *Variety*, 15 March 1932, p. 3.

113 In his constant correspondence with Monoszon, he gave no indication of a desire to defect, and it is likely that this suspicion had little basis in fact. TsGALI, 2617/1/42. On 24 September 1931 he sent a request to Monoszon for permission to bring three Fords back to the Soviet Union to be used for filming there, and on 8 November 1931 he sent him a copy of his letter to the *New Republic.*

114 TsGALI, 1923/2/1833; see also Helprin, "Eisenstein's New Film," p. 6.

115 Anita Brenner, for example, said she would be glad to "tell the truth" about Kimbrough's drinking and insulting behavior if he thought it would do any good; letter of 18 January 1932, TsGALI, 1923/1/1675. Eisenstein had seven teeth extracted at the end of January. He had some premonition of what was up: it was during this period that he did a large number of "Martyr" sketches, for example, showing both the bull and the matador being crucified.

116 Geduld and Gottesman (pp. 285–86) have offered a number of plausible reasons for why Eisenstein might wish to stay; a completed film would be a justification for his extended absence from the Soviet Union; returning with a film would allow him to reestablish his position and authority in what was a changing Soviet film industry; it was even possible he feared a purge. They added as well that he was in love with Mexico and might have kept shooting in Mexico indefinitely, if only as a way of justifying his remaining permanently in the country. Bixby tends to support this idea: "*Que Viva Mexico!* as a single text is a chimera; Eisenstein realized before his friends did and long before his death that *Que Viva Mexico!* was only a haunting vision, never to be a realized film"; "The Weave of the Serape," p. 271.

117 See "Eisenstein Is Barred Under the Alien Law," *New York Times*, 22 February 1932, section 15, p. 2. On the sketches, see Barna, *Eisenstein*, p. 182, and Geduld and Gottesman, pp. 309–10. For Sinclair's comments on the drawings, see ibid., p. 309. Once again, Eisenstein's sketches showed his frame of mind, especially one entitled "Yo—autoritratto," showing a two-headed figure, half male, half female, being crucified. Another equally revealing series was the one he did while staying in Nuevo Laredo entitled "Extasis." Seton wrote that Eisenstein underwent his own "ecstasis" while in Mexico, that by recognizing the unity of life and death there, Eisenstein found his own "spiritual soul"; Seton, *Eisenstein*, p. 194.

118 Leyda and Voynow, *Eisenstein at Work*, p. 71.

119 Ibid., p. 77. Eisenstein visited Charlot, Burliuk, Toor, and Susan Smith in New York. His parting words were published in the *Los Angeles Times*, quoted in Geduld and Gottesman, pp. 319–20. Seton has described best the significance of this departure from the New World: "As the Europa steamed out into the black void of a long night, the Sergei Eisenstein of legend began to die. He had come to

America a young man full of enthusiasm with a sensual delight in laughter, but two years had added ten to his appearance. He appeared a middle-aged man, whose austere face might never be humanized by a smile which was not wry" (Seton, *Eisenstein*, p. 244).

120 Norman Swallow, *Eisenstein—A Documentary Portrait* (New York: Dutton, 1977), p. 71.

121 The situation was not quite as bad as the rumors Stern had heard from Hollywood that Eisenstein was in Siberia, condemned for five years as a counterrevolutionary, that he had lost his mind and was incarcerated in an asylum near Moscow, and that he was dead. Lincoln Kirstein letter to Eisenstein, 2 September 1932, TsGALI, 1923/2/1812.

122 Kirstein wrote him in February 1933, for example, that "I really think there is an excellent possibility of your getting the picture to cut." TsGALI, 1923/1/1857.

123 TsGALI, 1923/2/1797; letters from Enos S. Booth to Eisenstein, summer 1933. Eisenstein apparently had some thought at this time of getting Shostakovich to do the music, basing it on Indian and Spanish themes as well as using solo and choral voices to comment on the action of the film.

124 The journal was building on the publicity it had given the film two years before. Their special issue of 1932 had called the film the "first in the Western hemisphere to assume the mantle of maturity" (Helprin, "Que Viva Mexico," *Experimental Cinema* 1, no. 4, p. 13), one that had "practically stolen from the Mexican nation all her secrets, dreams, and feelings accumulated during five thousand years" (A. A. Leiva, "Eisenstein's Film on Mexico," ibid., p. 5).

125 Helprin, "Eisenstein's New Film," p. 6; Richard Watts, Jr., "Mexico as Done by Eisenstein," *New York Herald Tribune*, 15 May 1932; A. F. Bustamente, "Eisenstein en México," *Nuestro México* 1, no. 1 (March 1932), p. 14. Not everyone was so overwhelming in their praise. Weston saw the stills from the film published in *Experimental Cinema* and commented on them negatively in his *Daybooks*, vol. 2, p. 247. Even so, he wrote some time later (6 April 1932) that "I eagerly await Eisenstein's new film on Mexico." Ibid., p. 254.

126 Modotti had been active in PCM politics in Mexico and had been involved with Julio Antonio Mella (see Pestkovsky's "Ubiistvo Khulio Melia," *Put MOPRa*, 1929, no. 3 [1–15 April 1929], pp. 2–3) before arriving in Moscow in October 1930. Leyda asked Eisenstein about Modotti, and according to her biographer Eisenstein "explained to Leyda that while he knew and admired Tina he had seen relatively little of her, since he was protecting his Mexican film and did not want information about his friendship with Tina to filter back to Mexico or to his American critics." Mildred Constantine, *Tina Modotti: A Fragile Life* (New York: Paddington Press Ltd., 1975), p. 195. Eisenstein's apartment has one of the few copies of Modotti's pamphlet, *Meksikanskie peony* (Moscow: Izdatelstvo TsK MOPR SSSR, 1932) in Moscow.

127 *New Republic*, 6 September 1933, p. 104.

128 Letter to Kenneth Macpherson, ed. of *Close-up*, 13 October 1932 (reprinted in Leyda and Voynow, *Eisenstein at Work*, p. 77); letter to Viertel, ibid., p. 71.

129 See Geduld and Gottesman, pp. 317–77, and for a sample of the attacks, Seymour

Stern, "The Greatest Thing Done on This Side of the Atlantic: Eisenstein's Original Version of Mexico," *Modern Monthly* 7 (1933): 525–32. The shorts were *Death Day, Land and Freedom, Mexico Marches, Idol of Hope, Spanish and Indian, Zapotec Village, Conquering Cross;* on these, see Geduld and Gottesman, pp. 421–23. There was general belief abroad that some of the film was used in the making of *Viva Villa!* (Aleksandrov, *Epokha*, p. 155), and later for an Eddie Cantor comedy (ibid., p. 156). Jean Mitry, *S. M. Eisenstein* (Paris: 1961), agrees. Geduld and Gottesman, on the other hand, say this is not the case (p. 330). When Eisenstein saw the film during World War II at the American Embassy in Moscow, he recognized the hacienda of Tetlapayac but did not comment on whether or not his film was used; he did say that he thought Wallace Beery's depiction of Villa was wrong because he tried to play both Villa and Zapata. Leiva was at the hacienda during the filming and wrote Eisenstein about how people had changed, about the tremendous amounts of money MGM was spending (in contrast to Eisenstein), and about how everyone at the hacienda asked about Eisenstein (letters of 1 August 1934 and 29 August 1934, TsGALI, 1923/2/1817).

130   See Jay Leyda, "'Que Viva Mexico', ein unvollendetes Werk," in Herman Herlinghaus, Heinz Baumert, and Renate Georgi, eds., *Sergei Eisenstein, Künstler der Revolution* (Berlin: Henschelverlag, 1960), pp. 192–201; also his "Eisenstein's Mexican Tragedy," *Sight and Sound* 27 (Autumn 1958): pp. 305–08, 329.

131   The open letter was published first in *Iskusstvo kino*, 1957, no. 7: 105–08; many believed that completing the film without Eisenstein's mind and personal participation was not possible; see Jacques Rivette, "Que Viva Eisenstein," *Cahiers du cinéma* 14 (January 1958): 20–21.

132   Tom Luddy, quoted in Edward Guthmann, "The Battle Behind a Mexican Documentary: Eisenstein's *Que Viva Mexico*," *San Francisco Examiner and Chronicle*, 30 October 1983, p. 29. Aleksandrov, of course, had done the editing, and Eisenstein's script was read by the Soviet film director Sergei Bondarchuk. Aleksandrov made no pretense of the film's being complete. He approached it as a documentary, showing photos of the team at work in Mexico and discussing the events that took place behind the scenes during the filming, and only then attempting to recreate as much as possible what Eisenstein had in mind originally. Aleksandrov's version presented the following sections of the film: the Prologue, Tehuantepec, the Fiesta, Maguey, a description of the Soldadera episode using documentary photographs from the Casasola collection, and an Epilogue using the Death Day shots.

133   While working on *Ivan the Terrible* in Central Asia he returned to drawing Mexico, something he had not done for several years; Karetnikova, "Eizenshtein i Sikeiros," p. 9. His reading included Tannenbaum's *Peace by Revolution*, with its drawings by Covarrubias; Prescott's *Conquest of Mexico*; Huxley's *Beyond the Mexique Bay*; and Pestkovsky's *Istoriia meksikanskikh revoliutsii*.

134   Barna, *Eisenstein*, p. 185.

135   Ibid., p. 183.

136   *Vacilada* was a concept that appealed to Eisenstein greatly, and the sections discussing it in Smith's *Venus* (pp. 88–89), Carleton Beals's *Mexican Maze* (Philadel-

phia: Lippincott, 1931, p. 238), and Brenner's *Idols Behind Altars* (p. 28) were all marked in some detail in Eisenstein's copies of the books. Brenner identified *vacilada* with the mestizo race of Mexico, as part of what she called the three heroisms of thought, emotion, and expression.

5 Postscript: Trotsky's Mexico

1 Isaac Deutscher, *The Prophet Outcast: Trotsky, 1929–1940* (London: Oxford University Press, 1963), p. 509.

2 He painted Trotsky's portrait in the New York City Trotskyite headquarters and had included Trotsky in his second version of the Rockefeller Center mural, for example. See Bertram D. Wolfe, *The Fabulous Life of Diego Rivera* (New York: Stein and Day, 1963), pp. 237–39, 338–39.

3 See Alice Rühle-Gerstel, "No Verses for Trotsky: A Diary in Mexico (1937)," *Encounter*, April 1982, p. 29.

4 Leon Trotsky, *Writings of Leon Trotsky, 1936–37* (New York: Pathfinder Press, 1970), pp. 79–84.

5 Diego Rivera, *My Art, My Life* (New York: Citadel Press, 1960), p. 229.

6 Trotsky, *Writings, 1936–37*, p. 179.

7 Rühle-Gerstel, "No Verses for Trotsky," p. 29.

8 Manuel Márquez Fuentes and Octavio Rodríguez Araujo, *El partido comunista mexicano (en el período de la Internacional Comunista: 1919–1943)* (Mexico City: Ediciones "El caballito," 1973), p. 208. It is interesting that while there was censure of Cárdenas from the Mexican Communists, the general assessment of his presidency by contemporaries in the USSR was quite favorable; see A. Volkov, "Agrarnaia reforma v Meksike," *Mirovoe khoziaistvo i mirovaia politika*, 1939, no. 6: pp. 113–18, and to a lesser extent, E. Menzhinskii, *Meksika* (Moscow: Gosudarstvennoe sotsialno-ekonomicheskoe izdatelstvo, 1937).

9 Rühle-Gerstel, "No Verses for Trotsky," p. 29.

10 Victor Serge and Natalia Sedova Trotsky, *The Life and Death of Leon Trotsky*, trans. Arnold J. Pomerans (New York: Basic Books, 1975), p. 211. Rühle-Gerstel remembers this somewhat differently, saying that the crowd was a group of newspapermen who had learned of Trotsky's arrival and wished to interview him, and that to avoid the crush, they raced their car into the city at "60 miles per hour." Rühle-Gerstel, "No Verses for Trotsky," p. 28.

11 Trotsky, *Writings, 1938–39* (New York: Pathfinder Press, 1969) pp. 79–80.

12 Trotsky, *Writings, 1938–39*, p. 46.

13 Trotsky, *Writings, 1939–40* (New York: Pathfinder Press, 19?), p. 172. Trotsky may have been more than a little enthusiastic in his bending of the truth here. For a more moderate evaluation of Lombardo during these years, although admittedly at times an overly worshipful one, see Robert Paul Millan, *Vicente Lombardo Toledano* (Chapel Hill: University of North Carolina Press, 1966), pp. 128–29.

14 See Carleton Beals, " The Fewer Outsiders the Better," *Saturday Evening Post*, 12 June 1937, pp. 77–78. For Trotsky's response, see his "Mr. Beals as a Witness," *Writings, 1936–37*, pp. 291–97.

15 Jean van Heijenoort, *With Trotsky in Exile: From Prinkipo to Coyoacán* (Cambridge: Harvard University Press, 1978), pp. 208–09.

16 Hayden Herrera, *Frida: A Biography of Frida Kahlo* (New York: Harper and Row, 1983), p. 208.

17 See ibid., pp. 192–214.

18 Rühle-Gerstel, "No Verses for Trotsky," p. 39.

19 He was currently working on a biography of Stalin, to raise money to support himself and his family. His son, Leon Sedov, died in 1937 after an appendix operation in a Paris clinic of mysterious and probably not natural causes, according to Rühle-Gerstel, "No Verses for Trotsky," p. 35. Trotsky's other children also died before he did: his two daughters from natural causes and suicide, and his younger son was condemned in 1936 in the USSR for his "Trotskyist" activities, sent into internal exile, and probably shot in 1938.

20 See Deutscher, *Prophet*, p. 357; also, "Answers to the Lies of the New York Daily News," 28 December 1938, in Trotsky, *Writings, 1938–39*, pp. 159–63.

21 Serge, *Trotsky*, p. 253. Trotsky did meet with Cárdenas's political adviser, General Mújica (Heijenoort, *With Trotsky*, p. 106), however. It was through Mújica that Cárdenas learned of the death of Trotsky's son, for example, and sent Trotsky a note of condolence. Serge, *Trotsky*, p. 253.

22 See "To the Representatives of the Mexican Press," 12 January 1937, in Trotsky, *Writings, 1936–37*, pp. 89–92.

23 Ibid., p. 234.

24 "On Mexico's Second Six-Year Plan," 14 March 1939, in Trotsky, *Writings, 1939–40*, pp. 221–28.

25 Deutscher, *Prophet*, pp. 431–35.

26 Heijenoort, *With Trotsky*, p. 126.

27 Leon Trotsky, "Art and Politics," *Partisan Review* 5, no. 3 (August–September 1938): 7–8.

28 Trotsky found it was not easy to view Rivera's murals, since many of his frescoes were inside the Secretariat of Public Education, in the later 1930s a "stronghold of Mexican Stalinists" (Rühle-Gerstel, "No Verses for Trotsky," p. 39), who were not overly hospitable to Trotsky.

29 "Letter to the Mexican Attorney General," 27 May 1940, in Trotsky, *Writings, 1939–40*, pp. 223–27. The book was eventually published as *Los Gangsters de Stalin*.

30 "Supplementary and Indispensable Explanations of My July 2 Statements," dated 5 July 1940, in Trotsky, *Writings, 1939–40*, pp. 305–15.

BIBLIOGRAPHY

Archival Material

1. Tsentralnyi gosudarstvennyi arkhiv literatury i iskusstva (TsGALI), Moscow.

f[ond] 56 Valerii Iakovlevich Briusov
f.   57 Konstantin Dmitrievich Balmont
f.   336 Vladimir Vladimirovich Maiakovskii
f.   389 Sergei Dmitrievich Protopopov
f.   571 Tatiana Lvovna Shchepkina-Kupernik
f.   1923 Sergei Mikhailovich Eisenstein
f.   2617 Lev Isaakovich Monoszon

2. Nauchnyi memorialnyi kabinet S. M. Eizenshteina pri soiuzu kinomatografistov SSSR, Moscow.

3. Museum of Modern Art, New York.

Material on Eisenstein and *Que Viva Mexico!* in Special Collections Division and Film Archive

Printed Material

1. Early Nineteenth Century

Alekseev, Aleksandr Ivanovich. *Ilia Gavrilovich Voznesenskii (1816–1871).* Moscow: Nauka, 1977.

———. *Russkie geograficheskie issledovaniia na dalnem vostoke i v severnoi Amerike (XIX–nachala XX v.).* Moscow: Nauka, 1976.

Andreev, A. I. *Russian Discoveries in the Pacific and in North America in the Eighteenth and Nineteenth Centuries: A Collection of Materials.* Translated by Carol Ginsburg. Ann Arbor: University of Michigan, 1952.

Andrews, Clarence L. "Russian Plans for American Domination." *Washington Histori-cal Quarterly* 18, no. 2 (1927): 81–92.

Bancroft, Hubert Howe. *Works.* Vol. 19. *History of California.* San Francisco: The History Company, 1886.

Barratt, Glynn. *Russia in Pacific Waters, 1715–1825.* Vancouver: University of British Columbia Press, 1981.

Bartley, Russell H. *Imperial Russia and the Struggle for Latin American Independence, 1808–1828.* Austin: Institute for Latin American Studies, 1978.

Blomkvist, E. E. "A Russian Scientific Expedition to California and Alaska, 1839–1849." Translated by Basil Dmytryshyn and E.A.P. Crownhart-Vaughan. *Oregon Histori-cal Quarterly* 73, no. 2 (1972): 101–70.

Calderón y Enríquez, Pedro. "The Memorial of Pedro Calderón y Henríquez Recom-mending Monterey as a Port for the Philippine Galleons, with a View to Prevent-ing Russian Enroachment in California." Edited and translated by H. Wagner. *California Historical Society Quarterly* 23 (1944): 219–25.

Chevigny, Hector. *Lost Empire: The Life and Adventures of Nikolai Petrovich Rezanov.* New York: Macmillan, 1937.

———. *Russian America: The Great Alaskan Adventure, 1741–1867.* New York: Viking, 1965.

Chikhachev, Platon Aleksandrovich. "Poezdka cherez Buenos-Airesskie pampy." *Otechestvennye zapiski* 34, pt. 2 (1844): 1–77.

Davydov, Iurii Vladimirovich. *Ferdinand Vrangel.* Moscow: Molodaia gvardiia, 1968.

———. *Golovnin.* Moscow: Molodaia gvardiia, 1968.

Divin, V. A. *Povest o slavnom moreplavatele (k 200-letiiu so dnia rozhdeniia V. M. Golov-nina).* Moscow: Mysl, 1976.

Du Four, Clarence John; E. O. Essig, et al. "The Russian Withdrawal from California." *California Historical Quarterly,* September 1933, pp. 240–76.

Essig, E. O. "The Russian Settlement at Ross." *Quarterly of the California Historical So-ciety* 13, no. 3 (September 1933): 191–209.

Fedorova, Svetlana Grigorevna. *Russkoe naselenie Aliaski i Kalifornii (konets XVIII veka–1867 g.).* Moscow: Nauka, 1971.

García Treviño, Rodrigo. *La ingerencia rusa en México (y Sudamérica).* Mexico City: Editorial América, 1959.

Gibson, James R. *Imperial Russia in Frontier America: The Changing Geography of Sup-ply of Russian America, 1784–1867.* New York: Oxford University Press, 1976.

———. "Russia in California, 1833: Report of Governor Wrangell." *Pacific Northwest Quarterly,* October 1969, pp. 205–15.

———. "Russian America in 1833: The Survey of Kirill Khlebnikov." *Pacific Northwest Quarterly,* January 1972, pp. 1–13.

———. "A Russian Orthodox Priest in a Mexican Catholic Parish." *The Pacific Histo-rian,* Summer 1971, pp. 57–66.

Golder, Frank Alfred. *Russian Expansion on the Pacific, 1641–1850.* Cleveland: The Ar-thur H. Clark Co., 1914.

Golovin, Pavel Nikolaevich. *Civil and Strange Encounters: The Worldly Travel Letters of an Imperial Russian Navy Officer, 1860–1861.* Translated and annotated by Basil

Dmytryshyn and E.A.P. Crownhart-Vaughan. Portland: Western Imprints (Oregon Historical Society), 1983.

———. *The End of Russian America: Captain P. N. Golovin's Last Report, 1862.* Translated with an introduction and notes by Basil Dmytryshyn and E.A.P. Crownhart-Vaughan. Portland: Oregon Historical Society, 1983.

———. *Iz putevykh pisem P. N. Golovina.* St. Petersburg: Ministerstvo morskogo flota, 1863.

Golovnin, Vasilii Mikhailovich. *Around the World on the "Kamchatka," 1817–1819.* Translated with an introduction and notes by Ella Lury Wiswell. Honolulu: Hawaii Historical Society and the University Press of Hawaii, 1979.

Hatch, Flora Faith. *The Russian Advance Into California.* San Francisco: R. and E. Research Associates, 1971.

Hutchinson, C. Alan. *Frontier Settlement in Mexican California.* New Haven: Yale University Press, 1969.

Khlebnikov, Kirill Timofeevich. *Colonial Russian America: Kyrill T. Khlebnikov's Reports, 1817–1832.* Translated with an introduction and notes by Basil Dmytryshyn and E.A.P. Crownhart-Vaughan. Portland: Oregon Historical Society, 1976.

———. "Memoirs of California." Translated by Anatole G. Mazour. *Pacific Historical Review,* September 1940, pp. 307–36.

———. "Vzgliad na polveka moei zhizni." *Syn otechestva* 175 (1836): 299–324, 345–75, 413–28.

———. "Zapiski o Kalifornii." *Syn otechestva* 174 (1829), bk. 2:208–27, 276–88, 336–47, 400–10; bk. 3: 25–35.

Kotzebue, Otto Von. *A New Voyage Round the World in the Years 1823, 24, 25, and 26.* 2 vols. New York: Da Capo Press, 1967.

Krylov, Ivan Andreevich. "Amerikantsy." *Polnoe sobranie sochinenii.* Edited by D. Bednyi. Vol. 2, pp. 631–86. Moscow: Khudozhestvennaia literatura, 1946.

Langsdorff, G. H. Von. *Langsdorff's Narrative of the Rezanov Voyage to Nueva California in 1806.* Revised English translation by Thomas C. Russell. San Francisco: Private Press of T. C. Russell, 1927.

———. *Voyages and Travels in Various Parts of the World, During the Years 1803, 1804, 1805, 1806, and 1807.* 2 vols. London: H. Colburn, 1813–1814.

Lomonosov, Mikhail Vasilevich. *Polnoe sobranie sochinenii.* Vol. 8. Moscow-Leningrad: Akademiia nauk SSSR, 1959.

Mahr, August C. *The Visit of the "Rurik" to San Francisco in 1816.* Stanford: Stanford University Press, 1932.

Makarova, Raisa Vsevolodovna. *Russians on the Pacific, 1743–1799.* Translated by Richard A. Pierce and Alton S. Donnelly. Kingston, Ontario: Limestone Press, 1975.

Markov, Alexei [Alexander]. *The Russians on the Pacific Ocean [California 1845].* Translated by Ivan Petroff with foreword by Arthur Woodward. Los Angeles: Glen Dawson, 1955.

Markov, Aleksandr. *Russkie na vostochnom okeane.* 2d ed. St. Petersburg, 1856.

Mazour, Anatole G. "Dmitrii Zavalishin, Dreamer of a Russian American Empire." *Pacific Historical Review* 5 (1936): 26–37.

"O Meksike." *Vestnik Evropy* 57 (1811): 75–80.

Okun, S. B. *The Russian American Company.* Translated by Carl Ginsburg, edited and with an introduction by B. D. Grekov. Cambridge: Harvard University Press, 1951.

Pasetskii, Vasilii Mikhailovich. *Ferdinand Petrovich Vrangel, 1796–1870.* Moscow: Nauka, 1975.

Pierce, Richard A., ed. *Rezanov Reconnoiters California, 1806.* San Francisco: The Book Club of California, 1972.

Rezanov, Nikolai Petrovich. *The Rezanov Voyage to Nueva California in 1806.* Translated by Thomas C. Russell. San Francisco: Thomas C. Russell, 1926.

Richardson, William. "Wrangell's Journey of 1836: 'From Sitka to Saint Petersburg by Way of Mexico.'" *The Pacific Historian* 28, no. 4 (Winter 1984): 43–54.

Rotchev, A. G. "Vospominaniia russkogo puteshestvennika o Vest-Indii, Kalifornii i Ost-Indii." *Panteon,* 1854, no. 1:79–108; no. 2: 93–114.

"The Russian Colonies in California: A Russian Version." *Quarterly of the California Historical Society* 12, no. 3 (September 1933): 189–90.

Schanzer, George O. *A Russian Visit to the Spanish Franciscans in California, 1836.* Washington, D.C.: 1953.

Shur, Leonid Avelevich. "Iz istorii ustanovleniia diplomaticheskikh otnoshenii Rossii so stranami Latinskoi Ameriki." *Voprosy istorii,* August 1964, pp. 211–15.

———. "Latinoamerikanskie literatury v Rossii v nachale XIX v." In *Mezhdunarodnye sviazi russkoi literatury: sbornik statei,* edited by M. P. Alekseev, pp. 175–91. Moscow: Akademiia nauk SSSR, 1963.

———. "Materialy russkikh puteshestvennikov XVIII–XIX vv. kak istochnik po geografii, istorii, i etnografii stran Latinskoi Ameriki." *Izvestiia Vsesoiuznogo geograficheskogo obshchestva* 100 (1968): 230–36. Published in English in *Soviet Historians on Latin America: Recent Scholarly Contributions,* edited and translated by Russell H. Bartley, pp. 109–19. Madison: University of Wisconsin, 1978.

———. "Russian Travel Notes and Journals as Sources for the History of California, 1800–1850." Translated by James R. Gibson. *California Historical Quarterly* 52, no. 1 (Spring 1973): 38–63.

Slezkin, L. Iu. "Pozitsiia Rossii v otnoshenii Ispanskoi Ameriki na rubezhe 18–19 vekov." *Voprosy istorii* 38, no. 6 (June 1963): pp. 47–59.

Spencer-Hancock, Diane, and William E. Pritchard. "Notes to the 1817 Treaty Between the Russian American Company and the Kashaya Pomo Indians." Translated by Ina Kaliakin. *California History* 59, no. 4 (Winter 1980–1981): 306–33.

Stepanova, M. V. "I. G. Voznesenskii i etnograficheskoe izuchenie Severo-zapadnoi Ameriki." *Izvestiia vsesoiuznogo geograficheskogo obshchestva* 76, no. 5 (1944): 277–81.

Tarakanov, Vasilii Petrovich. *Statement of My Captivity Among the Californians.* Los Angeles: Glen Dawson, 1953.

Taylor, George P. "Spanish-Russian Rivalry in the Pacific, 1769–1820." *The Americas,* 1958, pp. 109–27.

Tikhmenev, P. A. *A History of the Russian American Company.* Translated and edited by Richard A. Pierce and Alton S. Donnelly. Seattle: University of Washington Press, 1978.

Tompkins, Stuart R., and Max L. Moorhead. "Russia's Approach to America." *British Columbia Historical Quarterly* 13 (1949), no. 1–2, pp. 55–66; no. 3–4, pp. 231–55.

Vishnevskii, Boris Nikolaevich. *Puteshestvennik Kirill Khlebnikov.* Perm: Permskoe knizhnoe izdatelstvo, 1957.

Vishniakov, N. "Rossiia, Kaliforniia i Sandvichevy ostrova." *Russkaia starina* 124 (1905): 249–89.

Völkl, Ekkehard. *Russland und Lateinamerika, 1741–1841.* Wiesbaden: Harrasowitz, 1968.

Wrangell, Ferdinand Petrovich. "Dnevnik puteshestviia iz Sitkhi v Sankt-Petersburg cherez Meksiku." In *K beregam Novogo Sveta,* edited by Leonid Avelevich Shur, pp. 190–277. Moscow: Nauka, 1971.

———. *Ocherk puti iz Sitkhi v S. Peterburg.* St. Petersburg: N. Grech, 1836.

———. "Puteshestvie iz Sitkhi v Sankt-Peterburg." *Severniaia pchela,* 1836, no. 240–46, 259–64.

Yarmolinsky, Avrahm. *Russian Americana, Sixteenth to Eighteenth Centuries: A Bibliographical and Historical Study.* New York: New York Public Library, 1943.

Zavalishin, Dmitrii Irinarkhovich. "California in 1824." Translated and edited by J. R. Gibson. *Southern California Quarterly* 55 (Winter 1973): 369–412.

———. "Delo o kolonii Ross." *Russkii vestnik* 62, no. 3–4 (1866): 36–65.

———. "Kaliforniia v 1824 godu." *Russkii vestnik* 60 (1865): 322–68.

———. "Krugotsvetnoe plavanie fregata 'Kreiser' v 1822–1825 gg. pod komandoiu Mikhaila Petrovicha Lazareva." *Drevniaia i novaia Rossiia,* 1877, no. 5, pp. 54–67; no. 6, pp. 115–25; no. 7, pp. 199–214; no. 10, pp. 143–58; no. 11, pp. 210–23.

2. Porfiriato

Balmont, Konstantin Dmitrievich. *Belye zarnitsy.* St. Petersburg: M. V. Pirozhkov, 1908.

———. *Ptitsy v vozdukhe: stroki napevnye.* St. Petersburg: Shipovnik, 1908.

———. *Visions solaires: Mexique—Egypte, Inde—Japon—Océanie.* Translated by Ludmila Savitzky. Paris: Editions Brossard, 1923.

———. *Zmeinye tsvety.* Moscow: Skorpion, 1910.

———. *Zovy drevnosti: Gimny, pesni, i zamysli drevnikh.* St. Petersburg: 1908.

Danevskaia, S. *Otkrytie i zavoevanie Meksiki: Istoricheskii rasskaz dlia detei,* 4th ed. Moscow: V. K. Karchagin, 1903.

Devollan, Grigorii Aleksandrovich. "V tsarstve Montezumy." *Istoricheskii vestnik* 100 (1905): 285–307, 631–57.

Kogan, Galina. "Fiodor Dostoievski, el pensamiento social ruso y la 'cuestión mexicana' en los años sesenta del siglo XIX." *América Latina,* 1975, no. 2:128–45.

Kuteishchikova, Vera Nikolaevna. "Leon Tolstoi y México." *El Día,* 7 August 1978.

Levin, I. O. "Novyi perevorot v Meksiko." *Russkaia mysl,* 1913, no. 3:12–14.

"Literaturnoe dvizhenie v Meksike." *Obrazovanie,* 1900, no. 2, pt. 2:19–23.

Lukin, B. V. "Ekspeditsiia Peterburgskoi Akademii nauk v Meksiku i na Kubu." *Vestnik Akademii nauk SSSR,* 1966, no. 7:109–12.

Markov, Vladimir. "Balmont: A Reappraisal." *Slavic Review* 28, no. 2 (June 1969): 221–64.

"Meksikanskie legendy." *Vestnik inostrannoi literatury,* 1906, no. 2:143–48.

Orlov, Vladimir Nikolaevich. "Balmont: Zhizn i stikhi." In *Stikhotvoreniia*, by Konstantin Balmont, pp. 5–76. Leningrad: Sovetskii pisatel, 1969.

Patkanov, S. K. "Po gatsiendam i ruinam Iukatana." *Zemlevedenie* 3 (1896): bk. 1, pp. 79–110; bk 2, pp. 93–130; bk. 3, pp. 111–42.

———. "V strane maiasov." *Nabliudatel*, 1895, no. 6:98–130.

Patterson, Rodney L. "Balmont." In *Izbrannye stikhotvoreniia i poemy*, by K. D. Balmont, pp. 15–76. Munich: Wilhelm Fink Verlag, 1975.

Protopopov, Sergei Dmitrievich. "Proezdom po Meksike (iz zapisnoi knizhki puteshestvennika)." *Russkoe bogatstvo*, 1896, no. 9:82–108.

Rice, Martin P. *Valery Briusov and the Rise of Russian Symbolism*. Ann Arbor: Ardis, 1975.

Rozhdestvenskaia, I. "K. D. Balmont: Pisma k E. A. Liatskomu." *Russkaia literatura*, 1975, no. 2:194–201.

Rusanov, N. S. "Obozrenie inostrannoi zhizni: 3. Meksikanskaia revoliutsiia." *Russkoe bogatstvo*, 1913, no. 2:365–72.

Tverskoi, P. A. [Peter A. Demens]. "Sovremennoe Meksiko." *Russkaia mysl*, 1913, no. 3:65–89.

Voeikov, Aleksandr Ivanovich. *Klimaty zemnogo shara*. St. Petersburg, 1884.

———. "Puteshestvie A. I. Voeikova v tsentralnoi Amerike." *Izvestiia imperatorskogo russkogo geograficheskogo obshchestva* 11, pt. 2 (1875): 152–55.

Zemskov, Valerii. "Y México surgió cual inspirada visión . . . Konstantin Balmont y la poesía india." *América Latina*, 1977, no. 3:180–92. Published originally in Russian as "I Meksika voznikla, videne vdokhnovennoe . . . K. D. Balmont i poeziia indeitsev." *Latinskaia Amerika*, 1976, no. 3:170–82.

Zhanve, Tomas. "Meksikanskie legendy." *Novyi zhurnal literatury, iskusstva i nauki*, 1907, no. 5:142–49.

3. The 1920s

a. General Works

Bukasov, Sergei Mikhailovich. *Vozdelyvaemye rasteniia Meksiki, Gvatemaly, i Kolumbii*. Leningrad: Akademiia nauk SSSR, 1930.

Dandré, V. *Anna Pavlova in Art and Life*. New York: B. Blom, 1972.

Dobrynin, Boris Fedorovich. "Meksika (geograficheskii etiud)." *Zemlevedenie* 28 (1926): no. 1–2, pp. 35–56; no. 3–4, pp. 45–66.

Fainshtein, M. Sh. "K 50-letiiu pervoi sovetskoi ekspeditsii v Latinskuiu Ameriku (1925–1928)." *Latinskaia Amerika*, 1975, no. 5 (September–October): 134–42.

Hyden, Walford. *Pavlova*. Boston: Little, Brown, and Company, 1931.

Kahán, Salomón, and Gabino A. Palma. "Dos aspectos de Alexander Block." *Antorcha*, 11 July 1925, pp. 5–7.

———. "Los escitas ('Skify')." *Antorcha*, 11 July 1925, pp. 7–8.

Kniazev, A. G. and I. M. Freidberg. *Vokrug sveta na velosipede*. Moscow-Leningrad: Molodaia gvardiia, 1929.

Lazzarini, John, and Roberta Lazzarini. *Pavlova: Repertoire of a Legend*. New York: Schirmer Books, 1980.

Medvedev, Zhores A. *The Rise and Fall of T. D. Lysenko.* Translated by I. Michael Lerner with the editorial assistance of Lucy G. Lawrence. Garden City, N.J.: Anchor Books, 1971.

Meyer, Jean, with Enrique Krauze and Cayetano Reyes. *Historia de la revolución mexicana, período 1924–1928: Estado y sociedad con Calles.* Mexico City: El Colegio de México, 1977.

Meyer, Lorenzo. *Historia de la revolución mexicana 1928–1934 (el conflicto social y los gobiernos del maximato).* Mexico City: El Colegio de México, 1978.

Meyer, Lorenzo, Rafael Segovia, and Alejandro Lajous. *Historia de la revolución mexicana 1928–1934: Los inícios de la institucionalización.* Mexico City: El Colegio de México, 1978.

Popovsky, Mark. *The Vavilov Affair.* Hamden, Connecticut: Archon Books, 1984.

Reed, Alma. *The Mexican Muralists.* New York: Crown Publishers, 1960.

Revenkova, Anna Ignatevna. *Nikolai Ivanovich Vavilov, 1887–1943.* Moscow: Izdatelstvo selskokhoziaistvennoi literatury, zhurnalov i plakatov, 1962.

Reznik, Semen. *Nikolai Vavilov.* Moscow: Molodaia gvardiia, 1968.

Tugendkhold, Ia. "Diego de Riveira: Khudozhnik meksikanskogo proletariata." *Krasnaia niva,* 1926, no. 6.

Vasilkova, I. A. "Kniga, posviashchennaia vsem, kto delal revoliutsiiu." *Latinskaia Amerika,* 1984, no. 8 (August): 74–80.

Vavilov, Nikolai Ivanovich. "Velikie zemledelcheskie kultury dokolumbovoi Ameriki i ikh vzaimootnosheniia." *Izvestiia gosudarstvennogo geograficheskogo obshchestva* 71, no. 10 (1939): 1487–515.

Velázquez Bringas, Esperanza. *El arte en la Rusia actual.* Mexico City: 1923.

Vygodskii, D. "Sovetskaia literatura v stranakh Latinskoi Ameriki." *Zvezda,* 1931, no. 10:135.

b. *Pestkovsky*

Pestkovskii, Stanislav Stanislavovich [Andrei Volskii]. "Agrarnyi vopros i krestianskoe dvizhenie v Meksike." *Na agrarnom fronte,* 1927, no. 2 (February): 46–59.

————. [Diego Ortega]. *Agrarnyi vopros i krestianskoe dvizhenie v Meksike.* Moscow-Leningrad: Gosudarstvennoe izdatelstvo, 1928.

————. [Diego Ortega]. "Grazhdanskaia voina v Meksike." *Mirovoe khoziaistvo i mirovaia politika,* 1929, no. 7 (July): 45–61.

————. [Andrei Volskii]. *Istoriia meksikanskikh revoliutsii.* Moscow-Leningrad: Gosudarstvennoe izdatelstvo, 1928.

————. [Andrei Volskii]. "Meksika." In *Entsiklopedicheskii slovar russkogo bibliograficheskogo instituta Granat,* 7th edition, vol. 48, pp. 245–50.

————. [Andrei Volskii]. "Raskol v rabochem dvizhenii." *Krasnyi internatsional profsoiuzov,* 1927, no. 4:316–25.

————. [Andrei Volskii]. "Reaktsiia v Meksike." *Put MOPRa,* 1929, no. 11–12 (1–30 July): 107–08.

————. [Andrei Volskii]. "Ubiistvo Khulio Melia." *Put MOPRa,* 1929, no. 3 (1–15 April 1929): 23.

————. "Vospominaniia o rabote v narkomnatse (1917–1919 gg.)." *Proletarskaia revo-liutsiia,* 1930, no. 6 (June): 124–31.

————. [Stanislaw Pestkowski]. *Wspomnienia rewolucjonisty.* Lodz: Wydawnictwo Lodzkie, 1961.

c. *Mayakovsky*

Arutcheva, V. A. "Zapisnye knizhki Maiakovskogo." *Literaturnoe nasledstvo* 65 (1958): 325–96.

Barooshian, Vahan D. *Brik and Mayakovsky.* The Hague: Mouton, 1978.

Brown, Edward J. *Mayakovsky: A Poet in the Revolution.* Princeton: Princeton University Press, 1973.

Charters, Ann, and Samuel Charters. *I Love: The Story of Vladimir Mayakovsky and Lili Brik.* New York: Farrar, Strauss, Giroux, 1979.

Frías, José D. "El poeta ruso, Vladimiro Mayakowsky." *El Universal Ilustrado,* 23 July 1925, pp. 25, 54.

Kahán, Salomón. "La poesía rusa de la revolución frente a la poesía 'Este Tica'." *Antorcha,* August 1925, pp. 17–20.

Katanian, Vasilii Abramovich. *Maiakovskii: Literaturnaia khronika.* 3d ed. Moscow: Gosudarstvennoe izdatelstvo khudozhestvennoi literatury, 1956.

————. *Maiakovskii–khudozhnik.* Moscow: Sovetskii khudozhnik, 1963.

————. "Poezdki Maiakovskogo za granitsu." In *Polnoe sobranie sochinenii v dvenadtsati tomakh,* by V. V. Maiakovskii, vol. 7, pp. 540–79. Moscow: Khudozhestvennaia literatura, 1940.

Kemrad, Salomon. *Maiakovskii v Amerike: Stranitsy biografii.* Moscow: Sovetskii pisatel, 1970.

————. "'Polpred stikha' (k 65-letiiu so dnia rozhdeniia V. V. Maiakovskogo): Maiakovskii v Amerike." *Druzhba narodov,* 1958, no. 7:201–18.

————. "'Polpred stikha'–Maiakovskii v Amerike." *Druzhba narodov,* 1959, no. 10: 198–212.

Khardzhiev, Nikolai. "Zametki o Maiakovskom. 4. Puteshestvie v Meksiku." *Den poezii.* Moscow: Izdatelstvo sovetskii pisatel, 1969, p. 239.

Mayakovsky, Vladimir Vladimirovich. *Maiakovskii ob Amerike.* Compiled by V. Katanian. 2d ed. Moscow: Sovetskii pisatel, 1949.

————. "Meksika; iz knigi." *Krasnaia nov,* 1926, no. 1 (January): 194–212.

————. *Moe otkrytie Ameriki.* Moscow-Leningrad: Gosudarstvennoe izdatelstvo, 1926. Republished in his *Polnoe sobranie sochinenii,* vol. 7. Moscow: Gosudarstvennoe izdatelstvo khudozhestvennoi literatury, 1958.

————. "Nuestra Marcha," "Marcha a la izquierda." *Antorcha,* August 1925, pp. 21–22.

Metchenko, Aleksei Ivanovich. *Tvorchestvo Maiakovskogo 1925–1930 gg.* Moscow: Sovetskii pisatel, 1961.

"Mexican Communist Deputy Murdered." *Daily Worker,* 21 September 1925, p. 5.

"Mexican Politician Is Assassinated, Causing Sensation." *Daily Worker,* 16 September 1925, p. 2.

Moser, Charles A. "Mayakovsky and America." *Russian Review* 25, no. 3 (July 1966): pp. 242–56.

———. "Mayakovsky's Unsentimental Journeys." *American Slavic and East European Review* 19 (1960): 84–100.

"Notable poeta ruso que llegó a esta capital." *Excélsior*, 10 July 1925, pp. 1, 4.

"Novoe o Maiakovskom." *Literaturnoe nasledstvo* 65 (1958).

Pertsov, Viktor Osipovich. *Maiakovskii v poslednie gody: Zhizn i tvorchestvo (1925–1930 gg)*. Moscow: Nauka, 1965.

"Pisma Maiakovskogo k L. Iu. Brik (1917–30)." *Literaturnoe nasledstvo* 65 (1958): 101–74.

Richardson, William. "Maiakovskii en México." *Historia Mexicana* 29, no. 4 (April–June 1980): 623–39.

Rougle, Charles. *Three Russians Consider America: America in the Works of Maksim Gorkij, Aleksandr Blok, and Vladimir Majakovskij*. Stockholm: Almqvist and Wiksell International, 1977.

Schneider, Luis Mario. *Dos poetas rusos en México: Balmont y Mayakovski*. Mexico City: Secretaría de Educación Pública, 1973.

Snegovskaia, S. "Maiakovskii za granitsei." *Zvezda*, 1949, no. 4:157–64.

Talnikov, D. "Literaturnye zametki." *Krasnaia nov*, 1928, no. 8:259–81.

Tregub, S. *Maiakovskii gazetchik*. Moscow: Gosudarstvennoe izdatelstvo politicheskoi literatury, 1939.

"Trotzki y el poeta Mayakovsky." *Antorcha* 2, no. 2 (September 1925): 20–21.

Uspenskii, I. I. *Maiakovskii o burzhuaznoi "kulture" zapada i Ameriki*. Moscow: Gosudarstvennoe izdatelstvo kulturno-prosvetitelnoi literatury, 1950.

"V. V. Maiakovskii v Meksike." *Inostrannaia literatura*, 1963, no. 7:242.

Vygodskii, D. "Vladimir Maiakovskii v Ispanii i Ispanskoi Amerike." *Zvezda*, 1931, no. 4:207.

Zakharov, Iakov Ivanovich. *Maiakovskii v gazete*. Sverdlovsk: Sverdlovskoe knizhnoe izdatelstvo, 1963.

d. Kollontai

Beals, Carleton. *Glass House: Ten Years of Freelancing*. Philadelphia: J. B. Lippincott, 1938.

Breslav, Eva Ivanovna. *Aleksandra Mikhailovna Kollontai*. Moscow: Mysl, 1974.

Clements, Barbara Evans. *Bolshevik Feminist: The Life of Aleksandra Kollontai*. Bloomington: University of Indiana Press, 1979.

Farnsworth, Beatrice. *Aleksandra Kollontai: Socialism, Feminism, and the Bolshevik Revolution*. Stanford: Stanford University Press, 1980.

Itkina, A. M. *Revoliutsioner, tribun, diplomat*. Moscow: Izdatelstvo politicheskoi literatury, 1970.

Kollontai, Aleksandra Mikhailovna. *Autobiography*. Translated by Salvator Attanasio, edited by Irving Fletscher. New York: Herder and Herder, 1971.

———. *Iz moei zhizni i raboty*. Moscow: Sovetskaia rossiia, 1974.

———. *Izbrannye stati i rechi*. Moscow: Politizdat, 1972.

———. "Meksikanskii dnevnik Aleksandry Kollontai." Edited and with an introduction by I. A. Vasilkova. *Latinskaia Amerika*, 1979, no. 5 (September–October): 186–96.

"Madame Kollontai on Mexico." *America: A Catholic Review of the Week* 37, no. 15 (23 July 1927): 342–43.

Mindlin, Emilii Lvovich. *Ne dom, no mir: Povest ob Aleksandre Kollontai.* Moscow: Politizdat, 1969.

Palencia, Isabel. *Alexandra Kollontai: Ambassadress from Moscow.* New York: Longman's, Green and Company, 1947.

Porter, Cathy. *Alexandra Kollontai: The Lonely Struggle of the Woman Who Defied Lenin.* New York: Dial Press, 1980.

"Reds of Mexico City Hail Mme. Kollontai." *New York Times,* 9 December 1926, section 1, p. 3.

"Want Mme. Kollontai Expelled from Mexico." *New York Times,* 12 April 1927, section 1, p. 23.

"Woman Envoy Hits Intrigue: New Soviet Minister to Mexico Says Business Is Her Aim." *New York Times,* 19 October 1926, section 1, p. 26.

"Woman Envoy's Books Far Outnumber Gowns." *New York Times,* 10 December 1926, section 1, p. 3.

4. Eisenstein

Aleksandrov, Grigorii Vasilevich. *Le cinéaste et son temps.* Translated by Antoine García. Moscow: Progress Publishers, 1976.

———. *Epokha v kino.* Moscow: Izdatelstvo politicheskoi literatury, 1976.

———. *Gody poiskov i truda.* Moscow: Soiuz kinomatografistov SSSR, Biuro propagandy sovetskogo kinoiskusstva, 1975.

———. "Mexico." *Kultura i zhizn* 4, no. 8 (1960): 26–27.

———. "Vpechatleniia o poezdke." *Iskusstvo kino,* 1956, no. 6 (June): 119.

———. "Working with Eisenstein." In *Cinema in Revolution,* edited by Luda and Jean Schnitzler and Marcel Martin, pp. 53–63. Translated by David Robinson. London: Secker and Warburg, 1973.

"Backers Need Eisenstein or No Film." *Variety,* 1 March 1932, p. 3.

Baguez, Salvador. "Sergio Eisenstein ha sido descubierto en México." *La Opinión* (Los Angeles), 5 July 1931, p. 5 (special illustrated section).

Barna, Yon. *Eisenstein.* Translated by Lise Hunter, edited by Oliver Stallybrass. Bloomington: Indiana University Press, 1973.

"Barred from U.S. Serge Will Cut Film Abroad." *Variety,* 15 March 1932, p. 3.

"Beau Geste." *Outlook and Independent* 156 (12 November 1930): 406.

Berlein, Henry. *Mexico: The Land of Unrest.* Philadelphia: J. B. Lippincott, 1914.

Best Maugard, Adolfo. *Metodo de dibujo—tradición, resurgimento y evolución del arte mexicano.* Mexico City: Secretaría de Educación Pública, 1923.

———. "Mexico Into Cinema." *Theatre Arts* 16 (November 1932): 926–33.

———. "To the Editors of *Close-Up.*" *Close Up* 10 (September 1933): 256–57.

Bixby, Barbara Evans. "The Weave of the Serape: Sergei Eisenstein's *Que Viva Mexico* as a Multitext." Ph.D. diss., University of Florida, 1979.

Brenner, Anita. *Idols Behind Altars.* Boston: Beacon Press, 1970.

Brodman, Barbara L. C. *The Mexican Cult of Death in Myth and Literature*. Gainesville: University of Florida, 1976.

Bustamente, A. F. "Eisenstein el magnífico." *El Ilustrado*, 11 June 1931, pp. 24–25, 47.

———. "Eisenstein en México." *Nuestro México* 1, no. 1 (March 1932): 10–11, 14–15.

———. [A.F.B.]. "Lo que en México hace Eisenstein." *El Ilustrado*, 18 June 1931, pp. 24–25, 46.

———. "Los Indios del señor Eisenstein." *El Ilustrado*, 25 June 1931, pp. 24–25, 43.

Chaplin, Charles. *My Autobiography*. New York: Simon and Schuster, 1964.

Conger, Amy. *Edward Weston in Mexico, 1923–1926*. Albuquerque: University of New Mexico, 1983.

Constantine, Mildred. *Tina Modotti: A Fragile Life*. New York: Paddington Press Ltd., 1975.

de la Colina, José. "Los *Dibujos mexicanos* de Eisenstein, el otro yo del cineasta reflejado en el espejo de obsidiano." *Uno más uno*, 3 September 1978, p. 17.

Eagle, Herbert. "Eisenstein as a Semiotician of the Cinema." In *Semiotics Around the World*, edited by R.W. Bailey, pp. 173–93. Ann Arbor: University of Michigan, 1978.

Eisenstein 1898–1948: Suite de dessins. Lyon: Musée des Beaux-Arts, 1978.

"Eisenstein in Mexico." *Experimental Cinema* 1, no. 3 (1931): 22.

"Eisenstein Is Barred Under the Alien Law." *New York Times*, 22 February 1932, section 15, p. 2.

"Eisenstein Predicts New Type of Film." *Boston Globe*, 27 May 1930, p. 17.

"Eisenstein Says 'Adios'." *Los Angeles Times*, 7 December 1930, pt. 3, p. 1.

"Eisenstein's Monster." *Time*, 2 May 1932, p. 24.

"Eisenstein's Plans." *Living Age*, July 1932, pp. 462–63.

Eisenstein, Sergei Mikhailovich. "Correspondencia." *Sur*, 1974, no. 334–35.

———. *Dibujos mexicanos inéditos*. Mexico City: Cineteca nacional, Secretaría de Gobernación, 1978.

———. *Eizenshtein: Risunki*. Vol. 3. *Meksikanskie motivy*. Moscow: Soiuz kinematografistov SSSR, Biuro propagandy sovetskogo kinoiskusstva, 1971.

———. *Film Form*. Translated by Jay Leyda. New York: Harcourt, Brace, and World, 1949.

———. *Immoral Memories: An Autobiography*. Translated by Herbert Marshall. Boston: Houghton Mifflin, 1983.

———. *Izbrannye proizvedeniia*. Vols. 1–6. Moscow: Iskusstvo, 1964–.

———. *Meksikanskie risunki Eizenshteina*. Moscow: Sovetskii khudozhnik, 1969.

———. "A Mexican Film and Marxian Theory: A Communication." *New Republic*, 9 December 1931, pp. 99–100.

———. *Notes of a Film Director*. Translated by X. Danko. Moscow: Foreign Languages Publishing House, 1960.

———. "El prometeo de la pintura mexicana (Serguei Eisenstein sobre José Clemente Orozco)." *América Latina*, 1978, no. 2:161–64.

———. *Que Viva Mexico!* Introduction by Ernest Lindgren. London: Vision, 1972.

———. *Risunki/dessins/drawings*. Moscow: Iskusstvo, 1961.

Eisenstein, Sergei Mikhailovich, and G. V. Aleksandrov. "Que Viva Mexico." *Experimental Cinema* 1, no. 5 (1934): pp. 5–13, 52.

Fernández, Dominique. *Eisenstein*. Paris: Bernard Grasset, 1975.

Gardies, René. "Que Viva Mexico." *Image et son* 187 (October 1965): 75–82.

Gardner, Paul A. "Soviet Gathers Fragments of Eisenstein's Lost Films: Plans a Belated Tribute." *Variety*, 1 November 1972, pp. 2, 62.

Geduld, Harry M., and Ronald Gottesman, eds. *Sergei Eisenstein and Upton Sinclair: The Making and Unmaking of "Que Viva Mexico!"* Bloomington: Indiana University Press, 1970.

Gruening, Ernest. *Mexico and Its Heritage*. New York: The Century Company, 1928.

Guthmann, Edward. "The Battle Behind a Mexican Documentary: Eisenstein's *Que Viva Mexico*." *San Francisco Examiner and Chronicle*, 30 October 1983, pp. 26–27, 29.

Gutman, Walter. "News and Gossip." *Creative Art* 8 (March 1931): 94.

Helprin, Morris. "Eisenstein's New Film." *New York Times*, 29 November 1931, p. 6.

———. "Que Viva Mexico." *Experimental Cinema* 1, no. 4 (1932): 13–17.

Honig, Erwin, "In Eisenstein's Domain." *Experimental Cinema* 1, no. 2 (June 1930): 4–5.

Howard, Clifford. "Eisenstein in Hollywood." *Close Up* 7 (August 1930): 139–42.

"In a Lean Year, Soviets Dust Off Eisenstein Epic for Fest Circuit." *Variety*, 28 February 1979, pp. 4, 40.

Iurenev, R. "S. Eizenshtein–pisma iz Meksiki." *Prometei*, 1972, no. 9:185–99.

Karetnikova, Inga Abramovna. "Eizenshtein i Sikeiros." *Latinskaia Amerika*, 1970, no. 5:146–61.

Kepley, Vance, Jr. "The Evolution of Eisenstein's *Old and New*." *Cinema Journal* 14, no. 1 (Fall 1974): 34–50.

Kuteishchikova, Vera Nikolaevna. "Serguei Eisenstein y México." *Revolución y cultura*, November 1978, pp. 32–36.

Lasky, Jesse L. (with Don Weldon). *I Blow My Own Horn*. Garden City, New York: Doubleday, 1957.

Leiva, Agustín Aragón. "The Destruction of Eisenstein's Mexican Film." Typescript from Gottesman file, Museum of Modern Art, New York.

———. "Eisenstein en Mexico." *Orbe*, no. 21 (31 July 1931): 10–11.

———. "Eisenstein's Film on Mexico." *Experimental Cinema* 1, no. 4 (1932): 5–6.

———. "Eisenstein's Political Conceptions in Mexico." Manuscript in Gottesman file, Museum of Modern Art, New York.

———. "Sergio M. Eisenstein en México." *Orbe*, no. 17 (3 July 1931).

———. "What's Eisenstein Doing in Mexico?" Manuscript from Tetlapayac Hacienda dated 14 June 1931, to be sent to *Experimental Cinema*. Museum of Modern Art, New York.

Leyda, Jay. "Eisenstein's Mexican Tragedy." *Sight and Sound* 27 (Autumn 1958): 305–08, 329.

———. *Kino*. New York: Collier, 1973.

———. "'Que Viva Mexico,' ein unvollendetes Werk." In *Sergei Eisenstein, Künstler der Revolution*, edited by Herman Herlinghaus, Heinz Baumert, and Renate Georgi, pp. 192–201. Berlin: Henschelverlag, 1960.

Leyda, Jay, and Zina Voynow. *Eisenstein at Work*. Introduction by Ted Perry. New York: Pantheon and the Museum of Modern Art, 1982.

"M. Eisenstein's Next Film." *New York Times*, 16 February 1930, p. 6.

Marshall, Herbert. *Masters of the Soviet Cinema: Crippled Creative Biographies*. London: Routledge and Kegan Paul, 1983.

—————. "Moscow Invited to Hollywood." *Moscow News*, 5 October 1930, p. 7.

"May Deport Eisenstein: Mexico Considers Action on Soviet Film Man After Freeing Him." *New York Times*, 24 December 1930, section 4, p. 5.

Miller, G. E. "Meksikanskii film Eizenshteina." In *Meksika: Politika, ekonomika, kultura*, Akademiia nauk SSSR, Institut Latinskoi Ameriki, pp. 317–26. Moscow: Nauka, 1968.

Mitry, Jean. *S. M. Eisenstein*. Paris: Editions universitaires, 1961.

Moen, Lars. "The Fate of Eisenstein's Mexican Film." *Moscow News*, 10 June 1933, p. 3.

Monoszon, Lev Isaakovich. [L. M.] "Gruppa Eizenshteina v Meksike." *Proletarskoe kino*, 1931, no. 1:49.

Montagu, Ivor. *With Eisenstein in Hollywood*. Berlin: Seven Seas, 1968.

Moussinac, Leon. *Sergei Eisenstein*. Translated by D. Sandy Petrey. New York: Crown, 1970.

"Ob odnom nezavershennom filme." *Iskusstvo kino*, 1957, no. 5 (May): 104–17.

O'Rik, R. "Amerikanskaia tragediia." *Proletarskoe kino*, 1931, no. 9:59–62.

Porter, Katherine Ann. *Flowering Judas and Other Stories*. New York: New American Library, 1963.

Reed, John. *Insurgent Mexico*. New York: International Publishers, 1969.

Reyes, Alfonso. "México en el cine—la obra de Eisenstein, perdida." In his *A Lápiz: 1923–1946*, pp. 94–99. Mexico City: Editorial stylo, 1947.

Richardson, William. "Eisenstein and California: The *Sutter's Gold* Episode." *California History*, Fall 1980, pp. 194–203.

Rivette, Jacques. "Que Viva Eisenstein." *Cahiers du cinéma* 14 (January 1958): 20–21.

Robinson, Ione. *A Wall to Paint On*. New York: E. P. Dutton and Company, 1946.

Segal, Abraham. *S. M. Eisenstein*. Tübingen: Ernst Wasmuth, 1973.

Sergei Mikhailovich Eizenshtein: Spektakli, filmy, risunki, zamysli, knigi. Moscow: Gosfilmofond, 1966.

Seton, Marie. "Eisenstein." In *Eisenstein, 1898–1948*. Lyon: Musée des Beaux Arts, 1978.

—————. "Eisenstein's Images and Mexican Art." *Sight and Sound*, July–September 1953, pp. 8–13.

—————. "Histoire du film inachevé d'Eisenstein." *Revue du cinéma*, October 1948, pp. 3–18.

—————. *Sergei M. Eisenstein*. New York: Grove Press, 1960.

—————. "Treasure Trove." *Sight and Sound* 8, no. 31 (1939): 89–92.

Shklovskii, Viktor. *Eizenshtein*. Moscow: Iskusstvo, 1976.

Sinclair, Upton. *The Autobiography of Upton Sinclair*. New York: Harcourt, Brace and World, 1962.

Stern, Seymour. "The Greatest Thing Done on This Side of the Atlantic: Eisenstein's Original Version of Mexico." *Modern Monthly* 7 (1933): 525–32.

————. "Introduction to Synopsis for 'Que Viva Mexico!'" *Experimental Cinema* 1, no. 5 (1934): 3–4.

————. "*Que Viva Mexico!* The Fate of Eisenstein's American Film." *Cinema Quarterly* 1 (Winter 1932): 73–80.

Sudendorff, Werner. *Sergej M. Eisenstein: Materialen zu Leben und Werk.* Munich: Hanser, 1975.

Swallow, Norman. *Eisenstein—A Documentary Portrait.* New York: Dutton, 1977.

Troy, W. "Eisenstein Muddle." *Nation,* 19 July 1933, pp. 83–84.

Viertel, Salka. *The Kindness of Strangers.* New York: Holt, Rinehart, and Winston, 1969.

"Vpechatleniia o poezdke." *Iskusstvo kino,* 1956, no. 6:119.

Watts, Richard, Jr. "Mexico as Done by Eisenstein." *New York Herald Tribune,* 15 May 1932.

————. "The Passing of Eisenstein." *Film Mercury* 14 (November 1930): 8.

Weston, Edward. *The Daybooks of Edward Weston.* 2 vols. Edited by Nancy Newhall. New York: Millerton, 1973.

"Why Soviets' Film Genius Went Home." *St. Louis Post Dispatch,* 10 May 1932.

Wilson, Edmund, *The American Earthquake.* Garden City, N.Y.: Doubleday, 1958.

————. "Eisenstein in Hollywood." *New Republic,* 4 November 1931, pp. 320–22.

5. Trotsky

Alexander, Robert J. *Communism in Latin America.* New Brunswick, N.J.: Rutgers University Press, 1957.

Beals, Carleton. "The Fewer Outsiders the Better." *Saturday Evening Post,* 12 June 1937, pp. 23, 74–78.

Carmichael, Joel. *Trotsky: An Appreciation of His Life.* London: Hodder and Stoughton, 1975.

Deutscher, Isaac. *The Prophet Outcast: Trotsky, 1929–1940.* London: Oxford University Press, 1963.

Heijenoort, Jean van. *With Trotsky in Exile: From Prinkipo to Coyoacán.* Cambridge: Harvard University Press, 1978.

Herrera, Hayden. *Frida: A Biography of Frida Kahlo.* New York: Harper and Row, 1983.

Menzhinskii, E. *Meksika.* Moscow: Gosudarstvennoe sotsialno-ekonomicheskoe izdatelstvo, 1937.

Millan, Robert Paul. *Vincente Lombardo Toledano.* Chapel Hill: University of North Carolina Press, 1966.

Payne, Robert. *The Life and Death of Trotsky.* New York: McGraw Hill, 1977.

Powell, T. G. *Mexico and the Spanish Civil War.* Albuquerque: University of New Mexico Press, 1981.

Rühle-Gerstel, Alice [Alice Rühle]. "No Verses for Trotsky: A Diary in Mexico (1937)." *Encounter,* April 1982, pp. 27–41.

Sánchez Salazar, Leandro. *Murder in Mexico: The Assassination of Leon Trotsky.* With the collaboration of Julian Gorkin, translated by Phyllis Hawley. London: Secker and Warburg, 1950.

Serge, Victor, and Natalia Sedova Trotsky. *The Life and Death of Leon Trotsky.* Translated by Arnold J. Pomerans. New York: Basic Books, 1975.

Trotsky, Leon. "Art and Politics." *Partisan Review* 5, no. 3 (August–September 1938): 3–10.

————. *Stalin's Gangsters.* London: New Park Publications, 1977.

————. *Writings of Leon Trotsky.* 13 vols. New York: Pathfinder Press, 1969–1973.

Volkov, A. "Agrarnaia reforma v Meksike." *Mirovoe khoziaistvo i mirovaia politika,* 1939, no. 6:113–18.

Warth, Robert D. *Leon Trotsky.* Boston: Twayne Publishers, 1977.

Weiss, Peter. *Trotsky in Exile.* Translated by Geoffrey Skelton. New York: Atheneum, 1972.

Wyndham, Francis, and David King. *Trotsky: A Documentary.* New York: Praeger, 1972.

6. Diplomatic Relations

Akademiia nauk SSSR. Institut Latinskoi Ameriki. Ministerstvo inostrannykh del Meksiki. *Sovetsko-meksikanskie otnosheniia (1917–1980): Sbornik dokumentov.* Moscow: Mezhdunarodnye otnosheniia, 1981.

Aleksandrov, A. E. "Revoliutsioner, diplomat, uchenii." *Latinskaia Amerika,* 1982, no. 2:142–44.

Bassols, Narciso. *Obras.* Mexico City: Fondo de Cultura Económica, 1964.

————. *Las relaciones entre México y la URSS y Inglaterra.* Mexico City: Liga de Acción Política, 1941.

Blasier, Cole. *The Giant's Rival: The USSR and Latin America.* Pittsburgh: University of Pittsburgh Press, 1983.

Cárdenas, Héctor. *Las relaciones mexicano-soviéticas: Antecedentes y primeros contactos diplomáticos (1789–1927).* Mexico City: Secretaría de Relaciones Exteriores, 1974.

Cheston, T. Stephen. "Diplomatic Sideshow: A Study of Soviet Relations with Latin America, 1918–1936." Ph.D. diss. Georgetown University, 1972.

Chicherin, Georgii Vasilevich. *Stati i rechi po voprosam mezhdunarodnoi politiki.* Moscow: Izdatelstvo sotsialno-ekonomicheskoi literatury, 1961.

Clissold, Stephen, ed. *Soviet Relations with Latin America, 1918–1968: A Documentary Survey.* London: Oxford University Press, 1970.

Cuadros Caldos, J. *México-Soviet.* Puebla: Santiago Loyo, 1926.

Donskii, Grigorii Markovich. *Borba za Latinskuiu Ameriku.* Moscow: Moskovskii rabochii, 1928.

————. *Meksika, Kuba, Argentina.* Moscow-Leningrad: Moskovskii rabochii, 1929.

Jacobs, Dan N. *Borodin: Stalin's Man in China.* Cambridge: Harvard University Press, 1981.

Kruszewski, Z. Anthony, and William Richardson. *Mexico and the Socialist Bloc: The Foreign Policy of a Middle Power.* Boulder: Westview, 1987.

Lavrov, Nikolai Matveevich. "La revolución mexicana de 1910–1917 en los documentos del archivo de la política exterior de Rusia." *Latinoamérica,* 1979, no. 12:13–25.

Marchenko, V. M. "Sovetsko-meksikanskie diplomaticheskie i torgovye otnosheniia 20-e i 30-e gody." In *Problemy otechestvennoi i vseobshchei istorii,* edited by

V. G. Revunenkov, pp. 183–94. Leningrad: Izdatelstvo Leningradskogo universiteta, 1969.

Ministerstvo inostrannykh del SSSR, Ministerstvo inostrannykh del Meksiki. *Sovetsko-meksikanskie otnosheniia, 1968–1980.* Moscow: Izdatelstvo politicheskoi literatury, 1981.

Ministerstvo inostrannykh del SSSR. *Dokumenty vneshnei politiki SSSR.* Moscow: Izdatelstvo politicheskoi literatury, 1957–.

Muñíz Ortega, Carlos. *La URSS y América Latina (50 años de relaciones diplomáticos y económicas).* Lima: Francisco Moncloa editores, 1968.

Portes Gil, Emilio. *Quince años de política mexicana.* 3rd ed. Mexico City: Ediciones Botas, 1954.

Rámos Pedrueza, Rafael. *La estrella roja: Doce años de la vida soviética.* Mexico City, 1929.

Relaciones mexicano-soviéticas, 1968–1980. Archivo Historico Diplomático Mexicano no. 3. Mexico City: Secretaría de Relaciones Exteriores, 1981.

Relaciones mexicano-soviéticas, 1917–1980. Archivo Historico Diplomático Mexicano no. 4. Mexico City: Secretaría de Relaciones Exteriores, 1981.

Silva Herzog, Jesús. *Aspectos económicos de la Union Soviética.* Mexico City: Partido Nacional Revolucionario, 1930.

———. *Una vida en la vida de México.* Mexico City: Siglo veintiuno editores, 1972.

Sizonenko, Aleksandr Ivanovich. "Kak falsifitsiruiutsia na zapade sovetsko-latinoamerikanskie otnosheniia." *Latinskaia Amerika,* 1978, no. 3 (May–June): 97–108.

———. "Meksika-SSSR: Iz istorii otnoshenii." *Latinskaia Amerika,* 1981, no. 7 (July): 98–104.

———. *Ocherki istorii sovetsko-latinoamerikanskikh otnoshenii.* Moscow: Nauka, 1971.

———. "Sovetskaia Rossiia i Latinskaia Amerika." *Voprosy istorii,* 1973, no. 6 (November–December): 81–92.

———. *Sovetskii soiuz i Meksika—50 let.* Moscow: Mezhdunarodnye otnosheniia, 1974.

———. "Sovetsko-meksikanskim otnosheniiam—50 let." *Latinskaia Amerika,* 1974, no. 4 (July–August): 6–23.

———. *Stanovleniia otnoshenii SSSR so stranami Latinskoi Ameriki (1917–1945 gg.).* Moscow: Nauka: 1981.

———. "U istokov sovetsko-meksikanskikh otnoshenii." *Novaia i noveishaia istoriia,* 1980, no. 5 (May): 136–43.

———. *URSS y América Latina.* Moscow: Novosti, 1971.

———. *V strane atstekskogo orla.* Moscow: Mezhdunarodnye otnosheniia, 1969.

Un Siglo de relaciones internacionales de México (A través de los mensajes presidenciales). Archivo Historico Diplomático Mexicano, no. 39. Mexico City: Editorial Porrúa, 1970.

Volskii, Viktor Vatslavovich, ed. *SSSR i Latinskaia Amerika, 1917–1967.* Moscow: Mezhdunarodnye otnosheniia, Moscow: 1967.

7. Communism

Campa Salazar, Valentín. *Mi testimonio: Experiencias de un comunista mexicano.* Mexico City: Ediciones de cultura popular, 1978.

Carr, Barry. "Marxism and Anarchism in the Formation of the Mexican Communist Party, 1910–1919." *Hispanic American Historical Review* 63, no. 2 (May 1983): 277–305.

Cuadros Caldos, J. *El Comunismo criollo.* Puebla: Santiago Loyo, 1930.

Encina, Dionisio. *Vliianie oktiabrskoi revoliutsii na razvitie revoliutsionnogo dvizheniia v Meksike.* Moscow: Gosudarstvennoe izdatelstvo politicheskoi literatury, 1957.

Gill, Mario. *México y la revolución de octubre.* Mexico City: Ediciones de cultura popular, 1976.

Goldenberg, Boris. *Komunismus in Lateinamerika.* Stuttgart: W. Kohlhammer, 1971.

Halperin, Ernst. *Communism in Mexico.* Cambridge: Massachusetts Institute of Technology, 1963.

Herman, Donald L. *The Comintern in Mexico.* Washington, D.C.: Public Affairs Press, 1974.

Herman, Donald L., ed. *The Communist Tide in Latin America.* Austin: University of Texas Press, 1973.

Márquez Fuentes, Manuel, and Octavio Rodríguez Araujo. *El partido comunista mexicano (en el período de la Internacional Comunista: 1919–1943).* Mexico City: Ediciones "El caballito," 1973.

Meyer, Jean. "Los obreros en la Revolución mexicana: Los 'batallones rojos'." *Historia Mexicana* 21, no. 1 (1971): 1–37.

Modotti, Tina. *Meksikanskie peony (ocherki krestianskogo dvizheniia v Meksike).* Moscow: Izdatelstvo TsK MOPR SSSR, 1932.

Neymet, Marcela de. *Cronologia del Partido comunista mexicano: Primera parte, 1919–1939.* Mexico City: Ediciones de cultura popular, 1981.

Ospovat, Lev Samoilovich. "Guterres Krus Karlos." *Kratkaia literaturnaia entsiklopediia,* vol. 2, p. 466.

Phillips, Charles [Manuel Gomez]. "From Mexico to Moscow." *Survey* 53 (October 1964): 33–47.

Poppino, Rollie. *International Communism in Latin America: A History of the Movement, 1917–1963.* New York: Free Press of Glencoe, 1964.

Ramírez, M. *Meksika.* Moscow: Izdatelstvo TsK MOPR SSSR, 1929.

Rámos Pedrueza, Rafael. "Rusia Soviet y México revolucionario: Vicente Guerrero precursor del socialismo." Mexico City: Secretaría de Educación Pública, 1922.

Rivera, Diego. "AKhRR i stil proletarskogo revoliutsionnogo iskusstva (otkrytoe pismo v redaktsiiu)." *Revoliutsiia i kultura,* 1928, no. 6:43–44.

———. *Arte y política.* Edited by Raquel Tibol. Mexico City: Grijalbo, 1979.

Roy, Manabendra Nath. *Memoirs.* Bombay: Allied Publishers Private Ltd., 1964.

Rypins, Stanley. "Revolutions: Mexican and Russian." In *Renascent Mexico,* edited by Hubert Herring and Herbert Weinstock, pp. 151–67. New York: Covici, Friede, 1935.

Schmitt, Karl M. *Communism in Mexico: A Study in Political Frustration.* Austin: University of Texas Press, 1965.

Siqueiros, David Alfaro. *Art and Revolution.* Translated by Sylvia Calles. London: Lawrence and Wishart, 1975.

Sokolov, Andrei Aleksandrovich. *Rabochee dvizhenie Meksiki (1917–1929 gg.).* Moscow: Izdatelstvo Moskovskogo universiteta, 1978.

Tibol, Raquel. *Julio Antonio Mella en El Machete*. Mexico City: Fondo de cultura popular, 1968.

Wolfe, Bertram D. *A Life in Two Centuries*. Introduction by Leonard Shapiro. New York: Stein and Day, 1981.

8. Miscellaneous

Akademiia nauk SSSR. Institut Latinskoi Ameriki. *Latinskaia Amerika v sovetskikh issledovaniiakh 1973–1974 gg*. Moscow: Nauka, 1976.

———. *Meksika: politika, ekonomika, kultura*. Moscow: Nauka, 1968.

———. *Sovetskaia latinoamerikanistika posle kubinskoi revoliutsii*. V. V. Volskii, main editor. Moscow: Institut Latinskoi Ameriki, 1981.

Alperovich, Moisei Samoilovich, and Nikolai Matveevich Lavrov, eds. *Ocherki novoi i noveishei istorii Meksiki, 1810–1945*. Moscow: Sotsekgiz, 1960.

B. Z. "Diego Rivera—zhizn i tvorchestvo." *Iskusstvo*, no. 1–2 (March–April 1929): 53–67.

Beilin, A. "Proshloe, nastoiashchee, budushchee." *Neva*, 1967, no. 10:197.

"Bibliograficheskii ukazatel periodicheskoi i neperiodicheskoi literatury o stranakh Latinskoi Ameriki." *Revoliutsionnyi vostok*, 1932, no. 3–4:346–64.

Brodsky, Joseph. *A Part of Speech*. New York: Farrar, Strauss, Giroux, 1980.

Castels, Manuel. *The City and the Grassroots: A Cross-Cultural Theory of Urban Social Movements*. Berkeley and Los Angeles: University of California Press, 1983.

Charlot, Jean. *The Mexican Mural Renaissance, 1920–1925*. New Haven: Yale University Press, 1963.

De Micheli, Mario. *Siqueiros*. Translated by Ron Storm. New York: Harry N. Abrams, 1968.

"Diego Rivera: K risunku na oblozhke." *Krasnaia niva*, 17 March 1928, p. 3.

Dulles, John W. F. *Yesterday in Mexico: A Chronicle of the Revolution, 1919–1936*. Austin: University of Texas Press, 1961.

Ganelin, R. Sh. "Iz istorii ekonomicheskikh sviazei Rossii s Meksikoi i Braziliei v seredine 19 veka." *Novaia i noveishaia istoriia*, no. 6 (November–December 1963): 59–64.

Gardiner, Clinton Harvey. "Foreign Travelers' Accounts of Mexico, 1810–1910." *Americas* 8, no. 3 (January 1952): 321–51.

Grigulevich, Iosif Romualdovich. *Sikeiros*. Moscow: Iskusstvo, 1980.

Gunn, Drewey Wayne. *American and British Writers in Mexico, 1556–1973*. Austin: University of Texas Press, 1974.

Gunn, Drewey Wayne, comp. *Mexico in American and British Letters*. Metuchen, N.J.: Scarecrow Press, 1974.

Guzmán, Daniel de. *Aesthetic Currents in Mexico Between 1910 and 1940: A Cultural Appraisal of the Revolution*. New Haven: Yale University Press, 1957.

Ioffe, A. E. "SSSR i Latinskaia Amerika (kulturnye sviazi do vtoroi mirovoi voiny)." *Novaia i noveishaia istoriia*, 1967, no. 3 (May–June): 81–89.

Kautsky, John H. *Patterns of Modernizing Revolutions: Mexico and the Soviet Union*. Beverly Hills: Sage Publications, 1975.

Kostenevich, Albert Grigorevich. *Orosko*. Leningrad: Izdatelstvo iskusstvo, 1969.

Kuteishchikova, Vera Nikolaevna. "Diego Rivera y la revolución de octubre." *Plural* 1 (1978): 47–49.

———. "'Epokha vysshego napriazheniia' (zametki o meksikanskom iskusstve XX veka)." *Voprosy literatury,* 1967, no. 11:170–90.

———. "Ia nikogda ne smogu zabyt . . ." *Latinskaia Amerika,* 1977, no. 2 (March–April): 186–90.

———. "Meksika: Roman i natsiia." *Latinskaia Amerika,* 1970, no. 6:101–25.

———. "Meksika v moei zhizni." *Latinskaia Amerika,* 1984, no. 8 (August): 65–73.

———. *Meksikanskii roman: Formirovanie, svoebrazie, sovremennyi etap.* Moscow: Nauka, 1971.

———. "La novela de la revolución mexicana y la primera narrativa soviética." In *Recopilación de textos sobre la novela de la Revolución mexicana,* compiled by Rogelio Rodrigo Coronel, pp. 114–31. Havana: Casa de las Américas, 1975.

———. "El tema ruso en la obra de Diego Rivera." *Gallo Illustrado,* 19 December 1976, p. 5.

Kuteishchikova, Vera Nikolaevna, ed. *Meksikanskii realisticheskii roman XX veka: Sbornik statei.* Moscow: Izdatelstvo Akademii nauk SSSR, 1960.

Kuzmishchev, V. A., principal ed. *Kultura Meksiki.* Moscow: Nauka, 1980.

Miamlin, Igor Gavrilovich. *Skulptor Veniamin Borisovich Pinchuk.* Leningrad: Khudozhnik SSSR, 1965.

Mikhailov, A. "Diego Rivera." *Vestnik inostrannoi literatury,* 1929, no. 5:198–211.

"Nasha anketa: Diego Rivera." *Kultura i zhizn,* 1957, no. 6 (June): 54–55.

Okinshevich, Leo, comp., Robert Carlton, ed. *Latin America in Soviet Writings: A Bibliography.* 2 vols.: v. 1, 1917–1958; v. 2, 1959–1964. Baltimore: Published for the Library of Congress by The Johns Hopkins University Press, 1966.

Ospovat, Lev Samoilovich. *Diego Rivera.* Moscow: Molodaia gvardiia, 1969.

Parmenter, Ross. *Lawrence in Oaxaca: A Quest for the Novelist in Mexico.* Salt Lake City: Gibbs M. Smith, Inc., Peregrine Smith Books, 1984.

Pavlenko, A. V. "V poiskakh uteriannykh pisem." *Novoe vremia* 22, no. 47 (November 1964): 26–28.

Rivera, Diego. *My Art, My Life.* With Gladis March. New York: Citadel Press, 1960.

———. "Narodnoe iskusstvo Meksiki." *Vestnik inostrannoi literatury,* 1928, no. 8:151–52.

Riza, Bayram, and Catherine Quirk. "Cultural Relations Between the Soviet Union and Latin America." In *The Soviet Union and Latin America,* edited by J. Gregory Oswald and Anthony J. Strover, pp. 30–39. New York: Praeger, 1970.

Rogger, Hans. "America in the Russian Mind—or Russian Discoveries of America." *Pacific Historical Review* 47, no. 1 (February 1978): 27–51.

Sánchez, Héctor, ed. *México nueve veces contado, por narradores extranjeros.* Mexico City: Secretaría de Educación Pública, 1974.

Semenov, Oleg Sergeevich. *David Alfaro Sikeiros.* Moscow: Detskaia literatura. 1980.

Sevin, S. E. *Meksika.* Moscow: Molodaia gvardiia, 1931.

Shulgovskii, A. F., main editor. *Meksika: Politika, ekonomika, kultura.* Moscow: Nauka, 1968.

Shur, Leonid Avelevich. *Rossiia i Latinskaia Amerika: Ocherki politicheskikh, ekonomicheskikh i kulturnikh otnoshenii.* Moscow: Mysl, 1964.

Shur, Leonid Avelevich, comp. *Khudozhestvennaia literatura Latinskoi Ameriki v russkoi pechati, 1765–1959.* Moscow: Izdatelstvo vsesoiuznoi knizhnoi palaty, 1960.

Siqueiros, David Alfaro. *Me llamaban el coronelazo.* Mexico City: Grijalbo, 1977.

Solís, Ruth, ed., prologue by Angelica Arenal de Siqueiros. *Vida y obra de David Álfaro Siqueiros: Juicios críticos.* Mexico City: Fondo de cultura económica, 1975.

Tibol, Raquel, *Siqueiros (Introductor de realidades).* Mexico City: UNAM, 1961.

Volskii, Viktor Vatslavovich; I. R. Grigulevich; Iu. V. Dashkevich; L. Iu. Slezkin, eds. *Latinskaia Amerika v proshlom i nastoiashchem: Sbornik statei po ekonomike, istorii i kulture stran Latinskoi Ameriki.* Moscow: Izdatelstvo sotsialno-ekonomicheskoi literatury, 1960.

Voronina, T. S. *David Alfaro Sikeiros.* Moscow: Izobrazitelnoe iskusstvo, 1976.

Walker, Ronald G. *Infernal Paradise: Mexico and the Modern English Novel.* Berkeley and Los Angeles: University of California Press, 1978.

Williams, Robert C. *Artists in Revolution: Portraits of the Russian Avant-Garde, 1905–1925.* Bloomington: University of Indiana Press, 1977.

Wolfe, Bertram D. *The Fabulous Life of Diego Rivera.* New York: Stein and Day, 1963.

INDEX

Pitt Latin American Series

Cole Blasier, Editor

PLAS
PITT
LATIN
AMERICAN
SERIES

Argentina

Argentina in the Twentieth Century
David Rock, Editor

Discreet Partners: Argentina and the USSR Since 1917
Aldo César Vacs

Juan Perón and the Reshaping of Argentina
Frederick C. Turner and José Enrique Miguens, Editors

The Life, Music, and Times of Carlos Gardel
Simon Collier

The Political Economy of Argentina, 1946–1983
Guido DiTella and Rudiger Dornbusch, Editors

Brazil

External Constraints on Economic Policy in Brazil, 1899–1930
Winston Fritsch

The Film Industry in Brazil: Culture and the State
Randal Johnson

The Politics of Social Security in Brazil
James M. Malloy

Urban Politics in Brazil: The Rise of Populism, 1925–1945
Michael L. Conniff

Colombia

Gaitán of Colombia: A Political Biography
Richard E. Sharpless

Roads to Reason: Transportation, Administration, and Rationality in Colombia
Richard E. Hartwig

Cuba

Cuba Between Empires, 1878–1902
Louis A. Pérez, Jr.

Cuba, Castro, and the United States
Philip W. Bonsal

Cuba in the World
Cole Blasier and Carmelo Mesa-Lago, Editors

Cuba Under the Platt Amendment
Louis A. Pérez, Jr.

Cuban Studies, Vols. 16–17
Carmelo Mesa-Lago, Editor

The Overthrow of Allende and the Politics of Chile, 1964–1976
Paul E. Sigmund

Panajachel: A Guatemalan Town in Thirty-Year Perspective
Robert E. Hinshaw

Peru and the International Monetary Fund
Thomas Scheetz

Primary Medical Care in Chile: Accessibility Under Military Rule
Joseph L. Scarpaci

Rebirth of the Paraguayan Republic: The First Colorado Era, 1878–1904
Harris G. Warren

Social Security

The Politics of Social Security in Brazil
James M. Malloy

Social Security in Latin America: Pressure Groups, Stratification, and Inequality
Carmelo Mesa-Lago

Other Studies

Adventurers and Proletarians: The Story of Migrants in Latin America
Magnus Mörner, with the collaboration of Harold Sims

Authoritarianism and Corporatism in Latin America
James M. Malloy, Editor

Authoritarians and Democrats: Regime Transition in Latin America
James M. Malloy and Mitchell A. Seligson, Editors

Female and Male in Latin America: Essays
Ann Pescatello, Editor

Latin American Debt and the Adjustment Crisis
Rosemary Thorp and Laurence Whitehead, Editors

Public Policy in Latin America: A Comparative Survey
John W. Sloan

Selected Latin American One-Act Plays
Francesca Colecchia and Julio Matas, Editors and Translators

The State and Capital Accumulation in Latin America: Brazil, Chile, Mexico
Christian Anglade and Carlos Fortin, Editors

Transnational Corporations and the Latin American Automobile Industry
Rhys Jenkins